Global Politics

Global Politics

James Lee Ray

UNIVERSITY OF NEW MEXICO

HOUGHTON MIFFLIN COMPANY
BOSTON

Dallas   Geneva, Ill.   Hopewell, N.J.
Palo Alto   London

Library of Congress Catalog Card Number: 78-69552
ISBN: 0-395-26542-8

Contents

CONTENTS

Preface

Global Politics is designed for use in an introductory course in world politics. It has three major thrusts. First, it should give readers a basic understanding of the contemporary history of the international system from the First World War to the present. Second, it should help students understand the current crises in the global political system that are likely to have the greatest impact on the future. Finally, it should impress on students the possibility of developing generalizations about and discovering patterns in the foreign policies of states, the behavior of other important political entities (such as multinational corporations), and the operation of the global system.

This book has been inspired by the view that current texts, which tend to emphasize (1) traditional historical concerns, (2) relevant topics, such as the population explosion, famine, the energy crisis, or (3) scientific findings and methods—all leave out something of real value to beginning students. Historically oriented texts usually ignore, or deny the possibility of discovering, patterns in foreign policies and international relations. Books that emphasize these patterns tend to entangle students in methodological jargon, or they are based on an assumption that students know more about recent history and current events than they actually do. Texts that emphasize the relevant topics mentioned earlier tend to become outdated quickly by the rush of events and mislead students by creating the impression that the past is irrelevant to an understanding of the future.

If beginning students are to be exposed to history and the science of world politics, as well as information concerning current crises, does this mean they must take two, or possibly three, introductory courses? I hope not, because the majority of students will not take more than one course in world politics. In *Global Politics,* I have attempted to integrate history, science, and what might be called "futurology" in such a way that the material can be covered in one course. To this end, the historical thrust of the book is condensed; major events are covered in sufficient depth to give students a basic understanding of recent history. Scientific methods are discussed only briefly and statistics very rarely. Rather, the possibility of studying world politics scientifically is explained and defended; the argument is buttressed by discussion of simple, predictable patterns that can be discerned in the context of world politics without the use of sophisticated statistical techniques and computerized analyses. I have made no attempt to provide complete coverage of the findings of quantitative research. Some examples of this kind of research are integrated into the text in order to give students a clearer idea of what is involved in such endeavors. Students who plan to specialize in world politics will eventually want to delve more deeply into quantitative research. But there are few such students in an introductory course, and although *Global Politics* should serve to encourage their interest in the field, the text is based on the assumption that future specialists will have ample opportunity to review the quantitative literature in courses to come.

Finally, there will be a relatively brief discussion of contemporary crises, with special emphasis on what has become known as the Limits to Growth controversy. I find this controversy especially important, not only because it persists, but because it highlights in a useful way the basic divisions among those who propose solutions to contemporary crises. *The Limits to Growth** may fade into the background in the not too distant future, but the issues it has raised will be with us for many years to come, and beginning students of world politics should be familiar with them.

I will, of course, gladly accept most of the credit, and dutifully bear most of the blame, for the material that appears in the following pages. I will not, though, accept all the credit (nor all the blame). Several secretaries in the Political Science Department at the University of New Mexico typed and retyped hundreds of pages and helped me meet every deadline. Students in my introductory courses in international relations, over the last few years, have taught me at least as much about global politics as I have taught them. Bruce Bueno de Mesquita, of the University of Rochester, helped sharpen my original manuscript, and suggested several revisions that, I believe, add significantly to the quality of the text. Louis René Beres, of Purdue University, provided lavish encouragement when I needed it most, and exerted beneficial pressure on me to move into areas of global politics about which I was ignorant, or apathetic. If he did not succeed in "reforming" me as much as he would have liked, I am still grateful for his efforts. Howard Lentner, of Baruch College-CUNY, analyzed my

---

*Donella Meadows, Dennis L. Meadows, Jorgen Randers, and William W. Behrens, III, *The Limits to Growth: A Report for the Club of Rome's Project on the Predicament of Mankind.* Universe Books, New York, 1972.

arguments with amazing thoroughness, and the accuracy of his criticisms, as well as the quality of his suggestions, was a constant source of satisfaction for me. Finally, J. David Singer accounts for most of the "variance" in my knowledge about global politics; despite a very busy schedule, he read all of the manuscript and helped me improve many pages. Professors Bueno de Mesquita, Beres, Lentner, and Singer together, with their comments and criticisms, made writing *Global Politics* an educational experience from which I shall benefit for years to come. My hope is that students will find reading *Global Politics* a rewarding and enjoyable educational experience.

J. L. R.

ONE

The Historical Setting

HISTORY CAN BE DULL. SERMONS ABOUT THE IMPORTANCE OF
history are usually worse. I hope, however, a short sermon will
be acceptable.

The major purpose of *Global Politics* is to help the reader understand the world politics of today and tomorrow. But the best
way to begin such a process is to look at the world politics of
yesterday, for two basic reasons. First, today is, and tomorrow will
be, unique. But not totally so. For example, the wars that occur in
the future will not be exactly like any that have occurred in the past,
but neither will they be entirely different. The statement that history repeats itself is an oversimplification, but it is not completely
false. Recurring patterns are clearly visible in the historical record
of the global political system. In brief, history often provides situations that are comparable in important ways to those that create
today's headlines. To achieve the best possible understanding of

today's headlines and the ones to follow, it is important to be knowledgeable about comparable past situations.

The second reason is that, at least until very recently, global politics has been dominated by nation-states and the people who control them. These people, whether official decision-makers or powerful behind-the-scenes operators of various kinds, have had a very important characteristic in common. They have been (and are), almost without exception, steeped in the history of their respective countries and thoroughly informed about the world political system. The decisions they make and the policies they formulate have been shaped, often in obvious and predictable ways, by the lessons they draw from history. Any fruitful attempt to understand their decisions and policies must involve not only a knowledge of history but also a knowledge of how it has been interpreted by the most important scholars and leaders in the world.

A third reason for beginning with a historical analysis is less important but deserves to be mentioned. The author was not able to write such an analysis without revealing biases and some ignorance. The aggressive, intelligent reader will want to keep these shortcomings in mind as he or she begins reading and takes from the following pages what seems worthwhile.

The Transformation
of the Contemporary System:
The First World War

June 28, 1914, is a logical time to begin an analysis of contemporary world politics, because the war sparked by events on that day brought about fundamental changes in the international system that are still clearly visible. Serbian nationalists, apparently hoping for the liberation of fellow Slavs under Austrian rule, assassinated the Austrian heir apparent, Archduke Franz Ferdinand. Austrian leaders had long been concerned about separatist movements in their empire, and they were determined to strike back at Serbia, a nation that, in the Austrian view, sympathized with and supported these movements. Austria's determination was heightened when Germany, on July 5, assured Austria of support if conflict with Serbia brought Austria into conflict with Russia. Austria delivered an ultimatum to Serbia on July 23 and Serbia made a very conciliatory reply. Even so, on July 28, Austria declared war on Serbia. By

August 6, 1914, France, Great Britain, and Russia were at war with Germany and Austria-Hungary. The Allies were later joined by Japan, Italy, and the United States, while Bulgaria and Turkey fought on the side of the Germans and the Austrians.

Alternative Explanations

How could a small conflict between an unimportant country such as Serbia and the declining Austro-Hungarian empire lead to a war involving all the most powerful nations in the world? Possible answers to the question of how the First World War started fill many volumes, and only a few can be discussed here. One prominent answer emphasizes the importance of the system of alliances that existed at the time of the quarrel between Austria-Hungary and Serbia. Germany, of course, was allied with Austria-Hungary, one reason that Germany became involved in the conflict immediately. Russia was not formally allied with Serbia; rather, the Russians became involved in the conflict as defenders of pan-Slavic nationalism and because of a fear that Austria-Hungary would, if not checked, dominate an area that lay in the path of a possible Russian outlet to the sea. Russia was allied with France, though. The Germans knew this and had for years assumed that if they became involved in a war with Russia, they would have to fight France. Finally, England was allied with France and Russia; although England's alliances did not require going to the aid of Russia and France in the event of war, there is little doubt that they made it more likely. Thus, one can see sense in the argument that the conflict between Austria-Hungary and Serbia was transformed into a major conflagration by the complex interlocking system of alliances built up by the major powers of the system.

Another explanation of the outbreak of the First World War emphasizes the importance of the state of military technology and the bureaucracies that administered the technology. Generals of the time, for reasons I will discuss later, were convinced that rapid mobilization of forces would be crucial in determining who would win the next war. Accordingly, in Germany and Russia particularly, but also in Austria-Hungary and France, the armies made elaborate plans to ensure rapid mobilization. After Austria-Hungary attacked Serbia, Russia mobilized. Germany did not respond immediately; Kaiser Wilhelm sent a telegram to the Russian czar requesting that he show some sign of good faith that would allow the kaiser to avoid issuing his own mobilization orders. The czar canceled a general mobilization order and substituted another one for partial mobilization. But the Russian military bureaucracy would not respond to a change of plans. They feared the consequences of trying to convert to partial mobilization once general mobilization had been initiated. The czar became convinced that such a sudden change of plans might throw his military organization into chaos, and the original general mobilization order was reinstated.

Kaiser Wilhelm realized that Russia was not going to pull back from its general mobilization, and he and his advisors decided they must proceed quickly with their own. But because the German army was aware that France and Russia were allied, and it was assumed that the Russian army would take longer than the French army to mobilize effectively, the German plan called for mobilization and attack against the French first. The French would be quickly defeated, and the Russians could be dealt with in turn.

Even though the *Russians* were responding to the threat of Germany's ally, Austria, the German war plans called for an attack against *France*. At the last moment, Kaiser Wilhelm was led to believe (with help from the British) that France might be kept out of the war, even if Germany became involved against the Russians. Wilhelm decided that, in order to give France a chance to stay out, Germany ought to turn its troops around and attack Russia instead. But the German generals were as reluctant as the Russian generals to change their plans at the last moment. Moltke, the German chief of staff, reportedly broke into tears at the suggestion that such a thing might be attempted.

Kaiser Wilhelm and German chief of staff Helmuth von Moltke. Radio Times Hulton Picture Library.

The fact that Austria and France also had rapid mobilization schedules, an important element in the pressure on Russia and Germany, adds strength to the argument that the state of military technology and the bureaucratic organizations administering it were important causes of the war. With all sides so intent on rapid mobilization, had the assassination at Sarajevo not taken place, *some* crisis was bound to lead to war sooner or later.

Another explanation of the outbreak of the First World War was offered by Lenin in 1917. Lenin, of course, believed that capitalist states were necessarily imperialistic in order to ensure access to markets, fields of investment, and raw materials. All the important capitalist states in the world were in constant competition to establish imperialistic bases. Such competition led to instability, Lenin argued, because of the operation of what became known as the law of uneven development. The capitalist states might approach some clear definition of their respective spheres of influence, but that delineation would eventually become unsatisfactory to states that were growing more rapidly than others. Dissatisfaction on the part of the up-and-coming states, according to Lenin, would lead to war and did lead, in his view, to the First World War. The spat between Austria-Hungary and Serbia served as an excuse to engage in a battle that the major capitalist powers were intent on for more important reasons.

Other scholars and writers blamed the Great War on German militarism; munitions makers in all the countries involved; nationalism; the bipolarity of the international system in 1914; the press, especially the newspaper press in the European countries; and arms races, especially an arms race involving the navies of Germany and Great Britain. In short, plausible explanations at the time concerning the causes of the First World War were numerous and diverse. But there was widespread agreement after the war that steps must be taken to prevent its repetition.

Effects of the War
Perhaps the most important impact of the First World War on international politics involved the weakening of Europe. The European states had been in unquestioned command of the global political system up to 1914. By 1917, one important European state (Russia) was on the verge of dropping out of the war, and the rest were locked in a seemingly endless stalemate. It took a non-European state (the United States), to break the deadlock. By then, the Austro-Hungárian empire had been destroyed, and Germany, Britain, and France had been severely damaged.

The Russians had had their revolution, in no small part another effect of the war. It might have occurred in any case, but the war made the inefficient and outmoded aspects of the czarist regime more obvious and subjected the Russian people to such hardships that they became less tolerant. Alone among the major combatants, the United States emerged more powerful than it had been at the beginning of the war. It was, in fact, according to many tangible indicators, already the most powerful state in the world. The First World War significantly enlarged the role of the United States in the global political system.

Another important impact of the war involved the realm of political ideas. The war had been fought, according to the leader of its most powerful victor, to make the world safe for democracy. It had been won, as no one could fail to notice, by the more democratic states (the United States, Great Britain, and France), while the nondemocratic states (Germany, Austria-Hungary, and Russia) had fallen to pieces. The war served to enshrine the intertwined (but not synonymous) values of democracy and national self-determination; the other side of the coin was the beginning of the process of the delegitimization of empires. Empires were antidemocratic, and national self-determination was democracy on the level of international politics. It was therefore to be cherished and protected.

National self-determination was to become an especially important issue in the Middle East in the years following the war. In Turkey, a flamboyant military officer named Mustafa Kemal Ataturk first organized resistance to a Greek effort to annex a large portion of Asia Minor, and then led a modernizing nationalistic revolution. He abolished many of the institutions based on Islam and introduced a republican, secular form of government. In short, he established a reputation as one of the earliest Westernizers in a non-Western culture. Reza Shah Pahlavi, in neighboring Iran, modeled himself after Ataturk, doing much to rid Iran of foreign control (for a while) and to modernize his homeland. He did not move against Islamic traditions with the same fervor as Ataturk, but under his leadership "a vigorous program of modernization in the army, the government bureaucracy, the judicial system, and the educational system, and construction of an economic infrastructure (including roads, cross-country railroads, public finance, banking, and public health) was undertaken."[1]

[1] Abid A. Al-Marayati et al., *The Middle East: Its Governments and Politics,* Duxbury Press, Belmont, Calif., 1972, p. 405.

National self-determination was to become a hot issue in another part of the Middle East because Great Britain had issued the Balfour Declaration during the First World War. Balfour was Britain's foreign secretary at the time, and in a letter to a leader of the British Jewish community, he stated that the British government "view with favor the establishment in Palestine of a national home for the Jewish people." The declaration encouraged Jewish emigration to Palestine, brought Jews into increasingly bitter conflict with Palestinian Arabs as the emigration continued, and helped create a problem for Britain in Palestine that it was never able to resolve.

Finally, any discussion of the effects of the First World War would be incomplete without an emphasis on the extent to which it created conditions conducive to the next world war. In addition to the lasting hatreds it created (or reinforced), the First World War had several important effects on the international economic system that shaped the process leading to the Second World War. The United States emerged, by a considerable margin, as the most important economic unit in the world, and Great Britain, France, and Germany became dependent on it. Furthermore, the war (and, perhaps, the provisions of the treaty) devastated the German economy in a manner that paved the way for the appearance, and later the success, of Adolf Hitler.

The First World War and the Study of International Relations

A widespread American view is that the discipline of international relations was created by Americans as a result of their experience in the First World War.[2] This view might be criticized for its ethnocentrism, tending to ignore, as it does, such famous scholars as Thucydides, Kautilya, Machiavelli, and Clausewitz. Still, it is not without foundation.

Before the First World War nearly all ideas about the global system were neatly filed away under the box for international law, or diplomatic history, or the parent discipline of political

[2]For example, Fred Warner Neal and Bruce P. Hamlett state that "international relations is an American invention dating from the time after World War I when the American intellectual community discovered the world." See F. Neal and B. Hamlett, "The Never-Never Land of International Relations," *International Studies Quarterly* 13, (September 1969), 283.

thought itself. After 1918, however, a generation of scholars and writers, appalled by the horrors of the conflict just past, began to scrutinize interstate politics in systematic terms.[3]

Many of these writers, such as Brierly, Eagleton, Lauterpacht, and Potter,[4] continued to write about international relations in terms of international law and organization. But other writers, analyzing the causes of the First World War, broke from this tradition and attempted to bring a knowledge of political, historical, economic, demographic, and geographic factors to the understanding of foreign policies and international politics.[5] All were most concerned with steps that should be taken to avoid another world war. By the 1930s, a split emerged between those who advocated reliance on ideals, moral principles, and the "world court of public opinion," and other writers who were basically suspicious of idealistic principles as guides for action in international politics, and who stressed the importance of power and conflict. The best known analysis of the controversy between the idealists and the realists, as they became known, was written by Edward H. Carr in *The Twenty Year's Crisis, 1919–1939.*[6] This debate came to dominate the study of international relations in the United States after the Second World War.

Postwar Settlements

In the months immediately after the First World War, the idealists appeared to have more influence on the actual conduct of international relations, thanks largely to a very powerful advocate of their views, Woodrow Wilson. Wilson was anxious to move beyond the days of balance-of-power and sphere-of-influence politics, which he saw as the dangerous kinds of principles that had led Europe to

[3] Ralph Pettman, *Human Behavior and World Politics,* St. Martin's Press, New York, 1975, p. 2.

[4] James L. Brierly, *The Law of Nations,* 2d ed., Oxford University Press, New York, 1936; Clyde Eagleton, *International Government,* Ronald Press, New York, 1932; Hersch Lauterpacht, *The Function of Law in the International Community,* Oxford University Press, New York, 1933; Pittman B. Potter, *An Introduction to the Study of International Organization,* 3d ed., D. Appleton-Century, New York, 1928.

[5] Two famous examples would be Frederick L. Schuman, *International Politics: An Introduction to the Western State System,* McGraw-Hill, New York, 1933, and Frederick S. Dunn, *Peaceful Change: A Study of International Procedures,* Council on Foreign Relations, New York, 1937. These two, as well as the authors in the previous footnote, are cited by James Dougherty and Robert Pfaltzgraff, (eds.) *Contending Theories of International Relations,* Lippincott, Philadelphia, 1971.

[6] Macmillan, London, 1939.

near total collapse. The major instrument through which such principles would be replaced was the League of Nations. As the president of the strongest victor in the war, Wilson provided the major impetus behind the creation of such an organization, but there was widespread agreement on the need for such a body. Many European leaders were of the opinion that "the war came into being largely by default, because the forces of negotiation and peaceful settlement marshalled against it suddenly collapsed. . . ."[7] In short, the war occurred because the leaders had had no time or place to talk things over when the crisis began. The League of Nations would provide the opportunity for a cooling-off period that would have crowned with success the efforts to avoid the Great War.

Beyond that very general conception of the league, though, there lay important areas of disagreement among the victorious powers. One area became obvious when the disposition of Germany's colonies was discussed. Wilson wanted to make the colonies common property of the league, and have them administered by small nations. The British, along with their dominions, Australia, New Zealand, and South Africa, wanted to annex the colonies outright. A compromise was accomplished whereby the British dominions obtained the territories they desired under a loose mandate from the league. In fact, the distribution of the German colonies followed closely the provisions of the secret treaties concluded among the victorious European powers during the war. In adhering to the treaties, based on old spheres-of-influence ideas, the British and the other European powers demonstrated that their view of how international relations should be conducted in the postwar era was perhaps not as revolutionary as idealists such as Wilson might have hoped.

The French were even less idealistically inclined than the British. Their major concern was that Germany be kept under control, and they were not willing to rely on Wilson's idea of collective security without a solid basis of concrete force behind it. "There is an old system of alliances," the French Premier Clemenceau had said before the Paris Peace Conference, "called the Balance of Power—this system of alliances, which I do not renounce, will be my guiding thought at the Peace Conference."[8]

In pursuit of security against Germany, the French proposed the establishment of an international peace force. President Wilson

[7] Arthur Sweetser, *The League of Nations at Work,* Macmillan, New York, 1920, p.5. Cited by Inis L. Claude, *Swords into Plowshares,* 3d ed., Random House, New York, 1964, p. 40.

[8] Alexander De Conde, *A History of American Foreign Policy.* Scribner's, New York, 1963, p. 474.

rejected the proposal on the grounds that once the facts of a dispute had been made clear by such an august body as the league, world public opinion would be sufficient to deter aggression. The British shared some of Wilson's optimism regarding world public opinion, but they had a more practical reason for being opposed to an international peace force; they needed all of their armed forces, in particular their navy, to defend the far-flung British empire. So, the French proposal to "put some teeth" into "collective security" to be established by the league was a failure.[9]

The French also wanted to take all Germany's land west of the Rhine, an area containing some 5 million people, and create one or two republics that would be under French control. Wilson considered this a violation of the principle of self-determination. The peace conference came perilously close to breaking up over the point, but the French lost this argument, too. Germany was allowed to keep the Rhineland, although it was to be permanently demilitarized to about thirty-one miles east of the Rhine.

Another, eventually crucial, disagreement between idealistic Wilson and realistic Britain and France concerned the matter of reparations. Before the peace conference, Wilson had promised there would be no punitive damages. Germany had signed the armistice on the condition that the Allies would ask for payment only of damages to civilians and their property. But the British and the French were inclined to make Germany pay the whole cost of the war. This was understandable, since the British and the French had suffered much more from the war than the Americans had. Realizing this, and despite his reservations, Wilson agreed that Germany should be made to pay for pensions to disabled Allied soldiers and their relatives. The definition of civilian damages that Germany had agreed to pay was expanded considerably, and an increase of about 100 percent in reparations resulted. The debate over the justice of the reparations became a key element in Adolf Hitler's rise to power.

Germany and Adolf Hitler

On the eleventh hour, eleventh day, eleventh month of 1918, the armistice that ended the First World War was signed. Three days earlier, a new German republic, replacing the old Hohenzollern dynasty, was proclaimed. It could not have been born at a less

[9]F. S. Northedge and M. J. Grieve, *A Hundred Years of International Relations*, Praeger, New York, 1971, p. 150.

propitious time. Within a matter of seven months, the new government, led by Social Democrats, was faced with the responsibility of signing the Versailles peace treaty. The publication of the treaty in Germany, in May 1919, caused an outcry throughout the country; mass meetings were organized, the provisional president of the republic called the terms "unrealizable and unbearable," and the German delegates to Versailles called the treaty "intolerable for any nation."[10]

Yet, what choice did the new government have? Could it resist the demands? There was reason to believe it could, because the German army had been far from total defeat in November 1918. "The German army capitulated when it still occupied scores of square miles of enemy soil. It marched home as an integrated force."[11] In view of this, the provisional president asked Field Marshal von Hindenburg if military resistance was possible. He replied that it was not. The new government took him at his word, and the National Assembly accepted the peace treaty by a large majority.

Hindenburg's choice was wise because the Americans were in command of the situation. Even if the Allied troops in the field could not have crushed the Germans, the troops and artillery yet to be deployed by the United States were an obviously insuperable barrier to further German resistance. But the myth grew in Germany, a myth Hitler would use to advantage, that the German army had been stabbed in the back by the new democratic republic. The first basis of the myth was that the German army had not been destroyed physically at the end of the war. Also, after the crucial days had passed, the leaders of the German army forgot, unintentionally or not, that they had asked for the end of the war and had told the government that resistance was useless. For example, almost exactly one year after the armistice, Hindenburg himself testified to a committee of inquiry of the National Assembly that the German army had been stabbed in the back.

This (imaginary) stab was especially hard to accept because of what the German people considered the unreasonable demands of the Versailles treaty. It took land away from them. Seven million people were lost. Germany was virtually disarmed. Article 231 of the treaty held Germany responsible for the war. But the provision of the treaty that had perhaps the most lasting impact concerned reparations. The exact amount was not stipulated in the treaty, but the Germans were to make a preliminary payment of $5 billion

[10]William L. Shirer, *The Rise and Fall of the Third Reich,* Simon and Schuster, New York, 1960, pp. 57–58.
[11]Northedge and Grieve, *Hundred Years,* p. 207.

between 1919 and 1921. That gave some indication of what was to come. In April 1921, the Allies presented Germany with a total reparations bill of $33 billion. By that time the German mark had begun to fall in value. It was normally valued at 4 to the dollar, but by the end of 1921 it had fallen to a value of 75 to the dollar.

That was merely the beginning of what can be described as the most spectacular inflationary binge in the history of the industrialized Western world. In 1922 the value of the mark fell to 400 to the dollar, an inflationary rate of around 500 percent for one year. By the beginning of 1923, it took 7,000 marks to buy a dollar's worth of goods. In January 1923, the French occupied the Ruhr Valley, the industrial heart of Germany, because Germany had defaulted on part of its scheduled reparations deliveries. That sent the value of the mark to 18,000 to the dollar. By July, it was 160,000 to the dollar, by August a million to the dollar, by November four billion. From then on, the value of the mark compared to the dollar had to be calculated in the trillions. It took a wheelbarrow full of money to buy a simple loaf of bread, assuming either were to be found.

This was the scene in Germany when Hitler made his first marked impression on the body politic. He staged what became known as the Beer Hall Putsch in Bavaria, a ludicrously premature attempt to begin his ascent to power in Germany. He was arrested, tried, convicted, and sentenced to five years in prison on April 1, 1924.[12] A normal man would have been discouraged, but Hitler was neither. He spent his time in prison dictating a book that described in some detail his plans for the establishment of a Thousand Year Reich.

In time, Germany recovered from its inflationary binge, and things began to go well for the country both domestically and internationally. On the international scene, Germany signed an agreement with the other isolated state in the system, the Soviet Union, in 1922 at Rapallo. The treaty provided Germany with several benefits, but perhaps the most important effect was on Germany's relationships with Britain and France. Both states saw that Germany need not remain isolated any longer, and they did not want it to join forces with the Soviets. In 1925, the European allies proposed guarantees of the borders between Germany and its former enemies on the West. The French and the Belgians were guaranteed support by the British and the Italians in case of an attack by Germany. On the other hand, the treaty signed at

---

[12]He became eligible for parole in six months and was released after only nine months in prison.

Locarno also protected Germany from a French reoccupation of the Ruhr. The symbolic importance of the Locarno Treaty was that it marked the end of Germany's isolation from the West.

Domestically, the German economy began an impressive recovery, due in large part to a flow of American capital, used to pay reparations and renew Germany's productive capacities. Unemployment dropped, wages rose, and neither Hitler nor his Nazi party were noticeably heard from.

But the importance of the American economy to German prosperity was soon to become forcefully apparent. In fact, Great Britain and France as well as Germany had become heavily dependent on the United States economically. In the 1920s, American investors and Wall Street banks poured money into Germany, which used much of it to pay reparations to Great Britain and France, which in turn used the money to pay First World War debts to the United States. This interesting arrangement was, perhaps, harmless enough, until the stock market crash in 1929 when the supply of money in the circular flow from Wall Street and other sources in the United States suddenly stopped. Then, the Germans could no longer pay their reparations, which meant that Great Britain and France could not pay their war debts. The only possible alternatives for the Germans, the British, and the French were to default on their debts or to increase their exports to the United States in order to accumulate dollars to pay the debts. President Hoover and Congress moved to eliminate the second possibility (and to assure the first) by putting the Hawley-Smoot Act into effect in June 1930, raising American tariff rates to their highest point in history. "Over a thousand economists had pleaded with the president not to sign the bill, pointing out that higher rates would hamper foreign exports, block collection of the war debts, invite foreign retaliation, and embitter foreign relations. The predictions proved true."[13]

The effect of the depression on German electoral politics was immediate and dramatic. In 1928, before the crash, the Nazis had received 810,000 votes and elected 12 of their members to the Reichstag. In the September 1930 elections, after millions of people had been thrown out of work and thousands of small businesses had failed, Hitler's party won almost 6.5 million votes and 107 seats in the Reichstag, thus becoming the second largest party in the Parliament. Another political party in Germany gained as a result of the depression. Although its gains were not as spectacular (from 3.2

[13]De Conde, *History*, pp. 559–560.

million votes in 1928 to 4.6 million in 1930), the rise of the Communist party would undoubtedly smooth the way for Hitler in the years to come.

By 1932, the Nazis were the largest single political party in the country. In January 1933, Hitler was named chancellor. On March 27, 1933, the German Parliament passed what was called the Enabling Act, which served as the formal basis for the establishment of Hitler's dictatorship.

How did Hitler do it? He never received a majority of the votes of the German people (the Nazis received 44 percent of the total vote in a March 1933 election), but, again, Hitler's party did become the single largest in Germany and served as the base for Hitler's rise to power. The Nazis used terror and intimidation, there can be no quarrel about that, but they also attracted millions of uncoerced voters. Who were they?

Many of them, it appears, were the kind of lower-middle-class people (that is, white-collar workers, small investors, self-employed businessmen, and lower-level government officials)[14] who would have been hurt most by the terrible inflation that Germany suffered in the early 1920's. The lower-class workers were hurt by inflation, no doubt, but they had never had much money on hand so that when it became worthless, they did not lose very much, relatively speaking. (In any case, many responded to their frustrations by voting Communist.) The upper class held much of its wealth in the form of land and other kinds of property, so the drop in the value of money, while inconvenient, was usually much less than a tragedy. (In several cases it was not even inconvenient. Several industrialists who were deep in debt at the end of the war found their debts, in effect, liquidated by inflation.) But many people in the lower middle-classes did not own large amounts of property and were heavily dependent on money in savings accounts. When money became worthless, these people, in relative terms, fell harder and farther than anybody. They were just recovering from the disastrous effects of the inflation of the early 1920s when they were hit again by the Great Depression. They were desperate, and Hitler must have seemed the only solution in sight.

But Hitler could not have risen to power on this basis alone. He appealed to many Germans of all classes with his denunciation of the Versailles treaty, his condemnation of Jews, and as an alternative to the assumption of power by the Communists.

[14]See Seymour Martin Lipset, *Political Man,* Anchor Books, Garden City, N.Y., 1959, pp. 140–149. See also Witt Bowden, Michael Karpovich, and Abbot P. Usher, *Economic History of Europe Since 1750,* American Book, New York, 1937, p. 835.

Japan, Italy, and Germany:
Challenges to the Status Quo

Japan

To scholars of international politics, the 1930s (to 1939 at least) will always be remembered vividly for the successful challenges to the international status quo mounted by Japan, Italy, and Germany. The first challenge was made by Japan with the invasion of Manchuria in 1931. Japan was a rapidly growing power in the decades before 1931, and had taken advantage of the First World War to acquire several German colonial outposts, and to extend economic and political· privileges in China. Perhaps even more important, Japan dramatically increased exports to the Asian markets cut off from their traditional European suppliers by the war. By the end of the war, Japanese strength had become so apparent that it was accorded great-power status at the Paris Peace Conference.

All did not go well for Japan at the peace conference. Japan insisted on the inclusion of an article in the league covenant committing the league to the principle of racial equality. Great Britain and its dominions opposed the plank, mainly because Australia's domestic laws prohibited the immigration of Asians. Wilson, rather than see the league fall apart over this issue, felt it necessary to rule against the article on racial equality in his position as chairman of the League of Nations Commission.

That was not the end of international racial discrimination against Japan. In 1920, the platform of both the Republican and Democratic parties in the United States had oriental-exclusion planks. California, soon joined by Arizona, Washington, and Texas, passed laws that forbade Japanese from owning or even renting land. In 1921, the United States Congress passed the Emergency Quota Act, which cut off Japanese immigration into the United States entirely. Such discriminatory policies on the part of the most powerful nation in the world, in addition to the lack of commitment to racial equality in the Covenant of the League of Nations, were not calculated to increase Japan's respect for the international status quo.

Even so, the early 1920s were good years for Japan, both economically and politically. But in 1927, Japan began to have domestic economic problems that were exacerbated by the onset of the depression. The reaction of all the industrialized states to the depression, as we have seen, was to throw up high tariff walls in order to protect jobs. Japan was hit hard, since it was particularly dependent on international trade.

While Japan was feeling the pressure of the high tariff barriers around the world, China began an effort to recover Manchuria, which China considered its three northwestern provinces in spite of important Russian and Japanese influence in the area. Japanese interests were quite extensive; Manchuria accounted for some 40 percent of Japan's foreign trade and investment at the time.[15] In reaction to the increased flow of Chinese into the area, as well as anti-Japanese propaganda and incidents, the Japanese military took matters into its own hands. Manufacturing an incident involving the dynamiting of a Japanese-controlled railroad track, the army moved to clear Manchuria of Chinese troops and establish complete control.

The League of Nations urged China and Japan to restore normal relations. It took great pains to avoid taking sides on the issue, despite the rather obvious nature of Japan's aggression. A commission was formed to go to East Asia to study the matter. The commission issued a report one year later, and the league did not adopt the report until February 1933, almost a year and a half after the Japanese invasion. It was not a one-sided report. It called for an autonomous Manchuria under the control of China, but it also contained safeguards for Japanese interests there. But, when the league adopted the report, the Japanese delegation walked out and announced that Japan was resigning from the league. In the meantime, the Japanese had set up the puppet state of Manchukuo and recognized it officially in September 1932.[16]

The incident set an unfortunate precedent for the league, and the United States did not help the situation. Speeches were made and warnings were given, but it was obvious to the Japanese from the beginning that the United States' resistance to Japan's actions would go no further than that. Needless to say, words did not cause the Japanese to withdraw from Manchuria.

Italy

The next challenge to the league's collective security came from Italy. Italy, like Japan, became organized as a modern nation-state relatively late, in 1861, and engaged in several foreign adventures in the first decades of its existence. Italy joined Bismarck in a war against Austria in 1866 to acquire Venetia. In 1895, putting into action the idea that Italy, like other European States, deserved to have an African empire, the Italians attacked Ethiopia. To everyone's amazement, especially the Italians', Italy lost. In 1911,

[15]De Conde, *History*, p. 526.
[16]Edwin O. Reischauer, *Japan: Past and Present,* Knopf, New York, 1964.

Italy attacked Turkish holdings in Tripoli (later Libya) for the purpose of taking them over. This effort was successful. Fortunately for Italy, it decided not to join its German and Austrian allies in the First World War, and ended up instead fighting on the side of the Allies. For its contribution to the Allied effort, it expected much more in the way of territorial rewards from the Paris Peace Conference than it actually received.

In 1922, Mussolini came to power. He benefited almost immediately from the general worldwide economic advance, and by 1929, he could claim that he had saved the lira, put an end to inflation, and reduced unemployment. However, Italy, like Japan, suffered from the Great Depression.

> The underlying immobility and rigidity of the Italian economy under Fascism was to prove a matter of first-rate importance for the world. For international depression deprived Fascism of its only real claim to material success: as the world began to go under after 1929, the fraudulence of Mussolini's claims to have found the secret of prosperity were stunningly revealed, and the security of the regime was accordingly endangered.[17]

By 1935, Mussolini was ready, the necessary incidents had been engineered, and Italy attacked Ethiopia. The league responded, initially, with surprising forcefulness. Italy was officially branded the aggressor, and the league voted to institute an embargo of arms, ammunition, and implements of war against Italy. But this embargo was never effectively enforced. First, the league failed to classify oil, coal, and steel as implements of war. Further, the United States refused to cooperate with the league in imposing effective sanctions. The most important states within the league, Britain and France, were apparently motivated by the fear that strong action against Italy might drive Mussolini into the arms of Hitler. They still hoped, at this point, that Italy might be an ally against Germany if the need arose in the future. Roosevelt was unwilling to go against the tide of isolationism in the United States in order to cooperate with the league in opposition to Italian aggression.

Not surprisingly, the Italian venture was successful. By June 1936, Ethiopia was defeated, and Mussolini proclaimed it an Italian province. In December 1937, Italy followed Japan out of the League of Nations.

[17]James Dugan and Laurence Lafore, *Days of Emperor and Clown*, Doubleday, Garden City, N.Y., 1973, p. 80.

Germany

If Mussolini killed the league in Ethiopia, Hitler buried it, along with the Versailles peace treaty. First, he violated the disarmament provisions of the Versailles treaty. Then, in March of 1936, he occupied the Rhineland which, according to the peace settlement, was supposed to be a demilitarized zone. At this early stage, Germany's military strength was quite modest, and it is clear that Hitler would have had to back down in the face of any substantial resistance. But he met virtually no resistance at all.

In 1938, Hitler officially incorporated Austria into the Third Reich. Later that year he began to demand a solution to the "problem" of the Sudeten Germans who lived in Czechoslovakia. In March, under threat of military action, the British and the French gave in to Hitler's demands, and Czechoslovakia was forced to cede Germany 11,000 square miles of territory, containing all the fortifications in the Czech defensive line; the loss of it left the country helpless. By April 1939, Hitler had absorbed the rest of the Czechoslovakian state into his empire. Still Hitler was not satisfied. There was one more territorial change that he considered necessary. On September 1, 1939, Hitler attacked Poland in an effort to bring about that change, and the Second World War was under way.

Factors Leading to Appeasement

Why did the Japanese, Italians, and Germans meet with only feeble resistance until September 1939? Perhaps the most important reason was the impression made by the First World War on the leaders and the people of those states that might have defended the status quo. Britain and France in particular had suffered horrendous losses in the First World War, and none of the changes demanded by the three opponents of the international status quo seemed so important as to warrant the risk of another such horrifying experience. The First World War, many concluded, had been brought about largely by a regrettable lack of patience on the part of the national leaders of the time. None had really wanted war, yet they had somehow stumbled into it. The lesson learned was that such catastrophes might be avoided if leaders would only be flexible and compromise.

The role of the United States in the international politics of the 1930s must also be emphasized. The First World War had been brought to a conclusion because the United States had contributed its strength to the Allied coalition. The peace settlement was constructed on the assumption that the United States would be one of its principal guarantors. But the United States refused to join the

League of Nations, refused to sign the Versailles peace treaty, and withdrew from the international stage on which it had entered so dramatically.[18] The defenders of the status quo that resulted from the First World War were left in a weak position, and they knew it. Their policies reflected that weakness.

The impact of the Great Depression should not be overlooked. It seemed to have opposite effects on Japan, Italy, and Germany on the one hand, and on Britain, France, and the United States on the other. The latter seemed to react to the depression by turning inward, concentrating on domestic economic problems and avoiding "entanglements" in foreign affairs. But Japan, Italy, and Germany reacted to the depression by pursuing a more active foreign policy; they seemed to believe that a solution to their domestic economic problems could be found through foreign conquest.

In relation to Germany in particular, Britain and France were also contending with guilt feelings concerning the Versailles peace treaty. Hitler had, of course, branded it a diktat, but his opinion was shared by influential, thoughtful people in Britain and France.[19] Thus when Hitler began to challenge various provisions of the treaty, enthusiastic defenders of it were hard to find.

Finally, there is a tendency to forget the strength of the political arguments with which Britain and France were faced at the crucial meeting in Munich. The territory that Germany demanded contained some 2,800,000 people of German extraction, compared to only 800,000 Czechs.[20] National self-determination was a principle much revered in the aftermath of the First World War, and Hitler seemed to have it on his side in his quarrel with Czechoslovakia. And it should not be forgotten that the First World War had been precipitated by resistance to nationalist aspirations in this very part of the world. I do not mean to imply that the British and the French made the right decision at Munich. But to argue that, on the contrary, such leaders as Neville Chamberlain, prime minister of Great Britain, were extraordinarily stupid or cowardly, is an overly simple and misleading explanation of the agreement arrived

[18]Some revisionist historians dispute this statement. It is true that *economically* the United States did not demonstrate any reluctance to venture overseas. But it did refuse to take any strong action against the activities of Japan, Italy, and Germany.

[19]Perhaps the most influential was John Maynard Keynes in Great Britain. His *Economic Consequences of the Peace,* published in 1920, argued that the economic demands on Germany were unreasonable and did not serve as a sound basis for a peaceful settlement. The book was read widely and its thesis accepted by many. Keynes's arguments were not effectively countered until after the Second World War. See Étienne Mantoux, *The Carthaginian Peace,* University of Pittsburgh Press, Pittsburgh, 1952.

[20]Shirer, *Rise and Fall,* p. 421.

at in Munich. Chamberlain was reacting in a not unreasonable manner to historical forces and to his interpretation of history only too recently past.

The Emergence of the Big Two: The Second World War

The Nazi-Soviet Pact

One of the most crucial turning points in the process that led to the Second World War involved a contest between Germany and the Western democracies of Britain and France, for an alliance with the Soviet Union. Britain and France, once Hitler had eliminated Czechoslovakia, both pledged to protect Poland from the same fate. Realistically, they could not hope to do so without the aid of the Soviet Union. Besides, it was clear that Britain and France could use Russian help to dissuade Hitler from whatever aggressive designs he might have.

From the beginning, the Western powers seemed to have a better chance of obtaining the Soviet signature on a treaty than did the Germans. Ideologically, the British and French democracies were hardly compatible with the Soviet Union, but neither were they so unremittingly hostile as Nazi Germany. And the Soviet Union had an old score to settle with the Germans. When the Soviets dropped out of the First World War, their departure was formalized by the Treaty of Brest Litovsk, which they signed with the Germans. Lenin at the time was desperate to get out of the war, and the terms of the treaty reflected his desperation. Russia gave up 32 percent of its population, or 56 million people. The territory Russia lost contained 73 percent of its iron ore, 89 percent of its coal, and a third of its railway mileage. In addition, Russia agreed to pay an indemnity of 6 billion marks. Thus, in the 1930s the Soviets felt that some revision of boundaries and spheres of influence was desirable. Hitler did not seem likely to allow such revisions; perhaps with the help of the Western powers, the Soviets could bring them about.

Despite the advantages the British and the French had, the Germans won the contest. In August 1939, the Nazi-Soviet pact was announced. What brought the two dictators together? Hitler's motives, in retrospect, were quite obvious. Given his actions during the war, one may surmise that he never gave up his idea of acquiring Lebensraum in the east. And he knew that his planned attack on Poland might involve him in a war with Britain and France, especially if the two could count on a Russian ally. Once the Nazi-Soviet pact was signed, Hitler did not have to worry that his attack on Poland would lead him into a two-front war, and he could hope that without a Russian ally, Britain and France would refrain from serious opposition to his Polish venture. Even as he signed the pact with the Russians, Hitler almost certainly knew that he would, some day, violate it.

Stalin's motives are not quite as easily discerned as Hitler's. It is clear that Stalin was reluctant to sign a pact with the Western powers, because he was not at all sure that they would abide by it in the event of a German attack on Russia. He suspected that both Britain and France might be happy to see the Nazis and the Communists engage in prolonged bloodletting. Furthermore, France and Britain were unable to get Poland to agree to allow Russian troops onto Polish soil if Germany attacked Poland. This heightened Stalin's suspicion that the pact proposed by the West was a ruse designed to bring about war between Germany and the Soviet Union. Finally, Stalin, like Hitler, was worried about a two-front war. Germany's ally, Japan, was much on Stalin's mind as he signed the pact with Hitler.

Some argue that Stalin signed the pact with the idea that Hitler would get involved in a war with the Western powers first, thus ensuring that when Hitler turned his troops on the Soviets, the West would be irrevocably committed against the Germans. Stalin may have had that in mind, but there is a problem with the argument. If Stalin calculated that the pact he had signed with Hitler would assure that Germany and the democracies were at war by the time Germany attacked Russia, Stalin should have expected Hitler's attack. But according to every available indicator, Stalin and his army were caught entirely by surprise when the German attack came in June 1941. It is possible that what surprised Stalin was the timing of the attack rather than its occurrence. Still, the fact that he was so surprised by it lends credence to the argument that Stalin hoped his pact with Hitler would allow him to stay out of the war altogether.

Hitler's Attack on Russia
If Stalin's plan was to stay out of world war, it seemed to work for a while. By agreement both the Germans and the Russians moved against Poland, and the state ceased to exist as an independent entity. Despite their failure to obtain Russian allegiance, the British and the French decided they could not tolerate another Hitlerian adventure and declared war on Germany. Hitler's initial successes in the ensuing months were spectacular. It took him a little over two weeks to defeat Poland. Denmark, Norway, Belgium, the

Netherlands, and most surprisingly, France fell in quick succession. After one year of fighting, Hitler seemed invincible and well on his way to adding Great Britain to his list of victims. But Great Britain's resistance proved more substantial than Hitler had planned and may have influenced him to make the decision that ultimately led to disaster. He decided to attack the Soviet Union.

To some extent the decision was a strategic calculation on Hitler's part. His idea was that once he had defeated the Soviet Union, he could turn the full force of his military might against the British, thus finally accomplishing the victory that so far had eluded him. But the importance of these more or less rational calculations can be overstressed. At bottom, Hitler's decision to forsake his attack against the British seems to have been an ideological one. Fifteen years earlier, in *Mein Kampf,* he had written:

> And so we National Socialists take up where we broke off six hundred years ago. We stop the endless German movement toward the south and west of Europe and turn our gaze toward the lands of the East. . . . When we speak of new territory in Europe today we must think principally of Russia and her border vassal states. Destiny itself seems to wish to point out the way to us here. . . . This colossal empire in the East is ripe for dissolution, and the end of Jewish domination in Russia will also be the end of Russia as a state.[21]

Hitler's attack on Russia, like Napoleon's in the nineteenth century, was a disaster. The Russians managed to hold off the German onslaught until the Russian winter destroyed much of the German army. That alone might have been enough, in the long run, to be Hitler's undoing. But just about the time the German troops began to have trouble in Russia, one of Germany's allies took the step that assured the premature dissolution of the Thousand Year Reich.

Pearl Harbor
The Germans did not know about, nor did they approve Japan's attack on Pearl Harbor. Rather, they had hoped that Japan would be menacing enough to keep the United States out of the war. They did give assurances to the Japanese government that if it became involved in a war with the United States, it would have the support of Germany. But these assurances were apparently calculated only

[21]Cited by Shirer, *Rise and Fall,* p. 796.

to encourage the Japanese to bravely assume a menacing posture toward the United States and not to attack.

Despite their renowned zeal for combat, the Japanese did not feel that they could defeat the United States, march into Washington, D.C., and dictate peace terms to their liking. They did, perhaps, underestimate the military potential of the United States, but not to such an extent. Their idea was to deliver a punishing blow to the Unitd States at Pearl Harbor, then resist the American counterattack so vigorously and persistently that the United States would tire of the struggle and allow the Japanese the free hand in China, Southeast Asia, and Indonesia that they felt was necessary for the sustenance of the Japanese economy. From the Japanese point of view, the United States had for years expressed unreasonable opposition to their economic and political expansion in East Asia, and there is little doubt that many Japanese sincerely felt the slogan "Asia for Asians" accurately expressed the laudable goal of their country's policies.

The Japanese plan, of course, did not work. The productive and military potential of the United States eventually overwhelmed Japan, especially when the Americans added nuclear weapons to their arsenal. The Germans, having already suffered a grievous blow in the Soviet Union, found themselves totally unable to withstand the combined weight of the Russians from the east, and the Americans from the west. By the end of 1945, both Japan and Germany were occupied countries. Italy had fallen in 1943.

The Impact of the Second World War
Aside from the total defeat of the three challengers to the international status quo, probably the most important impact of the Second World War on the global political system involved the emergence of two superpowers, the United States and the Soviet Union. When the Germans attacked the Soviet Union in 1941, there was a widespread expectation that Soviet resistance would be shortlived. When these expectations proved wrong, and the Soviets defeated the Germans, their true strength came to light and was, perhaps, even exaggerated. The performance of the United States in the war made clear the identity of the other superpower.

The emergence of the Big Two was especially dramatic in comparison to the fate of Europe. The fall of Europe had begun in the First World War, but this fact was at least partially hidden by the withdrawal of the United States into isolationism, and the revolution in the Soviet Union. After the Second World War, the only European state with credible pretensions to great-power status was Great Britain. The weaknesses of Germany, Italy, and France were apparent to everyone. But in two or three years after the war, Great Britain's pretensions proved unwarranted. She found herself no longer able to fulfill her previous global responsibilities, and by 1948, India had gained its independence, followed by Ceylon and Burma, and the British had withdrawn from Greece and Palestine. Europe, the center of world political power for at least three hundred years, gave way to the Big Two.

The Cold War

It was inevitable, at the climax of a gigantic struggle such as the Second World War, that the settlements and agreements arrived at by the victorious coalition would shape the primary conflicts in the years to follow. And no matter what these settlements contained, some of the involved parties would be dissatisfied, and their dissatisfactions would form the basis of future conflicts.

Conflict over Eastern Europe

Perhaps the most heated and important conflict in the months immediately following the war involved Poland and the rest of the East European countries. Great Britain, after all, had resorted to war in the first place in order to ensure the existence of an independent Poland. Roosevelt, after the United States entered the war, was anxious to protect the interests of the Poles at least partly because of a desire to avoid alienating an important voting bloc in the United States. So both countries began to press the Soviets about the future of Poland well before the Soviets had established their presence in that country. Conflict centered first on what government-in-exile would be recognized as the official representative of Poland. The British and the Americans favored one group in London, while the Russians set up one more to their liking. The Russians had several reasons to be suspicious of the Poles in London. Poland had grabbed off territory the Russians considered their own in the years following the First World War, when the Russians were weak and unable to resist successfully. Later, many of the elements now represented in the government-in-exile in London had refused to agree to allow Russian troops on Polish soil in the event of a German attack, thus throwing an important roadblock in the way of the movement that might have resulted in an alliance between Great Britain and France, on the one hand, and Russia, on the other. Mutual suspicions between the Poles in London and the

Russians were solidified by a controversy surrounding the "discovery" by German soldiers of a mass grave for Polish army officers in the Katyn Forest. The Nazis accused the Russians of these mass executions, and the Russians blamed the Nazis. The Polish government-in-exile in London seemed to side with the Nazi charges against the Russians. If there had ever been any chance of compromise between the Poles in London and the Soviets (and it is not clear that there was), this incident certainly diminished the probability of such an occurrence.

The future of Poland, and the other East European states, was one of many topics discussed at a 1945 meeting of the Big Three (Roosevelt, Stalin, and Churchill) at Yalta in the Russian Crimea. One result of this discussion was the Declaration on Liberated Europe, in which Stalin promised that free elections would be held in East European countries that were, at the time, the site of Red Army victories over the Nazis. Roosevelt's acceptance of this promise was to provoke controversy in the years following the war, because, certainly from the American point of view, Stalin did not abide by his promise. Elections were not held in Poland until 1947, and even then they were not what the Western powers considered the free and unfettered elections that had been promised in the declaration.

Critics of Roosevelt have argued vociferously that the American president had to be incredibly naive to accept Russian promises with regard to Eastern Europe after the Second World War, and that he did so paved the way for a Communist takeover in these countries. In support of such critics it must be said that there is good evidence that Roosevelt was, during the war, more optimistic about the prospects for American-Russian postwar cooperation than subsequent events proved to be warranted. But it is important not to overlook the basic, if obvious, fact that at the time that Roosevelt accepted Stalin's pledge concerning free elections in Eastern Europe, the Russians had troops there and the Americans did not. What if Roosevelt had refused to accept Stalin's word on this matter? The only effective alternative would have been to send American troops through Germany to take on the Russians in Eastern Europe. This was hardly a politically viable option, and so it is hard to see what Roosevelt gave away in Eastern Europe that the Soviets did not already have, or were soon to have the power to grasp.

In any case, the Russians' "satellization" of Eastern Europe was an important step down the road toward the cold war with the

United States. But the view that the cold war was a result of aggressive Russian actions in Eastern Europe and elsewhere is a hotly disputed one. Several American writers,[22] for example, argue that Russian policies in Eastern Europe were essentially defensive, and that it was the American hostility toward the Soviets that was primarily responsible for the onset of the cold war. This controversy often turns on the question of which country took the *first* action that precipitated the cold war conflict. Defenders of American foreign policy point to the Soviet refusal to remove their troops from Iran in 1945 as the precipitating event. Revisionists, in response, point to some earlier occurrence, such as the refusal by the Americans and the British to allow full Russian participation in the governing of Italy when it fell to their troops in 1943. Discussion of the who-did-what-first question, carried to its logical extreme, leads one side to emphasize the hostility of Bolshevik propaganda against the Western states from the earliest days of the Russian Revolution, and the other to point out that several Western nations invaded the Soviet Union in an attempt to dismantle the Revolution in the years when it was born and struggling to survive.

The origins of the cold war will be examined in later chapters. I will conclude this discussion with reference to an important attribute of the structure of the international system after the Second World War. By the end of 1945, there was only one country in the world which was strong enough to pose a threat of any kind to the Soviet Union, and that was the United States. The only country in the world strong enough to resist the American will in any part of the globe at the end of 1945 was the Soviet Union. The development by the Soviets of an atom bomb in 1949 served to exacerbate dramatically the tensions inherent in such a situation. Perhaps the cold war was not inevitable, but given the structure of the international system at the end of the war, it was a probable development regardless of which country was more aggressive or hostile to the other.

Civil War in China

The conflict over Eastern Europe was mainly the result of the fact that German power had been crushed in that area, thus creating a "power vacuum" into which the Russians entered against the resistance of the Americans, the British, and at least some groups in the East European countries. But Eastern Europe was certainly not the only sector of the globe where such a vacuum had been created by

[22]Gabriel Kolko and Joyce Kolko, *The Limits of Power,* Harper and Row, New York, 1972. David Horowitz, *The Free World Colossus,* Wang and Hill, New York, 1965. Gar Alperowitz, *Atomic Diplomacy,* Vintage, New York, 1965.

the Second World War. A broadly similar process took place in China. The Japanese had taken over large areas of that country during the war, pushing the Nationalist government of Chiang Kai-shek farther into the hinterlands. As Chiang retreated, he became progressively more isolated from his more moderate sources of support and increasingly dependent on the more conservative classes. In the meantime, the Communists, under Mao Tse-tung, took advantage of the Japanese invasion to strengthen their organization. The Japanese, as they took over Chinese territory, tended to concentrate on the cities, leaving the peasants in the countryside more or less on their own. The Communists were to move into this particular vacuum, organizing the peasants, carrying out some land reform measures, and generally strengthening this important part of their power base.

In addition, the Communists did a good job of fighting the Japanese, especially in comparison with the forces of Chiang Kai-shek. Chiang's troops were perhaps less well trained and motivated in any case, but even if they were not, Chiang often showed himself to be more concerned with the Communists in his country than the Japanese invaders. So, while the Communists assumed a patriotic stance, and seemed to concentrate more on the foreign invaders, Chiang devoted much of his energies to the civil conflict and must have appeared to many Chinese to be less patriotic and heroic than his Communist counterparts.

When the Japanese evacuated the country, the stage was set for the culmination of the struggle between Mao and Chiang. Mao might have been successful eventually without the inadvertent aid of the Japanese, just as Lenin could conceivably have carried off his revolution even if the Russians had not experienced the disaster of the First World War. But there is little doubt that the Japanese invasion and evacuation created a fluid situation in China of which Mao took good advantage. Despite considerable financial aid and free advice from the United States, Chiang was unable to quash the Communist rebellion, and in 1949 he was forced to flee to the island of Formosa, leaving the world's most populous state in the hands of Mao Tse-tung.

The Korean War

Another area in which the defeat of the Japanese created conditions conducive to conflict was Korea. Korea had been formally annexed by Japan in 1910. In the final days of the war the Soviets and the Americans came to an agreement that the Soviets would accept the surrender of the Japanese troops to the north of the thirty-eighth parallel, while the Americans would accept similar surrenders south of that parallel. The agreement was carried out by both sides without serious problems. But problems were soon to develop. The Americans and the Russians ruled their zones separately, and by 1948 North Korea and South Korea had become two separate nations. Border tensions between the new nations were constant, with both sides threatening to "liberate" the other, and the Americans arming the South while the North received military aid from the Russians.

Finally, in June 1950, the North Koreans invaded the South.[23] The motives for this invasion have been the topic of lively speculation. There is widespread agreement that the North Korean government was controlled by the Russians, and so the Russians must have known about and approved the North Korean invasion plan. But why? At the time, the Americans and the West Europeans were fearful that the attack was a diversionary tactic adopted by Stalin to pin down the Americans in Asia so that he could move against Western Europe. Later, with the benefit of hindsight, and knowledge of the conflict between Communist China and the Soviet Union, some surmised that the Korean war was Stalin's scheme to get the Americans and the Chinese into a prolonged land war in Asia, thus weakening both. In his memoirs, Nikita Khrushchev insists that the invasion was the idea of North Korean Premier Kim Il Sung, who managed to convince Stalin that the South Koreans would greet the Northerners as liberators, thus ensuring an easy, quick victory for the North.[24]

Whatever the motivation, the attack by the North Koreans met with immediate success. With the South Koreans rapidly reaching desperate straits, the United States urged the United Nations to resist the invasion. Success for this effort was assured by the great influence of the United States in the United Nations of that time and by the absence of the Soviet Union from the Security Council. (The Soviets were boycotting the council to protest the exclusion of China from that body.) Eventually the United States and sixteen other nations sent troops to Korea; they managed to halt the progress of the North Koreans.

In fact the success of the United Nations forces (of which the United States' contingent was by far the largest) was so substantial and relatively easy that it brought about a change in American

[23]This version of the event is accepted by most Western sources, although the North Koreans claimed that they were responding to an attack by the South, and one well-known Western journalist argues that the United States was at least partially responsible for the onset of the Korean War. See I. F. Stone, *The Hidden History of the Korean War,* Monthly Review Press, New York, 1952.
[24]Cited by Richard J. Barnet, *The Roots of War,* Penguin, Baltimore, 1971, p. 274.

policy in the middle of the war. When the intervention began, Secretary of State Dean Acheson had explained that the United Nations troops were in Korea "solely for the purpose of restoring the Republic of Korea to its status prior to the invasion from the North. . . ."[25] But as the American forces moved up the peninsula, the temptation to bring about a more permanent solution to the problem posed by the Korean situation proved decisive. Instead of merely pushing the North Koreans back into their own territory, the United Nations troops moved to unify all of Korea by force. The risk that China would enter the war was accepted willingly by General MacArthur, the head of the U.N. troops, and by the United States government, as troops moved ever closer to the Chinese border. MacArthur was sure, and he convinced officials in Washington, that the Chinese would not intervene, despite Chinese warnings to the United States government (using the British, the Indians, the Swedes, and the Russians as intermediaries)[26] that they would not allow the U.N. troops to eliminate the North Korean government next to their border.

MacArthur was, of course, wrong, and the Chinese did intervene in the Korean War, with immediate and dramatic success. Only after many months of hard fighting were the Chinese forced to halt their advance. As the war dragged on, its unpopularity in the United States grew, and the election of 1952 resulted in the victory of Dwight Eisenhower, who promised to end the conflict. The new president did manage to bring about an armistice, which ended the fighting in July 1953, but which did little or nothing to solve the problems that had brought about the conflict in the first place.

The War in Vietnam

Another area where Japanese withdrawal left a vacuum to be filled was Indochina, and more specifically, Vietnam. Before the war, Vietnam had been a French colony. It remained officially so (but under the pro-Nazi Vichy regime) even during the Japanese occupation. Vietnamese nationalists, known as the Vietminh, had staged uprisings against the French, before the Japanese arrived. The Japanese, after their arrival, cooperated with the French in an attempt to stamp out the Vietminh. Finally, in March 1945, the Japanese staged a coup against the French and took over formal control of the country. This presented the Vietminh with an opportunity, since the Japanese had never had the chance to develop a

[25]"Review of U.N. and U.S. Action to Restore Peace," *Department of State Bulletin*, 23 (July 10, 1950), 46.
[26]Allen Whiting, *China Crosses the Yalu*, Macmillan, New York, 1960, pp. 108–109.

police apparatus as efficient as that assembled by the French. By September 1945 the Vietminh had effective de facto control of the country, and they issued a declaration of independence.

The reign of the Vietminh was to be short-lived. At the Potsdam Conference, the United States, Russia, and Great Britain had agreed that Southeast Asia was within the British sphere of influence, and thus the British were given the responsibility of establishing law and order in the area. But in Vietnam the British were to share that responsibility with the Chinese. For this purpose the former French colony was divided at the sixteenth parallel, with the Chinese zone in the North, and the British zone in the South.

The Chinese and the British interpreted their mandates to restore law and order in dramatically different ways. The Chinese recognized the de facto Vietminh regime. The British set about dismantling the Vietminh regime in the South in order to return control of that area to the former French colonialists. In this effort they were successful, but not without the cooperation of Japanese troops that were still in the country.[27]

The French began to have problems with their rebellious subjects in Southeast Asia almost from the moment that they reassumed control of the area. For the first few troubled years after the war, the United States opposed the efforts of the French, viewing them as dedicated to reimposition of an outdated colonial regime, and the Vietminh as fighters for national liberation. As late as 1947, President Truman was so opposed to the French policy in Vietnam that he insisted that American-produced propellers be removed from British aircraft sent by the British to French troops in Vietnam.[28] This attitude was to change quite rapidly without any essential change in the war taking place in Southeast Asia. In 1948, tension between the Russians and the Americans increased dramatically. In 1949, China came under Communist control. By 1950, the Americans saw the French as defenders of the free world, and the Vietnamese rebels as agents of a worldwide Communist conspiracy. Accordingly, the American government began to support the French military in Vietnam economically, and by 1954, the United

[27]General Douglas MacArthur, in Tokyo at the time, was outraged by the use of Japanese troops against the Vietnamese people. He stated, "If there is anything that makes my blood boil it is to see our allies in Indochina and Java deploying Japanese troops to reconquer the little people we promised to liberate. It is the most ignoble kind of betrayal." Cited by Harold Isaacs, "Independence for Vietnam?" in *Vietnam,* ed. Marvin E. Gettlemen, Fawcett, New York, 1965, p. 46.

[28]John G. Stoessinger, *Why Nations Go to War,* St. Martin's Press, New York, p. 107.

States was paying between 50 percent and 80 percent of the cost of the war against the forces of Ho Chi Minh.[29]

The British Retreat

The British were not defeated in the Second World War, but it soon became obvious that they had been severely weakened. As a result, they were forced to pull back from areas of the world where they had previously exerted influence and/or control. Further vacuums were created, and none was filled without conflict. In February 1947, Britain announced to the United States government that it could no longer support the government of Greece, then under attack by rebels, some of whom were Communists. Truman decided to take over British responsibilities there but the decision concerning Greece was imbedded in and overshadowed by a decision of much wider application, the decision to institute the policy of containment. Henceforth, Truman announced, "It must be the policy of the United States to support free peoples who are resisting attempted subjugation by armed minorities or by outside pressures."[30] If this did not mark the beginning of the cold war, it was at least an official pronouncement of it.

At about the same time the British also decided they could no longer hold on to their colony of India. They pulled out in 1947. During their rule, they had managed to keep the lid on conflict between the Hindu majority and the Moslem minority, even though they did nothing to bring about harmony between the groups. When the British left, the lid flew off and the pot boiled over. The Hindus and Moslems established two separate nations, India and Pakistan. These nations fought two wars over disputed territory (Kashmir), and then a Pakistani civil war in 1971 led to Indian intervention, a third bloody Pakistani-Indian war, and the creation of a third nation, Bangladesh.

Finally, in 1948, the British pulled out of Palestine. This area had been the scene of civil strife between Jews and Arabs from the time the British had established their rule after the First World War. After the Second World War the Jews were anxious to proclaim an independent state for themselves, the Arabs were equally anxious to prevent it, and the British found themselves unable to mediate

[29]For the lower estimate, see Miriam S. Farley, *United States Relations with Southeast Asia with Special Reference to Indochina,* Institute of Pacific Relations, New York, 1955, p. 4. The higher figure is given by Ellen J. Hammer, *The Struggle for Indochina,* Stanford University Press, Stanford, 1954, p. 313.

[30]Louis W. Koenig, ed., *The Truman Administration, Its Principles and Practice,* New York University Press, New York, 1956, pp. 296–301.

this conflict. They appealed to the United States and the United Nations for help but got only speeches encouraging to the Jews from the former, and resolutions impossible to enforce from the latter. So they simply announced that they were withdrawing their troops in May 1948. When they did, the Jews proclaimed the state of Israel, the Arabs tried to crush it, and the Jews won the ensuing war. In the process, the Jews created the bases for constant conflict for at least the next thirty years. That conflict erupted into actual war between Israel and her Arab neighbors in 1956, 1967, and 1973.

The Hungarian Crisis

By 1955, the first of the power vacuums, Eastern Europe, had been thoroughly eliminated by the Soviet Union. But in 1956 the ties between Soviet Union and the East Europeans began to weaken dangerously, from the Soviet point of view. One event that accelerated this process was a secret speech given by Khrushchev in 1956, in which he criticized Stalin and Stalinist policies in harsh terms. The contents of the speech became known in Eastern Europe, where hope began that a denunciation of Stalin might be a signal of renunciation of Stalinist control over Eastern Europe by the Soviet Union.

Workers' riots in Poland in June 1956 led to some limited measures of independence for that country. In October a more uncompromising rebellion took place in Hungary, aimed at the elimination of the domestic Communist regime as well as escape from the Communist international bloc. The Hungarians' pleas for help went unheeded by the United Nations and the United States; the Russians invaded Hungary and crushed the rebellion.

Neither the United States nor the Soviet Union escaped from this crisis unscathed. Soviet protestations that they were merely trying to save the Hungarians from reactionary capitalist elements were undoubtedly sincere in some measure, but their actions spoke louder than their words. Whatever the motivation, Soviet actions in Hungary appeared to be imperialistic, and the Soviet reputation as the leader of the anti-imperialist forces suffered accordingly. The reputation of the United States was not helped by the fact that President Eisenhower and Secretary of State Dulles had, in the past, proclaimed their intent to "liberate" the captive peoples of Eastern Europe. Their reaction to the pleas from Hungary during the Russian invasion, limited to denunciatory speeches, revealed the emptiness of earlier rhetoric.

Despite the embarrassment suffered by both superpowers as a result of the rebellion in Hungary, the crisis marked an important turning point in the cold war. Wisely or not, the United States had never clearly accepted the Soviets' firmly defined sphere of influence in Eastern Europe. The Eisenhower administration had emphasized this attitude with talk of rolling back the Iron Curtain. But when the United States stood by passively while the Soviets reestablished their control of Hungary, the government implicitly accepted the fact of Soviet hegemony in Eastern Europe, even if reluctantly. The cold war did not end in 1956, but the Hungarian crisis, in retrospect, can be seen as the point when movement began in that direction. This movement was to be halted periodically, even pushed back on occasion, in the years to come, but the trend toward the détente of the 1970s may well have been born in Hungary in 1956.

Sputniks, Kennedy, and Vietnam

Russian Success in Space

One of the setbacks in the movement toward détente coincided with a spectacular success in outer space by the Soviet Union in 1957. The Russians launched the world's first earth satellite in October 1957 and followed it one month later with a satellite some 6 times heavier than the first. The space program of the United States had literally not yet gotten off the ground. The Americans had plans to launch a satellite, but the one they were about to send off weighed only 31 pounds, 153 pounds lighter than *Sputnik I* and more than 1,000 pounds lighter than *Sputnik II*.

The Russian reaction to their stellar accomplishments was to assume a bolder stance in the cold war conflict. Khrushchev, for example, began to put verbal diplomatic pressure on West Berlin, threatening to give East Germany control of supply routes to the city unless the Western powers removed their troops. The American reaction bordered on panic: smug confidence that American technological superiority in the world was unquestionable was replaced by fears that the country had "fallen behind" the Russians in several strategically crucial areas. The sputniks were also to have an important impact on presidential politics, because they provided a basis for the myth of the missile gap. Kennedy ran against Nixon with a promise to get the country moving again and claimed one reason this was necessary was that the Eisenhower administration had allowed the United States to fall behind the Russians in the development and production of intercontinental ballistic missiles. The charge may have seemed credible to some voters because of *Sputnik I* and *Sputnik II*.

Kennedy's Defense Strategy

Curiously, once Kennedy was elected, his defense strategy did not focus on missiles. (This may have been partly because Kennedy's secretary of defense concluded that no missile gap existed.) On the contrary, Kennedy made a concerted effort to have the defense posture of the United States less reliant on missiles. Eisenhower and Dulles had decided that the United States could not, and did not need to, compete with the Soviet Union in maintaining large infantries. They concluded that the United States should rely heavily on missiles and nuclear weapons, thus confronting any Communist move anywhere in the globe with the threat of massive retaliation. (The policy was advocated on the grounds that it would provide more "bang for the buck.") After Kennedy was elected, he concluded that this policy was insufficiently flexible. He feared that there were many kinds of subtle yet effective probes which the Communists could make for which the threat of massive retaliation was not credible. The subtle kind of probe that worried him most, apparently, was that involving Communist-organized subversion and guerrilla warfare in Third World countries. Such efforts could not be countered with nuclear weapons, because the destruction caused by these weapons would be out of proportion to the nature of the threat, and in any case, guerrillas were hard to locate and separate from the local civilian population of the country being defended. In order to combat the threat of subtle probes Kennedy developed a more flexible defense posture, utilizing techniques more appropriate for counterguerrilla warfare, leading to the creation of such units as the Green Berets.

Two Cuban Crises

Kennedy's thousand days were marked by several dramatic events in the realm of international affairs. One involved the invasion of Cuba at the Bay of Pigs. The plan for this invasion originated in the Eisenhower administration shortly after Castro assumed power. The invasion was carried out by a small number of Cuban exiles, financed, organized, and led into combat by agents of the Central Intelligence Agency (CIA).[31] It was assumed that the invasion would spur massive numbers of Cubans opposed to Castro to active rebellion. This did not happen, because of poor coordination between the invading forces and the Cuban anti-Castro underground, and almost certainly because there was less opposition to Castro than the CIA supposed. The total failure of the invasion was

[31] Haynes Johnson, *The Bay of Pigs,* Norton, New York, 1964, pp. 103–106.

assured when President Kennedy decided not to approve overt and substantial support for the effort by the United States Air Force.

The Bay of Pigs fiasco, along with the construction of a wall between East and West Berlin by the government of East Germany, set the stage for the Cuban Missile Crisis in 1962. The Russians, of course, tried to slip missiles into Cuba secretly, for reasons that to this day remain somewhat mysterious.[32] The Americans discovered the missiles as they were being installed, and put a blockade (called a quarantine) into effect to prevent the Russians from delivering more missiles. In the end, the Russians backed down, turning around ships headed for Cuba with additional missiles, and agreeing to remove those already in Cuba.

Kennedy might well have firmly resisted this Russian move in any case; but his opposition was stiffened by the fear that, having cut off air support to the Bay of Pigs invaders and failing to take effective action against the construction of the wall in East Berlin, he could not acquiesce in the secret shipment of missiles to Cuba without leading Khrushchev to believe that the United States would not actively resist other bold moves on the part of the Soviets. Khrushchev put the best possible light on the affair, arguing that his primary aim was the defense of Cuba, and that since, in return for the removal of the missiles, he had obtained a promise from the United States not to attack the island, his aim was accomplished. All agreed that the crisis had brought the world the closest it had ever been to a nuclear holocaust.

The effects of the missile crisis on relationships between the Big Two were mixed, but apparently beneficial, at least in the short run. The close brush with nuclear war seemed to have a sobering effect on both sides. It is possible that the crisis led both sides to more earnest attempts to avoid confrontations of that kind. (The Nuclear Test Ban Treaty of 1963 might be an example.) On the other hand, in retrospect one can see that the Russians may have resolved to avoid ever being caught again in a position of strategic inferiority with regard to nuclear missiles, or any other military hardware.[33] The result of that resolution may be visible in the military budgets of the Soviets in the years since the crisis; the Russians have consistently devoted a tremendous portion of their national budget to defense, and in the 1970s began to catch up with

[32]Graham T. Allison, *Essence of Decision,* Little, Brown, Boston, 1971, pp. 40–55.
[33]James A. Nathan, "The Missile Crisis: His Finest Hour Now," *World Politics,* 27 (January 1975), 273.

TABLE 1.1   The military balance

	U.S.	U.S.S.R.
Armed forces	2,084,350	4,412,000
Tanks	10,000	42,000
Strategic missiles	1,710	2,378
Megatonnage	4,000	10,000
Strategic aircraft	463	135
Tactical aircraft	8,500	6,100
Major combat ships	182	226
Aircraft carriers	14	1
Missile submarines	41	73
Attack submarines	73	253

Source: Newsweek, March 1, 1976, p. 38. Reprinted with permission.

and pass the United States in several categories of military equipment. (See Table 1.1.) To trace all such defense effort to the Russian experience in the Cuban Missile Crisis wold undoubtedly be an error (especially in light of the Chinese threat so clearly perceived by the Soviet Union), but the crisis may well have made some significant contribution to Russian determination.

The Growing War in Vietnam
While the attention of Americans was focused on more dramatic events such as the Bay of Pigs invasion, Berlin crises, and the missile crisis, quieter but important developments were taking place in Vietnam. Kennedy inherited from the Eisenhower Administration a commitment to the government of Ngo Dinh Diem in South Vietnam that already involved, by 1960, the presence of some 1,000 American advisors in that country. When Kennedy's aides recommended that he send 8,000 military troops to Vietnam, he sent instead 15,000 more advisors, who were supposed to avoid actual combat. They did not seem to help the situation substantially, and Kennedy became increasingly convinced that nothing would unless Diem, the Catholic leader of a predominantly Buddhist Vietnam, were replaced. The United States government looked the other way when a coup d'état in South Vietnam resulted in not only Diem's removal from office but also his death.

Unfortunately, from the American point of view, the removal of Diem did not bring stability to the government of South Vietnam. Instead, a seemingly never ending series of generals succeeded

Diem, and the situation deteriorated further. When Kennedy was assassinated some three weeks after the death of Diem, Lyndon Johnson was faced with a problem in South Vietnam that he ultimately found insoluble. Kennedy's role in the process that created this problem for Johnson should not be overlooked; on the other hand, it should not be forgotten that when Kennedy died, there were 17,000 Americans in South Vietnam, but only about 70 had been killed.

Johnson delayed any serious increase in American involvement during the election year of 1964. Then, in 1965 he became convinced that some forceful response to the deteriorating situation in South Vietnam was necessary, and he committed large numbers of American combat troops. This was the beginning of the escalation and counter-escalation that ended in disaster for President Johnson. His military advisors would request additional troops, and Johnson would grant only half of the number requested, feeling that he was following a wise middle-of-the-road course. The air force would submit an ever expanding list of targets in the North to be bombed, and Johnson would trim that list at least partially, again feeling that his strategy was a moderate, reasonable one. The problem was that, no matter how strongly Johnson resisted the pressures from the military, the escalatory trend continued. It reached the point where the army wanted 1,000,000 men, and Johnson could barely hold the line at 550,000. The reaction from the North Vietnamese was always the same: no movement toward the bargaining table, which the Americans were trying to bring about, and counterescalation with infiltration of more men and supplies into the South. Finally, in March 1968, following months of domestic unrest in the United States, and precipitously falling ratings in the public opinion polls, President Johnson announced that he would not seek re-election. At the same time, he announced that he would dedicate the remaining days of his term to an intensive effort to bring peace in Vietnam. At that moment, a prediction that Johnson would not be successful in his effort, and that the next president would not be able to accomplish peace within the span of a full four-year term, would have struck most Americans as unreasonably gloomy and pessimistic.

Détente and Tripolarity

President Nixon did manage to get a peace settlement, but only after incursions into Laos and Cambodia, a bombing campaign against North Vietnam unprecedented for its scope and intensity, and thousands of additional American and Asian deaths. The prolongation of agony on all sides seemed especially pointless, in the American view, when a little more than a year after the peace settlement was accomplished, Saigon was taken by Communist forces.

But Richard Nixon was nothing if not a paradoxical man. While he fought the war against the small Communist nation of North Vietnam to its bitter conclusion, he took significant steps toward improving relationships between the United States and the leading Communist nations: the Soviet Union and China. Rapprochement with China was particularly dramatic and significant, because formal diplomatic communication between China and the United States had been almost nonexistent for more than two decades. What brought about the sudden improvement in relations between Richard Nixon, known for his rigid, vigorous anti-Communism, and the leaders in China as well as those in the Soviet Union?

One factor may well have been the flexible position Nixon found himself in during the early 1970s. His personal anti-Communism was, of course, unquestionable. Perhaps even more important was the solid anti-Communist reputation of Nixon's Republican party. The flexibility that this reputation gives Republican presidents was perhaps revealed when President Eisenhower accepted a peace settlement in Korea that might have been impossible for a Democratic president in the days of McCarthyism to accept. Eisenhower also stood by while the Russians crushed a rebellion in Hungary. In contrast Kennedy authorized an invasion of Communist Cuba shortly after the beginning of his administration and followed with a more determined resistance to Communist activities in South Vietnam than Eisenhower had ever mounted. President Johnson, of course, escalated the anti-Communist crusade in Vietnam dramatically, and also staged an invasion of the Dominican Republic in opposition to a Communist threat of dubious validity.[34] In short, when Nixon became president, he was not at all vulnerable to the charge of being soft on communism, and this may have eased the way for his move toward détente.

Henry Kissinger's role in the creation of détente should not be overlooked. It is clear that Kissinger recognized that the United States could not maintain its predominant position of the 1950s,

[34]Abraham F. Lowenthal, *The Dominican Intervention,* Harvard University Press, Cambridge, Mass., 1972, p. 155.

and that it had to accommodate the rising power of the Soviet Union and China. He had written that,

> for the two decades after 1945, our international activities were based on the assumption that technology plus managerial skills gave us the ability to reshape the international system and to bring about domestic transformations in "emerging countries." This direct "operational" concept of international order has proved too simple. Political multipolarity makes it impossible to impose an American design.[35]

In order to conform to this reality Kissinger advocated a normalization of relations with the Soviet Union and China, and a concomitant recognition of the legitimate spheres of influence of those two great powers.

But almost certainly the most important factors contributing to the improvement in relations between the Soviet Union and China on the one hand, and the United States on the other, were the continuing conflict between the two Communist states and their rising military-industrial might. The conflict between the Soviet Union and China led both countries to fear isolation from each other and from the United States. This made both amenable to any move by the United States to improve relations. In turn, the United States could not view the rising power of the two great Communist states with equanimity, especially if there were to be continued antagonism with them. From the point of view of the United States, the logic of the saying "If you can't beat 'em, join 'em," was inherent in the situation. The pressures on the United States, the Soviet Union, and China would have exerted their force regardless of the preferences and idiosyncrasies of the leaders of the Big Three. I do not mean that the structure of the international system in the 1970s made détente inevitable, but it certainly did increase the probability of such an improvement in the relations between the United States and the Communist states.

The probability of serious conflict between the United States and one of the great Communist states, or between the Soviet Union and China, has certainly not fallen to zero. Neither is an improvement in relations between the Soviet Union and China an impossibility. The death of Mao in 1976, for example, sparked

[35]Henry A. Kissinger, *American Foreign Policy,* expanded ed. Norton, New York, 1974, pp. 57–58.

speculation that antagonism between Russia and China might decrease. Indeed, what seems likely to occur in such a tripolar situation is intermittent cooling and warming of all three bilateral relationships. The warming of one will put strains on the other two, leaving the one state in danger of isolation and probably in a conciliatory mood. This state is likely to make concessions to one of the other two states in oder to break the collusion between them.[36]

Important territorial disputes (or, ambiguously defined spheres of influence) are likely to exert periodic strains on at least one of the Big Three bilateral relationships in the years to come. Probably the most bitter of these disputes will involve the longest common border in the world, that between the Soviet Union and China. The unification of Korea remains troublesome unfinished business going back to the end of the Second World War. Both the Soviet Union and the United States appear to feel entitled to rights and responsibilities in the Middle East that are not entirely compatible. Finally, the whole continent of Africa, but especially the southern half, with its two white regimes in the predominantly black countries of Rhodesia and South Africa, seems full of potential for conflict that could attract the competitive efforts of the major powers.

The Study of World Politics after the Second World War

The reaction of scholars to the Second World War was quite different from that to the First World War. After the first war, as has been seen, the idea that world government, or at least some form of strong international organization, was essential to preserve international peace, was very popular in academic circles. The second war, and the death of the League of Nations, seemed to indicate to most scholars that the approach taken after the First World War, involving reliance on the League of Nations, and measures such as the Kellogg-Briand Treaty, which "outlawed" war, had been too idealistic. Successful foreign policies, according to this train of thought, must be built on a realistic appraisal of the world; men hunger for power, and the primary goal of national foreign-policy makers is to serve the national interest defined in terms of power.

[36] Michael Tatu, "The Great Power Triangle: Washington-Moscow-Peking," in *International Politics,* ed. Robert J. Art and Robert Jervis, Little, Brown, Boston, 1973, pp. 452–474.

Realism Versus Idealism

The chief advocate of the realist theory of international politics was Hans Morgenthau. His classic text, *Politics Among Nations*,[37] contained a thoughtful explanation of his theory, which many teachers and students of the post– Second World War era found convincing. But critics pointed out that states and their individual leaders have many important goals in addition to the national interest defined in terms of power. For example, sometimes an increase in the defense budget of a state may increase a state's power, but if it sparks an arms race, it may also decrease a state's security. Decision makers (at least in some cases) are aware of such a possibility, and they do not always seek to increase a nation's power when confronted with such a choice.

Decision makers also often become painfully aware of a choice between guns and butter; they may devote more resources to military equipment or to consumer goods. They may opt for the latter, even if that decreases the power of their state, because they feel it necessary to keep themselves in power. In other words, they will act not in the national interest defined in terms of power, but in their personal interest defined in terms of their power.

Another reason that an assumption that national leaders will act in the national interest defined in terms of power may be misleading is that so few interests are truly national in scope. Virtually every foreign policy decision hurts some people and benefits others. If the military budget is increased, that may well mean that there is less money for social welfare programs or education. A large military budget can also lead to inflation, hurting, in particular, those on fixed incomes. A decision to go to war can help weapons manufacturers and may even serve to protect the security of all those who are too young or too old to fight. But it will hurt all those young men who will be drafted to serve unwillingly in the military, and it will lead to the deaths of many of them. If national leaders decide to raise tariffs against foreign imports, protected manufacturers and workers will be happy, but consumers will pay higher prices.

Perhaps when Morgenthau says that leaders act in the national interest, he means they choose the policies that bring the greatest good to the greatest number. That hardly seems a realistic theory. But if that is not what he means, it is difficult, at best, to figure out what he does mean. It is certainly true, as Morgenthau implies, that foreign policy makers will not often knowingly take steps that

[37]Hans Morgenthau, *Politics Among Nations,* 1st ed. Knopf, New York, 1948.

endanger national security. But there is such a wide range of decisions that can be perceived to be congruent with national security, or the national interest, that using Morgenthau's criterion gives us, in the final analysis, very little guidance in our attempts to understand world politics.

Another aspect of the controversy surrounding Morgenthau's theory in the early 1950s deserves at least a brief mention, if only because President Carter brought a similar debate into the limelight. Morgenthau argues that ideals are a bad guide for foreign-policy makers. He warns that if decision makers select policies in order to defend or promote ideals (such as democracy, freedom, or national self-determination), they will lead nations into moralistic crusades, resulting, ultimately, in conflicts, and even wars that need not and should not be fought. President Carter's foreign policy, at least in the first months of his administration, included a strong component of idealism; he spoke out in favor of human rights, especially but not exclusively in the Soviet Union.

As a realist like Morgenthau would undoubtedly have predicted, the president's admonitions on human rights seemed to exacerbate tension between the Soviet Union and the United States. Critics of the president argued that Carter was actually hurting the cause of human rights in the Soviet Union, because the response by the Soviet leaders involved a crackdown on dissidents in their country.

In the wake of Vietnam, and a series of revelations about the activities of the CIA in other parts of the world (such as Chile), there was, perhaps, more than a touch of realism in Carter's stand on human rights. The American public (and, for that matter, world public opinion), one can reasonably surmise, was disillusioned by American foreign policy and foreign policy makers when Carter came into office. By basing his own policies, in part, on a morally appealing defense of human rights, he was trying to distinguish his policies from those of his immediate predecessors and evoke enthusiastic public support for those policies (in the United States and elsewhere). If he does this successfully and promotes respect for human rights in the Soviet Union, and in the world generally, he will have accomplished the interesting feat of utilizing idealistic appeals for idealistic as well as realistic purposes.

Studying World Politics Scientifically

Beginning about the late 1950s, another controversy began to compete with realists and idealists for attention. This new controversy focused on the question of whether or not it is possible, or desirable, to develop a scientific study of world politics. Those who were convinced that this is possible were sufficiently numerous that the next decade saw a growing number of articles and research projects in world politics based on scientific methods. (Or, as some would insist, allegedly scientific methods.)

Is it possible to study world politics, or human behavior in any context, scientifically? The answer depends, of course, on what is meant by *science*. Generally, those who have tried to develop a science of world politics are aiming to discover patterns in the making of foreign policies, the behavior of various social entities in the global political system, and the operation of that system. Any study that aims at the discovery of such patterns, and that is based on reproducible comparisons, is in my view scientific. Reproducible comparisons, the heart of the scientific method, are based on procedures so clearly defined that any qualified scientist, in addition to the original researcher, can carry them out.

The steadily increasing amount of research in world politics based on such procedures makes it progressively more difficult to argue that it is impossible to apply scientific methods to this field. Such arguments are, indeed, becoming increasingly rare. Many still believe, though, that scientific methods will not produce findings of real interest to scholars of world politics. Is it not true, for example, that the behavior of people, since they vary so significantly in background, beliefs, and character, is essentially unpredictable?

There is no doubt that it is difficult to accurately predict the behavior of people, but it is obviously not impossible. One can confidently predict, for example, that most people will stop at stop signs, flee burning buildings, and come in out of the rain. On a more significant level, it has been found in several countries that wealthy people are more likely to vote for more conservative parties than poor voters.

The basic social scientific assumption is that similar people under similar circumstances will behave in similar ways, and this assumption is borne out in an increasing number of studies of world politics. Even so, which similarities in people, and in circumstances, are crucial to explanations of the behavior of people in the context of world politics is not a question to which we have a great many answers as yet. But there are tentative answers, some of which I will discuss in the following pages. While some of these answers are based on too few cases, or are defined with insufficient clarity to be worthy of great confidence, they will provide some evidence in favor of the scientific argument that people's behavior in the context of world politics is, within limits, predictable. It is hoped these simple patterns will also stimulate interest in more complex, specifically defined patterns that lead researchers to depend on sophisticated statistical techniques and scientific procedures.

Radical Theories and Futuristic Concerns

At least two other post– Second World War developments in the discipline of international relations deserve mention. One of these is clearly related to the experience of the United States in Vietnam. To many people, in the United States and elsewhere, official explanations of American policy with regard to the war in Vietnam did not make much sense. North Vietnam did not present a credible security threat to the United States. The South Vietnamese government was not democratic, and so the argument that the United States was defending democracy, or freedom of choice, was unconvincing. Despite the fact that official reasons for doing so seemed less than compelling, the United States government showed great determination in Vietnam, spending billions of dollars, sacrificing thousands of American lives, and provoking serious domestic unrest. Why?

Many, predominantly young, scholars in the United States and elsewhere concluded that the real reason, as opposed to the stated reasons, for the determination in Vietnam involved the economic interests of the United States. Vietnam itself was of some economic value to the United States, and of even greater value to an important American ally, Japan. More important, according to this argument, American officials, and the business interests they represented, were concerned that if the "liberation" movement in South Vietnam were successful, others would be sure to follow, which would cut off ever greater areas of the globe from business interests in the United States and other important industrial societies of the free world. Foreign markets, fields of investment, and sources of raw materials are absolutely essential to capitalist economic systems, and the United States government realized this. It was these kinds of concerns that accounted for the determination the government demonstrated in Vietnam.

The plausibility of this argument inspired several books and articles that analyzed American foreign policy from this point of view.[38] It also led to a reanalysis of relationships between the United States and Third World countries, and the emergence of the dependency theory. The major tenet of this theory is that economic

[38]See, for example, Harry Magdoff, *The Age of Imperialism,* Monthly Review Press, New York, 1969; Gabriel Kolko, *The Roots of American Foreign Policy,* Beacon Press, Boston, 1969; K. T. Fann and Donald C. Hodges, eds., *Readings in U.S. Imperialism,* P. Sargent, Boston, 1971.

contact between Third World countries and rich industrialized countries, whether in the form of international trade, foreign investment, or foreign aid, works to the disadvantage of Third World countries and will continue to do so until the international economic and political system under which these activities take place is radically altered. Later, we will analyze the validity of theories that insist that American foreign policy (and the foreign policies of capitalist states in general) is dedicated primarily to protecting the interests of expansive American capitalism, as well as dependency theory as it applies to Third World countries.

Another post–Second World War development in the study of world politics involves a de-emphasis of the importance of nation-states, and a corresponding stress on the importance of other kinds of entities and organizations in the global political system. Perhaps it was the threat of nuclear war, and the realization that states now command sufficient power to destroy the world, that gave new impetus to an old idea, that is, that the world organized and dominated by states is a dangerous place, and that states should at least share responsibility for the economic and political activities of the global system with other kinds of organizations. In the late 1960s, and continuing into the 1970s, the dissatisfaction with states was reinforced by the realization that the global system is faced with several problems of crisis proportions, such as the depletion of natural resources, pollution of the world's atmosphere, rivers, lakes, and oceans; inequalities in the distribution of wealth; and the population explosion, which states, for several reasons, are ill-equipped to handle. This dissatisfaction with states, and the simultaneous realization that "state-centric" theories of world politics have for some time masked the importance of other types of political entities, have led to new interest in nonstate actors, such as intergovernmental organizations, multinational corporations, subnational "liberation" groups, and other transnational organizations.[39] While the continuing impact of nation-states on global politics will be reflected in the pages that follow, the emergence and increased importance of nonstate actors will also be emphasized.

[39]Richard W. Mansbach, Yale H. Ferguson, and Donald E. Lampert, *The Web of World Politics,* Prentice-Hall, Englewood Cliffs, N.J. 1976. See also Robert O. Keohane and Joseph S. Nye, Jr., eds. "Transnational Relations and World Politics," spec. ed. of *International Organization,* 25 (Summer 1971).

TWO

People and International Politics

THE DISCUSSION OF THE IMPACT PEOPLE HAVE ON WORLD
politics as they occupy different roles within the structure of
nation-states, will include (1) a look at "ordinary" citizens and the
effects their opinions might have on the foreign policies of states,
(2) an analysis of various kinds of specialized interest groups that
are concerned with foreign policy, (3) an analysis of the people in
foreign-policy making bureaucracies who make the important decisions regarding a state's foreign relations, and (4) an examination of
the impact of individual national leaders on foreign policy and the
course of world politics in general.

Public Opinion
and International Politics

Most people do not know or care very much about international
politics. That is the conclusion found in a number of thoughtful

essays and some empirical research on the subject.[1] Examples abound. At no time in the postwar period could more than a small number of Americans describe accurately the history of the dispute over Berlin, identify the ownership of Quemoy and Matsu, or describe the basic contents of the Geneva Accords of 1954.[2] Probably a majority of social scientists would agree with the conclusion of political scientist John P. Robinson:

> Survey researchers and other social scientists who have examined the results of typical poll data have found that the vast majority of citizens hold pictures of the world that are at best sketchy, blurred, and without detail, or at worst so impoverished as to beggar description. These restricted horizons become particularly evident when one examines the public's inability to give satisfactory answers to objective questions related to world affairs.[3]

In any society, individuals are most likely to be concerned about problems that affect them directly, and over which they feel they have some control. Problems on the scale of international politics often seem to fail on both counts. But wars, economic crises, and coups in one part of the world can have a dramatic impact on the lives of individuals in other parts of the world. A war in the Middle East, for example, can lead to a sizable increase in the price of gasoline in Europe, Japan, and the United States. But the connection between events in certain countries and the impact on individuals in other countries is seldom so clear. Often, even if the impact of foreign events is great, individuals in the countries affected do not have sufficient knowledge to be able to see the link between a foreign event and the local impact. Add to this the fact that, even when the link is clear, most individuals feel they have no control over the event or its impact, and it is not hard to see

[1]See, for example, Gabriel Almond, *The American People and Foreign Policy,* Harcourt Brace Jovanovich, New York, 1950; Gabriel Almond and Sidney Verba, *The Civic Culture,* Princeton University Press, Princeton, 1963; Richard M. Scammon and Ben J. Wattenberg, *The Real Majority,* Berkeley Publishing, New York, 1970, p. 299.

[2]Richard J. Barnet, *The Roots of War,* Penguin, Baltimore, 1971, p. 244.

[3]John P. Robinson, *Public Information About World Affairs,* Institute for Social Research, Ann Arbor, 1967, p. 1. There are, to be sure, political scientists who disagree with this assessment of the public's knowledge of world politics. See, for example, John C. Pierce and Douglas D. Rose, "Nonattitudes and American Public Opinion," *American Political Science Review,* 68, (June 1974), 626–649, and James Nathan and James K. Oliver, *United States Foreign Policy and World Order,* Little, Brown, Boston, 1976, pp. 564–570.

why most people do not know or care very much about international politics.

It would be logical to conclude, then, that people rarely do very much to let their opinions be known, or persuade others to accept their point of view. The logical conclusion is empirically supported. In the United States, for example, the Vietnam War provoked an unusual amount of interest for a foreign policy issue. Yet a survey of a representative sample of Americans in 1967 found that, although most people expressed a concern about the war, most had done nothing to reflect their concern. Only 13 percent reported they had made any attempt at all to convince someone to change his or her views on the war. Only 3 percent had bothered to write letters to newspapers or political officials, and only 1 percent had taken part in marches or demonstrations.[4]

The next logical conclusion would be that public opinion does not have much impact on foreign policy. Logic and empirical evidence seem to support one another, but the difficulty in assessing the impact of public opinion should be stressed. Broadly speaking, there often seems to be a correlation between what foreign-policy makers do and what the public prefers, in dictatorships as well as democracies. And diplomats and other foreign-policy officials are typically fond of saying that public opinion demanded a concession or hard-line stand with respect to a foreign policy issue. Difficulty arises when one attempts to interpret the correlation between public opinion and foreign policy decisions. Does the public influence decisions, or do government officials manipulate public opinion to support their point of view and then announce decisions they had settled on in advance? There is no easy way to answer this question, especially since the truth probably lies somewhere between the extremes. Undoubtedly, decision makers are influenced, to some degree, by public opinion, and the public is certainly influenced by the arguments and statements of public figures. In which direction is the flow of influence greater? A majority of scholars believe the elite influence the public more, especially with regard to foreign policy issues, rather than vice versa, and that in any case, the elite who deal with foreign policy issues usually do not feel very constrained by public opinion. Many agree with Richard Barnet, who claims that "no major foreign policy decision in the United States has ever been made in response to spontaneous public demand."[5]

[4]Sidney Verba and Richard A. Brody, "Participation, Policy Preferences, and the War in Vietnam," *Public Opinion Quarterly,* 34 No. 3 (1970), 325–332. Cited by K. J. Holsti, *International Politics,* 2d ed., Prentice-Hall, Englewood Cliffs, N.J., 1972, p. 383.
[5]Barnet, *Roots of War,* p. 243.

One interesting bit of evidence to support Barnet's view was uncovered in a 1963 study of the relationship between constituency attitudes and the votes of members of the United States Congress. If constituency attitudes do have an impact on voting in Congress, it follows that members of Congress from districts where the voters are, for example, isolationist, would be more likely to vote against foreign involvements of various kinds than members from districts where voters are more internationalist in their attitudes. In an analysis as in Table 2.1, showing a perfect relationship, every member of Congress from a district where voters are internationalist would cast votes in favor of foreign involvements, and every member of congress from districts where voters are isolationist would cast votes reflecting noninvolvement. Conversely, if there is no connection between constituency attitudes and votes in Congress, then one would obtain results resembling those in Table 2.2. Members of Congress from districts where voters are opposed

TABLE 2.1 Hypothetical analysis showing a perfect relationship between constituency attitudes and votes of members of Congress

| | Constituency Attitudes Regarding Foreign Involvement | |
	Pro	Con
Votes of members of Congress regarding foreign involvement		
Pro	200	0
Con	0	200

TABLE 2.2 Hypothetical analysis showing no relationship between constituency attitudes and votes of members of Congress

| | Constituency Attitudes Regarding Foreign Involvement | |
	Pro	Con
Votes of members of Congress regarding foreign involvement		
Pro	100	100
Con	100	100

to foreign involvements would be no more likely to vote against such involvements than members of Congress from districts where voters are internationalist in their attitudes.

In fact, however, it was found in the 1963 study that "on the question of foreign involvement there is no discernible agreement between legislator and district whatever."[6] The reason is that apparently people do not have clear-cut ideas about foreign affairs, and members of Congress do not accurately perceive the opinions of their constituents even when voters do have well-formed ideas on such matters. Another factor, perhaps eroded by occurrences since the study was published, involved the tendency for members of Congress of both parties to accept the advice of the president on foreign policy decisions. On civil rights issues and matters involving social welfare, the study did find a systematic relationship between constituency attitudes and the votes in Congress. The contrast between the findings related to those issues, and the findings relevant to foreign policy supplies evidence of how small the impact of public opinion on foreign policy is.

What impact public opinion does have on foreign policy, most analysts agree, is not very specific. Rather, public opinion sets broad limits within which policy makers feel they must operate. For example, having led the United States into a long war in Southeast Asia, resulting in 55,000 American deaths and disastrous failure, American foreign-policy makers may well find that public opinion will make it impossible for the United States to become involved in another prolonged land war in Southeast Asia (say, in Korea) for some time to come.

Should public opinion have an impact on foreign policy? If it does not, is this to be regretted, or is foreign policy a matter best left in the hands of "experts"? It is easy, especially for educated people, to adopt an elitist attitude regarding this question. The evidence clearly shows that the public is not well informed about world politics. Gabriel Almond, in his classic study published in 1950, argues further that public opinion on foreign policy is subject to wildly fluctuating moods, first in favor of activist policies, then

[6]Warren E. Miller and Donald E. Stokes, "Constituency Influence in Congress," *American Political Science Review,* 57, (March 1963), 49. In a study published in 1973, John Kingdon found that constituency attitudes are significantly related to voting in Congress. He does not discuss this relationship as it pertains to foreign policy issues per se, but one gets the impression from his discussion that such issues are not very salient to voters, and so their opinions do not have much of an impact on members of Congress. In any case, Kingdon's attempt to measure the impact depends on perceptions of constituency attitudes by members of Congress. The earlier study by Miller and Stokes gives reason to believe that these perceptions may be unusually inaccurate with respect to foreign policy issues. See John Kingdon, *Congressmen's Voting Decisions,* Harper & Row, New York, 1973, pp. 3–28.

clamoring for withdrawal and isolationism. Consequently, according to Almond, public opinion cannot be counted on for consistent, stable support of any foreign policy commitments.[7] Does it not seem obvious, given the ignorance and moodiness of public opinion, that a country's foreign policy should not be subject to the whims of that opinion?

"Open covenants openly arrived at" was one of President Woodrow Wilson's principles, adhered to in the belief that secret deals between professional diplomats and foreign-policy makers were a part of traditional international politics that led to disasters like the First World War. The trouble with that idea, according to anti-Wilsonians, is that diplomats are unable to exercise their talents for compromise if the public is a participant in the negotiating process. When the public looks on, diplomats are subject to political pressures that require them to take extreme positions that become virtually impossible to back off from as negotiations continue. If the uninformed and moody public is kept out of the process, the wisdom and talents of professional diplomats can be given full play, and the result will be a better foreign policy for a country, and decreased probability of violent conflict among different countries.

This argument is based on the assumption that better-informed, better-educated people are more likely to adopt wise positions on foreign policy issues. That is not necessarily the case. In retrospect, for example, most Americans would admit that their country's involvement in Vietnam was a mistake. Also, during the war, the most visible opponents of the war were on college campuses. It becomes tempting to conclude that better-educated people were, in their wisdom, against the war from the beginning, and therefore foreign policy matters should be left in the hands of a better-educated elite. But such a conclusion rests on weak empirical grounds. During the Vietnam War, opinion polls consistently showed that college-educated people were relatively hawkish in their attitudes. In contrast, people whose education did not go beyond grade school were distinctly dovish.[8]

The history of the Vietnam War in general must raise doubts about the thesis that foreign policy is best left in the hands of experts. David Halberstam's account of the decision-making processes that led the United States into that war, ironically entitled

[7]Gabriel Almond, *American People,* pp. 53– 55.

[8]Milton Rosenberg, Sidney Verba, and Philip Converse, *Vietnam and the Silent Majority,* Harper & Row, New York, 1971, p. 55. See also Robert L. Erikson and Norman R. Luttbeg, *American Public Opinion,* Wiley, New York, 1973, p. 177, and John E. Mueller, *War, Presidents, and Public Opinion,* Wiley, New York, 1973, p. 124.

The Best and the Brightest,[9] emphasizes the academic brilliance of the key people involved in the decision making, and their contempt for the knowledge and opinions of the general public outside of Washington, D.C. Their brilliance did not save them from, and their contempt helped lead them into, the mire of disastrous policies. And Vietnam is only one example, a Wilsonian might argue, in the long list of foreign policy disasters that have marked this century. Elite decision-makers have had their way, and they have shown themselves unable to cope with world political problems successfully. As for Almond's argument that public opinion on foreign policy is moody and subject to whimsical and rapid changes, the available empirical evidence does not necessarily support it. For example, William Caspary points out in an article published in 1970 that the average proportion of Americans favoring an active U.S. role in world affairs is remarkably stable, hovering consistently in the area of 70 percent.[10]

In the final analysis, this debate is largely academic in the disparaging sense. Wilsonians may be right about the possible beneficial impact public opinion could have on world politics. But since in fact public opinion apparently does not have much impact of any kind, there are obvious limits to the benefits it can generate. Similarly, anti-Wilsonian fears about the detrimental impact of public opinion on foreign policy are unfounded, since the impact of public opinion for good or evil is so limited, and also because there is slim evidence to support the idea that educated elites and diplomats, left to their own devices, are peculiarly able to deal successfully with world political problems.[11]

Subnational Groups and International Politics

If the general public does not have much influence on foreign policy, who does? One broad answer is that there are various *interest groups,* in any society, that exert a concentrated effort to influence foreign policy. Are their efforts successful? What are generally the most powerful interest groups in a society? How can one tell?

Actually, political scientists have had only limited success in answering such questions, either for "open" democratic societies,

[9]David Halberstam, *The Best and the Brightest,* Random House, New York, 1972.

[10]William Caspary, "The 'Mood Theory': A Study of Public Opinion and Foreign Policy," *American Political Science Review,* 64 (June 1970), 536–547.

[11]Inis Claude, *The Impact of Public Opinion upon Foreign Policy and Diplomacy,* Humanities Press, Atlantic Highlands, N.J., 1965.

or "closed" totalitarian ones. In the 1950s, many American political scientists were enthusiastic about group theory[12] and tried to develop ideas about how the various groups in a democratic society exert influence and which groups are most successful. But group theory in my view, met with limited success;[13] one major reason involves the nature of the influence process and the concept *influence*.

Certainly there are interest groups in every society that attempt to influence foreign policy, and many of their efforts are visible. Interest groups pay for advertisements in the media, support their lobbying personnel, and contribute to the campaigns of friendly politicians. Other activities of interest groups are less visible. Lobbyists talk to members of Congress at private lunches, secretly threaten to withdraw financial support from uncooperative senators, offer financial support for subversive CIA activities against unfriendly foreign governments, and so on. The impact they have is difficult to determine.

But it is almost as difficult to determine the effectiveness of the more open and visible activities of interest groups. If *influence* is the ability to affect behavior, how does one tell if an interest group is influential? The fact that a group favors a policy that is adopted is insufficient evidence of the adequacy of its efforts. The policy might have been adopted anyway. Or, the political decision-makers may have persuaded the lobbying groups to favor the adopted policy, and not vice versa. Finally, some powerful third group (for example, the "capitalists") may have influenced both the lobbying group in question and the political decision-makers to favor a given policy. Influence is difficult to trace. It is so difficult, in fact, that some political scientists have suggested that the concept is too vaguely defined to be useful, and that the temptation to rely on it so heavily should be resisted.[14]

Unfortunately, perhaps, the theoretical development that would persuade political scientists to do so has not occurred, and the question of what groups in a society are most influential still attracts great interest. The answer by group theorists of the 1950s emphasized the pluralistic nature of the American political system; they seemed satisfied that the outcome of pressure group competition in the system was beneficial. The happy conclusion was that the stronger organized groups would be prevented from taking

---

[12] A prominent example is David Truman, *The Governmental Process,* Knopf, New York, 1951.

[13] G. David Garson, "On the Origins of Interest-Group Theory: A Critique of a Process," *American Political Science Review,* 68 (December 1974), 1505.

[14] James G. March, "The Power of Power," in *Varieties of Political Theory,* ed., David Easton, Prentice-Hall, Englewood Cliffs, New Jersey, 1966, p. 68–70.

undue advantage of their strength because of overlapping membership; that is, some or most of the members would also belong to other groups, which the individuals in the strong groups with overlapping memberships would protect. And the group theorists of the 1950s were not worried about the fate of unorganized interests, arguing that they constituted "potential interest groups"[15] that could mobilize and become actual organized groups if their interests were seriously threatened.

Critics of such an optimistic conclusion pointed out that, in fact, the pressure group system operates with an upper-class bias, since wealthy, educated people are more likely to participate in any political process, and pressure groups heavily overrepresent, for example, business interests.[16] A more general criticism, which can be applied to competing groups in either open or closed societies, holds that there are certain crucial advantages enjoyed by smaller special interest groups. Large groups in pursuit of a goal such as influencing foreign policy have to deal with the serious problem that no individual member has a logical reason for contributing to the group effort. Since the group is large, the absence of one individual's effort is not likely to make much difference. And often large groups are not in a position to deny the benefit of their accomplishments to any of the members, even those who have not contributed to the group's success. If each member is likely to benefit from the large group's success no matter what, and an individual effort is not likely to make much difference one way or another to the probability of success, there is not much incentive for each member to contribute. Members of small groups are in a very different situation. Each one represents a significant portion of the whole, and the absence of his or her efforts may have a significant impact on the probability of the group's success. Since the group is small, if one of the group refuses to contribute to the group effort, he or she is easily identifiable and may be subject to penalties imposed by the rest of the group.[17]

[15] Truman, *Governmental Process,* pp. 34–35.
[16] E. E. Schattschneider, *The Semisovereign People,* Holt, Rinehart, and Winston, New York, 1960, pp. 31–32.
[17] Mancur Olson, *The Logic of Collective Action,* Schocken Books, New York, 1968, pp. 33–36. Readers familiar with Olson's arguments will recall that they apply, strictly speaking, only to groups in pursuit of public goods. A public good is any good that, if consumed by one person in a group, cannot be feasibly withheld from others in the group. In the example of tariffs, steel is not a public good as ordinarily defined, but I believe that the lower price of steel and the lower tariff-barrier *are* public goods. If the tariff is lowered, for example, the benefit cannot be feasibly withheld from any in the group of steel consumers. In short, Olson's arguments apply, if perhaps with less formal precision, to groups in pursuit of a wide variety of goods not ordinarily thought of as public.

Consider a concrete example. Imagine that the United States government is about to decide whether to raise the tariff against the import of foreign steel. Foreign steel-manufacturers have the benefit of cheaper labor, and they can produce steel for less and offer it for a lower price than American manufacturers can afford. Naturally, American steel manufacturers do not want this kind of competition, and they lobby for an increase in tariffs against foreign steel. American consumers, on the other hand, like lower-priced steel products (such as automobiles), and they form a potential group opposed to the increase in tariffs on foreign steel. Which group is likely to exert the most influence on the decision?

Every consumer of steel in the country has an interest in keeping the price of steel low, which might lead one to conclude that consumers will be able to defeat the much smaller number of steel producers. But, of course, no single steel consumer can contribute very much to the group effort. Whether or not Congress defeats, or the president decides against, higher tariffs on foreign steel is going to depend very little on the activities of one solitary consumer. Every consumer knows this and cannot be blamed for concluding that it really is not going to make much difference one way or the other if he or she writes a letter to a member of Congress, or contributes to a consumers' advocate group that is lobbying against higher tariffs. The clincher is that whether or not a particular steel consumer contributes to the effort to defeat higher tariffs, he or she will benefit if the effort is successful. There is no way that the steel consumers who do contribute to a successful effort to keep the tariff low can prevent the noncontributing steel consumers from purchasing lower-priced steel products.

The steel manufacturers, on the other hand, are small in number and can see that their own contribution might indeed make a difference in the outcome of the struggle. There is probably no way that contributing steel manufacturers can prevent noncontributing manufacturers from sharing the benefits of a higher tariff against foreign competition. But the number of steel producers is small enough that contributing manufacturers will be able to identify noncontributing ones, and the noncontributors may become the target of other kinds of reprisals from the manufacturers who do contribute to the support of lobbying efforts. The reprisals might range from social isolation (the noncontributors might be excluded from industry conventions, for example) to economic retaliation. (The other steel manufacturers might collaborate to make it difficult for noncontributors to get contracts from steel buyers.)

Probably more important, each steel producer is vitally concerned with the tariff on foreign steel, but the vast majority of steel consumers will be only vaguely aware of it, or more likely totally unaware. All that is at stake for the average steel consumer is a 5 or 10 percent difference in the price of steel products he or she buys. A lowered tariff will cut into the annual profits of the average steel producer, and it may drive him out of business completely. It is easy to see who has the greater incentive to participate actively in the political process involving the decision on the tariff against foreign steel.

I do not mean that those who oppose higher tariffs always lose.[18] But the advantages of special interest groups (like steel producers) do allow them to win most of the time. For example, in the United States "tariffs and import quotas on such things as petroleum, steel, sugar, fresh and frozen meat, and dairy products such as milk, cheese, and butter cost U.S. consumers an estimated $12 billion per year in higher prices."[19] This does not happen merely because the average manufacturer or producer of such products is rich and the average consumer less wealthy. To return to the example involving consumers of steel products versus steel producers, the potential group of consumers, numbering in the millions, commands economic clout that could easily overwhelm that of steel producers. The losses by the larger groups are not the result of insufficient funds with which to compete for the attention of political decision-makers. In short, it is not always the wealthiest or the largest pressure group that exerts the greatest influence on foreign policy.

The Military-Industrial Complex

One pressure group that is in a position to exert a tremendous influence on foreign policy in many countries is that involved in the production and utilization of a nation's military hardware. The military-industrial complex achieved particular notoriety in the United States during the Vietnam War, although the phrase itself was introduced into the American political lexicon several years earlier by President Eisenhower. And the idea (as opposed to the phrase) that munitions makers successfully plot to bring about large wars so that they can make a huge profit selling arms to the war makers goes back much further, in the United States and

---

[18]In 1976, for example, shoe manufacturers pressed for a higher tariff against Brazilian and Italian shoes, but President Ford decided not to grant this request. Shoe *retailers* apparently formed an effective lobby against this particular tariff increase.

[19]Lester Brown, *World Without Borders,* Vintage, New York, 1973, p. 234.

elsewhere. In 1934, some sixteen years after the close of the First World War, there was a flurry of interest in the United States in the substantial profits made by weapons manufacturers and banks through sales to the Allies in that war. A Senate committee, headed by Gerald P. Nye of North Dakota, for months held widely publicized hearings marked by revelations of spectacular profits, and it seems clear that many Americans were convinced by the revelations that they had been successfully maneuvered into the First World War for the sake of corporate profits. In Europe, the famous Krupp family has been held accountable for the slaughter of generations of soldiers in a series of European wars.[20]

The accusations made against the American military-industrial complex during the Vietnam War were not restricted to assertions that it had plotted to bring about the war. Rather, the organization and structure of the American military, and its relationship to industries which supply weapons, were probed for inherent biases in favor of larger defense budgets. Purchases by the military, for example, are often arranged by generals, on the one hand, and retired generals working for the weapons manufacturers, on the other. Such arrangements are especially cozy from the viewpoint of the complex, because the cost of any deals that are made, plus cost overruns that occur when the weapons turn out to be more expensive than originally estimated, are passed on to American taxpayers. Taxpayers are unlikely to complain, though, because many of them benefit from a large defense budget, when, for example, large defense contracts are awarded to industries in their districts, or military bases are established near their places of business. Members of Congress in the districts of taxpayers blessed with such defense budget largesse are naturally reluctant to trim the budget. Finally, universities that receive large research contracts out of the budget are another part of the complex which push for increasingly large defense budgets.

Adding to the dynamic upward force the American military-industrial complex exerts on the defense budget is the existence of a Russian counterpart in the Soviet Union.[21] The structure of the Soviet complex differs in detail from the American one, but in both countries virtually everybody involved benefits from increases in the defense budget. And the fact that each complex relies on the large defense budget generated by the other as a rationale for increasing its own makes the symbiotic nature of the relationship obvious.

[20] William Manchester, *The Arms of Krupp,* Little, Brown, Boston, 1968.
[21] Vernon A. Aspaturian, "The Soviet Military-Industrial Complex—Does It Exist?" *Journal of International Affairs* 26, No. 1 (1972), 2.

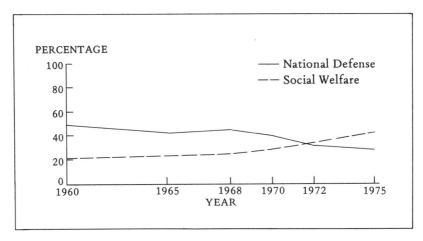

FIGURE 2.1 Proportions of the budget devoted to national defense and social welfare programs, United States, 1960–1975
Source: Budget of the United States Government, GPO, Washington, D.C., 1975.

A military-industrial complex undoubtedly has an important impact on the foreign policy of countries like the United States and the Soviet Union. In the United States, ever since the Second World War, the State Department has, in terms of size, budget, and apparent influence, been eclipsed by the Defense Department. Khrushchev may have lost his power in the Soviet Union because the Russian military-industrial complex was dissatisfied with his policies, especially the outcome of the Cuban Missile Crisis. But to say that military-industrial interests play an important role in foreign-policy-making processes is different from saying they dominate the processes; the difference should be stressed. In the United States, an example where the processes are easier to trace, there is clearly a range of powerful interests in favor of larger defense budgets (the military, industrialists, universities, labor unions, Congress) that make it difficult to control the budget. This seems especially true when one considers the groups that typically oppose larger defense budgets. A few liberal Congressmen, supported by a small number of college professors, students, and other people who believe that money should be diverted from military budgets and devoted to social welfare programs would not appear to stand much of a chance against the juggernaut in favor of increasing defense budgets. But the strength of the coalition against growing military budgets may well be stronger in the United States than it appears on the surface. Consider Figure 2.1, which shows the proportion of the budget of the United States government devoted to military expenditures as compared to the proportion invested in health and social welfare programs. The graph shows that the percentage of the budget successfully captured by the military-industrial complex is on the decline, and that expenditures on health and social welfare have now become significantly greater than defense expenditures. I do not mean that the military-industrial complex has, through some mysterious process, lost its political clout entirely, or that people on welfare have access to levers of power that are amazingly effective. One important reason the proportion of the budget devoted to defense has declined in recent years is that the Vietnam War ended in 1973, and American expenditures there started to decrease several years earlier. (Notice, though, that the percentage of the budget devoted to defense in 1960, also a year of peace, was 48.8, but in 1975, it was down to 28.8) In addition, the increases in health and welfare expenditures almost certainly do not reflect the increase in the political muscle of the groups that benefit from the expenditures as much as they do the more or less automatic nature of the increases. As the proportion of the population over 65 increases, for example, social security expenditures go up without a discrete decision made by Congress. But the decrease in the proportion of the budget devoted to defense, and the accompanying steady decline in the proportion of the gross national product (GNP) accorded to military expenditures (9.5 percent of the American GNP was devoted to defense in 1960; this figure fell to 6.3 percent in 1975) does indicate that there are limits to the influence of the military-industrial complex.[22]

Another indication of limits of influence is visible in voting patterns in the United States Senate. One way the military-industrial complex might exert influence is through the allocation of defense expenditures. Senators, for example, who consistently vote for defense expenditures and generally hawkish proposals,can be rewarded by the Defense Department when it awards lucrative contracts and locates military bases. States with cooperative, friendly senators can be awarded generous amounts of Defense Department money, while senators who are not so cooperative find that their states are overlooked. If this strategy is in effect, one would expect to find that senators whose states receive large amounts of Defense Department money would be substantially more likely to vote in favor of large defense expenditures than senators from states that only receive limited amounts.

But, as a matter of fact, if the Defense Department, and the military-industrial complex in general, follow such a strategy, it meets with limited success. A study published in 1970 reveals that

[22]The influence and defense budgets, of course, might both increase dramatically if the United States became involved in another war.

in the 1960s the relationship between the location of defense expenditures and Senate voting was, at best, very weak. Senators from states that received large amounts of Defense Department money were only slightly more likely to vote for larger defense expenditures than senators from states that received very little in the way of financial reward from the military-industrial complex.[23]

So far the discussion of the impact of military-industrial elements on a state's foreign policy has been limited to the United States and the Soviet Union. The second layer of major powers (China, Great Britain, France, and so on) also has military-industrial establishments that exert influence on the foreign policy of their respective countries. In the Third World, the military-industrial complex loses most of its industrial flavor because these nations are less industrialized and because the armies, navies, and air forces of Third World countries are not supplied by domestic firms. Rather, they get most of their weapons and equipment from one or more of the major powers. (Since the mid-1970s, the United States has been the largest supplier of arms in the world.) This weakens the symbiotic ties between the military and the industrial elements in most Third World countries.

It does not, though, obviously weaken the influence of the military on the foreign policies of Third World countries. States that fit into the Third World category differ greatly, and making generalizations about them is dangerous. But the prevalence of military influence and military governments throughout the Third World is clearly visible, despite dissimilarities. The military establishments of a great number of Third World countries have a tremendous influence not only on foreign policy but all policy.

Circumstances that lead to the influence of the military in the Third World can be divided, roughly, into those involving weaknesses in the domestic structures of the societies and those that involve penetration from outside. First, most countries in Latin America, Africa, and Asia do not have a strong tradition of con-

[23]Elsewhere, Russett claims his study showed that "legislators from districts with high proportionate military employment (but *not* contracting) were more likely to favor high levels of military spending than were other legislators." See Bruce M. Russett, "Apologia pro Vita Sua," in *In Search of Global Patterns,* ed. James N. Rosenau, Free Press, New York, 1976, p. 34. But Stephen Cobb claims that "the findings reported in this paper do not support the contention that defense spending concentrations have a significant influence on the manner in which senators vote. . . ." See Stephen Cobb, "The Impact of Defense Spending on Senatorial Voting Behavior," in *Sage International Yearbook of Foreign Policy Studies,* vol. 1, ed. Patrick J. McGowan, 1973, p. 150. In rebuttal, Russett cites other research (for example, Wayne Moyer, "Congress and Defense Policy, 1937–1972," Ph.D. Dissertation, Yale University, forthcoming) that supports his original finding. My conclusion is that defense expenditures may have some impact on congressional voting, but it is obviously not overwhelmingly important.

stitutional rule. There are no accepted procedures for seeking and assuming positions of political control. As a result, the various social groups interested in gaining positions of political power utilize techniques of confrontation rather than formal competition based on rules.

> Each group employs means which reflect its peculiar nature and capabilities. The wealthy bribe; students riot; workers strike; mobs demonstrate, and the military coup. . . . The techniques of military intervention are simply more dramatic and effective than others because as Hobbes put it, "When nothing else is turned up, clubs are trump."[24]

Even in an international political vacuum, it seems likely that the frequency of military coups and military governments in the Third World would be high. But these countries do not exist in a vacuum, of course, and the international political system provides several incentives and reinforcements for military elements to assume political power. The United States, for example, provides a steady supply of weaponry to a variety of military dictatorships. Great Britain and France join in the competition to make sophisticated military hardware available to Third World countries. And the Soviet Union has shown itself quite willing to supply military governments having even a vague anti-American or radical hue with great quantities of military equipment. One result of the easy availability of such equipment is that armies, navies, and air forces of virtually every country in the Third World are aware that they can stage a coup and be certain of substantial support from at least one major power. They know they will be able to obtain, probably on easy credit terms, enough equipment to intimidate the most fervent radical or reactionary domestic political opponents. Availability of weapons must surely be one factor leading to the large number of military governments in the Third World and the accompanying impact on the foreign policies of many of these countries.

Subnational Ethnic Groups
Ethnic minorities often constitute interest groups that are unusually concerned with and have a visible impact on, foreign policy. This is not a totally new phenomenon. For example, from 1815 until the

[24]Samuel P. Huntington, *Political Order in Changing Societies,* Yale University Press, New Haven, 1968, p. 196.

Second World War, Portugal, Spain, and Switzerland were the only European states that were not newly created, or did not have boundaries altered, as a result of ethnic aspirations.[25] But there may well have been an increase in the link between ethnic minorities and foreign policy in the twentieth century. "The technological revolution in communication permits previously isolated ethnic groups to become more visible, and, in certain cases, interact across national boundaries."[26]

The potential impact of these groups can only be described as astounding. There are an estimated 862 ethnic groups within the nation-states of the world,[27] and they are scattered about in such a way that all but fourteen of today's states contain at least one significant minority. And half of the fourteen are troubled by irredentist problems in which the dominant ethnic group extends beyond the borders of the homeland.[28]

A series of circumstances has made the Jewish people an ethnic minority of peculiar importance in international politics. First, Hitler's final solution led to the deaths of 6 million Jews, adding substantially to the Jewish drive for an independent Jewish homeland in Israel. In 1948, a homeland was created, but in a process that produced the bases for controversy and four wars since that time. Second, there are large Jewish minorities in the United States and the Soviet Union, the two most powerful countries in the world. Third, both the United States and the Soviet Union are vitally concerned with politics in the Middle East because of the presence of Israel and oil.

The effect of the Jewish minority on American foreign policy has been fairly clear, as these things go. When Israel proclaimed statehood, President Truman decided to accord diplomatic recognition immediately. He later allegedly explained his move with reference to the small number of Arab voters in his constituency. Since then, the Republicans and Democrats have disagreed over American policy in the Middle East only to the extent that each claims that it is more thoroughly committed to the defense of Israel. In the fifties and sixties, support seemed to require no more explanation than that provided by the influence of Jewish voters. But in the 1970s, with shortages of oil, and the Arab boycott, which cut off

[25] Walker Connor, "The Political Significance of Ethnonationalism Within Western Europe," in *Ethnicity in an International Context,* ed. Abdul Said and Luiz R. Simmons, Transaction Books, New Brunswick, N.J., 1976, p. 18.

[26] Abdul Said and Luiz R. Simmons, eds., "The Ethnic Factor in World Politics," in *Ethnicity in an International Context,* p. 18.

[27] Said and Simmons, "Ethnic Factor," p. 17.

[28] Walker Connor, "The Politics of Ethnonationalism," *Journal of International Affairs,* 27, No. 1 (1973), 1.

Middle Eastern oil from the United States in protest of American support of Israel, the reasons for support became less obvious. Could Jewish groups alone elicit American support for Israel if that support resulted in oil and gasoline shortages in the United States? The energy crisis of the early 1970s did decrease American enthusiasm for the Israeli cause, perhaps, but it did not result in any substantial change in American policy. Why?

To discount the influence of Jewish interest groups entirely would be almost as great a mistake as to give credence to myths that they dominate American banks or the American economic system.[29] Jewish voters are strategically concentrated in states that have large numbers of Electoral College votes, such as New York. Jews as a group are quite active politically, especially within the Democratic party organization. They have the advantage discussed earlier that most Americans are not interested in foreign policy issues, and a kind of vacuum is left into which those Americans who are interested can move. But the United States might well support Israel even if Jewish pressure groups were inept. The deaths of millions of Jews at the hands of the Nazis created a reservoir of sympathy. Also, there are, perhaps, many Christians who believe that since God did promise the land of Israel to the Jews, that settles the matter. Knowledge of, and sympathy for Palestinians, in contrast, is severely limited.

It is more difficult to gauge the impact of the Jewish minority in the Soviet Union. Clearly, Jews are less influential in the Soviet Union than they are in the United States. And the impact they have exerted on Soviet policy has often been of a negative variety. The Jews have, in other words, caused the Soviet government to react to their pressure, but to react in an undesirable manner.

When the state of Israel was created, the Soviet Union recognized it almost as rapidly as the United States did. Apparently the Soviets hoped there would be substantial Communist influence in the new state that could be used to counter British influence in the Middle East.[30] But after Stalin died, his successors could not fail to notice that Israel was not really needed as a counterweight against the British; in any case, the Israelis joined the British in the Suez War. The change of heart was undoubtedly reinforced by the ascent of military, nationalistic governments in the Middle East (such as

[29]That such myths die very hard indeed was demonstrated in 1974 when the *Washington Post* reported that the chairman of the American Joint Chiefs of Staff, General George Brown, had told an audience that Jews had an inordinate influence on American foreign policy because they controlled American banks and media. See the *Washington Post*, November 12, 1974.

[30]Richard Allen, *Imperialism and Nationalism in the Fertile Crescent*, Oxford University Press, New York, 1974, p. 423.

Nasser's in Egypt) that were not averse to receiving support from the Soviet Union. But an additional force leading to the change in Soviet policy may well have been the presence of the Soviet Jewish minority. Even in the earliest days of Israel's existence, Stalin had apparently been offended by the tumultuous welcome extended by Moscow's Jews to the first ambassador from the new Jewish state, Golda Meir. "He [Stalin] saw in her coreligionists—once all his other . . . opponents had been eliminated—potential conspirators."[31] The early fifties were years of substantial Jewish migration to Israel, and the Soviets allowed only a few to join this movement. In short, though one must rely largely on speculation in such matters, probably some of the animosity between the Soviet Union and Israel that developed after initially friendly relations between the two countries can be traced to the Jewish problem that this ethnic minority presents the Soviet government.

The subnational minority of greatest importance in post–Second World War world politics, after the Jews, has probably been the Palestinians. The wars between Israel and its Middle Eastern neighbors have left in their wake some 2 million Palestinian refugees, some in refugee camps, others spread from Lebanon to the Persian gulf to the United States. They have had a spectacular impact on world politics because of their homeless plight and because of the dramatic violence of their terrorist tactics, such as the murder of Israeli athletes at the 1972 Olympics in Munich and the hijacking of airplanes.

Palestinians who have left refugee camps have worked themselves into positions of importance in countries such as Kuwait and Saudi Arabia. They are credited with putting effective pressure on these governments to support the Palestinian cause. Whether the resettled Palestinians, plus those in refugee camps and those living in Israel, will ever gain anything resembling a victory depends on how they emerge from the disaster the Palestinian Liberation Organization suffered at the hands of the Syrians in Lebanon in 1976.

Though the Jews and the Palestinians have received the most publicity, a large number of additional ethnic groups have had an impact on world politics. "In recent years the antagonism of indigenous ethnic communities in Cyprus, Iraq, Malaysia, Guyana, Uganda, and Canada (to name only a few) have wrought changes in the international relations of nation-states."[32] The Catholic minority in Northern Ireland, the Croats in Yugoslavia, the Basques in Spain, and the blacks and Chicanos in the United States,

[31] André Fontaine, *History of the Cold War,* Pantheon, New York, 1969, p. 57.
[32] Said and Simmons, "Ethnic Factor," p. 16.

have all had their moments in the spotlight. Africa, with its new and badly integrated states, has been a veritable hotbed of ethnic international politics.

In the early 1970s, for example, the Libyan government was furnishing assistance to a separatist movement across its southern border in Chad. While deploring this intervention,

> the Chad government was offering aid and sanctuary to black insurrectionists in the southern Sudan. While trying to suppress this movement, the authorities at Khartoum were simultaneously supporting a separatist movement within the Eritrean sector of Ethiopia. Ethiopia, which was fighting a number of separatist movements in addition to that of Eritreans, was countering by joining Chad (as well as Uganda) in aiding the blacks of southern Sudan.[33]

In assessing the impact of ethnic groups on international politics, one might do well to keep in mind the point made by Schattschneider in his study of competition among pressure groups in domestic politics. "To understand any conflict it is necessary to keep constantly in mind the relations between the combatants and the audience, because the audience is likely to do things that determine the outcome of the fight."[34] Quite often, subnational ethnic groups have an interest in changing the scope of a conflict, because they believe that an enlarged scope will make it easier for them, or their ethnic compatriots in other states, to win. The Jews in the United States do not want the conflict in the Middle East to be fought in isolation between the opposing parties there. They want the United States involved in the conflict. The Palestinians retaliate with similar scope-widening tactics, trying to get other Arab nations involved and attempting to attract world opinion as it is reflected in the United Nations.

The Palestinians, as mentioned, have used terrorism on a worldwide scale to accomplish a change of scope. If other subnational groups learn similar tactics (and there are signs that this is happening already), these groups may pose a very serious problem for the present state-dominated system. The fragility of modern communication and transportation systems, and the increasing availability of nuclear materials could become, in the hands of various ethnic terrorist groups, an explosive combination indeed. At a

[33]Connor, "Politics," 15.
[34]Schattschneider, *Semisovereign People*, p. 2.

time when most scholars of global politics are urging a move beyond the nation-state to larger, less territorial kinds of political organizations, ethnic groups in virtually every part of the world are engaged in movements for "national liberation" that would move in the opposite direction. "The ethnic nation cannot yet compete with the state in nuclear warheads and warships, but it continues to exercise formidable influence over the primary authority patterns of men. It is from this exercise of power that revolutions are born."[35]

Foreign Policy Bureaucracies

Foreign policy decisions, and thus a significant portion of international politics, are in the hands of large bureaucracies. Consequently, the way large bureaucracies make decisions, and implement them, has an important effect on foreign policies and international politics.

The study of bureaucratic organizations in the last few decades has centered on two major questions: (1) Should bureaucracies make decisions in a rational manner? and (2) Do bureaucracies make decisions in a rational manner? The answer to the first question might seem obvious. Rationality must be an admirable goal to which bureaucracies and executives who administer them, should aspire. Who, for example, would deny that executives should step back, on occasion, from daily concerns and deal with issues and problems that have not yet reached the crisis stage? When confronted with a decision, it makes good sense (or so it seems) for an executive to consider every possible alternative solution to the problem at hand. Having done this, the executive should obviously turn to an assessment of the probabilities of success for each alternative and the costs involved in the implementation of each alternative. The final step in this rational process would be the selection of the alternative that offers the best combination of high probability of success and low cost.

Standard Operating Procedures and Prearranged Responses

Perhaps in the best of all possible worlds, the rational approach is the way decisions would be made by executives in large bureaucracies. But many organization theorists, led by Herbert Simon,[36]

[35] Abdul Said and Luiz R. Simmons, Introduction, p. 14.
[36] See Herbert Simon, *Administrative Behavior*, 2d ed., Free Press, New York, 1957, and *Models of Man*, Wiley, New York, 1957.

have argued plausibly that the actual process in which large bureaucracies come to decisions is not based on what might be called *comprehensive rationality*. First, whether they head organizations whose goal is to sell as many Wheaties as possible or to formulate foreign policies, executives typically do not have time to step back from daily crises, and anticipate problems looming in the future. Crises, ranging from minor to catastrophic, dominate the executive's ordinary day to the point that time for a broad philosophical approach to the goals of the organization is very scarce indeed. And the rational[37] approach to problem solving involves a strategy that is unrealistically thorough. An executive, even with the help of the organization, cannot possibly consider every alternative solution to a problem. There is literally an infinite number of such alternative solutions, and the search for information about them is costly. Also, estimating the probability of success and the costs of implementing each alternative solution, which the executive and the organization are already aware of, is a process that cannot be pressed to the end prescribed by comprehensive rationality. Even for the most brilliant executive, knowledge is limited, and increasing it costs time and money, both of which are in limited supply for every organization.

Faced with severe limitations in information, time, and resources, executives and large bureaucracies, according to Simon and others, will display a tendency to rely on standard operating procedures (SOPs) developed in the past, or on a *repertoire* of prearranged responses. SOPs and repertoires simplify the crucial problem of coordinating the different parts of the bureaucracy. The implementation of both will have been analyzed and coordinated. If it becomes obvious that the SOPs and the repertoire of prearranged responses will not suffice, the usual bureaucratic response will not involve a search for all possible alternatives but rather consideration of alternatives based on incremental changes in SOPs and prearranged responses.[38] And the solution chosen will not be the one that the executive and his or her subordinates believe is the best possible one, but one that is good enough, that allows the decision makers to "satisfice."[39]

[37]Defenders of rational-choice models argue, quite rightly, that such models are not necessarily based on an assumption of perfect information, that they can be based instead on an assumption of varying degrees of uncertainty. When I use the term *rational*, I will mean it in a restricted sense of comprehensive rationality, implying an assumption of perfect information, and unlimited capacity to process this information.

[38]Charles E. Lindblom, "The 'Science' of Muddling Through," *Public Administration Review*, 19 (Spring 1959), 81.

[39]Simon, *Models of Man*, p. 204.

Finally, many organization theorists have concluded that not only is it true executives and bureaucracies do behave and make decisions in this less-than-comprehensively rational manner, but that this is the way bureaucracies should deal with a very complicated world. Administrators and their subordinates should not feel guilty about their tendency to adhere to SOPs. If SOPs have worked in the past, there must be a reason. And if crises reach the point where SOPs must be modified, administrators should realize that they cannot possibly consider every possible alternative, and that it makes good sense to use the present SOPs as a criterion for consideration of alternatives. Gross changes will, first, be extremely difficult to coordinate and implement, and will be likely to produce novel, unexpected effects and reactions that the bureaucracy will find difficult to handle. *Incremental* changes in SOPs have several important advantages. Procedures based on such changes will be only marginally different from the original SOP, and their basic structure will benefit from the accumulated wisdom that has gone into the development of the SOP. Second, incremental changes will be easier to coordinate and implement. Third, the reactions of those outside the bureaucracy who are affected by the incremental changes are not likely to be drastically different from the reactions elicited by the original SOP, and the bureaucracy should be able to deal with those reactions.

Many of the same points can be made about the repertoire of prearranged responses that are developed by organizations to deal with anticipated *scenarios*.[40] Hospitals must work out a response enabling them to continue emergency care in the event of a loss of electric power. Defense departments, similarly, must develop a repertoire of prearranged responses to possible attacks by potential enemies. Developing such responses ahead of time involves a necessary loss of flexibility but, according to an extension of the logic of incrementalism as it applies to ongoing SOPs, this is a price worth paying. If the bureaucracy is not coordinated in the event that a scenario becomes reality, the chances that the bureaucracy will deal successfully with that reality approach zero. Last minute changes in prearranged responses, according to incrementalist logic, should be considered a last resort. If they involve large deviations from the original plans, such changes must almost certainly be rejected. The risks resulting from any attempt to implement rapid, large changes in prearranged responses are almost sure to outweigh any advantages that comprehensive rationality might indicate would result from such changes.

[40]Graham T. Allison, *Essence of Decision,* Little, Brown, Boston, 1971, p. 89.

Incrementalism, whether applied to ongoing SOPs or prearranged responses, is vulnerable to criticism, to be sure. It is inherently conservative, ruling out as a matter of principle any radical changes. It may also be too modest about the ability of mortals to deal with admittedly complex problems.[41] But as a description of the way bureaucracies do behave, it is, if certainly not perfect, at least less vulnerable. And it does provide insights into the formation of foreign policies and interaction among states that would be masked by any model resting on the assumption that bureaucratic behavior is based on comprehensive rationality.

Bureaucracies and the 1914 Crisis

Bureaucratic reliance on prearranged responses, for example, played an important role in the process that led to the First World War. Even a small dose of rational capability to deviate from prearranged procedures might well have altered the outcome of that process. But the Russians, to take a critical example, were set in their ways, even more than the average military bureaucracy. The minister of war, General Sukhomlinov, prided himself on not having read a military manual for the last twenty-five years, and believed that the military knowledge he had picked up as an officer in the Russian war against the Turks in 1877 would suffice for any future contingency.[42] By 1911, pursuant to the alliance formed between the two countries in 1894, Russia had joined with France in a plan to attack Germany simultaneously in case of war. The Austro-Serbian struggle sucked Germany in, so the Russians put in motion their prearranged response for the attack against Germany. As seen in Chapter 1, Kaiser Wilhelm put in a request to Czar Nicholas to delay, or at least reduce partially the Russian mobilization process. Nicholas attempted to do this. He issued an order for partial mobilization, but his generals refused to implement it. They were afraid that any delay would give their enemies a chance to get an insurmountable lead on the Russians in the mobilization process. But the Russian military bureaucracy was also responding in the way any incrementalist would expect. The Russian military had laid out its mobilization plan many years before the Austro-Serbian crisis in 1914. Once the process of implementing the plan was underway, the Russian generals stood as one in their reluctance to deviate from the plan. The chief of the mobilization section of the Russian general staff might have been speaking for the entire Russian military apparatus when he said that "the whole plan of

[41] Yehezkel Dror, *Public Policymaking Re-examined,* Chandler, San Francisco, 1968, p. 148.
[42] Barbara Tuchman, *The Guns of August,* Macmillan, New York, 1962, p. 61.

The Russian minister of war, General Sukhomlinov, and staff officers.
Imperial War Museum, London.

mobilization is worked out ahead to its final conclusion and in all its
detail . . . once the moment is chosen, everything is settled; there is
no going back; it determines mechanically the beginning of the
war."[43]

[43]John G. Stoessinger, *Why Nations Go to War,* St. Martin's Press, New York,
1974, p. 19.

The German military responded to the 1914 crisis with the same inflexibility. When the German troops were already in the process of mounting an attack against Belgium and France, the Kaiser thought he saw a chance to avoid a two-front war, if only the German army could be turned around and a last-minute change put into effect that would have involved an attack against Russia instead of France. The German chief of staff, Helmuth von Moltke, said that such a thing could not be done. Barbara Tuchman describes the process that the Kaiser wanted to modify in the hour of crisis:

> Once the button was pushed, the whole vast machinery for calling up, equipping, and transporting two million men began turning automatically. Reservists went to their designated depots, were issued uniforms, equipment, and arms, formed into companies and companies into battalions, were joined by cavalry, cyclists, artillery, medical units, cook wagons, blacksmith wagons, even postal wagons, moved according to prepared railway timetables to concentration points near the frontier where they would be formed into divisions, divisions into corps, and corps into armies ready to advance and fight. One army corps alone—out of the total 40 in the German forces—required 170 railway cars for officers, 965 for infantry, 2960 for cavalry, 1915 for artillery and supply wagons, 6010 in all, grouped in 140 trains and an equal number again for their supplies. From the moment the order was given, everything was to move at fixed times according to a schedule precise down to the number of train axles that would pass over a given bridge within a given time.[44]

Is it any wonder that Moltke was reluctant to try to rearrange these procedures at the last moment? As Tuchman points out, after the war, General von Staab, the chief of the German Railway Division, wrote a book in which he showed that he could have turned most of the German army around within a couple of weeks. And if bureaucracies operated in a rational fashion, it is at least conceivable that it could have and might have been done. But since bureaucracies typically do not operate in a rational fashion but deviate from standard operating procedures (or prepared responses) only with reluctance, and then only slightly, it does not seem likely that the German army would have turned around even if someone more flexible than Helmuth von Moltke had been German chief of staff.

[44]Tuchman, *Guns of August,* pp. 74–75.

Bureaucracies
and the Cuban Missile Crisis

Many writers have pointed to the impact bureaucratic rigidity had on the process that led to the First World War, but it is easy to gain the impression from these writings that the rigidity was unusual, a function of the peculiarities of the time or the personalities involved. This impression is, of course, mistaken. The reasons for bureaucracies to adhere to standard operating procedures, or prearranged responses, did not disappear with the end of the First World War. It is predictable that large foreign policy bureaucracies will do this, and the tendency has often had its impact on several crises since 1914.

For example, standard operating procedures and prearranged responses played an important role in the development of the Cuban Missile Crisis in 1962. The Russians sent the missiles to Cuba in utmost secrecy, with various devices of deception involved to mislead any observer. Yet, when the missiles arrived in Cuba, there was no attempt made to camouflage the sites, and even more incredible, the SAM, MRBM, and IRBM (types of ballistic missiles) sites constructed in Cuba were built to look exactly like the SAM, MRBM, and IRBM sites in the Soviet Union.[45] Also, the Soviet military personnel arrived in Cuba wearing slacks and sports shirts to hide their identity, but they left the Cuban docks formed in ranks of four and piled into truck convoys. Furthermore, they decorated their barracks with standard military insignia.[46] All of this, but especially the construction of the missile sites in Soviet style, made it rather easy for the Americans, by way of U-2 flights, to figure out what was happening.

What accounts for this seemingly irrational behavior? Why the great secrecy and deception on the one hand, and the blatant lack of secrecy on the other? The most plausible answer involves the bureaucratic tendency to adhere to standard operating procedures. The delivery of the missiles to Cuba, and from the docks to the sites, was the responsibility of the GRU (Soviet military intelligence) and the KGB (the Communist party intelligence organization). "Security is their standard operating procedure."[47] So, the missiles were hidden successfully until they reached their sites. Then the missiles were turned over to the military organizations, and secrecy was not part of the military repertoire of standard operating procedures. They built the missile sites in the way they

---

[45] Allison, *Essence of Decision*, p. 107. This discussion of the missile crisis relies heavily on Allison's work.

[46] Allison, *Essence of Decision*, p. 109.

[47] Allison, *Essence of Decision*, p. 110.

had always built them. Under emergency conditions, when there is a premium on speed and mistakes could be disastrous, what bureaucrat would do otherwise? As for the shirt-and-slack-clad soldiers arriving at the Cuban docks, it is reasonable to guess that their delivery was also the responsibility of organizations devoted to secrecy. But once they had arrived at their barracks, they adhered to procedures as if they were still in the Soviet Union.

The American bureaucracies involved in the crisis were not, of course, immune to the tendency to adhere to standard operating procedures or prearranged responses. The list of options that were considered by President Kennedy and his advisors was affected greatly by the repertoire of prearranged responses that the military had developed in the event of a crisis calling for an attack on Cuba. For example, one of the options considered by American decision-makers was a "surgical" air strike that would eliminate the Soviet missiles already in place. The air force insisted that this kind of strike would (1) result in extensive collateral damage and probably fairly large numbers of Soviet casualties and (2) not necessarily knock out all the Soviet missiles.

Both of these arguments may have been untrue from a rational point of view. The air force was not caught off guard by this opportunity to attack Cuba. Action against Castro by the United States had been anticipated and a standard operating response was carefully worked out for implementation when the opportunity arose. The trouble was, in the context of the missile crisis and the desire for a surgical air strike, the response called for an air strike of intolerable dimensions. "The 'air strike' option served up by the Air Force called for extensive bombardment of all storage depots, airports, and the artillery batteries opposite the naval base at Guantanamo Bay, as well as all missile sites."[48] In short, what the air force had done when asked about the feasibility of a surgical air strike was to modify its prearranged response, but only incrementally. It added the missile sites to the list of targets to be bombed. It subtracted nothing. To do so, the Joint Chiefs of Staff insisted, would pose an unacceptable risk.

Standard operating procedures also affected the imposition of the quarantine by the United States, designed to prevent missile-bearing Russian ships from getting to Cuba. The president and his advisors decided on the quarantine, and the navy set its standard operating procedures into motion. The complexity of the task should not be underestimated. The quarantine was designed to monitor almost 1 million square miles. The navy assigned 180 ships

[48] Allison, *Essence of Decision,* p. 125.

to the task. Then, virtually at the last moment, the British ambassador suggested to Kennedy that precious time might be gained if the quarantine were modified. Originally, it was designed to intercept Russian ships 800 miles from Cuba. If the quarantine procedures could be changed so that the Russian ships would not be intercepted until they got to within, say, 500 miles of Cuba, this would give the Russians a substantial amount of extra time in which, it was hoped, to change their minds. Kennedy agreed that it was a good idea and immediately issued an order to the navy to move the line of interception closer to Cuba.

The British ambassador's suggestion was unquestionably a rational one, and if bureaucracies behaved rationally, Kennedy's order would have been carried out without complaint. But the navy complained loudly. Procedures could not be modified at the last minute in such a major way without some colossal foul-up, which, under the circumstances of the missile crisis, would have repercussions of horrifying dimensions. But Kennedy and his Secretary of Defense, Robert McNamara, were insistent, and the navy finally gave in.

Or did it? The navy did verbally assure Kennedy that the line of interception had been pulled back, but an examination of the evidence involving timing of the sighting and boarding of the ships "confirms other suspicions. . . . Existing accounts to the contrary, the blockade was *not* moved as the President ordered.[49] In short, even when confronted with the possibility that much of the world might be devastated by a nuclear holocaust, the navy, according to some evidence, refused to modify substantially its standard operating procedures.[50]

If Kennedy had, despite the air force's warnings, issued the orders for the air strike, or if the navy, despite Kennedy's order, had intercepted Russian ships eight hundred miles from Cuba, and either of these events had proved instrumental in the outbreak of a Third World War, it seems likely that historians (if any were left) would have come to recognize a striking parallel between the First World War and the Third World War. The generals in 1914 would

[49] Allison, *Essence of Decision,* p. 130. The account of this episode involving the quarantine procedures can be found in Allison, pp. 127–132.

[50] At one point McNamara pressed Chief of Naval Operations George Anderson for details in the navy's procedures for boarding Russian ships. Anderson replied by picking up the *Manual of Naval Regulations* and waving it in McNamara's face, telling him that if he (McNamara) wanted to know what was to be done, he should simply refer to the *Manual*. McNamara is reported to have replied, "I don't give a damn what John Paul Jones would have done. I want to know what you are going to do, now." Allison, *Essence of Decision,* p. 131.

not modify their prearranged responses in order to narrow the scope of the developing crisis. And the American air force and navy, in 1962, would not modify their prearranged procedures in order to limit the damage of an air strike or give the Russians more time to consider alternatives. The fact that the Cuban Missile Crisis did not result in the Third World War should not obscure the similarity of the crises in 1914 and 1962, nor the effect that persistent adherence of large bureaucracies to SOPs and prearranged responses can have on international politics.

But the similarities in the two cases should not be overdrawn. Unlike the 1914 crisis, in the Cuban Missile Crisis, the behavior of the bureaucracies involved may have contributed to a peaceful resolution of the conflict, despite its irrational nature. If the air force had been more willing to modify its air-strike procedures, and the Americans had opted for that alternative, the violence could conceivably have sparked disaster. Similarly, if the navy had pulled its ships closer to Cuba, it is possible that a number of Russian ships might have slipped through the disorganized blockade, leading Americans to panic and potential disaster.

Bureaucratic Inertia
and the Vietnam War
In the Vietnam War, adherence to standard operating procedures did not have such a fortunate effect. The Vietnam case is instructive, because it demonstrates the role that standard operating procedures can play in the foreign-policy-making process in other than crisis situations. In both the 1914 and 1962 crises, it was largely prearranged responses that affected the outcomes. American policy in Vietnam was shaped to some extent by the tendency of large bureaucracies to adhere to procedures developed to handle routine problems. Henry Kissinger has pointed out that "the purpose of bureaucracy is to devise a standard operating procedure which can cope effectively with most problems. A bureaucracy is efficient if the matters which it handles routinely are, in fact, the most frequent, and if its procedures are relevant to their solution."[51] The United States government devoted the efforts of a huge, complex bureaucracy to the implementation of its policy in Vietnam. As the war continued, the rational reasons for the original intervention melted away. Despite this, as John Kenneth Galbraith explained at the time,

[51]Henry Kissinger, "Domestic Sources of Foreign Policy," in *Politics and the International System,* ed. Robert L. Pfaltzgraff, Lippincott, Philadelphia, 1972, pp. 388–389.

An American soldier in Vietnam. Wide World Photos.

> the war continues. This is because the bureaucracy, the military and intelligence bureaucracy in particular, operates not in response to national need but in response to its own need. . . . But it would be a mistake to picture bureaucratic need in terms of a too specific bureaucratic self-interest. A more important factor is pure organizational momentum. Bureaucracy can always continue to do what it is doing. It is incapable, on its own, of a drastic change of course.[52]

Bureaucratic inertia, an alternative incarnation of standard operating procedures, is often an important element accounting for the continuation of policies, good or bad.

Bureaucratic Politics and Policy Making

Inertia, though, is not always produced simply because of the bureaucratic preference for standard operating procedures. Sometimes current policies are adhered to because of the effects of competition among the various parts of the foreign policy bureaucracy. "Once the decision-making apparatus has disgorged a policy, it becomes very difficult to change it. The alternative to the status

[52]John Kenneth Galbraith, "Foreign Policy: The Plain Lessons of a Bad Decade," *Foreign Policy*, 1 (Winter 1970), 41.

quo is the prospect of repeating the whole anguishing process of arriving at a decision."[53] The process is anguishing because every decision made by complex government bureaucracies involves winners and losers within those bureaucracies. Once the decision is made, the winning coalition behind that decision has a vested interest in it. To change or reverse it is to admit that the losers may have been correct in the first place.

In the case of Vietnam, the complex bureaucracy involved in the implementation of the American policy persisted in that policy not only because of a normal bureaucratic preference for adhering to standard operating procedures, but also because changing policies would have constituted an admission that antiwar critics inside the bureaucracy (and outside, for that matter) had been right all along. Competition and resolve within the bureaucracy stiffened and information was produced for top decision-makers that was misleadingly optimistic. For example, both the navy and the air force were engaged in bombing missions. The navy feared that if later analyses showed its bombing had been less effective than that of the air force, the navy would lose its air wing. So, there was a tendency for the navy to overestimate the effectiveness of bombing raids. The air force, aware that the navy would engage in such tactics, added a dash of exaggeration to its reports. The process escalated, and as a result the Johnson administration received unreliably optimistic reports of the effectiveness of American bombing raids.[54] This may well have been one reason that Johnson continued the raids for so long.

Bureaucratic infighting can also introduce an element of irrationality to the foreign-policy-making process that does not necessarily involve persistence in the status quo or current policies. To return to the Cuban Missile Crisis for a moment, competition in both the American and Russian bureaucracies played a role. It is possible that the Russian Presidium ordered the Strategic Rocket Forces to place medium-range ballistic missiles in Cuba, but elements in the rocket forces decided on their own that intermediate-range missiles were preferable.[55] One of the reasons that Khrushchev insisted so vigorously during the crisis that the missiles his country had placed in Cuba were defensive in nature may have been that he was not aware of the range of the missiles that had actually been delivered and erected. And the American bureaucracy

[53]Kissinger, "Domestic Sources", p. 390.
[54]Morton H. Halperin, "Why Bureaucrats Play Games," *Foreign Policy*, 2 (Spring 1971), p. 83.
[55]Allison, *Essence of Decision*, p. 113.

had a difficult time deciding whether the U-2 flights aimed at acquiring photographic evidence of the presence of the Russian missiles in Cuba should be flown by air force pilots or CIA pilots. The Defense Department felt that air force pilots should do it, while the CIA felt that the task was within its jurisdiction, and therefore CIA agents should operate the flights. The argument raged for five days, and the Defense Department won. But the first flight in an air force U-2 apparently failed. A second round of competition between the Defense Department and the CIA ensued; the outcome was a decision to have air force pilots fly CIA U-2's, making necessary an additional five-day delay for the training of air force pilots to carry out the mission. The ten-day delay between the decision on how to send the flights and the actual flight is a good example of the kind of irrationality that can be introduced into international politics by competition in a large bureaucracy.

Bureaucratic Politics
and the Alliance for Progress

Finally, it is not only military bureaucracies that get involved in this kind of competition. An example of a day-to-day kind of policy that suffered from civilian bureaucratic competition is the Alliance for Progress effort. President Kennedy launched the alliance in 1961, partly in response to a personal interest in Latin America, but largely in response to the perceived threat posed by Fidel Castro. The idea of the alliance was conceived basically by liberal critics of American foreign policy in Latin America and the United States. It was hoped that American encouragement, and money, would help Latin American countries achieve a peaceful revolution that would alleviate the terrible problems of poverty, disease, illiteracy, and bad or nonexistent housing. The rhetoric in the first few months was exciting, but few would deny that the Alliance for Progress failed. There is, on the other hand, little agreement as to why it failed.

One of the alliance's many problems, though, was clearly a lack of coordination among the many government bureaus involved in the implementation of the alliance program. Each bureau looked at the alliance from the view of its own interests. The Treasury Department saw the alliance as a rather dangerous scheme that might damage American balance of payments. The main concern of the Commerce Department was to use the alliance to increase American exports to Latin America. The Agriculture Department feared that the alliance would encourage the production of agricultural commodities that would compete with American produce.

> Insofar as the Alliance for Progress was concerned . . . the U.S. government was divided among warring bureaucratic and political fiefdoms, each pursuing its own special interest. The Congress was at war with the executive; the Treasury was at war with AID, and AID was at war with itself. The Bureau of the Budget served as a sort of arbiter among the contenders. The Export-Import Bank, regarding the others with disdain, generally remained on the sidelines, while the Agriculture and Commerce Departments, parochial in outlook, entered the fray from time to time on behalf of beet-sugar producers, textile interests, and other nervous constituencies. The Alliance for Progress was merely a pawn in the interdepartmental competition for power and favor within the United States government.[56]

The results of these bureaucratic battles were disastrous for the Alliance for Progress and distorted it into a program that clearly served the various commercial interests of Americans more than the states of Latin America. For example, in 1964, the Agency for International Development (AID) authorized a $15 million loan to Brazil to be used to finance imports of fertilizer. But the fertilizer had to be American. Congress, responding to domestic pressures, had stipulated that AID money must be used to buy American products. Furthermore, 50 percent of the fertilizer had to be shipped on American vessels, according to another provision of the Foreign Assistance Act of 1962.

Brazil was particularly anxious to get the fertilizer in 1964, because the country was just recovering from political turmoil that had resulted in a military coup, inflation was spiraling, and foreign exchange reserves were gone. Brazil hoped to get the fertilizer in time for the beginning of the planting season in September. The highest levels of the United States government and AID were anxious to see Brazil get the fertilizer. President Johnson had shown unrestrained glee in 1964 when the Brazilian military coup d'état had overthrown a rather radical, but constitutional, government. There can be little doubt that he wanted to see the military receive support from the United States government. AID tried to see to it

[56]Jerome Levinson and Juan de Onís, *The Alliance that Lost Its Way,* Quadrangle Books, Chicago, 1970, p. 112.

that the Brazilian government got this support, but it ran into difficulties with other bureaus in the United States foreign policy bureaucracy.

The crux of the problem that AID confronted in the efforts to get fertilizer to Brazil involved the inefficiency and high cost of the U.S. merchant marine. The cost to the Brazilians of shipping the fertilizer on American ships was twice that of transporting on non-U.S. ships. The Brazilians, understandably, were reluctant to pay the cost, but after protracted negotiations, AID talked them into going along with the deal. But this was only the beginning of problems for AID and Brazil. In 1964 there was a food crisis in India, and the American involvement in Vietnam was growing. American vessels were busy carrying food to India and various commodities to Vietnam. There were no American ships available to transport the fertilizer to Brazil.

The AID mission in Brazil had to get the Office of Material Resources (a U.S. government bureau) to issue a certificate of nonavailability, which would verify that no American ships were available to the Brazilian government and that it could go ahead and ship the fertilizer in non-U.S. ships. Or at least that is what the AID mission in Brazil and the Brazilian government *thought* was meant by the certificate issued by the Office of Material Resources. But the office quickly pointed out that the Brazilian government would have to wait until American ships *were* available. When it was explained to the Office of Material Resources that the Brazilian planting season would begin in four months, and that there was little prospect that American ships would become available in time, the office ruled that even if all the fertilizer were shipped on non-U.S. bottoms, the government of Brazil would have to pay AID the difference between the actual shipping cost, and what it would have cost to transport half the fertilizer on American ships.

> The Brazilian government was reluctant to comply with this "Catch 22" ruling, and in the end the AID mission lawyer convinced the Office of Material Resources that its ruling was not only inconvenient, but not legally necessary. But the process took 6 months, and by that time the planting season in Brazil was over.[57]

The problem in Brazil was not an isolated incident. In July 1967, AID authorized a $24 million loan to Chile, $2 million of

[57]Levinson and de Onís, *Alliance*, pp. 117–119.

which was to be used to purchase tractors for the purpose of assisting Chile's program of agrarian reform. Here again, there is little doubt that the Johnson administration was anxious to see the government supported. During the 1960's, Chile received more economic aid per capita from the United States than any other country in the world, except Vietnam.[58] Eduardo Frei, president of Chile in 1967, had received financial aid from the CIA in his successful campaign of 1964. (One of his opponents was Salvador Allende.) Despite the generally favorable attitude of the United States government toward Chile, getting the tractors to that country proved very difficult. Once again the problem stemmed in large part from the fact that AID money was "tied"; it had to be spent on American products. The Chilean government, as a beginning in procuring the tractors, established a maximum acceptable price. The maximum price drove every American exporter out of the market, except the John Deere Company of Peoria, Illinois. Deere offered to sell the tractors to the Chilean government at a price of $5,700.

But the Ford Motor Company could sell equivalent tractors for a price of $3,900. Unfortunately, Ford tractors contained 50 percent English components, and regulations governing the dispensation of AID money required that no less than 90 percent of the components of products bought with such money be American. Chile preferred the Ford tractors, not only because they were cheaper but also because most of the tractors already in Chile were Fords, and the government had adopted a policy of rationalizing its tractor fleet by keeping the number of brands as low as possible. Since Chile was so reluctant to pay the higher price, and to add the unnecessary additional John Deere brand, the AID mission in Chile proposed that the 90 percent rule be changed so that tractors with 50 percent American components could qualify for purchase with AID funds. In order to encourage acceptance of this proposal, Ford agreed to begin making the tractors in the United States (instead of England), even though they would still have 50 percent English components.

The AID officials in Washington were reluctant to accept the change in the 90 percent rule. They pointed out that the change would cost the U.S. some $3 million in its balance of payments. The departments of treasury and commerce also became involved in the bargaining process, but after some initial wavering, and a conference with John Deere executives, the AID mission request on behalf of the Chilean government was denied.

[58]Miles D. Wolpin, *Cuban Foreign Policy and Chilean Politics,* Heath, Lexington, Mass., 1972, p. 71.

That is not quite the end of the story. The Chilean government finally became resigned to buying all-American tractors, but decided that International Harvester tractors met their needs better, even though the cost was $1,200 apiece more than the John Deere tractors. The AID mission in Chile agreed with this decision. But the procurement division of AID in Washington did not, and they feared that the U.S. Congress would be unhappy that Chile had opted for the more expensive tractors. They directed the AID mission in Chile to ask the Chilean government to reconsider its decision.

The Chilean government was reluctant to do so. Bargaining over this issue reached the highest levels of the Chilean government; at one point Chilean President Frei felt it necessary to explain the position of his government on the tractor issue to the United States ambassador. And the process took so long that although the original loan was authorized in July 1967, it was not until 1969 that the first International Harvester tractor arrived in Chile.[59] As Levinson and de Onís point out, "It is not surprising that Chilean officials, and Latin Americans in general, began to wonder whose development the Alliance for Progress was supposed to promote.[60]

The Alliance for Progress was designed by President Kennedy and his advisors to promote the development of Latin American countries.[61] This does not mean that the alliance was an entirely altruistic venture on the part of the United States. The alliance was supposed to deal with the threat of revolutions fostered by Fidel Castro, who might get help from other Communist countries. Kennedy and other top officials believed the best way to deal with the threat was to help Latin American countries develop economically. That the alliance achieved very little in this regard does not prove that it was really a plot against the welfare of Latin Americans. Rather, the history of the alliance provides another example supporting the important generalization that foreign policies are neither conceived nor implemented by unitary actors. Foreign policy decisions are made, and programs implemented, by complex bureaucracies divided into subbureaus, each with its own point of view regarding any foreign-policy issue. The subbureaus, in the

[59]Levinson and de Onís, *Alliance,* pp. 125–128.
[60]Levinson and de Onís, *Alliance,* pp. 127–128.
[61]Radical critics would argue that the alliance was designed for the purpose it best suited ultimately: to provide opportunities for American business to reap profits. But business executives were invited to attend the Punta del Este meeting that launched the alliance only as an afterthought, and were excluded from the original planning in Washington. That business executives and their allies in the Washington bureaucracy managed to turn the alliance into something that suited their purposes does not necessarily mean the original purpose was to aid American business.

United States and other countries, compete with each other in order to influence the resulting policies. The competition sometimes results in outcomes that are irrational if one views international politics as interaction between unitary actors. But, whether one's focus is on the Cuban Missile Crisis, the war in Vietnam, the Alliance for Progress, or any other major foreign policy decision or program, irrationality is often more apparent than real. It is the result of the foreign policy bureaucracies' pursuit of their aims in what may be, from their particular point of view, a quite rational manner.

SOPs, Bureaucratic Politics, and Foreign Policies

Having said that, I feel it is important to point out that those who emphasize the impact of organizational tendencies to adhere to SOPs and prearranged responses, and of bureaucratic politics, on foreign policies, may well exaggerate the impact. Knowledge of organizational procedures, and bureaucratic infighting, may give a better understanding of the events to which they pertain, but I would argue that usually neither the procedures nor the squabbling has a decisive effect on the shape of events. In virtually all of the examples just discussed, other factors played a more decisive role than SOPs, prearranged procedures, or bureaucratic politics.

Consider first the crisis leading to the First World War. The Russian generals were reluctant to call off general mobilization, not only because of an attachment to their SOPs, but because they calculated that, given the geographic expanse of Russia, and the relative inefficiency of its military organization, any delay in mobilization might put Russia at a considerable disadvantage in the opening weeks of a general war. And the German generals did not refuse to call off their attack on France purely out of some nonrational attachment to prearranged procedures. Those procedures were based on the reasonable calculation that France could mobilize more quickly than Russia, and thus must be dealt with first.

In the Cuban Missile Crisis, organizational procedures and bureaucratic politics may well account for some interesting anomalies, such as the Russian failure to camouflage the missile sites in Cuba, or the delay in the American U-2 flight. But it would be a mistake to attempt to understand the Cuban Missile Crisis solely, or even primarily, in terms of organizational procedures and bureaucratic politics. For example, as Allison points out, "The Soviet Union had never before stationed strategic nuclear weapons outside its own territorial borders."[62] Obviously, if one approaches

[62] Allison, *Essence of Decision*, p. 40.

the crisis convinced that bureaucracies are characterized by strict adherence to SOPs, one will find it difficult to understand why the Russians took the step that precipitated the crisis in the first place; furthermore, one will have no idea when to expect such drastic departures from SOPs.[63] And the American decision for a quarantine rather than a surgical air strike, may have been dictated to some extent by the navy's reluctance to modify its prearranged plans for an attack on Cuba. But the crucial calculation that such a strike might not destroy all the missiles in Cuba, and might result in Russian deaths, could well have emerged (and indeed, might have been more likely to emerge) even in the absence of the navy's prearranged plans. Finally, while bureaucratic squabbling probably did mar the Alliance for Progress effort, surely those squabbles were, in large part, merely a reflection of more important conflicts among various segments of the American society as a whole. It is almost certainly more important to come to grips with the reasons that, as Levinson and de Onís say, "business is the only interest group that consistently presents its viewpoint on Latin American affairs to U.S. government policy-makers,"[64] than to trace in detail all the differing positions of various parts of the bureaucracy that were responding, in large measure, to pressures from outside the government bureaus.

In short, organizational processes and bureaucratic politics do play a role in the foreign-policy-making process. But one must be careful, when focusing on the revelant bureaucratic organizations, not to lose sight of the larger factors that limit the natural tendencies of the organizations and shape their political maneuverings.

Great-Man Theories of History

In this chapter I have focused on the effects the general public has on foreign policies, narrowed the focus to the role of specific interest groups within the general public in foreign-policy making, and continued the narrowing process with a discussion of the impact of government bureaucracies on foreign policy. This process, carried to its logical extreme, arrives at a consideration of individual

[63]Ripley and Franklin suggest that foreign policy decisions be categorized for the purpose of analysis into structural-distributive, strategic-regulatory, and crisis decisions. Presumably, decisions in different categories would be marked by different degrees of susceptibility to the impact of SOPs and bureaucratic politics. See Randall B. Ripley and Grace A. Franklin, *Congress, the Bureaucracy, and Public Policy*, Dorsey Press, Homewood, Ill., 1976, p. 19.

[64]Levinson and de Onís, *Alliance*, p. 160.

leaders in foreign-policy making in particular, and world politics in general.

Great-man theories of history, which emphasize the impact of individual leaders on historical events, have an intuitive appeal. Explanations of important events in terms of abstract factors such as public opinion, bipolarity, and even military-industrial complex, seem lifeless and relatively difficult to understand. In contrast, explanations that emphasize the role that great leaders played in determining the outcome of important events are generally more interesting, partly because they reduce events to a human scale that is easier to understand and identify with. History, as a discipline, has a bias in the direction of great-man kinds of theories, in that it seeks out the unusual, the dramatic, and the memorable.[65] Tidbits about the impact of a leader's relationship with his mother or his mistress on momentous decisions enliven any historical account, and make the writer and the reader feel informed about the events being studied. In addition, historical accounts that emphasize the bravery and the wisdom of individual leaders make pleasant and inspiring reading, while those that stress the stupidity and wickedness of national leaders provide the pleasure of indulging in righteous indignation.

But great-man theories of history rely so heavily on the unique in explanations of the world's affairs that they obscure similarities among different and important events. If events really are determined to an important extent by idiosyncratic features of the personalities of the leaders that are involved, then they are essentially unpredictable. The factors that determine which particular individuals will be national leaders at particular times are obviously so numerous and random that making predictions about the process that brings individuals to the top is impossible. If it is impossible to predict which particular individual will emerge as the national leader, then it will obviously be impossible to predict what the foreign policies of a country will be, since, according to a great-man theory, the policies will be a function of the peculiar personality traits of the individual leader.

An approach contrary to great-man theories emphasizes the strength of constraints under which individual leaders operate. The contours of this approach will emerge in more detail in the pages that follow; for now it is sufficient to stress that explanations of behavior and events in the international political system that rely on visible, concrete factors such as the structure of the international

---

[65]George H. Quester, *The Continuing Problem of International Politics,* Dryden Press, New York, 1974, p. 249.

system, or the structure of the states involved, are more promising from a scientific point of view than great-man theories. If it is true that even leaders with very different idiosyncratic personality traits will react in similar ways to concrete, visible characteristics of the international system, or the structure of the domestic societies in which they live, behavior and events within the international system will be more predictable.

Consider an extreme, but instructive, example. In this century, the individual national leader whose particular personality characteristics seemed to have the greatest impact on the course of world politics was Adolf Hitler. His unique political genius enabled him to rise from lowly prisoner to a dictatorial leader of Germany in less than ten years. He built Germany into a formidable military force and used that force in ways he had personally planned well ahead of time, as described in the pages of *Mein Kampf*.

In the context of this discussion it is particularly interesting to note that Adolf Hitler fought and was wounded in action in the First World War. He could easily have been killed. If he had been, a great-man theory of history must lead us to conclude that events in the 1930s would have been dramatically different. There would have been no Adolf Hitler in Germany, and Germany's foreign policies might have been so different that the Second World War could have been avoided. In short, the course of world politics might have been changed crucially, and in an obviously and totally unpredictable manner, by the removal of one individual from the international system.

From a scientific point of view, it must be hoped that the world's political system does not operate in this fashion.[66] If momentous events such as the Second World War really do depend to a crucial extent on exactly where in Adolf Hitler's body a shell fragment hits, then theories that attempt to explain world politics in terms of larger, more visible, structural characteristics of the international system (or of the states involved) will be doomed to consistent failure by the tremendous impact of relatively trivial, randomly operating factors. An alternative explanation of events such as the Second World War that would not rely on random factors would point out that if a shell fragment had killed Adolf Hitler in the First World War, Germany would still have lost. Germany would still have been blamed officially for the war by the victorious powers and been charged the same substantial reparations. Hitler's death would not have saved Germany from the

[66]By this I do not mean that scientifically inclined scholars of world politics are glad that Hitler was not killed in the First World War, but that scientists must assume that events are not determined primarily by randomly operating factors.

traumatic experience of the inflation of the early 1920s, or the depression of the early 1930s. Having experienced all these devastating blows, Germany, or any important state, would, it seems likely, have produced and supported a Nazi, even if Hitler had died in the First World War. Finally, having such a leader, Germany's foreign policies in the late 1930s would not have been dramatically different even if Hitler had been dead for twenty years.

In short, the Second World War was predictable in the sense that it was brought about by concrete, visible factors, such as Germany's defeat in 1918, inflation, and worldwide depression and its impact on Germany, in a way that could not have been altered by the path of a random shell fragment. One objection to this argument is that it is beyond testing. One can say that if a state is subjected to the loss of a world war and official blame for it, to reparations, inflation, and depression, it will produce an Adolf Hitler (or someone like him). The prediction is totally safe because such a chain of events is highly unlikely to recur. But that chain of events not totally unlike others. Other nations have experienced depressions, for example, and there seems to be a fairly predictable tendency for radical political forces (such as naziism) to thrive under bad economic conditions. Even if there is not such a pattern, the fact that it is possible to look at the relationship between economic adversity and the strength of radical political parties means the assertion that Germany was likely to produce a Hitler can be subjected to a partial test, at least.

On the other hand, Hitler was not just any extremist; he was unusually talented, in a demonic way, and he was extraordinarily evil. The suggestion that Germany might have produced another Hitler if the original had been killed (of course, we do not know that he really was the original; perhaps somebody even worse was killed in the First World War) may strike some as ludicrous. And in truth, it might have been unlikely. But that does not mean that Germany's foreign policy, or the international political system of the 1930s would have been drastically different without Adolf Hitler. Whoever had been Germany's leader in the 1930's would have had to deal with the same problems. And Hitler was certainly not the only German who had ideas that led Germany to aggressive policies. For example, as early as 1922, one of the reasons that Germany signed the treaty with the Russians at Rapallo was that it gave them the opportunity to avoid the provisions of the Versailles peace treaty against rearmament. They were able to use Russian territory, which was beyond the scope of monitoring procedures set up by the peace treaty, for rearming purposes. And this was well before the time that Adolf Hitler had any influence on the

German government. Even if Hitler had not lived, Japan and Italy would have carried out their aggressive policies of the 1930s, thus demonstrating to any German leader the probable success of an aggressive policy on the part of Germany. Given the structure of the international system, and Germany's domestic structure, Germany might well have followed policies quite similar to Hitler's even if the personality of the leader of Germany had been quite different from Hitler's.

> Policy-makers occupy roles in the same sense that being a father or a child constitutes occupancy of a role. Such positions embrace certain responsibilities that have to be performed and expectations that have to be met if their occupants are to remain in them. Whatever prior experiences an official may have had, and regardless of the outlook and talents he may have previously developed, he has to make some adjustments which render his attributes and behavior compatible with the formal and informal requirements of his policy-making responsibilities.[67]

Many object to this kind of argument on philosophical grounds. If human behavior is predictably a function of environment, then there is no free will. Human beings cannot be blamed for their behavior, nor can they be given any credit. Particularly in the realm of world politics, where leaders are typically blamed for wars, and given credit for unusual wisdom and courage for victories, acceptance of the crucial role of environment in explanations of human behavior involves a radical departure from tradition. But in any realm, many are reluctant to accept a deterministic view of the world. It robs human beings of dignity.

The free will versus determinism question is, of course, an ancient philosophical one, and it is important to understand that for the present, at least, it cannot be settled on empirical grounds.[68] Still, any analysis of human behavior almost inevitably entails an assumption about whether that behavior is free or determined. The assumption here is that it is both. Human behavior is obviously determined to some degree by environment, but it is not necessarily totally determined. The goal of any social science, I believe, is to

[67] James N. Rosenau, "Private Preferences and Political Responsibilities," in *Quantitative International Politics*, ed. J. David Singer, Free Press, New York, 1968, p. 23.

[68] It is at least logically possible that social scientists, some day, might be able to specify what proportion of behavior is determined, and what is not.

discover the limits to the impact of environment (or heredity) on behavior. Pursuit of that goal does not imply a belief that the environment (or heredity) is totally determining.

Finally, it should be clear that the free-will-versus-determinism issue is related to but different from the question concerning the impact of idiosyncratic personality traits of individual leaders on world politics. One can believe that those personality traits have a tremendous impact, and yet have a deterministic philosophy. A leader, for example, might, in this view, be entirely unable to escape the influence of a domineering father or emasculating mother, and have a substantial effect on world politics. So belief in the importance of the environment provided by the international system, and the domestic political system in which a leader operates, as compared to the environment provided by a leader's private life, is not necessarily more deterministic than a philosophy of history that stresses the importance of idiosyncratic personality traits. And that belief might be wrong. To the extent that it is, attempts to analyze world politics in a way that de-emphasizes the role of individual personality characteristics of national leaders will be misleading. To the extent that the belief is correct, it will facilitate the development of a science of world politics.[69]

[69] This does not mean that, to the extent personality characteristics of leaders do have an impact on world politics, they are *impossible* to deal with scientifically. See, for example, Margaret G. Hermann, "When Leader Personality Will Affect Foreign Policy: Some Propositions," in *In Search of Global Patterns*, ed. James N. Rosenau, Free Press, New York, 1976, pp. 326–332.

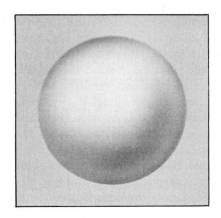

THREE

States, The Primary Actors

FOR AT LEAST THREE HUNDRED YEARS, SOVEREIGN STATES have been the most important political organizations in the global system. They have claimed a monopoly on legal violence within their boundaries and freedom from interference by forces outside their boundaries. Their pre-eminence has not gone unchallenged, and there are good reasons to believe that this particular kind of organization is outmoded, that it will not allow mankind to deal with problems that become more serious as the twenty-first century approaches. Even so, states are still a very important kind of political entity and are likely to remain significant even if other kinds of organizations become more influential. An understanding of the history of world politics necessarily involves some knowledge of the nature of states.

The Historical Origins
of the Modern State

Modern states were born in violence. They arose from the devastation of the Thirty Years' War in Germany, which lasted from 1618 to 1648. "About two-thirds of the total population had disappeared; the misery of those that survived was piteous in the extreme. Five-sixths of the villages in the empire had been destroyed. . . ."[1]

The Peace of Westphalia, signed in 1648, is widely recognized as the dividing line between the time when medieval Europe was dominated by small, localized political units, under the comprehensive authority of the Holy Roman Empire and/or the pope, and modern Europe, where states are recognized as sovereign. In a sense, the Peace of Westphalia marked the separation of church and state on the level of world politics. The Holy Roman Empire and the pope continued to exist, but their political power had been all but destroyed.

The Peace of Westphalia did not, of course, immediately transform Europe from a large collection of small local entities under universal authority into a small number of sovereign states. But the idea of states being hard-shelled, impenetrable units did develop in a short period of time surrounding 1648. As John Herz points out, shortly before 1648, scholars of international law such as Grotius still thought in terms of just and unjust wars, and considered it perfectly appropriate for one state to intervene in the affairs of another in order to protect the citizens from oppression. But some fifty years later, Pufendorf, another student of international law, writing with the benefit of the experience of the Thirty Years' War and the Peace of Westphalia, had decided that such interference by one state in the affairs of another was a violation of sovereignty.[2]

Religious Divisions
and Technological Developments
The process culminating in the Peace of Westphalia and the birth of modern states had been set in motion by two revolutionary developments, one in the realm of the spiritual, the other in the area of military technology. The spiritual unity of Europe had been rent by the Reformation. It was torn again when Calvinism added its

[1]Carlton J. H. Hayes, *A Political and Social History of Modern Europe,* Macmillan, New York, 1921, p. 231.

[2]John Herz, *International Politics in the Atomic Age,* Columbia University Press, New York, 1959, pp. 50–51.

anti-Catholic voice to Lutheranism. France, in an effort to weaken the hold of the Hapsburgs over the numerous principalities of the Holy Roman Empire, stirred up the religious divisions. Perhaps the divisions would have led to the violent horrors of the Thirty Years' War without the aid of France; in any case the horrors made it obvious that the Christian community of medieval Europe was a fragile edifice indeed and was in need of replacement. The replacement that came out of the Peace of Westphalia was the sovereign state. Unrestrained violence of the religious wars might be avoided if each ruler recognized the exclusive rights of others over their domestic realms. In the post-Westphalia period, the idea resulted in the extension of the concept of sovereignty beyond the dimensions described by Jean Bodin, the French legal scholar credited with the first systematic presentation of the concept in his *Six Books on the State,* published in 1586. Bodin's work was a defense of the divine right of the French king to rule in an absolute manner, but Bodin's concept of sovereignty did not imply a right to rule arbitrarily or above the law. Nor did it originally imply that a state fell under no superior obligations in its relations with other states.[3] But because of the urge to avoid catastrophes such as the Thirty Years' War, the concept of sovereignty came to imply that the state has an absolute power over its subjects, and an absolute right to be free from interference by other states in the exercise of that power.[4]

It is possible that if the divisions in Christendom in the fourteenth and fifteenth centuries had been unaccompanied by changes in military technology, the Thirty Years' War and the Westphalian peace might have established impenetrable sovereign units that were nevertheless similar in size to the numerous small units that went into that war. Around A.D. 1200 stone castles represented the ultimate in military defense, and they were scattered all over Western Europe. The rulers of these castles were often legally within the domain of superiors such as the Holy Roman Empire, or the king of France. But the fact that the castles or the fortified cities were self-sufficient militarily gave them independence, and the emperors and kings were rulers of the local barons in name only.

Military technology came to exert a strong force against this state of affairs. "The sudden maturation in 1450 A.D. of the cannon, after a long infancy, as the destroyers of castles made a further and larger change in the art of war in favor of the centralized state . . .

---

[3]James L. Brierly, *The Law of Nations,* 6th ed., Oxford University Press, 1963, p. 11.
[4]Edward Morse, *Modernization in the Transformation of International Relations,* The Free Press, New York, 1976, pp. 33–34.

and in favor of the monarch over the feudal barons."[5] The appearance of gunpowder on the battlefields accelerated the process of elimination of smaller political units in favor of larger units, such as states. Between 1400 and 1600, large numbers of the smaller entities lost their independence; the Thirty Years' War brought this process to a climax. After the Peace of Westphalia, fortified cities and castles gave way increasingly to fortresses lining the borders of states, at least partly because the cities and castles could no longer defend themselves against the new military technology.

The Eighteenth Century

These developments strengthened not only the states but also the monarchs of states. In the eighteenth century, wars between states were not infused with nationalism in the modern sense. They were usually fought on the basis of dynastic conflicts; one royal family would object to the accretion of power of another royal family. One important example involves the War of the Spanish Succession, from 1702 to 1713. The French Bourbons were on the verge of extending their influence by placing one of their number on the Spanish throne. The Hapsburgs, another European royal family, and the English objected, and they managed to make their objections effective. According to the Peace of Utrecht, which ended the war, a Bourbon was placed on the Spanish throne, but the treaty stipulated that the French and Spanish kingdoms were never to be united.

The Utrecht peace was based on the balance-of-power principle. The exact meaning of this principle has been debated since its formulation, but the principle served as the basis of conflict, and conflict resolution, in the eighteenth century despite its ambiguity. Clearly, the balance-of-power principle implied that it was dangerous for all states to allow any one state to become too powerful. Just what was too powerful was in constant dispute, of course, but in practice the balance-of-power principle usually served to preserve the existing distribution of power among the great powers (who became more clearly defined as the eighteenth century progressed). Any change in the status quo that worked to the detriment of a given great power made that state (or royal family) feel entitled to some compensation.[6]

[5]Richard Bean, "War and the Birth of the States," *Journal of Economic History,* 33, (March 1973), p. 208.

[6]Frederick L. Schuman, *International Politics,* 6th ed., McGraw-Hill, 1958, pp. 70–71.

The eighteenth century saw a series of balance-of-power wars, with the British and the French being the major opponents. The wars between kings were fought by soldiers of various nationalities employed for the purpose, and the diplomats who negotiated the peace settlements were virtually indifferent to nationalistic divisions.

> Foreign units of the French Army were composed typically of Swiss Guards, and Irish units were also used when the French could recruit them. Scottish regiments were regularly found in the service of Holland. . . . Frederick the Great's army some years later was more than half-filled with foreign mercenaries, prisoners of war and deserters from enemy armies.[7]

The same cosmopolitanism applied in the diplomatic corps of European states. Denmark used German diplomats, Russia employed Englishmen and Frenchmen, and Spain recruited diplomatic talent from Italy and Holland. Indeed, cosmopolitanism extended to heads of states. England had a German king, and the Spanish king was a grandson of Louis XIV of France. The intermingling of nationalities in the service of different states served to limit conflicts. One is reminded of the cross-pressuring idea as it is traditionally applied to domestic politics. In the eighteenth century, states were cross-pressured in the sense that their antagonism toward other states was softened by the possibility of relatives being in the service of opposing states.

The Impact of the French Revolution

The French Revolution, for better or worse, put an end to anational cosmopolitanism in Europe. The original aims of the Revolution were liberty, equality, and brotherhood for the French people. The aims implied the end of aristocratic rule in France, but more important, they implied that the state belonged to the people. Kings could no longer say *L'etat, c'est moi.*

> The acts of the government came to be viewed as acts of the citizenry, and the revolutionary French constitution of 1793 was ratified by a large popular majority. As popular will linked itself with the actions of its political representatives, tremendous support for the government ensued. As a consequence,

[7]Richard Rosecrance, *Action and Reaction in World Politics,* Little, Brown, Boston, 1963, p. 20.

the government came to be regarded as the head of a national society of Frenchmen, not as in the case of the "ancien regime," as the ruler of a mere "geographical expression."[8]

If the French Revolution had been self-contained, its impact on international politics might have been less dramatic. But under Napoleon the Revolution became expansionist. To be sure, this was to some extent a reaction to perceived threats from the outside. But the French became convinced that their ideals were too good and too important to be confined in application to one state, and with Napoleon's leadership they set out to spread those ideas throughout Europe.[9] In order to do this, Napoleon introduced the *levée en masse,* or conscription. From that point on, soldiers were no longer mercenaries, but patriots who fought in defense of, or for the glory of the state. Eventually the other states of Europe found they could not resist or defeat an army of patriots without copying its methods and its nationalism. France's enemies became nationalistic in self-defense. Even so, it took the combined forces of Napoleon's enemies over a decade to defeat him at Waterloo in 1815.

In the aftermath of the Napoleonic wars, the continental European states were anxious to quell the flame of nationalism, or at least liberal nationalism. A Bourbon king was restored to the throne of France. Somewhat ironically, France itself became the instrument used by the continental European powers to crush liberalism in Spain in 1823. But the efforts of conservatism to defend the principle of legitimacy against the onslaught of liberal nationalism were, in the long run, doomed to failure. Though no one of the conflicts was great enough to seriously disrupt the system set up at the end of the Napoleonic era, wars of national liberation became commonplace after Napoleon was finally banished from the European continent. The Greeks fought for liberation from the Turks. The Poles rose up against the Russians. The Hungarians and the Italians rebelled against the Austrians. An ocean away, the Latin American states obtained their freedom from Spain. And so it went until Serbian nationalistic aspirations helped to destroy the European system that traced its origins to the Congress of Vienna. Between the world wars, many colonies of European states began to show signs of restlessness; after the Second World War, peacefully or otherwise, colonies turned into states in

[8]Rosecrance, *Action and Reaction,* p. 34.
[9]"So convinced were the French of the blessings of the new nationalism for themselves that they could not conceive how it could fail to bless all other peoples." Carlton J. H. Hayes, *Essays on Nationalism,* Macmillan, New York, 1920, p. 45.

great profusion. The Vietnamese, the Algerians, the Angolans, the Hungarians, the Israelis, and the Palestinians, to name a few, have all engaged in violent conflict in the post–Second World War era, inflamed to some degree by the spirit of nationalism that was born in the era of the French Revolution and Napolean.

"Power"

If states have traditionally been considered the most important kind of political organization in the global system, the "power" of states has been treated as the most important concept in the study of world politics. The role that a state plays in world politics is clearly determined to a great extent by its "power." But what is *power?* Despite being central in the study of world politics, the concept has been defined in a confusing variety of ways. Perhaps the most common definition is given by Hans Morgenthau in his classic text *Politics Among Nations:* "When we speak of power, we mean man's control over the minds and actions of other men."[10] This kind of definition tends to equate power with influence or the ability to affect the behavior of others. It also makes the study of world politics unnecessarily complicated.

This is not to say that such a definition of power is wrong. "Power" is a symbol made up of letters (other symbols), and there is no meaning for the concept made in heaven. Definitions of concepts in general are neither true nor false, just more or less useful. There is, of course, no good reason to define concepts in such a way as to contradict widely accepted meanings ("Democracy is a form of government in which political parties are illegal"), but there may very well be a good reason to stipulate definitions of concepts that are somewhat different from generally accepted ones. Popular definitions may be very unclear. A definition of power that equates it with *influence,* though popular, is less useful for the purpose of understanding world politics than a definition that clearly distinguishes power from influence.

The Relationship Between
"Power" and "Influence"
If power is not distinguished from influence, it is almost impossible to measure, and this can make world politics seem mysterious.

---

[10] Hans Morgenthau, *Politics Among Nations,* 4th ed., Knopf, New York, 1967, p. 26. In a more recent text, John Spanier defines power as "The capacity to influence the behavior of others in accordance with one's objective." See John Spanier, *Games Nations Play,* 2d ed., Praeger, New York, 1975, p. 112.

Consider, for example, the contest between the United States and North Vietnam in the 1960s and the early 1970s. One would estimate, at first glance, that the United States, going into war, was clearly the more powerful of the two states. And yet North Vietnam won the war. There are (at least) two possible ways of dealing with this seeming anomaly. One is to persist in defining *power* as influence (the ability to affect behavior), and emphasize just how difficult it is to determine which state is, in this sense, more powerful. Even in cases as seemingly clear-cut as that involving the United States and North Vietnam, the great material advantages of the United States did not suffice to make it more powerful in the struggle over the fate of South Vietnam. Who would have guessed, at the outset of the contest, that North Vietnam would turn out to be more powerful?

Another, and I think more useful, way of dealing with situations like that presented by the outcome of the Vietnam War is to begin with a definition of power that clearly differentiates it from influence. I can (with tongue only slightly in cheek) define *power* as the relative ability to destroy things and kill people.[11] Then, according to this second strategy, I would emphasize that although power usually does lead to influence, this is by no means always the case. The fact that state A is more *powerful* (in our newly defined sense) than state B does not mean that state A will always be successful in its attempts to influence state B. State A might have problems, for example, if state B has powerful and influential friends. This is part of the explanation of the outcome of the Vietnam War. Hawks in the United States called for "bombing North Vietnam back to the stone age" or "turning it into a parking lot" (somewhat contradictory suggestions), and if the contest had been clearly confined to the United States and North Vietnam, there is not much doubt that the United States had the capability to do either. American policy-makers rejected those suggestions, and even more moderate ones, at least partly because they feared that the Chinese might intervene in the war if North Vietnam was threatened with total destruction.

Another reason why a more powerful state might have trouble influencing a less powerful state is that the latter might not be vulnerable to power. To cite another example from the Vietnam War, the North Vietnamese were able to withstand successfully the

[11]*Relative* is included in this definition to indicate that one state's power depends on how it relates, or compares to other states in the system at the time. Great Britain, because it possesses nuclear weapons, might well have a greater absolute ability to destroy things and kill people now than it did in 1910. But it is not more powerful now because its ability to destroy relative to the abilities of other states in the system is clearly much smaller now than it was decades ago.

massive bombing campaign waged against them by the Americans partly because North Vietnam's largely agrarian economy was not particularly vulnerable to that kind of strategy. If North Vietnam had been a more industrialized, more complex, society, it might have suffered more and been more easily influenced. Since industrialization generally leads to increased power, it is possible to argue that if North Vietnam had been more powerful, it might have been more easily influenced.

China's tremendous population may provide a similar ability to resist being influenced in the face of superior power. Or at least Mao Tse-tung seemed to have thought so. He explained on occasion that China was not particularly fearful of a nuclear war because China's millions would make it possible to emerge from such a war in an enviable position. If a nuclear war killed 200 million people in the Soviet Union or the United States, those states would be obliterated. But even if 300 million Chinese were killed, the nation would have a solid base of several hundred million on which to build. Mao's calculations may have been faulty; to the extent that they were not, China provides another example of a state that may be difficult to influence because of a degree of invulnerability to power.

There are several other examples of a more powerful state being unable to influence the behavior of a less powerful state. If the less powerful state has something desperately needed by the more powerful state, the latter might find its power not very effective. The Middle Eastern states, because of oil, are not only able to resist influence attempts; they can assert influence despite a lack of power. To take another example, a state might be very powerful, but not care to use its power to exert influence. Thus, although the United States was probably the most powerful state in the world in the 1920s, it was almost certainly not the most influential. Finally, nuclear weapons give a state tremendous *power,* defined as the relative ability to destroy things and kill people. But the power increment and the influence increment resulting from the possession of nuclear weapons may be substantially different. When the United States had an atomic power monopoly, for example, it was unable to prevent the Soviets from conducting a coup in Czechoslovakia in 1948, or blockading Berlin in the same year. American nuclear power did not enable the United States to influence China sufficiently to keep it out of the Korean War in 1950; the North Vietnamese seemed equally unimpressed by nuclear power in the 1960s.[12]

[12]A. F. K. Organski, *World Politics,* 2d ed., Knopf, New York, 1968, pp. 313–329.

In the cases just mentioned, power failed to lead to influence because the implied threat to actually unleash the power was not credible. This, of course, is not a phenomenon that is restricted to situations involving nuclear weapons. Great Britain and France together were clearly more powerful than Germany in the middle 1930s, but they failed to influence Hitler because he did not believe they would use their combined power against him.

"Power" as Brute Force

All the events and examples discussed become clouded and more difficult to understand if one works with a conceptual framework that treats power and influence as the same thing. That is one good reason to keep them separated. A second reason involves the importance of power by itself. It is sad but true that raw brute force plays an important role in world politics, and this crucial fact is in danger of being overlooked if power is conceptually intermingled with the more complicated concept of influence. As one example of the importance of simple destructive force in world politics, consider Table 3.1. During the Second World War, the Axis powers did all right as long as they produced more of the instruments that allowed them to destroy things and kill people. But as soon as their production of firepower was surpassed by Allied production, the Axis powers began to lose. The further behind they fell, the worse

TABLE 3.1 Percentage of total combat munitions output of the main belligerents, 1938–1943

Country	1938	1939	1940	1941	1942	1943
United States	6	4	7	14	30	40
Canada	0	0	0	1	2	2
Britain	6	10	18	19	15	13
U.S.S.R.	27	31	23	24	17	15
Total, Allied Countries	39	45	48	58	64	70
Germany	46	43	40	31	27	22
Italy	6	4	5	4	3	1
Japan	9	8	7	7	6	7
Total, Axis Countries	61	55	52	42	36	30

Source: Klaus Knorr, *The War Potential of Nations,* Princeton University Press, Princeton, 1956, p. 34. Copyright © 1956 by Princeton University Press. Reprinted by permission of Princeton University Press.

their position became. The point is no more complex than "God is always on the side of the biggest battalions." Discussions of the Second World War that compare the morale or the bravery of the soldiers on both sides, or the wisdom of the generals, are probably unnecessarily complex. The Allies won the war because in the end, they had a greater ability to destroy things and kill people.

It will occur to some readers that the reasons the Allies proved to have a greater ability to destroy things and kill people may have involved more subtle factors such as the superiority of the democratic form of government or better morale. Even if this is true, a focus on power as something distinguishable from influence serves at least two useful purposes. First, focusing on the distinction is a reminder that explanations of the outcome of events such as the Second World War must almost certainly include the ability to destroy things and kill people. Second, it highlights the measureability of power. Influence *is* difficult to measure, and predicting with complete accuracy when power will lead to influence may be almost as difficult. But measuring power, though hardly a trivial task, is not impossible. If power, as it is defined here, is measured, and power by itself, even if not inevitably associated with influence, plays an important role in world politics, there is a better chance to understand world politics.

Measuring "Power"

Despite widespread agreement that power is difficult to measure, both students and statesmen continue to try. And even if a simple definition of power is adopted that emphasizes its differences from influence, and the concrete aspects, measuring is not easy. There is a complex series of factors that determine a state's ability to destroy things and kill people; some factors are obviously more important than others, but it is difficult to determine which ones and by how much. In addition, the combination of factors that are most important changes over time.

The Ingredients of "Power"
One factor that has always been important, and will continue to be, is a large population. No state with a small population can be very powerful. This does not mean that there is a perfect relationship between power and size of population. The example of China makes clear the possibility of having too much of what is generally

a good thing. Even so, one of the most obvious criteria for distinguishing powerful nations from weak ones is the size of a state's population.

A second factor that determines a state's power is its industrial capacity. Since the death of Napoleon, it is probably safe to say that the most powerful nation on earth has been the nation with the greatest industrial capacity. Great Britain dominated most of the nineteenth century, not only because it had the world's largest navy but also because it industrialized first and faster than any other country on earth. The rise of the industrial might of the United States, and its status as the most powerful state in the world thus far in the twentieth century, are not coincidental. If the Soviet Union does surpass the United States in power in this century, one of the surest indicators of this will be the Soviet's industrial capacity vis-à-vis that of the United States.

The two world wars have accentuated the role of industrial capacity in determining a state's power. The introduction of nuclear weapons into modern military arsenals will continue the trend. The development and maintenance of delivery systems and a large number of nuclear weapons is a technologically and economically demanding task for any state. A large and sophisticated industrial plant is necessary if a state is to marshal a sufficient quality and quantity of technological ability and generate enough wealth to bear the cost of nuclear weapons and modern delivery systems.

A third crucial determinant of a state's power is the size and quality of its military establishment. The nation with the largest army, navy, and air force, though, is not necessarily the world's most powerful state. It may, for example, find that its ability to destroy things and kill people is overshadowed by another state in the long run (for example, in a long war) because the other state will be able, in time, to assemble and equip a larger military force. Perhaps even more important, the total supply of persons available is becoming progressively less important as military technology becomes more sophisticated and capable of greater destructive power. An army equipped with tactical nuclear weapons will probably be more than a match for a much larger force that is not so equipped. In a sense, war has become more automated, and the importance of sheer numbers of bodies in the military has become accordingly diminished.

If a state has a large population, a productive industrial sector, and a large, sophisticated military force, it is virtually certain to be quite powerful. There are other elements that go into making a state powerful, but the three discussed are probably most important. Of the additional factors, possession of large quantities of natural resources might be next. Modern wars, and modern economies, require large amounts of oil, coal, iron, and other raw materials. If a state has these within its boundaries, this is likely to enhance its power. But this factor may be less crucial than the previous ones. It is safe to say that no state in this century has obtained a very powerful status without a large population, a substantial industrial capacity, and a large, sophisticated military force. There have been, though, several instances of states achieving substantial power without the good fortune of having a large quantity of natural resources within their boundaries. Great Britain and Japan, both islands lacking in large supplies of most natural resources, achieved great power status in this century. And Germany has not been blessed with abundant natural resources. All of these states had to acquire access to substantial supplies of natural resources in order to become very powerful, which proved possible even though the resources had to be obtained from outside their national boundaries. The fact that the United States and the Soviet Union possess great supplies of natural resources within their boundaries does give them an advantage and may be an important reason that both have emerged as the most powerful states in the international system. But the history of this century indicates that access to, and not possession of, large quantities of natural resources is sufficient for a state to be powerful.

Geographic factors can have a bearing on a state's power. Large size gives a state an advantage, as the Russians have proved at least twice in the last two hundred years. But, again, this factor is not absolutely crucial. Great Britain and Japan became very powerful despite their small geographic area (as well as their lack of natural resources). The Soviet Union has been the largest country in the world for a very long time, but it has only recently emerged as one of the most powerful states in the world. Geographic location can also affect a state's power. The relative isolation of the United States in the nineteenth century may well have helped its growth. Poland's location seems, on the basis of sad history for the last two hundred years, to assure that its very existence will be precarious and its power limited. The narrow strip of water between the neighboring mainland continents and the islands of Japan and Great Britain may have helped them overcome the disadvantages already mentioned. And it is an often-noted fact that no great power in the modern era has been located in the southern hemisphere. This may be a coincidence. The industrial revolution occurred first in the northern hemisphere, and its impact has been concentrated there. There are a number of social, political, and economic differences between states in the southern hemisphere and those in the northern hemisphere, all of which are related to a state's power but none of which seems connected with the locations of the states, per se.

Intangible Factors and "Power"

A final set of factors that plays a role in the determination of a state's power are intangible, difficult to assess, and only rarely of great importance. I refer to qualitative factors such as national morale, national character, and quality of leadership. If two states are nearly equal in the possession of the concrete, measurable assets that give a state power, then it is certainly possible that these intangibles might make a difference. Within the confines of a single battle, the morale and bravery of soldiers, or the wisdom of generals, can certainly make a difference. But, in the long run, in all-out wars between states or coalitions of states, concrete factors are more important. Superior national morale or character or quality of leadership will only rarely suffice to make up for a deficit in such factors as population size, industrial capacity, and military capability.

This statement evokes numerous counterexamples. North Vietnam's victory over the United States is a recent one that might seem to indicate that morale, for example, can make a crucial difference. But other factors have been discussed (such as North Vietnam's potential allies) that were much more important than greater morale or superior national character in bringing North Vietnam success. I do not mean that the North Vietnamese morale was not better; it may well have been, at least partly because of the greater intrinsic worth of the goal for which the North Vietnamese were fighting compared to the goal toward which Americans were striving. For the North Vietnamese, the goal of unifying and "liberating" their country was more desirable, and easier to obtain than the goal of propping up an unpopular government several thousand miles away was for the Americans. But this does not indicate that the superior morale of the North Vietnamese enabled them to overcome a tremendous inferiority in power so much as it demonstrates that a lot more power is required to achieve some goals than others. If the North Vietnamese were to achieve a goal comparable in difficulty to the one the United States tried to achieve, such as imposing a Communist government in the southern half of the United States, then one might be justified in concluding that intangible factors made North Vietnam able to overcome the power gap between themselves and the United States.

Israel's victory in the 1948 war in the Middle East is another recent example often cited by those who like to emphasize the role of intangibles in the determination of a state's power. At the time, Israel was a new nation with a badly equipped army; nine Arab nations with a vast superiority in sheer numbers over the small Israeli nation, and superior military equipment to boot, set out to eliminate the new state immediately. They failed. Israel won. Surely this must be an example of morale and determination enabling a nation overwhelmed by the physical superiority of an opponent to exert greater power.

Not necessarily. There is little doubt that the morale and determination of the Israeli soldiers were greater than that of the largely uneducated and uninterested Arab peasants who made up the bulk of the Arab armies. But that was probably not the crucial difference between the two enemies. First, Israel sent some 70,000 troops into the field, 20,000 of whom were Second World War veterans. Though it is true that these troops took to the field against the armies of nine nations, the nations managed to assemble only somewhere around 25,000.[13] The 25,000 troops were, to repeat, better equipped than the Israeli army, but it seems clear that Arab soldiers did not know how to use much of their admittedly superior equipment. Almost certainly, the superior numbers put into the battle by the Israelis—plus the lack of ability by the Arabs to use the equipment they had—were more important determinants of the amounts of power exerted by the Israelis, and by the Arabs, than the differences in the morale of both sides.

To summarize, the tangible elements that make a state powerful are very important, and when isolated and studied can reveal important things about the structure of the international system.

A Simple Index of "Power"

The point can be further illustrated by constructing an index of power based on the three concrete factors given at the opening of the discussion. The index will measure a state's power in terms of demographic, industrial, and military dimensions. A state's total population will be the indicator that reflects the demographic component of power. Three indicators of industrial capacity will be included. The first is the total urban population living in the state (all those living in cities over 20,000 are classified as urban population), which gives a fairly accurate picture of the industrial potential of a state for the short, foreseeable future, or the industrial output that a state might achieve during a prolonged war. The second

[13]Fred J. Khouri, *The Arab-Israeli Dilemma*, Syracuse University Press, Syracuse, 1968, pp. 70–71.

indicator of industrial capacity is steel production. The capability to produce steel is an important part of what is meant by industrial capacity, and steel is necessary for the development of other capabilities involved in the industrial process. Also, a state must produce large quantities of steel if it is to develop and maintain modern weapons. A third indicator of a state's industrial capacity is its fuel consumption (in terms of metric tons of coal equivalents). This indicator complements nicely the one based on steel production, since it reflects the industrial progress of more diversified economies. Finally, the number of military personnel supported by a state, and the size of its military expenditures, will be the indicator of the military dimension of power.

These six indicators of power could be combined in a variety of ways to yield an overall index of power. Some could be weighted more heavily than others, and the indicators could be given different weights for different time periods. To avoid preconceptions about which states are more powerful than others, each indicator will be given an equal weight in the index.

The index can be applied to the major powers in the international system since 1900. At the beginning of the century there were, according to a fairly firm consensus among scholars of diplomatic history, the following major powers: Austria-Hungary, France, Great Britain, Italy, Japan, Germany, Russia, and the United States. Austria-Hungary's great-power status was permanently destroyed by 1918; Russia and Germany, having lost such status in the First World War, regained it in 1922 and 1925, respectively. The Second World War, according to consensus, resulted in the elimination of the Axis powers (Germany, Italy, and Japan) from major-power status until the present time, as well as the temporary removal of France from major-power status from 1940 to 1944. China appears on the list of major powers in 1950.[14]

The index is applied to the major powers every fifth year, starting in 1900 (with some exceptions around the years of the two world wars). Each state is given an index score that reflects the proportion of the "power factors" it possessed at the particular time. For example, in 1900 the total population of the United States comprised 16 percent of the population living in all the major power states at the time. Of the urban population living in one of the major powers, 21 percent lived in the United States at the time, and the United States accounted for 39 percent of the steel produced

---

[14]This list of major powers, as well as the index of power, is taken from J. David Singer, Stuart Bremer, and John Stuckey, "Capability Distribution, Uncertainty, and Major Power War, 1820–1965", in *Peace, War, and Numbers,* ed. Bruce M. Russett, Sage Publications, Beverly Hills, 1972, pp. 19–48.

TABLE 3.2   Distribution of "power" among major powers, 1900–1970

1900		1905	
State	Index Score	State	Index Score
United States	22	United States	25
England	20	Germany	16
Germany	16	Russia	16
Russia	15	England	15
France	10	Japan	10
Austria-Hungary	6	France	9
Italy	5	Austria-Hungary	6
Japan	5	Italy	4

1910		1913	
State	Index Score	State	Index Score
United States	26	United States	26
Russia	18	Germany	18
Germany	17	Russia	18
England	14	England	14
France	9	France	9
Japan	6	Austria-Hungary	6
Austria-Hungary	6	Japan	6
Italy	4	Italy	4

1920		1925	
State	Index Score	State	Index Score
United States	46	United States	35
England	22	England	15
France	13	Russia	13
Italy	11	Germany	12
Japan	8	France	11
		Japan	8
		Italy	7

1930		1935	
State	Index Score	State	Index Score
United States	31	Russia	27
England	20	United States	26
Russia	15	Germany	14
France	10	England	10
Germany	10	Japan	8
Japan	7	France	8
Italy	6	Italy	7

TABLE 3.2   Distribution of "power," 1900–1970 (cont.)

1938		1946	
State	Index Score	State	Index Score
Russia	25	United States	45
United States	24	Russia	34
Germany	20	England	14
England	10	France	7
Japan	10		
France	6		
Italy	5		

1950		1955	
State	Index Score	State	Index Score
United States	38	United States	39
Russia	30	Russia	30
China	17	China	17
England	9	England	9
France	5	France	5

1960		1965	
State	Index Score	State	Index Score
United States	35	United States	33
Russia	29	Russia	32
China	24	China	24
England	7	England	6
France	6	France	5

1970	
State	Index Score
United States	33
Russia	32
China	25
England	5
France	5

Source: The data for this table were supplied by the Correlates of War Project at the University of Michigan. (Sums for years that deviate from 100 are accounted for by rounding error.)

by major powers in that year as well as 38 percent of the major-power fuel consumed. Finally, in 1900, 4 percent of major-power military personnel were located in the United States, and the Americans' military expenditures were 12 percent of the total military expenditures made by major powers in that year. The single power index score assigned to the United States in that year is simply the average of the six figures. (16% + 21% + 39% + 38% + 4% + 12%), divided by 6 equals 22, which is the power index score for the United States in that year.)

There are several interesting things to point out about Table 3.2. It excludes, of course, all the intangible elements of *power* defined as influence, and yet it portrays quite clearly important changes in the structure of the international system from 1900 to 1970. Notice, for example, the increase in the power of Germany before the First World War. Germany surpasses Great Britain by 1905, and this unseating of the greatest power in the European system might well have been one of the unsettling elements that caused the system to collapse in 1914. Notice, too, the extent to which the United States benefits, in terms of its power advantage over the other major powers, as a result of the First World War. The dramatic increase in the power of Germany before the Second World War is reminiscent of that before the First World War, but in Table 3.2, Germany's defeat of France is foreshadowed in the figures for 1938, as well as the defeat of Germany by the Soviet Union. Also, if one calculates the combined power of the Axis coalition, and compares it to the power in the hands of the Allies, it is clear that the Axis faced a nearly impossible task. Finally, American supremacy in the international system is reflected quite clearly in the figures for the years immediately following the Second World War, and the emerging tripolarity in later years is also quite apparent.

The Major Powers:
A Brief History

In this section we are going to discuss briefly the most important states in the international system today. In some ways, the distinction between major powers and others is not quite as important, at least in a formal way, as it once was. Still, it is true, for example, that "thirteen . . . countries alone account for almost 77 percent of the world's mobilized wealth."[15] In addition, this economic gap has been increasing since the Second World War. In the 1970s, the two most powerful states alone accounted for over one-half of the military expenditures in the entire world. So, even if it is true that the formal distinction between major powers and the others has lost some of its significance in the modern era, the most powerful states still have plenty of clout, and no one can gain a deep understanding of the global political system today without a basic knowledge of the historical experiences of these important states.

The United States

The Americans entered the twentieth century, according to concrete indicators, as the most powerful state in the international system. It was clearly not, as already noted, the most influential state. Indeed, it only became generally recognized as a major power at all with its defeat of Spain in 1898. During the nineteenth century, the United States considered itself isolated from the European-dominated international system, and in most respects it was. The oceans separating it from Europe and Asia were important barriers throughout that century. But it would be a mistake to picture the nineteenth-century American nation as pacific, satisfied, and without interest in expansion. Its citizens devoted themselves to settling and integrating their considerable share of the North American continent, as well as resolving a bitter internal dispute. By the beginning of the twentieth century, the continent had been explored and settled from coast to coast, and the Indians had been subdued. Business interests and their lobbyists began to worry about a lack of room for expansion. A United States senator lamented that "today we are raising more than we can consume. Today, we are making more than we can use. Therefore we must find new markets for our produce, new occupation for our capital, new work for our labor."[16] Theodore Roosevelt wrote to his friend Henry Cabot Lodge that "this country needs a war." Whether purposely or not, the country found a war with Spain in 1898. In the process of fighting that war it acquired Cuba, Puerto Rico, and the Philippines. In the first decades of the twentieth century, the United States revealed a proprietary attitude about the Caribbean and Central America. Roosevelt "took" Panama from Colombia,

---

[15]Marshall R. Singer, "The Foreign Policies of Small Developing States", in *World Politics*, ed. James N. Rosenau, Kenneth W. Thompson, and Gavin Boyd, Free Press, New York, 1976, p. 264.

[16]Richard N. Current, T. Harry Williams, and Frank Freidel, *American History: A Survey*, 3d ed., Knopf, New York, 1971, p. 518.

and work was started on the canal. The Dominican Republic, Cuba, Haiti, Nicaragua, and Mexico were all invaded and militarily occupied for periods of time ranging from a few months to twenty years. These activities did not seem, to most Americans, to be a break with the past, or out of tune with the traditional American isolation from international politics. The Monroe Doctrine, proclaimed in 1823, had established the western hemisphere as an area divorced from ordinary international politics, as far as Americans were concerned. Most of the interventions that took place in the first three decades of this century were seen as extensions of a long-standing policy based on the Monroe Doctrine.

This vision of continuity in American policy was mostly an illusion. The Monroe Doctrine, excluding European powers from Latin America (except in those areas where they had colonies already established) was not effectively enforced in the nineteenth century. To the extent that it was enforced at all, the British, not the Americans, kept foreign interests out of Latin America. By the time Theodore Roosevelt became president, though, the United States was becoming the predominant power in Latin America, and his Corollary to the Monroe Doctrine served as an announcement of that fact.

The Americans Enter the First World War   While the American intention and capability to enforce its will south of the border was not seen as a break with the past, entry into the First World War certainly was. George Washington, of course, had warned his countrymen to avoid "permanent alliances with any portion of the foreign world," and Americans had taken that advice seriously. Woodrow Wilson had been elected in 1916 partly on the basis of his slogan "He kept us out of war." But the United States entered the war before the first year of Wilson's new term had expired. If the Germans won, some Americans feared, they threatened democracy and national freedom in Europe, the Old Country for the vast majority of Americans. Undoubtedly, many Americans were also concerned about what a formidable power Germany might become if it defeated Great Britain, France and Russia. Whatever the reasons, the Americans entered the First World War in an attempt to reform the anachronistic evils of the European international system. In retrospect, it is easy to see that most Americans viewed the war not as the beginning of deep American involvement in world politics, but as a brief heroic effort to set Europe right. Clearly, the Senate of the United States was reflecting public opinion when it refused to vote for entrance into the League of Nations. And the more Europe showed signs of slipping into its bad ways, the more the Americans showed determination to stay out of European quarrels. Not until 1941 did the Japanese successfully counter the arguments of the isolationists with their attack on Pearl Harbor.

After the Second World War   The United States emerged from the Second World War as the most powerful state in the world, and I have discussed at some length its role in post– Second World War international politics in Chapter 1; the basic outlines of the history are likely to be familiar (as the histories of the other major powers may not be) in any case. The Americans have continued to demonstrate, since 1945, that they consider the western hemisphere their special domain, but the methods used to maintain pre-eminence have been less obvious, on the whole, than those applied in the earlier part of the century. In 1954, for example, President Eisenhower authorized the CIA to aid in the overthrow of a government in Guatemala, which included some Communist officials, had received a shipment of arms from Czechoslovakia, and had expropriated a large quantity of land from the United Fruit Company. (The question of which of these factors was most important in spurring the CIA into action is the basis of a very lively controversy among students of American foreign policy.) President Kennedy went along with the CIA-organized invasion of the Bay of Pigs, the origins of which can be traced back to the Eisenhower administration. President Johnson sent the marines into the Dominican Republic, and President Nixon used the CIA, as well as an invisible blockade that cut off various sources of financial aid to the Allende government in Chile, in an effort to "destabilize" that government. (Were those efforts successful, or would Allende have been overthrown by a military coup in any case?)

The CIA and the United States military were busy in many areas in addition to Latin America during the postwar era. The former was apparently involved in governmental changes in Syria in the late forties, and in Iran in the early 50's. The Korean War occupied the Pentagon from 1950 to 1953. Eisenhower sent the marines into Lebanon in 1958. As the United States became progressively more involved in Vietnam, it also became progressively more committed to its role as policeman of the world, shoring up counterrevolutionary regimes in Latin America, Africa, the Middle East, and Asia with financial and military aid. Needless to say, the experience in Vietnam, plus revelations of CIA activities in other parts of the world, led many Americans to question the wisdom of such a policy.

What the alternative will be is not clear. In the early 1970s, Secretary of State Kissinger made some moves, as was observed in

Chapter 1, to accommodate the rising power of the Soviet Union and China. How, and if, the United States will continue the adaptation process vis-à-vis the Russians and Chinese, and whether it will be able to reach some kind of accommodation with Third World countries demanding drastic structural changes in the international economic system, seem to be the major questions facing American foreign-policy makers as they look forward to the 1980s.

The Soviet Union

Russia entered the twentieth century singularly unequipped to deal with it. Geographic distance from the liberalizing influence of Europe and the frequently experienced dangers of invasion from the east, south and west, left the country with an anachronistic, oppressive czarist regime. As outdated as it was, in the latter part of the nineteenth century, the regime was also expansionist. It completed the Trans-Siberian Railroad in the last decade of the century, and as it used this railway to extend its influence into Manchuria and Korea, it came into conflict with Japan. Japan attacked Russia's new naval base at Port Arthur in February 1904, and the war was on.

It was assumed in Russia and the rest of the "civilized" world that Russia would easily defeat Japan. Russia was a great power and Japan was not. In addition, the Japanese were Orientals and thus presumably inferior and backward. But the war proved that the Russians actually suffered from backwardness. The Japanese won an overwhelming victory, and the czarist regime was humiliated.

Humiliation encouraged rebellious domestic elements and the czar was forced to compromise with them. The Duma, a representative assembly, was created, the first significant crack in dynastic absolutism. Unfortunately for the cause of liberal democracy in Russia, the Duma was never given any significant responsibilities and the reform of the Russian government was skin-deep at best. On the foreign front, the Russsians, perforce, put a halt to their eastward expansion and turned their energies to the Balkans, where they hoped to strengthen the cause of pan-Slavism. This cause encroached on the interests of Turkey and Austria-Hungary. In 1912 Russia fought a "war by proxy" supporting the Balkan states of Serbia, Greece, Bulgaria, and Montenegro in their struggle for freedom from Turkish control. Then in 1914 Russia stood firmly behind Serbia in its dispute with Austria, an important element of which was Serbia's support of Slavic nationalists in the Austro-Hungarian empire.

The Russian Revolution   The Russians, it turned out, were no better

able to handle the Germans in the First World War than they had the Japanese in 1904–1905. Sheer superiority of numbers, and German concentration on the western front, allowed them to avoid immediate collapse. But by the fall of 1916, food shortages, equipment shortages, inflation, and political turmoil began to catch up with the czar. He finally abdicated in March 1917, and a provisional government, the key figure of which was Alexander Kerensky, took power.

The provisional government insisted on fighting the war. A substantial majority of Russians were opposed to this policy, and the provisional government fell to the Bolsheviks some nine months after it had come into existence. Lenin believed that the first priority of the Revolution had to be the consolidation of its power, and that to do this it had to get out of the war. So, despite the original opposition of the majority of his colleagues, Lenin accepted the Treaty of Brest Litovsk forced on him by the Germans.

Consolidation Lenin hoped that by surrendering vast amounts of territory to the Germans he would gain some breathing space for his revolution. And perhaps he did. But it was a very short one. Within a matter of months, the Bolsheviks were attacked not only by domestic enemies (the White Russians) but also by the Americans, British, Japanese, French, Canadians, and Italians. The initial, official explanation of these attacks was that they were necessary in order to destroy the government that had accepted the treaty with the Germans, and to put into power a government that would carry on the fight. This argument may not have been entirely specious, but it hardly seems, in retrospect, to have been the whole truth, either. The foreign enemies persisted in their attacks after Germany had surrendered, and it became increasingly obvious that the Allies' motivations were directed as much toward abolishing the specter of Communism as anything else. Poland later joined the attack against the Russians, and, aided by the French, was ultimately successful in getting the Russians to sign the Treaty of Riga in March 1921, which formalized the transfer of some 6 million Ukranians and Byelorussians. (The treaty remained in force until the outbreak of the Second World War.) The Bolsheviks managed to avoid ultimate disaster at the hands of their collective enemies, but not without enduring a three-year period of civil war, famine, and social chaos.[17] The Russian Marxists would have been predisposed by ideology and past history in any case to believe that the capitalist

[17]Robert P. Warth, *Soviet Russia in World Politics*, Twayne Publishers, New York, 1963, pp. 55–97.

states would be inevitably dedicated to the destruction of the Revolution. Undoubtedly, their experience in the first years after the Revolution reinforced their tendency to take to heart the warning of Lenin:

> We are living not merely in a state, but in a system of states, and the existence of the Soviet Republic side by side with imperialistic states for a long time is unthinkable. One or the other must triumph in the end. And before that end supervenes, a series of frightful collisions between the Soviet Republic and the bourgeois states will be inevitable.[18]

Immediately after the successful Revolution, the Bolsheviks had rejected "normal" international intercourse as part of the bourgeois system of oppression. Secret treaties concluded by the previous regime were renounced (and published), as well as all debts and liabilities incurred by that regime. In 1919, the Third International, or Comintern, was formed and given the responsibility of coordinating Communist revolutionary activities all over the world.

But by 1921, Lenin and his colleagues began to confront cold realities that led them to curb their ideological fervor. Lenin advocated the adoption of a new economic policy to replace "war communism"; the new policy involved the abandonment of forced requisitions in agriculture, some toleration of private ownership in trade and small-scale industry, and an attempt to attract foreign investment into the Soviet Union.[19] By 1922 the Soviets had signed the Treaty of Rapallo with Germany, which demonstrated that Russia was no longer a totally isolated pariah state. The treaty also gave the Soviets the benefit of German technological and military aid and was a symbolic (if only partial) renunciation of ties between German Communists and the Soviet government. By signing the treaty, the Russians formed ties with a government they had previously believed (and hoped) was about to fall prey to a Communist revolution. "In Soviet Russia the Rapallo agreement was, as a matter of course, acclaimed a diplomatic triumph despite its disturbing implication that the German workers had been abandoned as less desirable partners than their bourgeois rulers."[20] The Rapallo treaty, then, gave priority to the defense of the Soviet home of the

---

[18]V.I. Lenin, "Report of the Central Committee at the Eighth Party Congress of March 18, 1919," *Selected Works*, Vol. 8, p. 33. Cited by Frederick H. Hartmann, *The Relations of Nations*, 6th ed., Macmillan, New York, 1957, p. 444.

[19]Adam B. Ulam, *Expansion and Coexistence*, 2d ed., Praeger, New York, 1974, p. 127.

[20]Warth, *Soviet Russia*, p. 113.

first successful Communist revolution over the possibility of spreading that revolution elsewhere. Whether or not the Soviet Union should give priority to defense of the homeland, or to spreading revolution, was the major foreign policy issue of the 1920s for the Communist party. Lenin was inclined to sacrifice the Soviet national interest for the sake of revolution abroad. But Lenin became ill in the spring of 1922 and was a helpless invalid by December that year. (He died in January 1924.) The stage was set for the spectacular debate between Trotsky and Stalin. Trotsky advocated a theory of permanent revolution, calling on the Soviet Union to concentrate on helping Communist parties in promising states. Stalin argued that the first Soviet goal should be the defense of socialism in one country, that all would be lost unless the Soviet Communist state was preserved. When Lenin died, Trotsky was assumed to be the heir apparent. But Stalin worked quietly and effectively within the structure of the Communist party, and by 1928 he had not only won the debate, he had eliminated Trotsky and every other potential opponent from contention for the leadership of the Soviet Union.

Having gained a measure of security in his role as leader, Stalin inaugurated the first five-year plan for the Soviet Union in 1928. The goal of the plan was to modernize the Soviet Union; industrial capacity was to be greatly increased, inefficient small farms were to be collectivized, and kulaks (well-to-do peasants) were to be eliminated as an effective source of opposition. The plan degenerated into a virtual war between the regime and the peasants. It is still a matter of dispute whether the plan originally called for so much brute force to be applied to the peasants, or whether the unexpectedly stiff opposition mounted by the peasants brought about the violent reaction on the part of the Soviet government. It is clear that millions of peasants died as a result of the starvation and brutality that accompanied the first five-year plan.

Stalin's Prewar Foreign Policy In foreign affairs during the prewar period, Stalin was enjoying a reputation as a prophet. He had predicted that the capitalist world was headed for economic disaster, and in 1929–1930, the Great Depression served to bear him out. It served also to reinforce the policy of the Communist party to oppose moderate socialist elements in capitalist countries. This policy was carried to its logical extreme in Germany during the rise of Hitler. Following directions from Moscow, the German Communists attempted to destroy the Social Democrats, the Socialist trade unions, and any other reform-minded democratic elements, accusing them of being social fascists. The idea was that naziism (as well as other forms of fascism) was the last stage of dying capitalism.[21] Once the Nazis had taken over, the reasoning went, their rule would be so oppressive, reactionary, and repugnant that it would be a relatively simple matter to unite the people behind a Communist revolution. The depression, in Germany and elsewhere, seemed to provide a perfect setting for this kind of strategy. The greatest danger of failure for the strategy, it seemed to the Communists at the time, stemmed from the presence of Social Democrats and their ilk. They provided a less-than-revolutionary alternative to the Communists. Because of the danger they posed to a Communist takeover they must be vigorously opposed.

The Communist party of the Soviet Union adhered to this opinion until Hitler was firmly in power and obviously not about to be overthrown by the Communists or anyone else. Gradually, the Soviets began to change their strategy. They advocated the creation of popular fronts, coalitions between leftist and moderate elements, in order to stem the tide of fascism and other right-wing elements. Internationally, the Soviet Union took several steps toward respectability. In 1933, the Soviets agreed to curb the activities of the Comintern in the United States in negotiations that resulted in diplomatic recognition of the Soviet Union by that country. The Russians also entered the League of Nations in 1934. Finally, in May 1935, the Soviets signed a pact with France that provided that each would come to the aid of the other in the event of an unprovoked attack by a European power against either one.

All of these tactics, from the popular fronts to the pact with France, were attempts to join with the establishment, so to speak, against the revisionist powers of Germany, Japan, and Italy. But from the Soviet point of view, none of them worked very well. The French, under a popular front government, did not take effective steps against the possibility of a Nazi invasion. The United States refused to take a very strong stand against the aggressive designs of the Japanese in East Asia, as the Russians had apparently hoped they would. The League of Nations did nothing effective to curb the Italian actions in Ethiopia. And the Russians and the French never did get together to hammer out plans for military coordination that might have made their alliance effective.

The Nazi-Soviet Pact Perhaps it was the inability to organize a viable coalition with the anti-Fascist elements in the world that eventually persuaded Stalin to sign a pact with Hitler. In any case,

[21]William Shirer, *The Rise and Fall of the Third Reich*, Simon and Schuster, New York, 1960, p. 185.

in the middle of the 1930s Stalin proceeded to consolidate even further his own personal power by way of purges in the Soviet Union, which resulted in the deaths of thousands of top officials in the Communist party, Comintern, the diplomatic corps, the army, and the secret police. Having eliminated even potential opposition from these quarters, Stalin was certainly free to pursue almost any foreign policy he wished. It appears that he became convinced by 1938 that he had no chance of preventing an attack on the Soviet Union by Hitler unless he came to some kind of agreement with Hitler. As a result of the Nazi-Soviet pact, Stalin gained not only time but also valuable territory, in Poland, for example, which could serve as a buffer zone in the event of an attack by Germany. Even so, as discussed in Chapter 1, it is not clear that Stalin had these goals in mind when he signed the pact, for at least two reasons. First, if Stalin signed the pact to gain time, it seems logical to conclude that he would have begun an intense armaments program immediately. But as a matter of fact the Russians did not put their industry on a wartime basis until June 1940, after the fall of France.[22] And, as said in Chapter 1, Stalin and his army were apparently completely surprised by Hitler's attack in June of 1941.

The Russians in Eastern Europe   The German attack reached within thirteen miles of Moscow. In the total effort to defeat Hitler, the Soviets cooperated with the Western democracies. One concrete indication of Soviet cooperation was the disbanding of the Comintern in 1943. But even as early as 1943 the Russians and the Allied powers became involved in a dispute over the administration of conquered Italy. This was merely the first of a series of "jurisdictional" conflicts that reached its greatest intensity in Eastern Europe. The Russians were understandably nervous about the possibility of unfriendly governments coming to power in Eastern Europe and Germany. This does not mean, necessarily, that their postwar actions in Poland, East Germany, Bulgaria, Hungary, Rumania, and Czechoslovakia were justified. But any explanation of their actions that does not point out the historic danger of invasion from the west—two dramatic examples of which have occurred in this century—must be somewhat misleading. It is, perhaps, equally understandable that the United States, having defeated one totalitarian power in Europe, was not happy to see another impose its hegemony over a large part of the same continent.

[22] Ulam, *Expansion*, p. 297.

In any case, within two years after the war, the Soviet Union found itself once again in the position of a pariah state in the eyes of most of the major powers of the world, and particularly in the eyes of the most important one, the United States. In March 1947, President Truman announced his policy of containment, aimed at curbing any expansion of Soviet influence. In September that same year, the Russians organized a successor to the Comintern, which became known as the Communist Information Bureau, or Cominform. Stalin spent the last years of his life concentrating on the rebuilding of the Russian economy (at great expense to East Germany and the other East European countries) and consolidating the Russian position in Eastern Europe. One East European leader, Tito, resisted Stalin's control and Stalin retaliated by expelling him from the Cominform in 1949.

By the time Stalin died in 1953, the Russian command of Eastern Europe seemed invincible. And in 1950, the Russians had signed a thirty-year treaty of friendship with the new Communist government of China. To Western eyes, the Communist world appeared to be a unified monolithic structure stretching from Eastern Europe to China. But Stalin's successors were soon to discover that the monolith was fragile.

Within months after Stalin's death there was a general strike in East Germany that reached such a serious stage the Russians had to send troops and tanks into East Berlin to quell it. The situation seemed to convince the Soviets that they ought to try to de-Stalinize their control of Eastern Europe, that the Russian hand had been too heavy. Khrushchev visited Tito in 1955 and apologized for Stalin's anti-Yugoslav activities. Then, at the Twentieth Congress of the Communist Party of the Soviet Union in 1956, Khrushchev delivered a ringing denunciation of Stalin, accusing him of developing a cult of personality, liquidating faithful Communists, ignoring the party, demanding glorification of himself, and, at the time of his death, plotting another purge of his faithful comrades in arms. (one of whom was Khrushchev.)[23] Within a matter of weeks of the speech, there were workers' riots in Poland. In October 1956 the Polish Communist Party announced the intention of electing Wladyslaw Gomulka as first secretary of the party and dumping the present Russian leader. Khrushchev flew in from Moscow, the Red Army made threatening moves, but in the end Gomulka was accepted. In a matter of days, the Russians had to deal with a more serious revolt in Hungary, where nationalists were demanding

[23] Ulam, *Expansion*, p. 575.

freedom from Communist rule, not limited freedom within the confines of the Communist party. The Red Army squashed this rebellion and shortly thereafter Khrushchev proclaimed that "Stalinism, like Stalin himself, is inseparable from Communism. Where it was a question of the revolution, of the defense of the class interests of the Proletariat in the fight against the enemies of our class, Stalin defended the cause of Marxism-Leninism bravely and unyieldingly."[24]

Russia and China Khrushchev's statement did not signal a return to Stalinism. Temporarily, the Russians felt it necessary to crack down on dissident elements in Eastern Europe, but the general trend during Khrushchev's reign was toward liberalization and toward increasingly visible breaks in monolithic communism. After the Hungarian rebellion was put down, things were relatively quiet in Eastern Europe. In contrast, on the Russians' other flank, the Chinese showed increasing signs of dissatisfaction with the Soviet leadership of the Communist bloc. The alliance between the Soviets and the Chinese in the early fifties had, in retrospect, several powerful forces working against it. First, there is the simple geographic fact that the Soviets and the Chinese share the largest common border in the world and they are two of the most powerful states in the world. This combination of factors alone would seem likely to lead to distrust regardless of the personalities or historical events involved in the relationship between Russia and China. Then, too, the Chinese empire and the Russian empire had had unfriendly relations from the sixteenth century on. And the fact that the Chinese have for centuries regarded their country as the Middle Kingdom must have made it difficult for them to accept the leadership of another country under the best of conditions.

More recent historical events also helped bring about the breakup of the Chinese-Russian alliance. Mao Tse-tung and other Chinese Communists had no reason to be grateful to the Russians for the advice given to the Chinese Communist party in the 1920s and the 1930s that led to almost total disaster for the party (see page 123). And—although the Russians did apparently help the Chinese Communists by giving them Japanese weapons while departing from Manchuria after the Second World War—they did not, on the formation of the Russo-Chinese alliance in 1950, give Mao as much financial assistance as Mao had been hoping for.

[24]John Spanier, *World Politics in an Age of Revolution*, Praeger, New York, 1967, pp. 343–344.

By 1956 doctrinal disputes began to arise. Perhaps the most important one concerned the adaptation of Marxism-Leninism to the advent of nuclear weapons. At the twentieth party congress in 1956, in the same speech in which he denounced Stalin, Khrushchev announced that there is no inevitability of war between the Communist and capitalist worlds. From Khrushchev's point of view, this modification of Leninist doctrine was a reasonable compromise in the face of the possibility of nuclear destruction of the world. To the Chinese it smacked of inadmissible timidity.

Shortly after the Russians launched their first satellite in October 1957, Mao Tse-tung made a speech at an international Communist conference in Moscow in which he emphasized dogma. He talked of the "east wind prevailing over the west wind," and insisted that even if the imperialists did plunge the world into nuclear war, only they would be banished from the face of the earth; the socialists would survive. About a year later, the Chinese began what appeared to be an attempt to take over the offshore islands of Quemoy and Matsu. From the Chinese perspective, the Russians refused to back up these efforts with sufficient vigor. Convinced, perhaps, of the recklessness of their allies, in June 1959 the Russians renounced an earlier agreement to help the Chinese develop their own atomic weapons.[25]

Russo-Chinese relations deteriorated rapidly from that point, and by the time of the Cuban Missile Crisis the two countries were verbally tearing each other to pieces. (After the Russians backed away from confrontation with the United States over the missiles in Cuba, the Chinese accused the Russians of "adventurism" and "capitulationism.") At bottom, though, the dispute between the Russians and the Chinese is probably at least as much territorial as doctrinaire. A book published in Peking in 1954, *A Brief History of Modern China*, contains a map showing areas that have been wrongfully seized from the Chinese since 1840. Among these areas are Eastern Turkestan, Kazakhstan, Siberia west of the Amur River, the maritime provinces east of the Amur down to Vladivostok, and the island of Sakhalin, all presently held by the Soviet Union. And in 1964 Mao Tse-tung himself said: "There are too many places occupied by the Soviet Union. . . . The Soviet Union has an area of twenty-two million square kilometers and its population is only 220 million. It is about time to put and end to this allotment. . . ."[26]

[25]Geoffrey Stern, "Soviet Foreign Policy in Theory and Practice," in *The Foreign Policies of the Powers*, ed. F.S. Northedge, Free Press, New York, 1974, p. 134.

[26]Stern, "Soviet Foreign Policy" pp. 139–140.

The Brezhnev Era   Khrushchev, because of a combination of problems involving the Cuban Missile Crisis, the quarrel with the Chinese, and domestic economic failures, was ousted from leadership in October 1964. The new leadership, soon to be dominated by Leonid Brezhnev, was uncertain at first. The Cuban Missile Crisis had been a damaging blow to the prestige of the Russians. Within its own Communist world, the Chinese were challenging the leadership of the Soviet Union. The East European states seemed to be drifting, slowly but certainly, to increasingly closer ties with Western states.

This last discouraging trend came to a head in Czechoslovakia. The Czechs, under Alexander Dubcek, were going through a period of liberalization, including an unusual degree of freedom for the press, that disturbed the Soviets as well as the regimes of several East European countries. In the end, the Soviets felt that the liberalizing trend was so dangerous for the stability of all East European regimes, as well as their own, that it had to be crushed, permanently, with troops. This tactic worked surprisingly well for the Soviets. The problem was solved without much violence. In the aftermath the Russians announced the Brezhnev Doctrine, through which the Russians proclaimed that they will not tolerate deviations of the Czechoslovakian type in the future in Eastern Europe. The Helsinki Declaration, signed by the United States and thirty-five European states, certainly implies a Western acceptance of Soviet hegemony in Eastern Europe.

The Helsinki Agreement was also part of the arrangements and tacit agreements that served as a basis for détente between the United States and the Soviet Union. Generally speaking, the Soviets seem to have entered into this relationship with the United States with some confidence. They still have their fear of the Chinese and of possible American-Chinese cooperation against them. They also seem to have lost ground in the Middle East in the 1970s, particularly in Egypt. But the American experience in Vietnam, followed by Watergate, certainly had a demoralizing impact on the United States. Even if that is temporary the Soviets have acquired sufficient military strength that it seems unlikely that the United States will ever regain a predominant position such as it enjoyed in the 1950s or even the 1960s. Indeed, some analysts claim that "today there is little doubt that the Soviet Union, if it cannot boast a clear or even meaningful superiority, is at least no longer second to the United States in strategic weapons."[27] If the Soviet

[27] Vernon A. Aspaturian, "The Foreign Policy of the Soviet Union, in *World Politics*, ed. James N. Rosenau, Kenneth W. Thompson and Gavin Boyd, Free Press, New York, 1976, p. 89.

Union can support an expensive military force without succumbing to potentially disastrous domestic economic problems, it could conceivably become the most powerful state in the international system.

China

In 1900 the Chinese were ruled by the decrepit Manchu dynasty, and foreign powers were exerting steady pressure on whatever was left of China's sovereignty. Five years earlier the Japanese had annexed Formosa; then France obtained a naval base in south China, Germany took over a port and claimed extensive rights in the Shantung province, and Russia became well established in Manchuria. The British had long been entrenched in Hong Kong and elsewhere. The situation provoked the Boxer Rebellion in 1900 in which a number of foreigners were murdered. The rebellion was unsuccessful, and the foreign nations imposed a humiliating peace treaty on the Manchus. The signing of the treaty was one of the final blows against the imperial dynasty.

The Emergence of Modern China　The dynasty did manage to survive for slightly more than a decade after the Boxer Rebellion. In the middle of that decade Sun Yat-sen began his activities on behalf of Chinese nationalism and republicanism. In 1911 the imperial police came across a list of the membership of Sun's revolutionary organization and this provoked a crisis. Several officers in the imperial army had secretly supported the republican cause and they persuaded the head of the army to declare his support for this cause in the midst of the crisis. When he did so the empress dowager turned to an army general, Yuan Shih-k'ai, for support. Yuan proved himself to be an opportunist. He offered his support to the side that gave him the best offer; the republican revolutionaries offered to make him president of the new regime.

After he became president he deposed the Manchus quickly but shed his republicanism almost at the same time. He assumed dictatorial powers and gave the impression that he was attempting to establish a new imperial dynasty. His attempt failed, and when Yuan died in 1916 China no longer had even a semblance of an effective central government. Control of China fell to several warlords, each protecting his regional power base. In a weakened condition, China was forced to accept the imposition of several important privileges and concessions by the Japanese. According to Lucian Pye,

From 1916 to 1927 China was fragmented and ruled by war-lords who had separate provincial bases. For the Chinese this was a period of unrelieved humiliation because all the warlords seemed to be shortsighted, selfish and unconcerned about the national interest. The experience of the period convinced the intellectuals that China's salvation lay not in competing power centers but rather in the establishment of a monolithic, single-party hierarchy of power.[28]

Sun Yat-sen, meanwhile, was making an energetic effort to put an end to this humiliating state of affairs. He found a sympathetic warlord in Canton who allowed him to set up a revolutionary regime there in competition with the more widely recognized regime in Peking. Sun was never successful in getting the outside world to recognize his regime as the legitimate one in China, and by 1922 he had a violent falling out with the warlord in Canton. He began to look for support wherever he could find it, and Lenin's Comintern happened to be in contact with him at the time. Sun eventually agreed to accept Soviet financial aid and advisors, on the condition that the members of China's new Communist party join his Kuomintang and submit to its discipline. The condition was accepted because Lenin believed—and Stalin came to the same opinion—that Eastern countries generally were not sufficiently advanced for a Communist revolution. Nationalists like San Yat-sen, in the Russian view, had to carry out a bourgeois revolution in order to prepare a ground for Communists.

Sun Yat-sen died in 1925 and Chiang Kai-shek became the leader of the Kuomintang. Stalin insisted that the Communists cooperate with Chiang, and Chiang's reaction to this cooperation was decidedly lacking in gratitude. He all but eliminated the Communist party in China. He was not totally successful, though.

The elimination of the Communists was part of Chiang's greater effort to unify the country behind him. In 1928 he managed to take Peking and proclaim a new Republic of China, with Nanking the capital. The proclamation was far from effective in much of the country, but the warlord in Manchuria decided to accept the authority of the new republic. Acceptance by the warlord plus a stream of Chinese immigrants into Manchuria, led the Japanese to fear that Manchuria would be effectively integrated into the Chinese nation. The Japanese attack in 1931 prevented an assimilation.

[28]Lucian Pye, *China*, Little, Brown, Boston, 1972, p. 127.

Mao's Struggle   In the meantime, control of the Communist party of China was passing into the hands of Mao Tse-tung. He was elected chairman of a central Soviet government, putting him in nominal control of all Communist base areas in 1931. The party headquarters were in Shanghai. The party members there were supported by the Comintern and were Moscow oriented. These members were finally forced out of Shanghai by Kuomintang police and joined Mao in the countryside. There the Moscow-oriented party members apparently staged a struggle with Mao for control of the party, which Mao won in stages. While the struggle was taking place, the Communists suffered a series of military disasters at the hands of the Kuomintang. By 1934, Chiang had the "Soviet" surrounded, and Mao escaped only by means of the famous long march, which ended in Shensi, a new Communist base.

Chiang could never make up his mind entirely about his first priority. Was it to eliminate the Communist opposition in his country or to drive out the Japanese invaders? He was personally inclined to concentrate on the Communists, believing that Japan's other enemies would eventually defeat Japan. But in 1936, for example, he was kidnapped by his own generals and was literally forced to accept an agreement whereby the Kuomintang and the Communists would unite in an anti-Japanese effort. The Japanese began a war against the Chinese officially in 1937, and for a while the Communists and the Kuomintang did cooperate at least officially. But the Kuomintang suffered a long series of defeats that pushed them farther into the Chinese countryside, while the Communists effectively combined military and political operations against the Japanese and the Kuomintang. "Thus the Communists emerged from the war in 1945 in a far stronger position than when they had entered it, whereas the Nationalists were, in reality, so weakened by the strains of the war as to be far weaker relative to the CPC than they had been in 1937."[29]

After the Second World War was over, the Americans and the Russians had troops in China, and ostensibly, both tried to bring about some kind of settlement between the Communists and the Kuomintang. By 1946, the Russians and the Americans had pulled their troops out of China, and the full-scale civil war was on. The first crucial battles were in Manchuria and the Communists won them. Mao announced in 1947 that the position of the Communists was sufficiently strong to allow a transition from guerrilla warfare to conventional attacks against the Kuomintang. The Communists

[29]Harold C. Hinton, *Communist China in World Politics*, Houghton Mifflin, Boston, 1966, p. 19.

Mao Tse-Tung. Marc Riboud/Magnum.

took Peking in January 1949, and on October 1, 1949, the Chinese People's Republic was proclaimed.

The Early Years of the People's Republic   Within little more than a year after the Republic was born, Mao signed a thirty-year Treaty of Friendship, Alliance and Mutual Assistance with the Soviet Union and found himself at war with the United States. Mao had gone to Moscow in December 1949. The alliance with the Soviets was directed against Japan and at states allied with it. The latter target was clearly the United States, whom both the Soviets and the Chinese expected might launch an attack. In addition, the Russians agreed to give China a loan of $300 million over a period of five years, an amount that Mao apparently considered quite insufficient.

> There can be no doubt but that he was disappointed, and it seems probable that this first and only meeting between Mao and Stalin was not of the happiest. . . . All we know is that it took them two months to complete an agreement that ought to have been concluded in a few days.[30]

Not very long after suffering this disappointment, Mao found his country at war with the United States. Several possible explanations for the North Korean attack on South Korea have been discussed in Chapter 1. One more deserves mention here. The prolonged negotiations between Stalin and Mao for an alliance must have served as a warning to Stalin, if he needed one, that Mao was not going to be an easy person to keep in line. If Stalin could fortify a Russian position on China's border by unifying Korea, he might be able to deal with Mao.[31] Stalin must also have been influenced by the fact that, on January 12, 1950, Secretary of State Dean Acheson clearly affirmed that Korea was outside the defense perimeter of the United States; he was, finally, justifiably confident that the North Koreans would be able to defeat the South Koreans easily if the South Koreans did not get outside help.

These explanations are based on the assumption that Mao had very little to do with the launching of the North Korean attack, and that seems to be the case. Mao may have acquiesced in the decision to have the Koreans attack, but there is some evidence that he was not even informed of it until a day or two before it occurred.[32] Even if Mao had agreed to the attack, it must have been somewhat reluctantly, because he had many other problems to deal with. There were still isolated pockets of resistance to the revolution that he had to wipe out, and Chinese control had not yet been established in Tibet. Finally, there is clear evidence to indicate that the Chinese planned to invade Taiwan in the summer of 1950.[33]

[30]David Floyd, *Mao Against Khrushchev*, Praeger, New York, 1963, p. 13.
[31]Floyd, *Mao*, p. 14.
[32]Stuart Schram, *Mao Tse-Tung*, Penguin, Baltimore, 1968, p. 262.
[33]Allen S. Whiting, *China Crosses the Yalu*, Macmillan, New York, 1960, pp. 21-22.

Mao had to put off the invasion, especially since the United States, in June of 1950, neutralized the Taiwan Strait with the interposition of the Seventh Fleet. And when the United States army approached the Chinese border of vulnerable Manchuria, the Chinese must have felt that they had no choice but to respond. The nation was not entirely united behind the war effort or the revolution, and Mao took vigorous steps to unify the country and to rid it of domestic opposition even while trying to carry on in Korea. Thought-reform programs were instituted for intellectuals, and indoctrination programs were developed for those who had been involved with the Nationalist regime. By early 1951 "regulations regarding the punishment of counterrevolutionaries" were promulgated that provided the death sentence for a very broadly defined range of antiregime activities. Just how vigorously these "regulations" were enforced remains one of the most controversial aspects of the Chinese revolution. Estimates of the number of executions range from Chou En-lai's official statement of some 135,000 in early 1951 to as many as 10 to 15 million. One seemingly honest and impartial source estimates that there were 1 to 3 million executions all told.[34]

By 1952–1953 the war excitement had died down somewhat, and the Chinese turned their energies to domestic reform. A five-year plan, based on the Soviet model, was announced in 1952 and launched in 1953. One of the indicators of the spirit of getting down to work was the "five too manys" campaign against "too many meetings, too many organizations, too many concurrent posts for cadres, too many documents, and too many forms to be filled out."[35]

Steps were taken toward the collectivization of agriculture, and producers' cooperatives were established in the face of some opposition by the peasants. The opposition continued to grow, and by 1955 it was clear that production had declined since the beginning of the collectivization effort. It began to look as though the effort would be abandoned or at least carried out more slowly. But Mao intervened personally—as he was to do more than once in the coming years—to ensure that the revolution would stay on course. He called for a dramatic increase in the speed of the collectivization effort, and during the next year nearly three-fourths of the countryside was brought into advanced cooperatives.

At about the same time, China began to assert itself more confidently in foreign relations. China was allowed to participate as a major power in the Geneva Conference that drew up the peace

[34]Schram, *Mao Tse-tung*, p. 262.
[35]Pye, *China*, p. 190.

settlement necessitated by the departure of France from Vietnam in 1954. Also in 1954, the Chinese sent troops into the capital of Tibet, beginning the process of integrating the area into the Chinese nation that culminated in full Chinese control by 1959. They began putting pressure on the Nationalist regime in Taiwan; Chou En-lai made public statements about China's intention to liberate Taiwan, and Chinese troops began shelling the offshore island of Quemoy.

China began, too, the rise to a leadership role in the Third World. There was a conference of Third World nations at Bandung, Indonesia, in 1955, apparently inspired by the Chinese. Chou En-lai made an impressive showing among Third World leaders who gathered there. Until that time, India had been widely acknowledged, under Nehru, to be the leading state in the Third World. The Bandung Conference changed that. The Soviet Union, it should be noted, did not attend the meeting. China not only assumed a leadership role in the Third World at the Bandung Conference; it also began to demonstrate independence from the leader of the Communist world.

Mao felt even more independent and confident after the death of Stalin, which made him the elder statesman among the Communists. He began to advise the Soviets to be tolerant of liberalizing tendencies in Eastern Europe, especially after Khrushchev made his anti-Stalin speech. Mao also felt confident enough to allow more liberalization in his own country. Previously, intellectuals had been muzzled. Now, in 1956, Mao said, "Let one hundred schools of thought contend; let one hundred flowers bloom." The flowers were reluctant at first, but by the end of the year, intellectuals all over the country were expressing not only constructive criticism of the revolution but also fundamental criticism of communism itself.

Mao could not tolerate such criticism, and he took the offensive with a vengeance. He started an antirightist campaign, followed by a rectification campaign, aimed at the elimination of all improper thought. In 1958 Mao launched the Great Leap Forward, an attempt to use the fervor and energy of the masses to overcome the "objective" barriers standing between China and a truly Communist society. The countryside was organized into communes, and workers were called on to work consecutive shifts with no rest. Little steel mills were set up in backyards. With such tactics it was hoped that China would out-produce Great Britain within fifteen years.

At the same time, Mao became more aggressive on the foreign front. It was during this period (1957) that he made his east-wind-prevailing-over-the-west-wind speech. He dropped a previous emphasis on peaceful coexistence, and was incensed when Khrushchev went to meet with President Eisenhower at Camp David in an effort to lessen Soviet-American tensions. Also in 1958, China resumed its pressure on Taiwan, especially on the island of Quemoy, which, in effect, was blockaded with artillery fire and air action.

The Great Leap Forward and the aggressive foreign policies were ultimately failures. By the end of the first year of the Great Leap the Chinese had to pull back from some of the more revolutionary steps. In fact, the disasters were so great, it appears that, temporarily at least, Mao may have lost control of the Communist party. He was replaced as chairman of the government by Liu Shao-ch'i. The Great Leap created divisions in the party that were to surface again in the Great Proletarian Cultural Revolution.

Also, the Russians were not convinced by Mao's east-wind-over-the-west-wind philosophy. They refused, as seen earlier, to be as aggressive as Mao thought appropriate, especially with respect to Mao's campaign to liberate Taiwan, probably an important step toward the Soviet-Chinese schism.

If the Chinese could not regain Taiwan, they seemed determined to "recover" Tibet. In 1959, fighting broke out in the streets of the capital city of Tibet, and the Chinese moved to crush the rebellion. The Dalai Lama fled to India, where he was given something of a hero's welcome. Border skirmishes between China and India followed that were to drag on for years and finally result in a war in 1962. Through the whole affair the position of the Soviets ranged from neutrality to some sympathy with India's position. Sino-Soviet relations were thus subjected to another serious strain.

The Great Proletarian Cultural Revolution   While Mao carried out an almost personal propaganda campaign against Khrushchev in the early 1960s, other Chinese leaders tried to restore some element of rationality to the Chinese economy, suffering as it was from the ideological excesses of the Great Leap Forward. From Mao's point of view the leaders departed too far from the ideologically acceptable revolutionary path toward economic rationality. Party bureaucrats and technicians, more concerned with pragmatic goals than with revolutionary ideals, came to the point of taking over the party completely. In later years, Mao was to complain that the party leaders during this time had shunted him aside, treating him as a mere figurehead. Then, in the area of foreign policy, events seemed to be conspiring against Mao's preference to treat the Soviets rather than the United States as the primary enemy of China.

The United States was becoming deeply committed in South Vietnam, thus bringing American forces perilously close to the Chinese border. In addition, a countercoup in Indonesia, and the downfall of Nkrumah in Ghana, seemed to leave China in an increasingly isolated position.[36] Some Chinese leaders decided that now was not the time to add the Soviet Union to the list of China's enemies and began making a series of moves to improve relations between the two Communist powers. This meant that Mao was violently opposed to the drift of his revolution both at home and abroad. Mao had enough strength in the party to effectively call for a halt to this drift, and the result was the Great Proletarian Cultural Revolution.

The major purpose of the Cultural Revolution seemed to be to rid the Communist party, and the Chinese society for that matter, of the undesirable influence of leaders and bureaucrats insufficiently imbued with revolutionary zeal. "Better red than expert" was one slogan that symbolized the aim. Mao was never convinced that the Great Leap Forward had failed because it was badly planned or was just a bad idea to begin with. In his opinion it had failed because those charged with carrying out the plan had lacked revolutionary ardor. Even worse, the objectionable elements of the party had become stronger since the demise of the Great Leap.

The instrument used to weed out the undesirables was originally an organization that became known as the Red Guards. These were college and high school students who for two years terrorized large sectors of the Chinese society that Mao and other leaders of the Cultural Revolution had decided should be purged from the party, or, for example, the universities. By the end of this two-year period even Mao apparently decided that the students had gotten out of hand, and he, in effect, called on the People's Liberation Army to bring the Cultural Revolution to a close. In the process, the army replaced the party as the principal basis of political power in Chinese society. "The one unquestionable consequence of the Cultural Revolution was the elevation to power of the military. The People's Liberation Army was put in charge of managing China."[37]

China, Russia, and the United States   In the meantime, Mao's idea that the Soviet Union was a greater danger to China than the United States became increasingly credible. The United States was

[36]Coral Bell, "China: The Communists and the World," in *The Foreign Policies of the Powers,* ed. F. S. Northedge, Free Press, New York, 1974, p. 148.
[37]Pye, *China,* p. 294.

failing in Vietnam, and the 1968 Tet offensive helped to expose this failure to the world. The Soviet Union, on the other hand, had invaded Czechoslovakia and followed that with the promulgation of the Brezhnev Doctrine, which asserted a Soviet right to intervene in Communist countries whose domestic politics took an undesirable turn. By 1969, Russian and Chinese soldiers were shooting at each other across the border, and by the spring of 1971, the Soviets had deployed more troops against China than they had deployed in Eastern Europe against the North Atlantic Treaty Organization (NATO) forces in Europe. It is certainly no coincidence that 1971 was also the year of ping-pong diplomacy between the Chinese and the United States, culminating in the trip by President Nixon to China in 1972.

The deaths of Mao Tse-tung and Chou En-lai in the middle 1970s created an obvious crisis of leadership in the Communist party of China. That crisis brought to the surface some of the same conflicts that had convulsed China in the 1960s. In the months immediately following the death of Mao, Hua Kuo-feng seemed to have emerged as China's new leader. Whether he can maintain that position will depend at least in part on the resolution of two different but related issues. One involves the relationship between the Soviet Union and China. Mao's death brought a series of small conciliatory moves on the part of the Soviets, and the Chinese may reciprocate. On the other hand, the Chinese may also continue to attempt to develop closer ties with the United States. Which way they go might be influenced by a related contest between reds, or radicals, who carry on Mao's concern that the revolution might get lost in the pursuit of technological economic goals, and experts, who feel that technological, economic progress deserves top priority. If the latter group wins out—and if the United States is willing and able to help that group obtain its economic goals—then the prospects for increased normalization of relations between China and the United States seem good. If that does not happen, China may turn to the Soviet Union for aid or the radicals may re-emerge as a powerful force in Chinese politics.

France
A domestic political scandal was much on the minds of the French as they entered the twentieth century. In 1894 Captain Alfred Dreyfus had been found guilty of selling military secrets to Germany. Dreyfus was sentenced to life imprisonment on Devil's Island, a sweltering penal colony off the coast of South America.

The fact that Dreyfus was a Jew helped set off a wave of anti-Semitism in France and added an extra measure of passion to what was destined to be a fervent controversy in any case.

The Dreyfus affair would not die, even after Dreyfus had spent several years languishing on Devil's Island, because there was good evidence that kept coming to the surface that Dreyfus was not guilty. In addition, it became obvious that overzealous army officers had consciously forged documents and illegally presented them to the judges in the case in order to get a conviction. When this became known, a civilian court annulled Dreyfus's conviction and ordered that he be given a new military trial. The new trial, despite overwhelming evidence against the original verdict, resulted in the reaffirmation of the verdict.

By this time, the political right in France had become convinced that the fate of one individual was inconsequential compared to the necessity of upholding the honor of the army, the church, and the nation, all of which, they believed, would be disgraced if Dreyfus were now declared innocent. The left, on the other hand, felt that the honor of the nation was stained terribly by the conviction and continued imprisonment of an innocent man. The left won this contest, but it was not until twelve-and-one-half years after Dreyfus's original conviction that he was officially declared innocent. The army and the church were indeed disgraced, and the left took advantage of this. Several privileges of the church were abolished and new leaders less committed to anti-Republicanism were promoted in the army. The Dreyfus affair served to exacerbate the already serious split between the right and the left in France, and weakened the country in ways that the succeeding decades were to make obvious.

France Versus Germany   While the French were tearing themselves apart domestically, they kept a wary eye on Germany. France, of course, had suffered a stunning defeat in the Franco-Prussian War some thirty years earlier. Out of that war had come a united German state that became increasingly threatening to France. French leaders took several steps to deal with this threat. The first was taken in 1894, when France entered into a military alliance with Russia. By 1899, the alliance was strengthened by an agreement stipulating that France would come to the aid of Russia if Russia were attacked by either Germany or Austria-Hungary, while the Russians would come to the aid of France if France were attacked by Germany. In a few years, France also solidified ties with Great Britain, forming an entente in 1904, which had by 1907—with the inclusion of Russia—become the Triple Entente. The entente was faced with the Triple Alliance of Germany, Austria-Hungary, and Italy. But France had arranged an ace in the hole within this structure of alliances. In 1902 France and Italy came to a secret agreement in which each promised to remain neutral if the other were attacked. This was one of the reasons that Italy did not join its allies when the world war began in 1914.

In the first years of the new century, France enlarged its empire. Although there were other reasons, one motive clearly involved the idea that a large empire—by supplying soldiers, raw materials, and markets—would strengthen the country. Between 1875 and 1914 France added Tunisia, Morocco, Annam and Tonkin in Indochina, and large areas in western and equatorial Africa to its colonial holdings.

The first decade of the twentieth century was also marked by two crises over Morocco, both involving France. The two crises raised tension among the major powers of Europe and had an important impact on the relationship between France and Britain.

The first crisis occurred in 1905. In order to accomplish the entente with Great Britian, the French had given the British a free hand in the areas of Sudan and Egypt; in return, Great Britain promised support for French efforts to take over Morocco. Germany objected to this arrangement, and Kaiser Wilhelm traveled to Tangier, Morocco, in order to deliver a belligerent statement to the effect that Germany would insist that Morocco remain an independent state.

In 1911, the other crisis occurred when the Sultan of Morocco asked the French to send troops to the capital to protect him from rebels. When the French agreed, the Germans sent the gunboat *Panther* into the Moroccan port of Agadir to protect German interests. The result was a second war-scare over Morocco.

The French used both crises to help solidify their ties to the British. After the 1905 war-scare, the French persuaded the British to allow consultation between the military staffs of the two countries.[38] And

Seven weeks after the beginning of the Agadir crisis the Imperial Defense Committee held a secret meeting in London . . . in which it was agreed that in case of a German attack on France which brought Britain into the war, the British would immediately rush over an army of six infantry divisions and

[38]J. P. T. Bury, *France 1814–1940,* Barnes, New York, 1962, p. 216.

one cavalry division to fight on the left flank of the French armies. Staff talks between the two countries had already worked out the details.[39]

The agreement was to prove important in the first great battle of the First World War. The Germans were intent on defeating the French quickly and their first thrust brought them within sight of Paris. But, with critical help from the British, the French beat the Germans back at the Battle of the Marne, and the war settled down to a contest of attrition. France, with the help of the British—and at the end of the war, the Americans—won the contest.

But in an important sense, France was the real loser of the war. France lost 10 percent of its active male population, the highest of any of the major participants. France had mobilized 8,410,000 men to fight the Germans; of that number, 1,357,800 were killed, 4,260,000 were wounded, and 536,000 were taken prisoner or were missing. All these categories together accounted for 73 percent of the total number mobilized.[40] Furthermore, the largest, most dreadful battles had been fought on French soil. The added deliberate German destruction meant that fully a third of France was devastated. Almost 300,000 homes had been destroyed and some 3,000,000 acres of land made unfit for cultivation.[41] Finally, the French treasury had been emptied and its war debts were staggering. France suffered more than Germany in many ways, and its leaders were absolutely desperate to assure their people they would never have to battle the Germans again.

Recovery from the First World War   The rest of the world—Great Britain and the United States in particular—was surprisingly unsympathetic to French concerns. As seen earlier, the Americans and the British would not go along with French demands to give the League of Nations an army of its own to enforce collective security. This meant, as far as the French were concerned, that they would have to depend on their own army for security, and that now was the time to make sure that Germany would not rise again. So, France wanted Germany to be pushed back across the Rhine and the territory taken away from Germany formed into an autonomous republic, though clearly dominated by France. Neither Great Britain nor the United States would go along with the demand.

[39] William L. Shirer, *The Collapse of the Third Republic*, Simon and Schuster, New York, 1969, p. 114.
[40] Shirer, *Collapse*, p. 133.
[41] J. P. T. Bury, *France, 1814–1940*, p. 252.

The British suggested compromise. If the French would give up their demand to create a new republic out of part of the old Germany, the British and the Americans would, through what became known as the Anglo-American Guarantee Treaty, promise to defend France if Germany should ever attack again. The French were reluctant to accept this promise, arguing that "if we do not hold the Rhine permanently there is no neutralization, no disarmament, no written clause of any nature, which can prevent Germany from breaking out across it and gaining the upper hand."[42] But the British and the Americans would not be convinced, and the French decided in the end that they would trust their allies.

That trust was misplaced. The British parliament approved the Treaty of Guarantee, but in 1920 the United States Senate rejected it. British approval was contingent on that of the Americans, and the British refused to give France a unilateral guarantee. The French were furious, as they had every right to be. "It is unprofitable to argue about the might-have-beens of history, but it does seem that the collapse of the Anglo-American Guarantee Treaty marks the point at which the Western World took the path that led eventually to World War II."[43]

This was only the beginning of a succession of "raw deals" that the French suffered in the 1920s. In addition to the partition of Germany, the French wanted Germany to pay extensive reparations. More extensive, it turned out, than the British and the Americans were willing to agree to. The French had to give in again; the bill ultimately presented to Germany was not as great as the French wanted. And by the end of 1920 Germany began to default on payment of the reduced bill. Much to its chagrin, France could not even get London and Washington to go along with putting pressure on Germany to pay the reduced reparations. The Americans had, somewhat self-righteously, refused to take any reparations from Germany. The French suspected, and they may have been right, that the British had concluded that rebuilding the German market for their exports would be of greater benefit to them than soaking the Germans for large reparations. After about a year of bickering with erstwhile allies, France decided to move on its own. Having waited until the reparations commission had officially certified that Germany had defaulted on payments, the French president sent troops to occupy the Ruhr Valley.

The invasion did not work out well for France. Britain and the United States condemned French aggression. The Germans

[42]Shirer, *Collapse*, p. 145.
[43]Lennox Mills and Charles H. McLaughlin, *World Politics in Transition*, Holt, New York, 1956, p. 461.

adopted a policy of passive resistance in the Ruhr so that the French had problems getting the mines and the mills there to produce. The invasion also helped bring on a disastrous round of inflation in Germany, the effects of which were felt in France when the value of the franc dropped alarmingly.[44] The invasion did evoke sympathy for Germany, and the United States was moved to draw up the Dawes Plan, a series of loans that allowed Germany to make some payments on reparations that were reduced by the terms of the agreement. France enjoyed some residual benefits of the Dawes Plan, but the "bottom line" for France, as a result of all the financial wheelings and dealings between the Allies and Germany in the 1920s, was this: France received from Germany only enough to pay 20 percent of the cost of rebuilding its devastated war-torn regions. Germany, on the other hand, actually came out ahead. Germany borrowed more from American bankers than it paid in reparations, and those loans were never repaid.[45]

As if that were not enough to bear, the French suffered because the Americans refused to cancel French war debts. The Americans were so magnanimous to the defeated enemy that they did not charge reparations and helped pay those that were charged. But they would not cancel the French (or the British) war debts and even insisted on charging substantial interest. When the depression came, France offered to cancel German reparation debts if the United States would forgo the collection of war debts. The Americans refused.

Still, it would be a mistake to conclude that the 1920s were disastrous years for France. France found several states that shared its concern about developments in Germany, and between 1920 and 1927 France formed alliances with Belgium, Poland, Czechoslovakia, Yugoslavia, and Rumania. In 1925, of course, it also signed the Locarno Pact, thus finally succeeding in efforts to get a British guarantee against attack by Germany. France played a leading role in the establishment of the Kellogg-Briand Pact, which "outlawed" war and which was eventually signed by sixty-five nations. The French empire was augmented by the addition of territory taken from Germany and Turkey. In the latter half of the decade, the French economy showed signs of improvement and, all in all, it seemed as if France might recover quite well from the First World War.

The Depression This happy trend might have continued had it not been for the depression. Economic catastrophe seemed again to

[44]Ernest John Knapton, *France,* Scribner's, New York, 1971, p. 487.
[45]Shirer, *Collapse,* p. 150.

inflame relations between the left and the right in France. The right took to the streets, and the left won electoral victories.

In 1936 the Radical Socialists, the Socialists, and the Communists formed a popular front, which scored a substantial victory in the elections of that year. On the surface, the popular front accomplished several needed and long-delayed reforms. Collective bargaining was legalized, the forty-hour week was instituted, the Bank of France was brought under government control, and some of the militant right-wing groups such as the Croix de Feu were dissolved. But beneath the surface France was falling apart at the seams. The government continued to be plagued with instability. Prime ministers lasted only as long as they could hold together shaky coalitions of squabbling political parties. Instability rendered the government unable to back up the reforms that existed on paper. Still, the very existence of the popular front put fear into the hearts of many conservatives. The fear reached such heights that it led some of the French to sympathize more with foreign leaders than their own government. "Better Hitler than Blum" (Blum was a leader of the popular front) was a slogan that succinctly expressed the opinion of a significant segment of French society, which saw in Hitler someone who would protect their property from the Communist elements of the popular front.

"Better Hitler than Stalin" was another slogan that symbolized another serious problem for the popular front. Efforts to strengthen the French bond with the Soviet Union met with bitter opposition from those who feared the Communists in France would be strengthened. France did ratify a pact with the Russians, but the French never cooperated with them in ways that would have made the alliance militarily significant. Class divisions, focusing on the Communists, tormented France up to the moment of the German onslaught; French Communists, adhering to Moscow's position of the moment, opposed the war effort and had some success undermining the morale of the troops.

Prewar Military Strategy   French weakness was compounded, as the Second World War approached, by stagnation in the military. This was partly the responsibility of the popular front governments. Daladier, the prime minister in the last months of peace, failed to create a special armaments ministry and got around to appointing a ministerial council to coordinate war production only after the war had been under way for six months. Disorganization in the military bureaucracy and outmoded thinking among the leading generals were equally as severe. After the war there were bitter complaints that the government of the Third Republic had not provided sufficient funds for the military. But the fact was that in the crucial years of 1933 to 1935 the military bureaucracy was so inefficient that it could not even spend the amounts allotted to it. And the money that was spent was devoted to disastrously ineffective strategy. Strategic thinking in the French army was dominated by generals who had become heroes in the First World War. What they had learned in the First World War was that strategy based on all-out offensive had led to catastrophe. On the other hand, a defensive strategy, such as that used at the Battle of Verdun, had been successful. The French generals were convinced that none of the technological developments since Verdun had destroyed the legitimacy of that lesson. French strategy against a possible German attack was to be based on an impenetrable defense, the Maginot Line. Criticisms of this strategy, especially in the military, were very rare. One cogent voice did go against the tide of French military thought. It belonged to a rather obscure lieutenant colonel named Charles de Gaulle.

"To the everlasting credit of . . . the leading generals of the French army it must be said that one of the reasons for insisting on the defensive . . . was their determination to spare French blood in any future war."[46] Firmly in place in the back of the minds of the defense-oriented generals was the realization that France was the victim of a dramatically unfavorable demographic trend. In 1801 France had been the second most populous country in Europe. By 1939 it had fallen to fifth. In 1870 France could rely on some 4,400,000 men of military age, against Germany's 4,700,000. In the First World War, France was outnumbered by Germany in terms of men of military age by 4,500,000 to 7,700,000. And partly because of terrible losses in the First World War, France entered the Second World War with an available pool of military recruits roughly half as large as that available to the Germans.

Reliance on the Maginot Line led France to defeat. The French could have easily prevented Hitler from reoccupying the Rhineland in 1936, but they were, at that time, already in an overly defensive frame of mind. They could have discouraged Hitler from ravaging their eastern allies, such as Czechoslovakia, but what good would their Maginot line do them if they left it behind to launch an attack against Germany in retaliation for German aggression in Eastern Europe? In the end, the Germans utilized modern, mechanized warfare to go around and over the Maginot line. They did not deploy a vastly superior number of troops on the ground, but in the air the Luftwaffe enjoyed a 3–1 superiority over the combined forces of

[46]Shirer, *Collapse,* p. 182.

the British and the French. The German planes were also of superior quality. The Battle of France began on May 10, 1940. France lost by June 14, 1940.

Survival France disintegrated, roughly speaking, into three separate parts after the German victory. First there was the Vichy regime under Marshal Pétain, which collaborated with the Germans and was in return allowed to operate in a tenuously autonomous fashion in the south of France. Then there was an underground resistance movement, which did its best, through sabotage and other kinds of subversive activities to weaken the German hold on France. (Among the most effective groups in the resistance movement was the Communist party, and the Communists emerged from the war as the single largest party in France.) Finally, there was a combination movement and government-in-exile, usually referred to as the Free French, which formed a liberation army and after some wrangling came under the leadership of Charles de Gaulle.

After the war, de Gaulle emerged as the head of a provisional republic, but by October 1946, de Gaulle resigned from the presidency and French voters (narrowly) approved a new constitution. One of the serious problems of the Third Republic had been a lack of strength in the executive. Prime ministers lasted, on the average, less than a year in the Third Republic. One might suppose that the new constitution would have provided a remedy for this problem, but it did not. French governments lasted roughly half as long under the Fourth Republic as they had under the Third.

With this uncertain kind of leadership, the Fourth Republic had to work out two crucial problems in the area of international relations. First, arrangements had to be made to protect France from Germany. Second, France would have to come to terms with colonial holdings, which under the provisions of the new constitution, were included in the French Union.

The first problem was handled quite successfully. In 1950 two plans were proposed which, while dealing with what was perceived as an increasing threat from the Russians, might also have the benefit of protecting France from Germany. The first plan called for the creation of an all-European army under a European minister of defense. The European nations could combine their strength in opposition to the Russians and also prevent the Germans from building an independent armed force. German generals would command troops and German troops would be armed, but they would be so intermingled with generals and troops from other countries that it would, presumably, be impossible for them to

General Charles de Gaulle. Marcel/Viollet.

organize for any specifically German purposes. The second plan called for the economic integration of the coal and steel industries of France and Germany (and of Italy, Belgium, the Netherlands, and Luxembourg, as well). The plan would, it was hoped, aid the economic recovery of all the countries involved, increase the military strength of Europe by improving the prospects for two strategically vital industries, and prevent the Germans from independently controlling the same industries. The French rejected the first plan, embodied in what became known as the European Defense Community (EDC). The second plan served as the basis of the European Coal and Steel Community (ECSC), which was a resounding success and helped convince the French and other Europeans to launch a broader project, the European Economic Community (EEC).

The second problem, France's relations with its colonial holdings, was not handled so well. Perhaps the reason was partly that the French refused to see it as a colonial problem. As far as they were concerned, the overseas territories were part of the French Union and their relationship to France of indubitable benefit to the people who lived there. This kind of attitude has a long history in France.

> From the end of the eighteenth century onward, foreign policy attitudes have been increasingly colored by a . . . tradition which is not, strictly speaking, an aim, but an innate conviction. . . . It is the belief that France is not only a natural political leader in Europe but also a natural cultural leader, that French ideas and civilization should be exported to less favoured nations, at first in Europe, and with the coming of the colonial era, to overseas possessions.[47]

The extent to which France as a nation indulges in the assumption of cultural superiority can be easily exaggerated, and usually is by those who have a special interest in French foreign policy. (It is probably safe to say that every powerful state and empire in recorded history has been impressed by its own cultural superiority.) Still, even if France is not peculiar in this regard, it does seem that the French people have a full measure of national pride. This may account for some of the tenacity with which France held on to her overseas territories after the Second World War. After such an exhausting and humiliating experience as the French people suffered in that war, it would have seemed natural for them to turn inward and not show any enthusiasm for foreign adventures. If anything, the war seemed to have the opposite effect, making the French government, at least, determined not to suffer the added indignity of losing parts of the empire.

The Emergence of de Gaulle   France made a desperate effort to hold on to Indochina, losing 71,000 soldiers over an eight-year period in the process. This sad experience for France ended with a disastrous

---

[47]Dorothy Pickles, "France: Tradition and Change," in *The Foreign Policies of the Powers,* ed. F. S. Northedge, Free Press, New York, 1974, pp. 204–205.

defeat at Dien Bien Phu in 1954, but that year also marked the beginning of the tragic struggle between France and Algeria. The struggle destroyed the Fourth Republic and indirectly led to French embarrassment in the Suez War in 1956; the French hoped to destroy Nasser because they suspected (apparently with good reason) that he was aiding the rebels in Algeria. By 1958 France was on the verge of civil war over the future of Algeria. There was, by wide agreement, only one man who could restore order in France, and that was Charles de Gaulle. (This was partly because, as became apparent in the following years, no one knew for sure what he would do. It is clear, for example, that many Europeans living in Algeria believed that de Gaulle would not allow the Algerian rebellion to succeed.) De Gaulle had long been critical of the constitution of the Fourth Republic, and he became premier with the understanding that he would change the constitution. He did, and the result was the constitution of the Fifth Republic, which gives the chief executive more power than given under previous constitutions. One of the purposes to which de Gaulle put this power was the solution of the Algerian problem. It took him four years, but in 1962 the conflict was resolved, basically by giving Algeria its independence.

De Gaulle was to dominate French foreign policy for eleven years, and during that time he successfully made himself unpopular in several quarters. Franco-American relations were particularly strained. De Gaulle insisted on developing France's nuclear capability, in large part because he distrusted the reliability of the American nuclear umbrella. France exploded its first nuclear device in 1960 and continued nuclear testing in the following years, rejecting both the Test Ban Treaty and the Non-Proliferation Treaty advocated and signed by the United States. De Gaulle reduced dramatically France's commitment to NATO. The headquarters of the alliance had been built in France, there were American bases in various parts of the country, and the Americans also had nuclear weapons there. De Gaulle gradually limited French participation in the North Atlantic Treaty Organization (NATO), and then in 1966, he pulled out of NATO almost completely. He insisted that the NATO headquarters, as well as all American military bases and nuclear weapons, be removed from France. In the end, France remained part of NATO in a technical way only, although she would presumably fulfill her obligation to join the other members in any action against aggression.[48]

[48]Dorothy Pickles, "France," p. 219.

De Gaulle increased his unpopularity with the American government by becoming progressively more critical of that country's war in Vietnam. His vetoes of Britain's entry into the Common Market (1963 and 1967) were also aimed indirectly at the United States. He reportedly felt that if Britain were allowed to enter the EEC, it would serve as a Trojan horse for the United States, giving the Americans much greater influence in Europe than de Gaulle thought appropriate.

De Gaulle seemed to be, at least, the major obstacle in the way of the developing supranationalism in the European Economic Community. He firmly believed that states were the only realistic basis for political action and disapproved of any pretension to supranationality on the part of the Eurocrats on the Commission of the EEC. At one point he threatened to pull France out of the community altogether. He relented only after receiving guarantees of "states' rights" within the community.

De Gaulle did not make a point of antagonizing everybody. He did, for example, strive to improve relations between France and West Germany, negotiating a treaty with that country in 1963 in which the two historical enemies pledged to cooperate in foreign affairs, defense, and cultural matters. He also tried to strengthen French ties with Eastern Europe and the Soviet Union. This last effort was dealt a serious blow when the Soviets invaded Czechoslovakia in 1968.

The common thread running through all of de Gaulle's policies involved the grandeur of France. De Gaulle believed that France deserved to be a major power and that one way to maintain that status was to insist on an independent foreign policy. It was for this reason that de Gaulle insisted, for example, that France would not be part of the "American bloc," nor would it fade into a supranational EEC. Whether de Gaulle's ambitions for France were realistic can certainly be debated, but most of the French apparently approved of his policies.

Après de Gaulle Since de Gaulle's death in 1970 France has been visibly less active on the international stage. "France's nonparticipation in the East-West or American-Soviet negotiations, combined with the increasing pressure of internal problems, both political and economic, tended to make foreign policy of less interest to the general public."[49] The French government, as well as

[49]Dorothy Pickles, "The Decline of Gaullist Foreign Policy," *International Affairs,* 51, No. 2 (1975), p. 223.

the general public, seems preoccupied with domestic issues. The issues are more compelling because of the possibility that the Communist party may become strong enough to gain entrance into the government. The probability of this would undoubtedly be enhanced if Communists successfully achieve entry into the government of Italy. How such an event would affect France's relations with its NATO allies, or with its partners in the European Economic Community, is one of the more intriguing questions facing France in the 1980s. Perhaps even more intriguing is the question of whether or not France will be able to maintain any of the grandeur that de Gaulle strived so mightily to obtain for it.

Great Britain

The British dominated the international politics of the nineteenth century, and it is probably safe to say that most of the English who thought about such things rather assumed the twentieth century would be no different. Britain's power and security rested first on its navy, dominating the seas the world over and making any cross-channel attack on the home island very unlikely to succeed. The second solid basis for Britain's nineteenth century superiority was its manufacturing ability. She was the workshop of the world, and with its navy assuring access to the world's markets there seemed little reason to fear that this would change.

Britain Enters the Twentieth Century   In retrospect it is easy to see that the beginning of the twentieth century brought with it several developments that would prove to be detrimental to Great Britain. Probably the most important was the increasing power of three states. To the west, the United States was already superior to Britain in terms of economic productivity and would soon surpass Britain, too, in military strength. In the east, Japan was proving to be a major power in wars against China and Russia, making it very difficult for Britain to maintain its customary domination of the seas in that area. Most ominously, Germany began to challenge Britain's ability to preserve a balance of power on the European continent.

Great Britain accommodated the rising power of Japan in 1902 by signing an alliance, an unusual step for the British, who had traditionally avoided firm commitments of this kind. Britain's foreign policy had for several centuries been based on a conception of itself as the balancer in a balance-of-power system that was especially applicable to relations among the major powers of Europe. In order to make the system work, the British believed they must avoid tying their hands prematurely and should become involved in interstate conflicts only after it became clear which state posed the greatest threat of dominating the European continent. Britain would then join the alliance that formed against that state.

Russian threats to dominate Manchuria, and possibly China, after the Boxer Rebellion had been quashed, convinced the British to deviate from its policy of avoiding precommitments, in Asia at least. The British government was still inclined, though, to cling to that policy in Europe. For some time the British were unconcerned about the rise of Germany. Bismarck had long followed a policy of keeping the German navy small, and as long as Germany maintained that policy it did not seem threatening. In fact, at the beginning of the century the British, because of colonial rivalries, tended to regard the French with more suspicion than the Germans. The suspicion was strong enough that for a while the British tendency was rather to come to an understanding with Germany, and perhaps even to become aligned in some form with the Triple Alliance of Germany, Austria–Hungary, and Italy.[50] The tendency was wiped out by a combination of French conciliation and German belligerence. The French agreed to give the British a free hand in Sudan and Egypt (in return for giving the French a free hand in Morocco). The Germans made it obvious that they intended to build a navy that might challenge Britain's control of the seas. The result of these two developments was the Entente Cordiale between Britain and France in 1904.

In the beginning the entente involved no specific commitments. The Kaiser, by stirring up two crises over French influence in Morocco, strengthened the bond between Britain and France. By 1912, the British responded to the German naval threat by pulling out of the Mediterranean and concentrating ships in the North Sea, leaving France to protect joint interests in the Mediterranean. The French in turn, having transferred their navy to the Mediterranean, depended on Britain to protect their coast on the channel from any attack.[51] Such maneuvers demonstrated a rather remarkable amount of trust between two countries that were not formally committed to defend one another in case of war. And something of a moral obligation was created for Britain to come to the defense of France in the crisis of 1914.

The British Role in the First World War   When British policy-makers are criticized for their role in the crisis that led to the First World War, the criticism typically focuses on the reluctance of the British

[50] Anthony Haigh, *Congress of Vienna to Common Market,* Harrap, London, 1973, p. 67.
[51] Mills and McLaughlin, *World Politics,* p. 416.

to make a specific commitment to the defense of France. If such a commitment had been made, one argument goes, then Germany would have realized that an attack against France would add Great Britain to its enemies, and the realization might have made the Germans more cautious. The British view at the time, though, was that they could more successfully mediate the developing conflict if they avoided a clear alignment with one of the opposing sides. In any case, it is known that the Kaiser realized there was a good possibility that an attack against France (and Belgium) would bring the British into the war, and that he tried to alter the plans of the German army because of this. Whether he would have been successful if he had been certain that the British would fight unless the German plan to attack France and Belgium were changed, is at least doubtful.

In centuries past, the addition of British power to an alliance had been sufficient to deter aggression against that alliance altogether, or to assure the alliance ultimate victory. The First World War was to be different. Germany defeated Russia completely and almost succeeded in defeating the British and French armies in a German offensive in March 1918. This was a clear indication that the British were no longer able to play their traditional role as holder of the balance, and that when the United States withdrew from European international politics after the war, problems might arise.

Foreign Policy in the 1920s   Britain's foreign policy after the war reflected a desire to adhere to the basic assumptions on which its prewar policy had been based. It wanted to preserve a balance of power on the European continent, and in the 1920s there was only one clear threat to that balance. Germany had been defeated and humiliated. Russia was still trying to recover from a revolution and a civil war. Only France was threatening, and that is the way the British treated France. They would not go along with desires to dismember Germany, and disapproved heartily of the French occupation of the Ruhr in 1923. And, as before the First World War, Britain wanted to avoid any specific precommitments, even though the philosophy of collective security on which the League of Nations was based clearly called for such commitments. In addition to the forces of tradition, Britain's dominions pushed it away from being tied down in the name of collective security. Canada was particularly outspoken in its objections to any British commitment that might oblige Canadian troops to become involved in European quarrels. So, in 1924, when Britain was called on to approve the

Geneva Protocol (already accepted by France)—which would have explicitly committed league members to come to the aid of victims of aggression—Britain refused. At about the same time, Britain also accepted the rights of its dominions to make their own treaties with other states. It thus became clear that Britain regarded the League of Nations as little more than a convenient place for consultation, and that in case a league member was attacked, it was uncertain at best what Britain, or other members of the British commonwealth, would do.

Having rejected the Geneva Protocol, Britain did make a gesture toward France by signing the Locarno treaties, guaranteeing, along with Italy, that France would receive aid if attacked by Germany. (Actually, the treaties were worded in such a way that they amounted to a guarantee for both Germany and France against attack by the other.) The Locarno agreements were hailed in Britain as a great boon to mankind, finally accomplishing the real peace that had eluded the diplomats at Versailles. But, in retrospect, it is easy to see that the structure erected at Locarno had serious weaknesses. First, although Britain did commit itself to action in case of aggression on Germany's western border, it resolutely refused to become involved in guarantees of the frontiers of Germany's eastern neighbors. That was left up to France. And Britain's promises to France were not very valuable because the British did not have enough military strength to keep them. In effect, the treaty was

> no more than a hollow gesture to soothe the French, a bogus commitment, a fraudulent IOU that was given only because the English government never thought for a moment that they would ever have to make it good. . . . France was left alone except for the Locarno guarantees and for her weak allies in Eastern Europe.[52]

Chamberlain, Appeasement, and a Costly Victory The depression exacerbated the dangers in Locarno by making Britain even more hesitant to become involved internationally. In 1929 a Labour cabinet had come into power. Economic problems were to drive it out of office by 1931 and bring into power a national coalition consisting of all three major parties in Britain. The coalition fell apart when the Labour party, torn by internal dissension, left the government. The Conservatives ruled the country in the remaining

[52]Correlli Barnett, *The Collapse of British Power,* Morrow, New York, 1972, pp. 332–333.

prewar years, and the leaders of the Conservative party adopted an unwavering policy of appeasement. The name of Neville Chamberlain is most clearly associated with the policy, but it should be remembered that he had great popular support in Britain, and that it is unlikely that any prime minister who had adopted a much different policy would have lasted very long.

Chamberlain became prime minister in 1937. In 1938 Germany's military expenditures were roughly five times larger than Britain's. Chamberlain's deal with Hitler at Munich won for him a tumultuous hero's welcome when he returned to Great Britain. As late as April 1939, both the Labour and the Liberal parties voted against the introduction of conscription, thus reflecting the determination of many Britons to avoid war at any cost.

The British were, of course, on the winning side in the Second World War, but as the postwar decades unfold, it becomes progressively more clear that it was a Pyrrhic victory for them. Already in the nineteenth century, Great Britain had become so industrialized that it was unable to grow enough food domestically to feed itself. This was hardly a problem then, or even into the twentieth century, because the combination of Britain's industrial prowess and sure access to international markets secured by its navy meant that enough manufactured goods could be easily exported to pay for needed imports of food and raw materials. But even well before the Second World War Britain began to lose the ability to produce sufficient exports to pay for imports. Before the Second World War the difference was made up by profits on extensive foreign investments. In the 1940s Britain was forced to liquidate its foreign assets to pay for the war. This has meant that it has had to increase exports dramatically in the postwar years, and in the face of competition of unprecedented intensity from the United States immediately, and eventually from West Germany and Japan. Meeting this challenge has turned out to be the major concern for the British since the Second World War.

Postwar Adjustments   Despite obvious problems, in the first years after the Second World War Britain saw itself—and most of the world saw it—as one of the Big Three (with the United States and the Soviet Union). It was clearly third among the Three and yet was also clearly not in the same league as the rest of the second tier of powers. Postwar developments increased the difficulty for Britain to maintain this status. Britain lost control of its colonies, the biggest loss occurring in 1947 when India became independent. It had to pull out of Palestine in a hasty way that damaged its credibility as a Great Power. It also pulled out of Greece in a manner that emphasized the extent to which its global responsibilities were being passed on to the United States.

Despite troublesome omens, Britain did not see itself as being in such desperate straits as its neighbors in Western Europe. It showed little interest in joining the European Coal and Steel Community with six other European states, feeling that the benefits in joining were not worth whatever sacrifices in national sovereignty membership might entail. Britain at this time was also clearly relying on its special relationship with the United States to make available any aid Britain might need in its efforts to recover from the Second World War.

Britain's trust in the special relationship must have received a substantial blow in 1956. Nasser seized the Suez Canal. Responding to an instinct developed over the almost one hundred years of the canal's existence, the British felt that a life line vital to their security had been savaged, and they decided that they must not stand by and let another Hitler (their view of Nasser) get away with unpunished aggression. They sent troops to the Middle East to deal with Nasser, and, much to their dismay and disbelief, the United States did not support them. In fact, the Americans joined with the Russians in demanding that the British pull out of the Middle East. The British did so, reluctantly, and wondered aloud if the Americans would be so solicitous of the rights of small nations if Panama were to seize *that* canal.

In addition to shaking confidence in its American ally, the Suez incident also must have dealt a death blow to Britain's faith in its ability to maintain access to far-flung markets overseas. It was becoming less dependent on these markets in any case. Until the Second World War it had tried to build up trade with other members of the Commonwealth through a system of imperial preferences. Britain would allow foodstuffs to enter under very low tariffs, and in return the Commonwealth members would allow British manufactured goods to enter their countries under equally low tariffs. On paper, the system looked as though it had a promising future. But after the Second World War Britain began to abandon it. First, Britain desperately needed American trade and aid, and thus the Americans could and did put effective pressure on the British to lower the trade barriers protecting the imperial preferences. Then, too, it became increasingly obvious that Britain must depend more on Europe for its trade. The underdeveloped members of the Commonwealth were unlikely in the foreseeable future to demand substantial amounts of British goods. The English-speaking Commonwealth nations were sufficiently developed to be promising markets, but they were not large, they were close to competitors (Canada to the United States and Australia to Japan), and they were intent on developing their own manufacturing capabilities. By the 1960s British trade with Europe was more important than trade with Commonwealth nations, which must have been an important reason why Britain decided to apply for Common Market membership.[53]

Britain Enters the EEC   In 1961 Prime Minister Harold Wilson began negotiations for entry into the community. The negotiations proved fruitless when Charles de Gaulle vetoed Britain's entry in 1963; another British effort suffered the same fate in 1967. But in 1969 de Gaulle left the French government, and Britain's economic problems were growing worse. Prime Minister Heath decided to make one more effort to enter the community, despite the fact that public opinion polls at the time showed that most of his constituency opposed the idea. In addition to the increasingly apparent economic need for Britain to get into the Market, there were some international political factors that spurred Heath on. Perhaps the most important one involved the continually decreasing attractiveness of the special relationship with the United States. The Americans seemed to be on the verge of serious internal problems, but probably even more important to Britain, they seemed also quite willing to ignore the British as they pursued their own policies vis-à-vis the Russians and the Chinese. In short, the British were impressed by

> President Nixon's tendency in the early 1970s to leave Britain entirely behind in his dealings with Communist China and the Soviet Union, which he visited in March and May of 1972, respectively. . . . Hence, one of the strongest arguments for joining the West European Communities, in the eyes of the Heath government, was that, through a united Europe, Britain might secure its place at the great-power level.[54]

Heath did get Great Britain into the community, starting officially on January 1, 1973. The Labour party, though, objected to this step, and when it came into power in 1974, there was some

[53]Leon D. Epstein, "British Foreign Policy," in *Foreign Policy and World Politics,* 5th ed., ed. Roy C. Macridis, Prentice-Hall, Englewood Cliffs, N.J., 1976, pp. 64–65.
[54]F. S. Northedge, "The Adjustment of British Policy," in *The Foreign Policies of the Powers,* ed. F. S. Northedge, Free Press, New York, 1974, p. 189.

doubt as to the permanence of British membership. One of the primary objections of the Labour party had to do with the increased cost of food created by the British entry into the community. The British method of subsidizing agriculture had resulted in comparatively lower prices for food. The EEC method restricts imports of cheaper food and forces consumers to pay more of the actual cost of food production.[55] Trade union members of the Labour party also feared competition from more efficient continental firms. But once the Labour party did get into power, it renegotiated the terms of British membership in the community in 1975, obtaining some concessions involving the community's agriculture policy and reducing Britain's contribution to the EEC budget. As a result, the leaders of the Labour party announced that they could support community membership under the new terms. A referendum on the question was scheduled for June 1975, and 67 percent of the voters expressed their desire to stay in the community.

Painful Changes   During the decade that Britain was striving to get into the community, Britain was getting out of more of its global responsibilities. The British decided they would develop their own nuclear weapons, but they also decided that they could not afford to develop their own delivery system. For this they became totally dependent on the United States. By 1967 the British announced their intention to pull out all troops then stationed east of Suez and in the Mediterranean. In 1975 the only major British overseas military commitment left was NATO; British troops were stationed in West Germany, and there was increasing concern in Britain about the expense of this one last commitment. The British are in the uncomfortable position of realizing that their small island cannot be defended against nuclear attack and that the country cannot tolerate an extended conventional war, either. Since this means, in effect, that they cannot fight war at all, there are many Britons who wonder whether it is worth the expense to maintain any meaningful military force.

Unfortunately, Britain did find a use for its military troops in the 1970s. Many British soldiers committed to NATO in West Germany spent their time instead in Northern Ireland, trying to preserve some semblance of order there while the Protestants and the Catholics carried on their virtually perpetual feud. This was one of several signs that the disintegration of the British Empire may not stop when it reaches the shores of the British Isles. The 1960s were marked by outbursts of anti-English nationalism in Scotland

[55] Epstein, "British Foreign Policy," p. 62.

and Wales.[56] By the mid-1970s these movements had gained such strength that both Scotland and Wales were on the verge of obtaining some form of autonomy. Superimposed on this disintegration was the increasingly obvious and rapid economic decline of Britain. In the immediate postwar years Britain commanded some 20 percent of the world's trade; by the 1970s this figure had slipped to 6 percent. Inflation reached 20–25 percent a year. Britain had become the second poorest member of the EEC.[57]

On the bright side, it should be noted that England alone, even without Scotland and Wales, constitutes some 80 percent of the population of the United Kingdom, so that even if those areas do gain some measure of autonomy it will not mean total dismemberment. And the discovery of oil in the North Sea in the 1970s promises to deliver a substantial flow of wealth into the country by the 1980s. Certainly one of the key questions of the 1980s will be whether or not this flow will be handled wisely. Will it be used for purely ameliorative purposes, which will not, in the end, solve Britain's underlying problems? Or will at least some of it be used to modernize Britain's economic plant so that there will be a solid basis to build on after the oil runs out? There will, probably, always be an England, but it may be unrecognizable to those whose impressions of the country are based on memories of the nineteenth century.

Comparative Foreign Policy

The states discussed separately in the preceding brief history have two obvious characteristics in common. First, they all hold permanent seats (and the accompanying veto power) on the Security Council of the United Nations. Second, they all possess nuclear weapons. These two characteristics do not apply to any other state in the international system, and it is on this basis, largely, that major powers in the international system today are so designated.

But it is clear that the major power status of Great Britain and France is something of an anachronism; they were given permanent seats on the Security Council immediately after the Second World War because of the power and influence they wielded before the war. Since the war, as seen earlier, things have gone badly for both

[56]Amaury de Riencourt, *The American Empire,* Dial Press, New York, 1968, p. 138.
[57]Joseph Frankel, "Britain's Changing Role," *International Affairs,* 50, No. 4 (1974), p. 581.

states. In many ways, the major losers of the Second World War—Germany and Japan—have fared better, especially economically. Germany and Japan both have larger gross national products than either Great Britain or France, and if present trends continue the gap will grow in the coming years. Thus, perhaps, I should discuss the histories of Germany and Japan as I did those of the major powers. It would seem to make equal sense to analyze the past and future possibilities of potentially powerful states such as Brazil and India. But this is not my intent.

A serious student of global politics will want to become more familiar with the historical experiences of Germany, Japan, Brazil, and India, as well as several other states. And the entire text could be devoted to presenting such information. But such a text would be badly out of balance. It is true that each state is, to an extent, unique, and that the unique characteristics of each state have important effects on foreign policy. States are not entirely different from one another, though, and as the number of states grows larger it becomes apparent that the similarities shared by different groups of states may have an important impact on their foreign policies and their behavior in the global system. Concentration only on the unique characteristics of states, and their unique historical experiences, will obscure similarities among states and foreign policies, and make the study of global politics even more bewildering than it already is.

Categorizing States
If this is so, the compelling question becomes: How can states be categorized in such a way that nations within the same category will exhibit similarities in their foreign policy behavior, and states in different categories will be marked by substantial differences in foreign policy behavior? Or, to put the question in a slightly different way, which emphasizes another view of the comparative process: What are the differences among states that make a difference with regard to their foreign policy behavior? As a first step toward answering this question, a large number of national attributes can be eliminated. It seems unlikely, for example, that the percentage of redheaded people living in a state, or a predominance of maple trees, or the ratio of ugly to beautiful people, will have a significant impact on a state's foreign policy. Elimination of such qualities, though, still leaves a large number of characteristics of states that seem, logically and intuitively, to be related to a state's foreign policy. The type of government, level of education of the populace, number and kinds of political parties, the wisdom of

political leaders and their cultural background, the size and domestic influence of the military establishment, geographic location, the extent of freedom of the press, the sophistication of the scientific and technological establishments, the amount of internal unrest, and the mental and physical health of the population are merely a few national attributes that might plausibly be related to a state's foreign policy behavior. How do we choose the factors that are most important?

First, not all conceivably relevant factors can be considered. If it turns out that *all* factors are important, no matter what categories are defined, states will differ according to criteria other than those used to define a category, and thus, the foreign policy behavior of states within the same category would be so diverse as to defy any attempt to discover similarities. This could be the case. But I prefer to assume that some factors can be ignored, that others are much more important, and if they are discovered, states that are similar with respect to these factors will show important similarities in their foreign policy behavior.

Having adopted this assumption, the next step is to decide which factors, or national attributes, have the greatest impact on a state's foreign policy. This can be approached in two basic ways. The first depends on logic, intuition, and common sense and might be labeled the *theoretical approach* to the problem. The other approach concentrates on available data about states and involves the manipulation of data in such a way as to maximize the distinctions between categories of states. Interestingly, the empirical approach and theoretical analyses have shown a substantial convergence in the decade or so that scholars have devoted efforts to the comparative study of foreign policy.

In 1966 James Rosenau published an article[58] in which he discussed the difficulties of deciding which factors have the greatest impact on foreign policies, but also stressed the necessity of doing so if any progress is to be made in the scientific study of such policies. He then presented a pre-theory, a major feature of which was a set of categories into which he suggested states should be sorted for the purpose of analyzing their foreign policies. He did not discuss his choice of categories in any depth, but it is clear that he based his choices on a combination of his knowledge of traditional studies of foreign policy and an intuitive analysis of the contemporary international system. The first fundamental distinction that Rosenau emphasizes is that between large and small states. He

[58]James N. Rosenau, "Pre-theories and Theories of Foreign Policy," in *Approaches to Comparative and International Politics,* ed. R. Barry Farrel, Northwestern University Press, Evanston, 1966.

then stresses the importance of the distinction between developed and underdeveloped societies, and the difference between open and closed societies. These three distinctions serve to sort states into eight different categories, displayed in Table 3.3. The clear implication of this table, and Rosenau's article in general, is that of all the possible distinctions among states, these are the most fundamental and important for the purpose of studying foreign policy behavior.

Since that article appeared, there has been an accumulation of evidence that indicates Rosenau may have been right. For example, one year later, Jack Sawyer presented the results of an empirical analysis of 236 variables pertaining to eighty-two independent nations.[59] One of the purposes of this analysis was to sort nations into categories in such a way that nations within the same categories were as similar as possible with respect to the 236 variables used in the study, and at the same time, as distinct as possible from nations in different categories.[60] Sawyer used factor analysis to accomplish this. Interestingly, he found that the three factors best suited to the task were size (as measured by population), wealth (as measured by GNP per capita), and type of political system (as measured by political orientation, that is, Communists, neutral, or Western). This compares rather remarkably well with the intuitively derived set of factors proposed by Rosenau. (It should be noted that the two sets of factors are not completely identical, though, particularly with respect to the distinction between types of political systems. States with a Western political orientation, for example, are certainly not uniformly open, even though it is safe to assume that all Communist societies are closed, in Rosenau's sense of that word.) Bruce Russett[61] and Rudolph J. Rummel[62] have also performed factor analyses that indicate states differ from one another most fundamentally in terms of size, wealth, and type of political system.

Categorizing Foreign Policy Behavior
Impressive as this accumulation of evidence may be, it must be emphasized that the discovery that states fall most clearly into

[59]Jack Sawyer, "Dimensions of Nations: Size, Wealth, and Politics," *American Journal of Sociology,* 73 (September 1967) pp. 145–172.

[60]Aficionados of factor analysis may recognize this as rather a misstatement of the analysis performed by Sawyer. Actually, what Sawyer did was sort the variables into categories, not the states. But for the purpose of this discussion I believe it is safe to ignore for the moment the distinction between Q-factor and R-factor analysis. For a brief discussion, see Rudolph J. Rummel, "Understanding Factor Analysis," *Journal of Conflict Resolution,* 11 (December 1967), pp. 445–446.

[61]Bruce M. Russett, *International Regions and the International System,* Rand McNally, Chicago, 1967.

[62]Rudolph J. Rummel, "Indicators of Cross-National and International Patterns," *American Political Science Review,* 63 (March 1969), 127–147.

TABLE 3.3   Rosenau's typology of states

Geography and physical resources	Large Country				Small Country			
State of the economy	Developed		Underdeveloped		Developed		Underdeveloped	
State of the polity	Open	Closed	Open	Closed	Open	Closed	Open	Closed
Example	U.S.	U.S.S.R.	India	Red China	Holland	Czecho-slovakia	Kenya	Ghana

Source: James Rosenau, "Pre–Theories and Theories of Foreign Policy," *Approaches to Comparative and International Politics,* ed. R. Barry Farrel, Northwestern University Press, Evanston, Ill., 1966, p. 48. Reprinted with permission.

categories defined according to size, stage of economic development, and type of political system does not necessarily imply that
these are the national attributes with the greatest impact on foreign
policies. That conclusion must await a comparison of the foreign
policy behavior of the states that fall into the different categories.
And before we can do that we must decide just what kinds of
behavior we are going to look at. The difficulty of this task should
not be overlooked. As one critic of the field of comparative foreign
policy has put it, "getting a clear fix on what the actors do is darn
hard work—first there are lots of possible 'actors' and, second,
putting it bluntly, actors do one hell of a lot of things."[63]

This problem is similar to that leading to the categorization of
states. My aim is to generalize; to avoid devising a different explanation for each state, states will be categorized in ways, it is hoped,
that will allow the application of one kind of explanation to several
states. Similarly, to avoid constructing a unique explanation for
every example of a foreign policy behavior, these behaviors will be
categorized in such a way that behaviors within a single category
will have similar causes. If this is successful, then factors can be
isolated that account for classes of foreign policy behavior.

I will begin by specifying that "foreign policy consists of those
discrete official actions of the authoritative decision-maker of a
nation's government, or their agents, which are intended by the
decision makers to influence the behavior of international actors
external to their own polity."[64] The important question becomes,
How can foreign policies be categorized in such a way that policy
actions within the same category will have similar causes? As was
the case with categorizing states, there are several criteria that make
little sense and can be discarded immediately. Discrete official actions could be sorted into two categories, those promulgated on
Monday, Wednesday, and Friday, and those the other four days of
the week. Or, foreign policy actions could be divided into those
taking place in months containing the letter r, and those occurring
during other times of the year. Neither strategy seems very promising, though, since it is unlikely that policy actions categorized together in this way would have anything important in the way of
common origins. But what if foreign policy behaviors were divided into those that are cooperative and those that are conflictive?
This would make more sense and several scholars of international

[63]Patrick M. Morgan, *Theories and Approaches to International Politics,* 2d ed.,
Page-Ficklin, Palo Alto, 1975, p. 166.
[64]Charles Hermann, "Policy Classification: A Key to the Study of Foreign
Policy," in *The Analysis of International Politics,* ed. James N. Rosenau, Vincent
Davis, and Maurice East, Free Press, New York, 1972, p. 72.

politics have suggested that such a categorization of foreign policy is helpful for the purpose of understanding international politics.[65] Another frequent suggestion implies that the most fundamental and important distinction between foreign policy actions is that between actions aimed at preserving the status quo and those directed at changing it.

Modern foreign-policy analysts have tried to move beyond such broad general characterizations of foreign policies to more detailed and specific categorizations. One of the more ambitious attempts to do this is embodied in the World Event/Interaction Survey (WEIS) directed by Charles McClelland. McClelland and his associates began with a categorization scheme based on sixty-three types of foreign policy behavior, which they sorted into the following twenty-two categories

1	yield	12	accuse
2	comment	13	protest
3	consult	14	deny
4	approve	15	demand
5	promise	16	warn
6	grant	17	threaten
7	reward	18	demonstrate
8	agree	19	reduce relationship
9	request	20	expel
10	propose	21	seize
11	reject	22	force

Those categories are supposed to be mutually exclusive and exhaustive; that is, every foreign policy behavior should fit into one of the categories, and only one. What McClelland's project has done is to look at each significant actor in the international system since 1966, and record all their foreign policy actions, using the *New York Times* as their basic data source. This means that researchers, instead of relying entirely on intuitive appraisals of a nation's behavior, can calculate exactly what proportion of behaviors displayed fall into each of the twenty-two categories. The availability of this kind of data also means that it is possible to formulate and investigate quite specific questions about differences in the foreign policies of different kinds of states.

[65]See, for example, Arnold Wolfers, "The Pole of Power and the Pole of Indifference," in *International Politics and Foreign Policy,* ed. James N. Rosenau, Free Press, New York, 1961, and Raymond Aron, *Peace and War,* Doubleday, Garden City, N.Y., 1966.

TABLE 3.4   Six major categories of foreign policy behavior derived from a factor analysis of WEIS data, 73 nations, 1966—1968

Type of Behavior	Percentage of All Behavioral Events
1 Cooperative action	5.3
2 Participation	46.8
3 Diplomatic exchange	16.9
4 Verbal conflict	18.4
5 Nonmilitary conflict	8.0
6 Military conflict	4.6

Source: This table adapted from "An Empirically Based Typology of Foreign Policy Behaviors" by Stephen A. Salmore and Donald Munton is reprinted from *Comparing Foreign Policies: Theories, Findings, and Methods,* edited by James N. Rosenau © 1974, p. 344 by permission of the Publisher, Sage Publications, Inc. (Beverly Hills/London).

Relationships Between National Attributes
and Foreign Policies

And that is exactly what several researchers have done. Relying on such distinctions as those based on size, wealth, and politics, they have compared the foreign policy behavior of states in terms of the kinds of data recorded by WEIS and other similar data collections. Typically, the WEIS-type data is simplified; factor analysis is used to sort the original twenty-two categories into a few major kinds of behavior. Charles McClelland and Gary Hoggard found in their analysis that WEIS data falls rather neatly into three categories of behavior—one consisting basically of cooperative behavior, a second made up of routine interactions (named *participation*), and a final category containing behavior of a basically conflictive nature.[66] One later analysis of the same data led to the development of similar, but slightly more specific major categories described in Table 3.4.

Now, if Rosenau's typology of states is useful for the study of foreign policies, large states will be dramatically different from small states, developed states will differ substantially from underdeveloped states, and states with open political systems will contrast sharply with states controlled by closed political systems, in terms of the kind of foreign policy behavior recorded by WEIS, or, for example, in terms of voting behavior in the United Nations.

[66]Charles McClelland and Gary Hoggard, "Conflict Patterns in the Interaction Among Nations," in *International Politics and Foreign Policy,* rev. ed. James N. Rosenau, Free Press, New York, 1969, pp. 711–724.

David Moore has reported that the factors of size, wealth, and type of political system do indeed correlate more strongly with several variables in the WEIS data, as well as voting behavior in the United Nations, than such alternative national attributes as governmental stability, population density, and urbanism.[67] More specifically, it has been found by other researchers that large states, for example, are much more active participants in the international system. McClelland and Hoggard discovered that the five most active nations in the system (the U.S., and U.S.S.R., China, Great Britain, and France, all large states) initiated 40 percent of all the behavior in WEIS.[68] There also seems to be a clear pattern for larger states to issue more protests and accusations, and to engage in troop movements and take up arms. More developed states tend to sever relations less often and engage in a somewhat smaller proportion of conflictive acts than less developed states.[69]

Some of these findings are worth noting, but this kind of research provokes more interest when it is directed toward questions that have served as the bases for long-standing controversies. For example, probably one of the more persistent hypotheses in the literature on international relations since the First World War involves the idea that democratic states will adopt foreign policies that are different from the policies of dictatorial states. Because of that persistent idea, reiterated by Rosenau in his pre-theory, there have been several analyses of the differences between states with open and closed political systems. Zinnes and Wilkenfeld divided states into three categories: those with personalist political systems were primarily one-man governments, centrist systems were primarily socialist or Communist, and industrial democracies such as the United States, West Germany, and Sweden fell into the polyarchic category. Having done this, Zinnes and Wilkenfeld found that centrist countries exhibited more and polyarchic governments less, conflictive behavior than would have been expected given the proportion of countries that fall into these categories.[70] (In other words, the so-called null hypothesis was that centrist and polyarchic countries would exhibit a proportion of the overall conflictive behavior in the system equal to the proportion of the coun-

---

[67]David Moore, "National Attributes and Nation Typologies: A Look at the Rosenau Genotypes," in *Comparing Foreign Policies,* ed. James N. Rosenau, Wiley, New York, 1974, pp. 254–255.

[68]McClelland and Hoggard, "Conflict Patterns," p. 711–724.

[69]Michael Sullivan, *International Relations: Theories and Evidence,* Prentice-Hall, Englewood Cliffs, N.J. 1976, pp. 110–113.

[70]Dina Zinnes and Jonathan Wilkenfeld, "An Analysis of Foreign Conflict Behavior of Nations," *Comparative Foreign Policy: Theoretical Essays,* ed. Wolfram F. Hanreider, McKay, New York, 1971, p. 208.

tries in the international system they represented. What they found was that, given the proportion of centrist countries in the international system, the proportion of conflictive behavior engaged in by such countries was higher than expected.) East and Hermann also report that states with open political systems have a clear tendency to engage in a lower percentage of conflictive foreign policy acts than states with closed systems.[71]

Another hypothesis that has a long history among theorists of international relations points to a possible relationship between the amount of internal unrest in a country and the amount of foreign conflict in which it becomes involved. The idea is that societies with a lot of internal unrest, such as riots, strikes, coups, and the like, are societies in which the tenure of the ruling elite is likely to be insecure. This insecurity may tempt the elite to distract the attention of restless citizens by initiating quarrels, perhaps even wars, with other countries. It is hoped, from the point of view of the elite, this will take the minds of the people off their domestic grievances and focus their antagonism against foreign enemies.

This plausible idea has been investigated by Rudolph Rummel, who reported his findings in two articles in the early sixties. He gathered data on internal unrest and foreign conflict for seventy-seven sovereign nations for the years 1955 to 1957, relying on such sources as the *New York Times, Facts on File,* and *Keesings.* He then used factor analysis to sort the data on both kinds of conflict into categories of similar kinds of events that tend to occur at the same time and place. He found that both foreign and domestic conflict fall into three categories. One category of foreign conflict, which he labeled *war,* contained not only actual military conflict, but such activities as mobilization of troops. A second, called *diplomatic conflict,* consisted of such events as nonviolent personnel and troop movements. The third category, named *belligerency,* was made up of events such as the severance of relations, demonstrations, and negative sanctions. The three categories of domestic conflict were *turmoil* (spontaneous conflict, riots, crises) *revolution* (overt organized conflict, general strikes) and *subversion* (covert organized conflict, assassinations). Rummel found that there was only a very weak positive relationship between domestic conflict and foreign conflict, regardless of the categories analyzed.[72] A couple of years

[71]Maurice A. East and Charles F. Hermann, "Do Nation-Types Account for Foreign Policy Behavior?" in *Comparing Foreign Policies,* ed. James N. Rosenau, Wiley, New York, 1974, pp. 295–296.
[72]Rudolph J. Rummel, "Dimensions of Conflict Behavior Within and Between Nations," *General Systems Yearbook,* 8 (1963), 1–50, and "Testing Some Possible Predictors of Conflict Behavior Within and Between Nations," *Peace Research Society (International) Papers,* 1 (1964), pp. 79–111.

later, Raymond Tanter produced the same findings using the same data analytic techniques and data sources, but focusing on the years 1958 to 1960.[73] In short, both Rummel and Tanter found that nations with a lot of internal unrest and domestic conflict are not more likely to become involved in foreign conflict than states that do not suffer from this kind of unrest.

Given the plausibility and the persistence of the idea that there *is* a relationship between domestic and foreign conflict, this is a rather surprising finding. Jonathan Wilkenfeld concluded that it might be the result of lumping together all kinds of states into the same analysis. He decided to see whether different kinds of states might exhibit different types of relationships between domestic and foreign conflict. He categorized the same nations included in Rummel's analysis according to the type of political system they had, utilizing the three categories discussed earlier (personalist, centrist, and polyarchic). His suspicions proved to be well founded. States with personalist regimes, for example, do tend to have more foreign conflict if they are experiencing domestic conflict, and this is true for all types of both kinds of conflict. Among states with centrist regimes, revolutionary domestic conflict is related to all three types of foreign conflict, and among polyarchic regimes, all three forms of foreign conflict are consistently related to domestic turmoil. The specifics of these relationships are not particularly important, because no one has yet developed a theoretically logical explanation of the differences in the relationships among the different kinds of states. But it is important to note that there is some evidence to indicate that domestic conflict does lead to foreign conflict, and that the specific relationship between these variables is different for different kinds of states.[74]

Caveats

It would be appropriate to conclude with a few words of caution about the kinds of studies discussed in this section. First, all scien-

[73] Raymond Tanter, "Dimensions of Conflict Behavior Within and Between Nations, 1958–1960," *Journal of Conflict Resolution,* 10 (March 1966), 41–64.
[74] In later analyses, Wilkenfeld has found, in particular for centrist and polyarchic regimes, that previous levels of foreign conflict predict present levels far better than the amount of domestic conflict in these countries. This leads him to conclude that "domestic conflict in general appears to be only minimally related to foreign conflict behavior." See Jonathan Wilkenfeld, "Models for the Analysis of Foreign Conflict Behavior of States," in *Peace, War and Numbers,* ed. Bruce M. Russett, Sage Publications, Beverly Hills, 1972, p. 298. Personally, I would not be so eager to abandon domestic conflict as an explanatory factor simply because previous levels predict better to present levels of foreign conflict. That might merely be an indication that levels of foreign conflict do not change very rapidly, and not that there is any kind of causal connection between previous and present levels of foreign

tific knowledge is tentative, and that developed about foreign policy behavior is more tentative than most. Second, what has been discovered are correlations among variables. It is by now trite to say it, but it still must be remembered that correlation does not necessarily imply causation. This is especially so with regard to the correlations involving foreign policy behavior recorded in the *New York Times* or other similar sources. The "fit" between reality and what appears in newspapers may well be far less than perfect.[75] And even if the data sources have not severely contaminated the findings, the reported correlations between national attributes and foreign policy behavior have been uniformly small. This may well mean that factors other than national attributes have a larger impact on such behavior. Finally, the relevance of these scientific studies of foreign policy to the actual conduct of foreign policy has yet to be demonstrated. Foreign-policy makers are usually concerned with quite specific questions about particular states, and the scientific findings about foreign policy behavior are very general in nature.

This does not mean that scientific findings will never become "policy relevant." If the scientific study of foreign policy progresses and clearer patterns and relationships are discovered, it is possible that foreign-policy makers will become more interested in it. Basic research often turns out to have practical applications that are not immediately obvious; and policy makers may come to see that they will have a better chance of making wise decisions about particular problems if they are aware of scientific generalizations about the class of problems to which the one of immediate concern belongs.[76] And even if the scientific study of foreign policy does not become policy relevant in the near future, it may still uncover patterns and develop generalizations that will lead the scholar to a significantly better understanding of foreign policy and global politics.

conflict. See also Leo Hazlewood, "Diversion Mechanisms and Encapsulation Processes: The Domestic Conflict-Foreign Conflict Hypothesis Reconsidered," in *Sage International Yearbook of Foreign Policy Studies,* vol. 3, ed. Patrick J. McGowan, Sage Publications, Beverly Hills, 1975, 213–244.

[75] See, for example, Gary Hoggard, "Differential Source Coverage in Foreign Policy Analysis," in *Comparing Foreign Policies,* ed. James N. Rosenau, Wiley, New York, 1974, pp. 353–381.

[76] An analogue that comes to mind involves the kind of problems confronted by the manager of a baseball team. No scientific knowledge about baseball will necessarily lead him to the correct choice of a pinch hitter in a particular game, but if he is aware that, in general, left-handed hitters do better against right-handed pitchers than right-handed hitters, he is more likely to make a larger proportion of wise choices. Similarly, while it is unlikely that a foreign-policy maker will want to base any particular decision entirely on scientific findings, it is possible that familiarity with such findings might lead him to make a larger proportion of wise choices in the long run.

FOUR

International Actors:

The Recurrent Hope

IN THE TWO PREVIOUS CHAPTERS, CONCENTRATION WAS ON
factors that have an impact on the foreign policies of states. A
process of looking at states one at a time, for the purpose of analyzing their behavior, was involved to a certain degree. Now there
will be a shift to a focus on interaction among several states, especially as it takes place in coalitions and alliances, regional economic
integration organizations, and within the institutions of universal
peace-keeping organizations such as the United Nations.

International Alliances

Coalitions seem to be an inevitable result of interaction among
sovereign political units. "Wherever in recorded history a system of
multiple sovereignty has existed, some of the sovereign units involved in conflicts with others have entered into alliances."[1] Al-

[1] Arnold Wolfers, "Alliances," in *International Encyclopedia of the Social Sciences,*
ed. David Sills, Macmillan and Free Press, New York, 1968, p. 269.

liances were part of interstate relations in ancient India and China, in Greece during the era of city-states, and in Machiavellian Italy.

Why are coalitions such a prominent part of international relations? The most common answer given by policy makers is that they are a necessary defense against aggression. Often, perhaps most of the time, defense is the actual motive for the formation of alliances. But some alliances are also formed for more aggressive purposes. The pact between Nazi Germany and the Soviet Union in 1939, which resulted in the immediate dismemberment of Poland, is probably the most prominent twentieth-century example.

Balance of Power Theory Versus Game Theory

Whether for defensive or offensive purposes, alliances are usually formed to give members an advantage in interstate conflicts. But under what conditions states are most likely to form alliances, who will ally with whom, what kinds of alliances are most effective and cohesive, and what effects do alliances have on the stability of the international system are questions about which there is little agreement. The most traditional set of answers is supplied by the *balance-of-power theory*. According to the theory, nations will form alliances when any state in their midst becomes so powerful that it threatens to establish hegemony. Through the mechanism of alliances, the balance is preserved, and if war is not avoided, at least the powerful, aggressive state is denied victory. Most balance-of-power theorists would argue that alliances so used are beneficial, indeed necessary, for the stability of the international system.

Out of a very different tradition comes a contrasting view of alliance formation in the international system. Utilizing *game theory,* and small group laboratory experiments, several students of coalitions[2] have developed an idea that William Riker calls the *size principle*. This principle states that, in social situations meeting certain assumptions (to follow), "participants create coalitions just as large as they believe will ensure winning and no larger."[3] In effect, Riker predicts that the pattern of alliances that will appear in the international system will be the result of two contradictory intentions of states: (1) to join a winning coalition and (2) to win as much as possible. Obviously, the first aim will lead each state to prefer large alliances because they can ensure victory. The second leads each state to prefer small alliances because they can provide the

[2] See, for example, William Riker, *The Theory of Political Coalitions,* Yale University Press, New Haven, 1962, and Jerome Chertkoff, "A Revision of Caplow's Coalition Theory," *Journal of Experimental Social Psychology,* 3 (April 1967), 172–177.

[3] Riker, *Theory,* pp. 32–33.

biggest share of whatever there is to win. The result of such contradictory aims will be, according to Riker and others, alliances that are just as large as they must be to win, but no larger.

While balance of power theorists predict that states will form alliances to prevent the appearance of a winner, Riker predicts the opposite.[4] His theory predicts that winning alliances will appear and that they will be *minimum winning coalitions*.

Historical Evidence

The most convincing evidence in favor of the size principle involves the relatively rare occasions when grand coalitions have appeared in the international system. *Grand coalitions* can be defined as coalitions of almost everybody against almost nobody. A clear implication of the size principle is that such coalitions will soon fall apart. There is no way for such coalitions to win anything, since there is nobody left to win from; an advocate of the size principle would predict that such coalitions will break up so that member states can win something from each other. And that is exactly what has happened.

After the Napoleonic wars at the beginning of the nineteenth century, for example, the states of Great Britain, Austria, Prussia, and Russia constituted a grand coalition, since France was a defeated state and the only other great power in the world. The coalition began to show signs of disunity as early as the Congress of Vienna in 1815. Russia and Prussia both had territorial ambitions that were opposed by Austria and England. As a result, the grand coalition broke up, and Austria and England secretly allied with the French against the Russians and the Prussians.

> Hence followed this astonishing result: Austria and England, both of whom had been fighting France for nearly a generation, brought a reconstituted French government back into world politics and allied with it against their own former allies in the very moment of victory."[5]

The process was still visible, but not quite as clear-cut, after the First World War. Because of the revolution in Russia and the defeat of Germany, the United States, Great Britain, and France

[4]Dina Zinnes, "Coalition Theories and the Balance of Power," in *The Study of Coalition Behavior*, ed. Sven Groennings, E. W. Kelley, and Michael Leiserson, Holt, Rinehart, & Winston, New York, 1970, p. 359.
[5]Riker, *Theory*, p. 69.

constituted a grand coalition.[6] This coalition, too, began to break up almost immediately after its enemy was defeated. The United States refused to join the League of Nations. Great Britain and France began to disagree about how defeated Germany should be treated. France, in general, wanted to be much tougher than the British. This disagreement reached something of a climax when France invaded Germany in order to collect reparations, and the British angrily accused the French of aggression.

The most spectacular dissolution of a grand coalition took place after the Second World War. During the war, the Americans, the Russians, and the British (with some help from the French) constituted what was fairly close to a minimum-winning coalition. But after the war, with Italy defeated and Japan and Germany nearly prostrate, the Big Three became a grand coalition. A great controversy has raged, especially in the last ten or fifteen years, among American historians about the origins of the cold war. The orthodox Western view, briefly, is that the cold war was the result of Russian aggression and hostility, that Stalin was paranoid and took several steps, particularly in Eastern Europe, that gave the Americans no choice but hostile retaliation. The revisionist view is that the Americans, motivated by economic interests in Eastern Europe (and the economic interests of their West European allies), led by President Truman, whose anti-Communism bordered on the hysterical (especially when contrasted with the attitudes of President Roosevelt), made an unjustifiable attempt to prevent the Russians from consolidating their position in Eastern Europe. To adherents of the size principle, this controversy is largely sound and fury signifying nothing. The cold war occurred as a more or less inevitable result of the grand coalition falling apart. The fact that the only state in the world strong enough to threaten the United States was the Soviet Union, and vice versa, also played a role. Ideological differences may have exacerbated the split to a degree. Personality characteristics of Stalin and Truman were almost certainly trivial in impact in comparison to other factors. According to the size principle as it applies to grand coalitions, "Having defeated the Axis, the winners had nothing to win from unless they split up and tried to win from each other."[7]

[6]Japan and Italy might also be included in this coalition. Both of these states adhered to the pattern of rapidly becoming unhappy with the grand coalition, Japan largely because the league refused to adopt the principle of racial equality, and Italy because its territorial demands were not met.
[7]Riker, *Theory*, p. 71. All three of the examples are discussed on pages 69–71. Steven Brams points out that this evidence in favor of the size principle as it applies to international politics is "historical in nature and not particularly susceptible to quantification and rigorous empirical testing. Nonetheless, it has the virtue of being

British prime minister Attlee, President Truman, and Soviet premier Stalin, 1945. Wide World Photo.

The Importance of Pivotal Power

Like the size principle, another concept of the formal kind of coalition theory that may give some insight into the formation of alliances in the international system is *pivotal power*. In any coalition game, the greater the necessity to include a player in a coalition to make it a winning one, the greater that player's pivotal power. Consider a simple game in which player A has resources equal to 45, B equals 40, and C equals 15, and it takes a coalition with resources greater than 50 to win. Formally, the pivotal power of each player is equal to the percentage of potential winning coalitions of which it must be a member. In this three player game, there are only three possible winning coalitions; AB, AC, and BC.[8] The interesting thing to notice about this simple game is that despite the substantial inequality in the resource bases of the players, the pivotal power of each player is exactly the same. (Each player must be in exactly two-thirds of the potential winning coalitions to make

---

systematic: Riker did not ransack history for isolated examples that support the size principle but rather considered all instances of relevant cases within the spatially and temporally defined limits he set. To the extent that these cases . . . are representative of zero-sum situations generally, they allow him to draw more general conclusions than would be adduced from anecdotal evidence alone." See Brams, *Game Theory and Politics,* Free Press, New York, 1975, p. 224.

[8] There are four possible winning coalitions if one includes the grand coalition of ABC.

them winning, so each player's pivotal power equals 66.7 percent.[9])
So, despite C's relatively tiny resource base, C is as valuable a
member of a coalition as A or B, and can rationally demand a
payoff as big as A or B might demand.

The kind of situation in which "the tiny are mighty" occurs
regularly in multiparty parliaments. Two large parties may constitute by far the greater share of a potential ruling coalition, but if
they need a small third party to put them over the top, they may
well be willing to give that party political rewards out of proportion to the resources it will contribute to the coalition. "Coalition
theory . . . posits that pivot parties . . . will obtain payoffs greater
than their share of resource contribution."[10]

Similarly in international politics, states with very small resource bases may come to exert a disproportionate influence on the
process of international alliance formation if they find themselves in
a situation where they enjoy a generous portion of pivotal power.
France, after the Napoleonic wars, found itself in such a situation.
The French nation had been a gigantic pain in the neck for Europe
over the last fifteen to twenty years; even so, before Napoleon was
finally disposed of, France had the other states in the system competing for its allegiance, and it was generally restored to a position
of influence and prestige with amazing speed. One kind of explanation for this would heap praise upon the French foreign minister of
the time, Talleyrand.[11] According to this kind of theory (a great-
man theory), Talleyrand was so adroit, clever, and diplomatically
engaging that despite the atrocious behavior of the French nation,
he managed to get the major powers of Europe to treat France with
respect in the very moment of defeat. A game theory approach to
the success of France after Napoleon would be quite different. The
approach would point out that, despite France's recent defeat and
correspondingly meager resource base, the structure of the international system was such that France enjoyed a healthy measure of
pivotal power. England and Austria on the one hand, and Russia
and Prussia on the other, needed to include France in their coalition
to make it a winning one.

[9] This is a simplification of a more formal procedure for calculating pivotal
power, which also takes into account the sequence of additions to potential winning
coalitions. See Brams, *Game Theory and Politics*, pp. 162–163.

[10] Sven Groennings, "Patterns, Strategies, and Payoffs in Norwegian Coalition
Formation," in *The Study of Coalition Behavior*, ed. Sven Groennings, E. W. Kelley,
and Michael Leiserson, Holt, Rinehart & Winston, New York, 1970, p. 74.

[11] See, for example, Harold Nicolson, *The Congress of Vienna*, Methuen, London, 1961; Duff Cooper, *Talleyrand*, Jonathan Cape, London, 1964; Clarence Crane
Brinton, *The Lives of Talleyrand*, Norton, New York, 1963. Not all historically
minded analysts agree. See Henry Kissinger, *A World Restored*, Grossett and Dunlap,
New York, 1964, p. 148.

French foreign minister Talleyrand. Ary Scheffer/Musée Condé/Giraudon.

Germany was in a somewhat similar situation after the Second World War. Suffering two world wars led several in the victorious states to conclude that Germany deserved to be banished forever as a major nation-state. And yet in a few short years, Germany was the recipient of a generous amount of foreign aid, and the Americans even insisted that it be rearmed. Given Hitler's abominable behavior, how did this happen? Was Konrad Adenauer's genius or powerful personality responsible for this remarkable acceptance of

Germany after the Second World War? Certainly a game theorist would be no more impressed by Adenauer's genius than Talleyrand's allegedly clever diplomacy. Rather, a game theorist would be inclined to point out the similarity between the position of Germany after the Second World War, and of France after the Napoleonic wars. Germany, like France, largely because of the developing cold war conflict between the Soviet Union and the United States, found itself blessed with pivotal power, despite the devastation of its resource base suffered in the war. The Americans came to see quickly that Germany might be necessary to ensure that the Western coalition was a winning one. Third World nations, throughout the 1950s in particular, enjoyed similar good luck. Despite very small resource bases, they were perceived by the Soviet Union and the United States as having considerable pivotal power. The result was that these small nations were able to influence the policies of the two superpowers more than one might think possible on the basis of their small size.

The Utility of Formal Theories

The applicability of formal coalition, or game theories, to international politics should not be exaggerated. The conclusions of such theories are based on assumptions that are often highly unrealistic. For example, Riker's size principle is based on assumptions that the players are *rational,* that they have access to all relevant information, and that the game being played is zero sum.[12] A *zero-sum* game is one in which whatever one player wins, the other player loses. No cooperation is possible, because there is no solution to a game that allows all players to win something. States, and their decision makers act rationally at times, but they never have access to all relevant information, and conflict situations in international politics are virtually never zero sum. Even in total war, the game is usually *variable sum,* meaning that, depending on the strategies adopted by the players, the winnings and the losses need not necessarily add up to zero (as in zero-sum games). If all the players, for example, cooperate in order to avoid the use of poison gas, or in the treatment of prisoners, they may all win.

Since the assumptions on which formal theories are based are rarely met, the predictions they make may turn out to be inapplicable to reality. There are many reasons, for example, why coalitions in world politics are often much larger than minimum winning.

[12]*Rationality* is defined roughly as preferring winning to losing. Riker also assumes that side payments are permitted. Game theorists, of course, are not restricted to these assumptions. Not all games, for example, are based on the assumption of perfect information.

First, states are unlikely to want to take the risks involved in forming such coalitions. In a parliament, just forming a coalition big enough to win assures victory. In world politics, once the coalition is formed, it may well have to defeat an opposing coalition in a war. Also, any attempt to form a minimum winning coalition may be foiled by the difficulty of measuring power. What was thought to be just enough to win may turn out to be insufficient. Even if that does not occur, a minimum winning coalition may have to fight long and hard to win the war, while a much larger coalition might win easily.

For these reasons, one would expect larger-than-minimum-winning coalitions to be quite common, and that these coalitions might well not collapse as quickly as calculations based on the size principle would lead one to believe. And that is exactly what has been found. Larger international alliances do not, as a matter of fact, show any tendency to break up faster than small alliances.[13]

Such a lack of fit between reality and the predictions of formal theories should not, though, lead one to discard the theories as useless. They may point out patterns that would not have been apparent otherwise. And the fact that they are based on unrealistic assumptions is a quality shared with respectable theories in the hardest of sciences. For example, physicists use the following formula to describe the motion of a pendulum:

$$X = A \sin (mt)$$

where X equals the horizontal deflection of the bob, A equals the maximum deflection, t is time, and m is a constant. This formula is derived on the basis of assumptions that clearly distort reality. It is assumed, for example, that the bob has extension, but no mass. It is also assumed that there is no air resistance, that the supporting string has no mass, and that friction has no effect. All of these assumptions are false. Why does the physicist continue to make them? "In return for sacrificing precision . . . he gains simplicity, and what is more important he gets at the fundamentals . . . of the situation."[14] In other words, physicists as well as social scientists must use simplifying assumptions in order to understand a very complex world. And if physicists have to use such unrealistic assumptions in order to understand something as relatively simple as

[13] Bruce Bueno de Mesquita and J. David Singer, "Alliances, Capabilities, and War: A Review and Synthesis," in *Political Science Annual*, ed. Cornelius Cotter, 1973, p. 266. See also, William J. Horvath and Caxton C. Foster, "Stochastic Models of War Alliances," *Journal of Conflict Resolution*, 7 (June 1963), 110–116.

[14] Anatol Rapoport, "Various Meanings of 'Theory,' " in *International Politics and Foreign Policy*, ed. James N. Rosenau, Free Press, New York, 1961, p. 46.

the motion of a pendulum, similar kinds of assumptions must be even more necessary for social scientists who are trying to fathom the fundamentals of world politics.

Despite the simplifying assumptions on which it is based, the formula for describing the motion of a pendulum provides quite accurate predictions. This is not always the case, even for powerful theories. According to Newtonian physics, objects that fall to the earth should accelerate at the rate of 32 feet per second per second. It is probably true that, in any given year, over 90 percent of the objects that fall to earth are either raindrops, snowflakes, or leaves. Raindrops come closer than snowflakes and leaves, but it is still safe to say that not one of these objects, as it falls to earth, accelerates at the rate of 32 feet per second per second. Given the substantial inaccuracy of Newtonian predictions as they apply to reality, one might be inclined to conclude that Newton was a numbskull. That would, of course, be a mistake. Newton was a scientist who, when theorizing, relied on simplifying assumptions. No game theorist can claim to have matched Newton's accomplishments, but the fact that game theories, or other formal theories, rely on unrealistic assumptions, and often make predictions that turn out not to apply very well to actuality, should not lead us to ignore them. Formal theories in social sciences are only utilizing techniques developed in other sciences that may also prove helpful in a scientific study of world politics. They may, for example, highlight such patterns as the rapid dissolution of grand coalitions, or the effect of pivotal power, which might otherwise have been lost in the welter of data with which any scholar of world politics must deal.

Who Will Ally With Whom?
One perspective on alliances that is strikingly different from formal coalition-theory is based on the idea that alliances are formed between states that share a common ideology, common economic and political systems, or similar cultural characteristics. The contrast between this kind of theory and formal theories arises because the latter tend to treat all states as identical, each responding to system structure or some set of incentives, in a rational manner. This is another way in which such formal theories do not supply an accurate picture of reality, since it is clear that there is some tendency for states to prefer alliance partners with whom they share common national attributes. In the cold war era, there was a clear tendency for Communist states to ally with other Communist states, and democratic (or merely anti-Communist) states to do likewise. Unfortunately, there have been no studies of the kind that

would give a clear idea of how strong the tendency for states with bonds formed by common characteristics to ally with one another really is. "The lack of such a study is serious because . . . the most casual recall brings to mind many instances where these bonds failed to produce joint action or to prevent the states concerned from joining opposing alliances."[15] The United States, for example, refused to.ally with the British and French democracies before the two world wars until it was almost too late in both cases. And a common ideology has not served to cement the bond between the Soviet Union and the People's Republic of China. Conversely, radically different ideologies did not prevent Nazi Germany and Communist Russia from forming a coalition in 1939.

While it may be that states that are similar in terms of ideology, political systems, or culture are more likely to ally with one another than dissimilar states, there are plenty of exceptions to the rule. One important origin of such exceptions stems from another principle of coalition formation that can be summarized as my enemy's enemy is my friend. Republican France, for example, allied with czarist Russia in 1894 because they shared a common enemy, Germany. Republican France allied with Communist Russia in 1935 for the same reason. Many of the clearest examples of ideological similarities being overridden by the principle my enemy's enemy is my friend in post– Second World War international politics arose from the conflict between Pakistan and India. The two newly independent nations fought over Kashmir in 1947. In the ensuing decade, they developed sharply contrasting political systems. India was admirably democratic, while Pakistan was ruled by a military dictatorship. The dictatorship was, though, staunchly anti-Communist, and aligned itself with the Western world in not one but two alliances, the Central Treaty Organization (CENTO) and the Southeast Treaty Organization (SEATO). Despite membership in two strongly anti-Communist alliances, Pakistan soon found itself with a strong Communist ally. Pakistan's enemy India became involved in a border dispute with China, which erupted into a war in 1962. China thus emerged as the enemy of Pakistan's enemy, and "by the mid-1960s, Pakistan was in the unique position

[15]Bruce Russett, "Components of an Operational Theory of International Alliance Formation," *Journal of Conflict Resolution,* 12 (September 1968), 286. In the same article, Russett observes that the size principle alone only specifies a class of alliances out of which one will emerge, and that one might expect bonds of community to determine which of that class is more likely to be formed. In a similar vein, Robert Axelrod hypothesizes that in multiparty parliaments, for example, the coalitions that are formed will be minimal winning, and connected, in the sense that the parties in them will be adjacent to one another on an ideological spectrum or policy dimension. See Robert Axelrod, *Conflict of Interest,* Markham, Chicago, 1970, pp. 168– 171.

of being a member of two Western military alliances and, at the same time, enjoying the friendship of the People's Republic of China."[16]

This was not the end of coalitions of strange bedfellows in this conflict. While Pakistan developed into a military dictatorship strongly allied with the forces of Western democracy, democratic India remained resolutely neutral in the cold war conflict. But in 1971, as the civil war between West and East Pakistan became more serious, and the Indians decided they must intervene, Mrs. Gandhi (still a democratic leader at the time) abandoned India's long-standing policy of nonalignment and signed a treaty of friendship with the Communist regime of the Soviet Union. Why? Because by that time the Soviet Union was an enemy of India's enemy, China.

Alliances and War

At least equal in interest to the question of who will ally with whom are questions concerning the effect of alliances on international war. Alliances have usually been intended to help a state avoid war, or to help it win a war once the war started. Whether or not alliances serve the prior purpose well is a matter of some dispute in the literature of international relations. It may be true that a state threatened with aggression can deter the potential aggressor by acquiring one or more formal allies. But these alliances may also convince the potential aggressor that it is the victim of a strategy of encirclement, and this in turn can lead to several undesirable reactions. The target of the alliances, for example, may go out and seek its own alliance partners. Before the initial alliance was formed, the potential aggressor may have had trouble finding such partners, because the important states in the area were not aware of the lines of cleavage in the system. But an alliance or two could conceivably polarize the situation to the point that the potential aggressor will find it easy to form a counteralliance. At worst, the polarized situation can result in the very thing that the original alliance was designed to avoid, an enemy attack. The attack might be brought about either because of fear the original alliance provoked in the enemy or because of confidence the enemy now has, based on its own alliance brought about by the original coalition.

This is all highly speculative, of course, and it seems fairly clear that in the past, the conclusions of such speculation about alliances have been influenced heavily by the role that alliances played in the last big war. Take, for example, the Franco–Prussian

[16]John G. Stoessinger, *Why Nations Go to War,* St. Martin's Press, New York, 1974, p. 153.

War in 1870. France lost that war, badly, and one reason was that France did not receive help from potential allies. The leaders of France, in the months leading up to the war, believed that Austria, or perhaps Italy, might come to their aid if they became involved in a conflict with Prussia.[17] But when the time came, France found itself alone. Both Austria and Italy left the French to their sad fate.

World leaders could have concluded, as a result of the experience of France in 1870, that wisdom with respect to alliances lies in a policy of getting one's potential alliance partners to sign on the dotted line so that they are clearly committed when a crisis occurs. (France had relied on vague assurances of assistance before the Franco-Prussian War.) And that is the lesson that many decision-makers in leading European states seemed to have learned. In any case, by 1914, the European state system was virtually honeycombed with formal alliances. And those alliances seemed, in retrospect, to be an important part of the problem that caused the system to collapse because of an intrinsically unimportant spat between Austria and Serbia. Alliance ties sucked Germany into the conflict. After Russia became involved, alliances then entangled France and England. Suffice it to say that alliances came out of the First World War with a rather tarnished reputation.[18]

That alliances had a tainted reputation did not deter France from forming many of them in the interwar years, but there is the possibility that it did deter France from relying on alliances, or cultivating them to the point that they might have been useful. France had alliances with several Balkan states and with the Soviet Union but relied on the Maginot Line in a manner that was contradictory to the alliance commitments. The French, as seen previously, never did solidify the Russian alliance and abandoned their Balkan allies at the moment of crisis.

England avoided alliances in Eastern Europe altogether, and both England and France made only half-hearted and disastrously ineffective attempts to form an alliance with the Soviet Union. The United States did form an alliance of sorts with its Latin American neighbors in the 1930s, but refused to become involved in any arrangement that was more directly connected with the developing European (or Asian) conflict and more likely to deter aggression. Again, in retrospect, the *avoidance* of alliance bonds seemed disastrous. If only effective alliances had been formed against Hitler, he might not have even had the nerve to begin the Second World War.

[17]Michael Howard, *The Franco-Prussian War,* Rupert Hart Davis, London, 1961, pp. 46–48.
[18]Sidney B. Fay. *The Origins of the World War,* Macmillan, New York, 1928, p. 34.

In short, right or wrong, alliances came out of the Second World War with the reputation for deterring aggression restored, certainly in the eyes of American policy-makers, at any rate. The United States, in the years following the Second World War, formed the most extensive set of formal alliances in the history of the world. The Rio Pact in Latin America, the Central Treaty Organization in the Middle East, the Southeast Asia Treaty Organization in Asia, and a treaty between Australia, New Zealand, and the United States (ANZUS) in the South Pacific, were created by the United States to implement its policy of containment.[19] Several bilateral pacts were added. (See Table 4.1.) The keystone of the American system of alliances was, of course, the North Atlantic Treaty Organization, centered in Western Europe. Having already signed an alliance with Communist China, the Soviets organized the Warsaw Treaty Organization (WTO) to counterbalance NATO (and in response to the rearming of Germany), thus solidifying the bipolarization of the international system.

The bipolarization and the structure of these alliances, has changed considerably over the last two decades. The Russo-Chinese alliance ceased to exist in 1961. For several complicated reasons involving Middle Eastern politics at the time, the United States never did join CENTO, and this organization has become progressively less important. The Southeast Asia Treaty Organization was disbanded in 1975. Clearly, in the confrontation between the United States and the Soviet Union, NATO and WTO are by far the most important alliances for each of the superpowers.

As this brief historical account should make clear, decision makers have, over the years, changed their minds about the utility of alliances repeatedly, typically relying on very recent experience to determine whether they will depend on them or not. Is there evidence of a more systematic scientific nature that policy makers might rely on instead? Is it true, for example, that nations with many alliance ties are more likely to avoid war? Or can it be proved that states with alliances are more likely to win a war once it gets started?

Unfortunately, the evidence relevant to both of these questions is spotty. It is true, for example, that the experience of states in the international system from the Napoleonic wars to the end of the

[19] Although this was certainly an important motive for the United States in forming these alliances, the motives of the other states involved were not always so clear. Some Latin American states in the Rio Pact, for example, were at least as concerned about possible North American intervention as they were about attack or subversion by a Communist state, and Australia and New Zealand were enticed by the United States into signing a peace treaty with Japan with the guarantees they received in the ANZUS pact.

TABLE 4.1   Postwar alliances involving the United States
and the Soviet Union

North Atlantic Treaty Organization (1949–)		Rio Pact (1947–)	
Belgium	Italy	Argentina	Honduras
Canada	Luxembourg	Barbados	Mexico
Denmark	Netherlands	Bolivia	Nicaragua
Federal Republic	Norway	Brazil	Panama
of Germany	Portugal	Chile	Paraguay
France[a]	Turkey	Colombia	Peru
Greece	United Kingdom	Costa Rica	Trinidad
Iceland	United States	Cuba[b]	Tobago
		Dominican	United States
		Republic	Uruguay
		Educador	Venezuela
		Guatemala	
		Haiti	

Southeast Asia Treaty Organization (1954–1975)		ANZUS (1951–)	
Australia	United Kingdom	Australia	United States
France	United States	New Zealand	
New Zealand	Cambodia[c]		
Pakistan	Laos[c]	Central Treaty Organization[d] (1955–)	
Philippines	Vietnam[c]		
Thailand		Iran	Turkey
		Pakistan	United Kingdom

Second World War shows that states with more alliances did get involved in more war. But that correlation turns out to be largely the result of the fact that states that were part of the international system for most of those years became involved in more alliances *and* more war than states that were in the system for a shorter period of time. If, instead of looking at the relationship between total numbers of alliances and years of war, one correlates the number of alliances and the amount of war that states experienced *per year* they were members of the international system, one finds there is no strong tendency for states having more alliances to be more war prone.[20]

[20]J. David Singer and Melvin Small, "National Alliance Commitments and War Involvement, 1815–1945," *Peace Research Society Papers*, 5 (1966), 109–140.

TABLE 4.1   Postwar alliances involving the United States
and the Soviet Union *(cont.)*

Warsaw Pact (1955–)		
Albania[e]	German	Poland
Bulgaria	Democratic	Rumania
Czechoslovakia	Republic	Soviet Union
	Hungary	

Bilateral Pacts[f]	
Russia-Yugoslavia (1945–1948)	U.S.-Philippines (1951–)
Russia-China (1950–1961)	U.S.–South Korea (1953–)
Russia-North Korea (1961–)	U.S.-Taiwan (1954–)
Russia-India (1971–)	U.S.-Turkey (1969–1975)
Russia-Iraq (1972–)	
Russia-Somalia (1974–1977)	
Russia-Angola (1975–)	

[a]The French government withdrew its forces committed to NATO on July 1, 1966. Greece withdrew from military participation in NATO in 1974.

[b]Cuba was excluded from participation in the inter-American system by the Organization of American States (OAS) in 1962.

[c]Signed a protocol giving them some privileges according to the treaty.

[d]The United States played a key role in the formation of this organization, but then failed to join it formally. Iraq was an original member of the alliance, then known as the Baghdad Pact, but withdrew in 1958.

[e]Albania ceased active participation in 1961.

[f]Excluded are bilateral pacts between Russia and East European states that were superseded by the creation of the Warsaw Pact in 1955.

Sources: Francis A. Beer, ed., *Alliances: Latent War Communities in the Contemporary World,* Holt, Rinehart, & Winston, New York, 1970; Melvin Small and J. David Singer, "Formal Alliances, 1816–1965: An Extension of the Basic Data," *Journal of Peace Research,* 1 (1966), 1–32; several *State Department Background Notes.*

There is, on the other hand, a patterned relationship between the extent of alliance aggregation in the international system, and the amount of war in the system. But the relationship in the nineteenth century was different from that in the twentieth century. In the earlier century, the higher the percentage of states in alliances, the less international war there was. In this century (up to 1945 at least), the higher the percentage of states in alliances, the more war there was likely to be.[21] From the viewpoint of a theorist interested in the causes of war, these patterns are interesting, but their relevance to policy makers of individual states is uncertain at

[21]J. David Singer and Melvin Small, "Alliance Aggregation and the Onset of War, 1815–1945," in *Quantitative International Politics,* ed. J. David Singer, Free Press, New York, 1968, pp. 247–286.

best. Even if it is assumed that the pattern discovered for the period 1900 to 1945 still holds (that is, the more alliance aggregation, the more war), it is not safe to conclude that states wishing to avoid war should stay out of alliances. The systemic level pattern *might* have been brought about because unallied states fought more war during times when other states formed alliances. It is conceivable, for example, that during periods of high tension, smart states form alliances, while dumb states do not adopt this strategy and fight the wars. In any case, the systemic level correlation between alliances and war does not serve as a sound basis for the conclusion that states involved in alliances are more war prone.

There is even less evidence available that is relevant to the question of whether or not alliances help states win wars. About the most one can say is that formal alliance pacts do increase the likelihood that a state that becomes involved in a war will receive help from other states. A look at "major powers" (as defined in Chapter 3) from 1815 to 1945, shows that major powers without formal alliances received military help from other major powers on only 20 percent of the occasions when such help might have been provided. In contrast, major powers that went into war with formal alliances received help 33 percent of the time. In other words, "alliance commitments are meaningful and . . . they help influence the behavior of the signatories."[22] Whether or not, and how often, the aid of allies has been crucial to victories achieved by aided states is an open question.

Secondary Purposes

The primary purpose of alliances is to provide advantages for their members in interstate conflicts, either political or military. In the twentieth century especially, they have come to serve some secondary purposes that are only indirectly related to such conflicts. As Britain and France retreated from their colonial outposts, starting with the end of the First World War, they signed a number of alliances with their ex-colonies that were mainly a façade for the continuation of basically colonial relationships. For example in 1930, the British signed a treaty with Iraq that

> established a military alliance and pledged the Iraqi king to provide "all facilities and assistance in his power. . . ." Iraq granted to Britain sites for air bases and authorized Britain to

[22]J. David Singer and Melvin Small, "Formal Alliances, 1815–1939: A Quantitative Description," *Journal of Peace Research,* 1 (1966), 257–282.

maintain armed forces in Iraq for twenty-five years. Britain alone would furnish all foreign military schooling, advisers, and armaments required by Iraq.[23]

Since the Second World War, the United States and the Soviet Union have formed alliances that critics of both superpowers see as fulfilling imperialistic purposes in a manner not unlike the British-Iraqi Pact. The United States has utilized the institutions of the Organization of American States (OAS) to strengthen the military establishments of several Latin American states. The purpose of American-supplied military hardware is obviously only partially related to the dangers of external invasion. It is more often used against internal enemies of the present governments of the Latin American countries. Whether or not there is a "conspiracy" between the ruling elites in these countries and the government of the United States is certainly debatable, but there is little doubt that such military arrangements have served to strengthen Latin American governments more compatible with American preferences than might otherwise be the case. In addition, the United States has used the OAS on occasion to deal with, through harassment or outright invasion, Latin American governments it views as undesirable. Cuba and the Dominican Republic have been the most prominent targets of OAS activities in the postwar years.

In 1955 the Soviet Union and seven East European countries formed the Warsaw Treaty Organization, for the ostensible purpose of defending the members from outside attack. And from the viewpoint of the Soviet Union, the ostensible motive was no doubt at least partially sincere, just as the United States government genuinely believes that subversive threats to Latin American states are promoted by foreign Communist governments who would take advantage of successful subversion in ways detrimental to the United States. But "the true reason for the Warsaw Pact . . . probably was the desire of the U.S.S.R. to obtain legal justification for stationing its troops in East-Central Europe."[24] Troops are still stationed in East-Central Europe. And in 1968, the Soviet Union used the Warsaw Pact as a formal basis for the invasion of Czechoslovakia, the purpose of which was to depose the government in a manner reminiscent of the way the United States utilized the Organization of American States to legitimate the 1965 invasion of the Dominican Republic.

[23]P. Edward Haley, "Britain and the Middle East," in *The Middle East in World Politics,* ed. Tareq Y. Ismael, Syracuse University Press, Syracuse, 1974, p. 25.
[24]Richard F. Staar, "The Warsaw Treaty Organization," in *Alliances,* ed. Francis A. Beer, Holt, Rinehart, & Winston, New York, 1970, p. 159.

The Russians invade Prague, 1968. Wide World Photo.

Regional Economic Integration

Alliances are coalitions of states that have primarily political goals. Since the Second World War, numerous coalitions have arisen of states whose goals are more economic in nature. Of course, political and economic goals are often intertwined. This has been especially true of integration organizations in Europe.

Integration in Western Europe

Shortly after the Second World War, the threat of Russian domination led Winston Churchill to call for a United States of Europe. In the succeeding years there were several attempts to get Europe organized. Responding in part to Churchill's suggestion, sixteen west European nations, in 1947, formed the Congress of Europe, made up of members of parliaments of member countries.

Federalism Versus Functionalism   The impetus toward international organization in Europe received two important boosts in 1948. The Soviets backed a successful coup in Czechoslovakia. They also blockaded Berlin, making it necessary for the Americans to supply the city from the air. One of the immediate responses to the perceived Soviet threat was the creation of the North Atlantic Treaty Organization. By 1950, there were two separate but related movements to unify Europe to facilitate dealing with the Russians and at the same time ensure against any future trouble with a rejuvenated Germany. One movement was based on what became known as the *federalist* philosophy of integration. The heart of the philosophy is summarized neatly in the slogan "The worst way to cross a chasm is in little steps." This slogan implies that any attempt to unify several nation-states into a federal union must go to the heart of the matter directly. The incipient federal government must be given substantial political power from the beginning. René Pleven, French premier in 1950, suggested the creation of an all-European army. (The Americans were very much in favor of the idea, and may have suggested it to Pleven.) This was a federalist idea par excellence, going to the heart of the sovereignty of the separate European states, that is, the control of their armies. As discussed in Chapter 3, it was hoped that this plan would allow the Europeans to thwart any aggressive designs the Russians might have, and to rearm the Germans without giving them control of weapons or troops. Spurred on, perhaps, by the beginning of the Korean War, and the fear that North Korea's attack was a diversionary tactic devised by the Russians to gain a free hand in Europe, five out of the six states involved in the plan to create the integrated European army (the European Defense Community) approved it. But in 1954, France, the last country to vote on the matter, officially rejected the scheme.

Part of the reason was that by 1954 the Russian threat seemed less ominous than when the plan was first suggested in 1950. Also, there may well have been some in the other countries to be included in the European Defense Community who voted for the plan, in order to avoid displeasing the Americans, who confidently expected the French to take them off the hook by sabotaging the whole idea. In any case, the federalist philosophy of economic integration died with the European Defense Community in 1954, at least for the foreseeable future.[25]

The functionalist (or neofunctionalist) philosophy of integration fared better. Functionalists argued that integration of independent states could best be brought about by creating first a central organization with authority only over technical economic tasks. According to this argument, the strength of such a central organization will grow with time. In its effort to coordinate, for example, the coal and steel industries of several states, it will find that it needs to expand authority over other related areas. As the member states see the economic benefits resulting from the activities of the central

[25] A safe prediction, since, if the unforeseen occurs even immediately, this merely fulfills the prediction by taking the future out of the foreseeable category.

organization, they will be willing to give that organization broader authority. So the integrating organization will be given control of manganese, perhaps, because this is an important ingredient in the steel making process. One technical task will "spill over" into other tasks until the integrating forces are virtually overwhelming. The functionalist organization will end up running everything, and at this stage the process of giving it political power will be little more than a formality to which the formerly independent member-states will have no objections.[26]

These ideas were put into practice by way of the Schuman plan (named for Robert Schuman, the French foreign minister) proposed in 1950. Devised by Jean Monnet, the plan called for the creation of a common market in Europe for the coal and steel industries. Eventually, in 1951, France, West Germany, Italy, Belgium, the Netherlands, and Luxembourg, signed the Treaty of Paris, launching the European Coal and Steel Community.

By almost any standard, the ECSC was an immediate success. The benefits its members derived were sufficiently obvious that by 1955 negotiations were under way that led to a more comprehensive approach to European integration. Negotiations culminated in the Treaty of Rome, signed by the same six states in 1957, and the creation of two new organizations, the European Economic Community (EEC) and the European Atomic Energy Community (EURATOM). These two organizations, together with the ECSC, make up what is known as the European Community (EC).

The European Community   The treaty outlined the structure of institutions for the European Community in a manner reminiscent of the Treaty of Paris. The community has, in effect, executive, legislative, and judicial institutions. The European Court of Justice, for example, fulfills a role in the community that is not totally unlike that of the Supreme Court in the United States. The court consists of nine judges who serve terms of six years. The primary function of the court is to settle disputes concerning the provisions of the treaties that established the community, as well as laws passed with respect to the treaties.

Although the court is clearly one of the more obscure institutions in the community, it has acquired supranational powers of some significance. In ordinary courts of international law, only states can be heard. Individuals are not allowed to take legal complaints to such courts, and states have traditionally insisted that this

[26]For a fuller discussion of these ideas, see David Mitrany, *A Working Peace System,* Royal Institute of International Affairs, London, 1943, and Ernst Haas, *The Uniting of Europe,* Stanford University Press, Stanford, 1958, especially Chapter 8.

custom be adhered to rigorously. But individuals in the European Community *can* be heard before the Court of Justice, and there have been cases in which the supreme court of a member state has deferred to the judgment of the Court of Justice.

The Court of Justice can also hear cases brought by member states, by other institutions of the community, and by corporations affected by treaty provisions. For example, if France imposes tariffs on inexpensive Italian wines, complaints against the tariffs by the Italian government, or the affected Italian companies, may be taken to the court, which will decide if the tariffs are legal according to the Rome treaty. The court hears a number of such cases every year and appears to be developing the potential, at least, to become a supranational judicial institution.[27]

The executive functions of the community are shared by the Commission and the Council of Ministers. (Originally, the ECSC, the EEC, and EURATOM had separate commissions and councils, but in 1967 they were unified into a single body serving all three organizations.) The Commission is the supranational part of this executive branch. It consists of thirteen members, appointed for four-year renewable terms, and they are supposed to act independently, in the name and interests of the community as a whole. The Council of Ministers, clearly the most powerful body in the community, consists of one minister (usually, but not always, the foreign minister) from each country. These ministers, of course, represent the separate interests of the member nations, and it is clear that virtually every measure of substantial importance must be approved by the Council of Ministers. If the community does, some day, become supranational, one of the most obvious institutional changes that will be required will involve giving the Commission greater independence from control by the Council.

As things stand now, the Commission has two major duties. The first is to present the Council of Ministers with policy proposals, which the Council approves or disapproves. (There is a European Parliament, but its legislative powers are limited, as will be seen.) On the face of it, the Commission is entirely at the mercy of the Council, but the Rome treaty provides for several procedural rules that give the Commission more power than it might seem to have at first glance. For example, the Commission sets the agenda for the Council. The Council can discuss only proposals put to it by the Commission. Also, the Council can amend these proposals only by unanimous vote. (It can pass some proposals by a weighted majority.) This puts the Council in a position where it must either

[27] Andrew Axline, *European Community Law and Organizational Development*, Oceana, Dobbs Ferry, N.Y., 1968.

accept what the Commission proposes, or try to come up with an amended proposal on which there is unanimous agreement. In short, the Council is limited in its maneuverability vis-à-vis the Commission, and this gives the Commission added influence over the policy-making process in the community.

The other main duty of the Commission is to supervise the execution of the treaties. It calls member countries, and affected companies, to account if they fail to observe the provisions of the treaties. As we have seen, as a last resort, the Commission can refer disputed cases to the Court of Justice, but as a matter of course it tries to settle the disputes before they reach that stage.

"Imagine a United States Congress whose members can advise but neither consent to nor pass laws, who belong both to their state legislatures and the national body, who speak six different languages and spring from nine distinct countries."[28] That may be the best way for an American to begin to understand the European Parliament. It is, at the same time, clearly the most powerless, and yet the most intriguing, of the major institutions of the community. Its members have very limited powers over the legislative process that takes place in the dialogue between the Commission and the Council. It can express nonbinding opinions on most measures proposed by the Commission before they go to the Council. It can also put oral and written questions to the Commission and the Council, and it seems to be making more effective use of this procedure as time goes by.

At bottom, the Parliament has two concrete powers. It can, if it fundamentally disagrees with the Commission, censure it, and this entails the removal of the commissioners. Only one censure motion has been introduced into the Parliament, in December 1972, and it was withdrawn because a new Commission was scheduled to succeed in any event in January 1973. This does not necessarily mean that the power to censure is meaningless. It could mean that the Parliament has not chosen to use the power because the Commission has always been very careful not to propose measures of which the Parliament disapproves. To some extent this is true, but the Parliament's influence has been limited (at least up to 1978; see following) by the fact that its members are only part-time employees. They are full-time members of their own national parliaments, and they have been able to devote only limited time and energy to their community duties.

The other concrete power given to the Parliament involves control over a portion of the community budget. That power was

[28]Nancy Hoepli, Editor's Introduction, in *The Common Market,* ed. Nancy L. Hoepli, Wilson, New York, 1975, p. 22.

increased in April, 1970, at the same time that the member states voted to give the community its own independent financial resources. To date, the Parliament controls about 5 percent of the budget, not a very large sum, but that portion is strategically placed in such a way that the Parliament's power over finances is larger than might be assumed given this small figure.

One of the more intriguing characteristics of the Parliament is the way its delegates sit, vote, and caucus. For the most part, they do not organize themselves along national lines. Rather, the members are organized along party lines, with Christian Democrats, Social Democrats, and Liberals from all countries voting and caucusing together on many issues. This supranational aspect of the Parliament will undoubtedly be strengthened if the community goes ahead with plans to follow the provision of the Treaty of Rome stipulating that the member states "draw up proposals for election by direct universal suffrage." At this writing, such direct elections to the European Parliament are scheduled for 1979. There are several issues that remain to be settled, probably the most important being the allocation of seats among the member countries. If all the problems are ironed out, and the direct elections to the European Parliament are actually held in 1979, this should strengthen the Parliament and the supranational thrust of the community. If not, while it might not mean the demise of European integration, it would surely be a serious setback.

The Process of Integration   How have the institutions of the EEC worked? One step toward answering that question would involve a discussion of a prior question, namely, what exactly are they trying to accomplish? The ultimate goals of the community are political, but the intermediate steps are economic. The first step in the economic integration process is the creation of a *free trade area*. Tariffs among the members of the organization are eliminated. This is supposed to increase trade among member states, but free trade areas can be infiltrated easily. A state outside the organization can simply export goods into the member state with the lowest tariffs. Once that is done, the goods can be exported from the member state to the other members of the organization *and* escape the tariffs of the other states as if they had come from within the free trade area.

An obvious solution to this problem is having the states in the organization adopt a common tariff to be applied to all imports coming from the outside. If this is accomplished the organization has reached the status of a *customs union*. The next step up the ladder of economic integration is the establishment of a *common market*. In

TABLE 4.2   A comparison of the European Community with the Soviet Union and the United States, 1973

	EC	US	SU
Population (millions)	260	210	249
GNP (1972) (billions of dollars)	902	1,150	410.5[a]
Percentage of world exports	37.2[b]	11.9[b]	3.6
Percentage of world imports	35.6[b]	12.9[b]	3.7
Gold, SDR's, convertible currency reserves	43.9	13.19	n.a.

[a]Estimated net material product 1971.
[b]Excludes trade with Communist countries in Asia.
Sources: Vision, no. 8/9 (July-August): 38; Statistical Offices of the European Communities, Basic Statistics of the Community (1974), pp. 73, 116; U.N. Statistical Office, Yearbook of International Trade Statistics (1973); U.S. Department of Commerce, Survey of Current Business. From The European Community in World Affairs: Political Influence and Economic Reality by Werner Feld. Copyright © 1976 by Alfred Publishing Co., Inc. Reprinted by permission of Alfred Publishing Co., Inc.

addition to the abolition of intraorganization tariffs and the creation of a common external tariff, a common market allows the free movement of the components of production, that is, capital and labor, across national boundaries. Entrepreneurs from one member state can invest, without restriction, in another member state, and workers may freely migrate to any state in the organization to find work. If the member states can cooperate to the extent that they jointly plan monetary, fiscal, and social policies, they have formed an *economic union.* If they turn the planning of these policies over to a unified, supranational body (such as the Commission of the EC), then total economic integration has been accomplished. According to functionalist ideas, once economic integration has reached this advanced stage, the central integrating organization will be running virtually everything anyway, so there will be no strong objection to advances toward political integration and the emergence of a new statelike entity.[29]

The Development of the Community   How far along in this process has the European Community come? It is clear that the Europeans have forged a significant economic unit. (See Table 4.2.) The Community is only one-sixth the size of the United States, but it has fifty million more people. In the mid-1970s, the community's GNP was over three-fourths that of the United States, and, by a

[29]Bela Balassa, *The Theory of Economic Integration,* Richard B. Irwin, Homewood, Ill., 1961, p. 2.

healthy margin, the community engages in more international trade than any state in the world. (It might be argued, though, that to the extent this volume of trade is a reflection of dependence by Europe on imports of scarce resources such as oil, it is an indication of weakness rather than strength.) Intraorganization trade is up dramatically since 1958, somewhere in the neighborhood of 900 percent. By 1968, ahead of schedule, tariffs among the members had been abolished, and the common external tariff was established. The Rome treaty established freedom of movement for workers, and capital has moved with more, but not unrestricted, freedom within the organization since 1958.

This does not mean that the community has had smooth sailing all the way. Far from it. Almost simultaneous with the beginning of the EEC came the rise to power of Charles de Gaulle in France. First, de Gaulle proposed the Fouchet plan, the purpose of which was to rob the community of some of its supranational pretensions. The other five member states rejected this plan. Then, when the British decided that they would like to enter the community (in 1963) de Gaulle vetoed their application, largely on the grounds that Britain would serve as a Trojan horse for the United States. By 1965, de Gaulle was accusing the Commission of the EEC of acting like a government. He was particularly concerned because, by the beginning of 1966, the community was scheduled to settle an increasing number of issues by majority vote in the Council of Ministers. Faced with the prospect of being outvoted on matters crucial to France and an inability to veto proposals passed by an anti-French majority, de Gaulle decided to boycott the community in June 1965, walking out of the organization's meetings. The conflict between France and the rest of the community was not solved until January 1966. A compromise was reached which reduced the Commission's powers and increased the supervisory powers of the Council of Ministers. The document also instructed the Commission to stop acting like a government. France did agree to accept increased application of majority voting in the Council of Ministers, but stipulated that when vital national interests were at stake, discussions should continue until unanimity is reached. In short, it is doubtful that this agreement deserves the label *compromise*. In essence, France got its way, agreeing to an official acceptance of majority voting with very little substance.

De Gaulle vetoed a British move to enter the community again in 1967, but probably the most important developments for the community from 1966 (when the compromise bringing France back into the community was reached) to 1973 (when Britain, along with Denmark and Ireland, entered the community) involved its relationship with the United States. First, there was the invasion by the multinational corporations (MNCs), most of them American based. When the community was first formed, several business interests in the United States were rather concerned that the higher tariff barriers created by the community would be harmful to them. By 1965, the corporations had found a way around, or over this problem. Instead of relying on the export of goods from the United States to Europe, the MNCs set up subsidiaries inside the Common Market, and thus benefited as much, if not more, from the free trade area and the customs union as European firms. On the one hand, there is little doubt that these American subsidiaries helped stimulate the rapid economic growth that the Europeans enjoyed in the late 1960s. On the other hand, the multinational corporations were so successful that many Europeans began to worry about the influx of American money and technology. Jean Jacques Servan-Schreiber, in *The American Challenge,*[30] warned Europeans that if present trends continued, Europe would be threatened with thorough "Americanization," and this was a warning that some Europeans took to heart.

The Community and the United States   While Europeans worried about being smothered in an American economic embrace, they also began to be concerned about being relegated to a secondary status in terms of American international political commitments. This was, of course, because the United States became increasingly preoccupied with Southeast Asia, Vietnam in particular. At least some European political leaders had ideological objections to the American war effort, and they objected even more to the fact that the war meant the Americans had little in the way of resources and energy left over to devote to European matters.

But the most dramatic impact of the war in Vietnam on relations between the United States and Europe occurred because the Americans refused to pay for the war as they were fighting it. President Johnson insisted on adhering to a business-as-usual economic policy even as the costs of the war skyrocketed. One of the results of this policy was an increasingly bad balance of trade, from the American point of view, between the United States and Europe. In short, Americans were, month after month, importing much more from Europe than they were exporting there. According to the international economic system set up after the Second World War, there were two basic ways to settle accounts that became unbalanced. The state experiencing the trade deficit could pay

[30] Atheneum, New York, 1968.

off the debt with gold or dollars. The dollar was a universally accepted international currency, as good as gold, because the United States government backed dollars with a promise that they could be exchanged for gold at any time.

In the first decade after the war, this system worked fairly well because of the great strength of the American economy, and because the United States government possessed a large amount of gold. But by the time John Kennedy was elected president, pressures on the price of gold in terms of dollars increased substantially, and the United States formed a gold pool with several other industrialized countries in order to deal with these pressures. The countries in the pool sold gold in order to lower the price if it rose above a thirty-five-dollar-an-ounce standard, and bought gold to support the price if it fell below the standard. "But the Vietnam conflict and the refusal of the Johnson Administration to pay for it and for its Great Society programs through taxation resulted in an increased dollar outflow to pay for the military expenses and in rampant inflation, which led to a deterioration in the American balance of trade position."[31] The American solution to these problems was to print dollars faster. The trouble with the solution was that the Europeans (and others) found themselves flooded with dollars. By March 1968, the non-American members of the gold pool had lost all patience, the Americans had so little gold on hand that they were unable to meet another day's sales, and the gold pool was dissolved.[32]

President Nixon continued the war in Vietnam, and in 1970 decided to reinflate the American economy, apparently for domestic political reasons. (Specifically, to help Republicans get elected that year and to further his own chances in 1972.) By May 1971, there were an estimated fifty to sixty million Eurodollars in circulation, almost equal to the sum of dollars in the United States, and by late summer, for the first time in the twentieth century, the United States went into a balance of trade deficit. Nixon pressured the Europeans (and the Japanese) to revalue their own currencies to

[31]Joan Edelman Spero, *The Politics of International Economic Relations*, St. Martin's Press, New York, 1977, p. 48.

[32]Michael Hudson insists (on the basis, it must be admitted, of very little evidence) that as a result of this crisis, "On March 31, 1968, millions of Americans heard Lyndon Johnson announce over television that he would not run again for the presidency, and that he would not substantially escalate the Vietnam war despite the Tet Offensive. Unperceived by the public at large, the point had finally been reached at which depletion of U.S. gold holdings abruptly altered the country's military policy. As one expert noted, 'The European financiers are forcing peace on us. For the first time in American history, our European creditors have forced the resignation of an American president.' " See *Super Imperialism,* Holt, Rinehart, & Winston, New York, 1972, pp. 228–229.

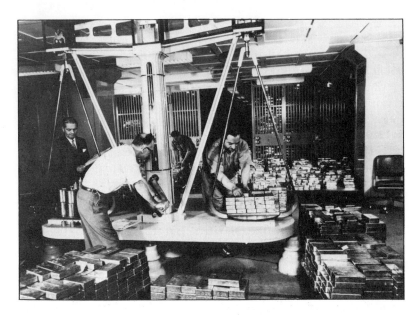

Gold bars such as these (at the Federal Reserve bank in New York) left the U.S. in large numbers during the Vietnam War. Wide World Photo.

take some of the pressure off the dollar. Finally, when they refused, in August 1971, President Nixon announced that the dollar would be unhinged from gold. Past promises were renounced: dollars could no longer be exchanged for gold.

If a "banana republic" had tried such a strategy, it would have been disastrous for its international economic standing. And even for the United States, the step represented an admission that it could not dominate international trade and finance in the manner to which it had become accustomed after the Second World War. But the results of the move proved to be much less than disastrous for the dollar, at least partly because neither the Europeans nor the Japanese nor any of the other countries with large dollar holdings could afford to make the United States pay for its broken promises. European countries in particular held such a significant portion of their reserves in dollars that any damage to the dollar would hurt them almost as much as the United States. And the Europeans are so dependent on the United States as an outlet for their exports that damage done to it by way of "revenge" would also be harmful to Europe. So, in the past, the dollar had been the pre-eminent international currency because the United States had an abundant supply of gold, and several countries owed it large debts. Now, paradoxically, the dollar became a powerful currency, in part, because the United States had lost a large portion of its gold holdings, and the United States owed, in effect, large debts (in the form of unredeemed, and now unredeemable, dollars) to the Europeans.[33]

New Problems for the Community   In the middle 1970s, the community wrestled with serious problems brought about by the Arab use of the "oil weapon" and a prolonged recession. Europe depends on the Middle East for about 60 percent of its oil, and when the Arab countries slowed down the production of oil and picked Holland as a target for a complete boycott, significant centrifugal pressures were put on the community. Each of the member states scrambled in a rather unseemly fashion to make separate deals with the Arabs, and the community took no effective steps, at least officially, to help Holland in its time of need. The recession exacerbated several already serious problems and, combined with the energy crisis, served to scuttle entirely (or so it seemed) the plans the community had to launch a monetary union, based on a common currency for all the members, by 1980. These problems were so grave that it seemed possible the community might be faced with total dissolution.

And there are several important factors that tend to pull the community apart. Aside from the obvious historical enmities and cultural differences (especially in religion and language), two of the most serious problems involve Germany. By 1975, the Germanization of Europe seemed to have almost replaced the vintage 1960s fear concerning possible Americanization. Germany's is the largest and strongest economy in the community, and it consistently sells more than it buys from its fellow community members. In addition, the Germans consistently contribute much more to the various redistributive programs sponsored by the community than they receive. "On the one hand, the affluent West Germans . . . are increasingly reluctant to finance the needs of the poorer members of the European Community. . . . On the other hand, the poorer countries in the Market are beginning to resent this excessive dependence on West Germany."[34]

The specter of German economic domination of the community would not be a welcome one in the best of times, but the problem threatens to dissolve the community during a recessionary period like the mid-1970s. If cheap German products flood the market of, say, Italy and put Italians out of work, the situation is tolerable if economic conditions in Italy allow the unemployed a

[33]Hudson, *Super Imperialism,* pp. 231–251.
[34]Tad Szulc, "Fractious Common Market," *The New Republic,* November 20, 1976, p. 17.

reasonable chance to find alternative employment. But in a recession, the influx of German goods may deprive Italians of jobs when they have no prospect of finding another. The pressure to keep German goods out of Italy in a situation such as this might well escalate to a point that Italian politicians could not withstand. If they give in to this pressure, it might ignite a process that could result in the dismantling of the community.

This would be especially true if Germany is also experiencing economic difficulties. One of the first retaliatory measures that would occur to the Germans in this scenario would probably be the deportation of Italian workers. Again, if times are good, the "guest workers" take only menial jobs and are not generally resented. But if jobs are scarce, they may well be seen as competitors for the few jobs available and as workers whose minimal wage demands exert a depressing effect on the wages of all workers. The pressure to get rid of them might well become irresistible.

The other potentially serious problem involving Germany's relationship with the rest of the community arises from the possibility that, instead of dominating it, Germany may leave it altogether. According to this scenario, the German departure would be brought about by the Soviets, who have rarely had anything good to say about the EC.

> The Soviet Union has the power to keep the Europeans from unifying. In its drive to accomplish this, it is trying first to woo Germany. . . . The specific bribe that Russia holds out to Bonn is the right to be the undisputed No. 1 country in trade with East Europe . . . when the trade has grown important enough, U.S.S.R. will make pointed suggestions about Germany's stand on East-West issues.[35]

In favor of the plausibility of this scenario, it might be pointed out that in addition to economic benefits, the Russians might offer West Germany the possibility of reunification with East Germany. Some West Germans have always worried about the impact of EC membership on the chances for reunification. If the Russians do successfully get the West Germans dependent on trade with Eastern Europe and then insist that they make a choice between the EC and reunification, might not the Germans choose the latter?

[35] Charles Cerami, *Crisis: The Loss of Europe,* Harcourt Brace Jovanovich, New York, 1975, pp. 166–167.

Possibly, but there are at least a couple of reasons why such a scenario seems unlikely to develop. First, it is rather difficult to believe that the Soviets would want the Germans to become that closely intertwined in East European economic affairs. Being good Marxists, they are fully aware of the power of economic forces and are likely to be sensitive to the possible detrimental effects of economic ties between Eastern Europe and West Germany. In 1968, one of the important reasons that the Soviet Union invaded Czechoslovakia was that the Czechs were on the verge of establishing closer economic bonds with West Germany. If the Soviets were so concerned about it then, why would they want to give West Germany free entry into all of Eastern Europe?

Second, even assuming that the Soviets would be inclined to set such a trap, it is unlikely that the West Germans could be enticed into it. True, they would probably benefit from increased trade with Eastern Europe, and there is little doubt that most West Germans would like to see their country reunified. But a West Germany that renounced the EC and the West, without possessing nuclear weapons, would be at the mercy of the Soviet Union. Such a prospect could not be attractive to West Germany, no matter how great the possible economic benefits of trade with Eastern Europe or how appealing reunification may be.

"Eurocommunism" is another possible threat to the future of the community. If the Communist party successfully achieves an important role in the governments of France or Italy, this might have an unsettling effect on other community members. The Communist party of Italy, in particular, has come around to a position ostensibly in favor of the EC, but even if it sticks to that position once its members get into the government, the distrust it might evoke elsewhere could prove to be an important obstacle to the progress of the community.

The Future of the Community   In the long run, though, this writer at least, expects the European Community to overcome the obstacles, for several reasons. One is that economies of the member states are becoming progressively more closely intertwined, despite the general gloom-and-doom attitude prevalent in European circles in the 1970s. Even though multinational corporations have sparked some fears in Europe, and monetary crises have hindered their freedom of movement, they continue to exploit markets all over Europe. They will not want to see access to the enlarged market provided by the EC taken away, and they can exert an important influence to keep it together. Labor unions, faced with these corporations

which can jump from one country to another to avoid union demands, are beginning to realize that the only way to deal with this
tactic successfully is to organize internationally. Intracommunity
trade is now so substantial that the member states export inflation
and other economic problems, as well as goods and services, to
each other. It is increasingly useless for them to attempt to deal
with these economic problems without consultation and joint planning.[36]

Even in bad economic times, there is a clear majority of Europeans who want to see the community continue to exist. Older
Europeans remember one or both world wars. Younger ones are
perhaps more impressed by the steady economic progress with
which the community has so far been associated. Public opinion is
fickle, of course, but for now at least it seems to be a force working
in the community's favor.

But probably the most important factors holding Europe together are political, economic, and military pressures from the outside world. In short, if the Europeans do not hang together, they
will hang separately. They are, for example, increasingly vulnerable to political and military pressures from the Soviet Union. If the
Americans do what they have been talking about for many years
now, that is, pull their troops out of Europe, this will increase
European vulnerability and the danger of "Finlandization." If the
European states break up economically, they are faced with the
prospect of being swamped by the United States, Japan, and maybe
even Brazil, in the future. Robbed of economic importance, they are
not likely to count for very much in international political terms,
either.

Of course, just because it might be irrational for the community to disband does not mean that it will not happen. Fears,
jealousies, and antagonisms have caused the Europeans to commit
irrational acts in the past. It is even possible that, far from pro-
gressing toward unity, the member states will fall apart. It is conceivable that Scotland, Wales, and Northern Ireland will separate
from England. The Flemish and the Walloons waste no love on one
another in Belgium. Relatively industrialized northern Italy has
never been particularly well integrated with rural southern Italy.

On the brighter side, it is also possible that the European
Community will expand dramatically. Greece has already officially
applied for full membership, and at this writing the application is
being studied by the community. Spain and Portugal have also
expressed a clear desire to join. Not too long ago, all of these states

[36]"Emu is dead: What next?" *The Economist,* August 23, 1975, p. 22.

would have been automatically excluded because of the dictatorial nature of their political systems. Now, it is their relatively under-developed economic systems that provide the major obstacle to entry. Most of the industries in these states could not compete with those in the rest of the community, and it is very likely that Greece, Portugal, and Spain will want to protect their industries. They might also want to protect some areas of agriculture. In short, what Greece, Portugal, and Spain would like to have is free access to the markets of the community while barring access by the community members to their markets. Even though they will certainly be willing to compromise in order to get into the community, neither Greece, Portugal, nor Spain is wealthy enough to provide first-rate markets for the manufacturers in the community. Further-more, these three countries would put additional demands on the various redistributive finds set up by the community in recent years. Countries like Germany, which contribute more to these funds than they collect, cannot be happy about this prospect. Brit-ain and Italy, which take more out of than they put in the social funds, must also worry about competition from even more needy states. Considering these problems, one cannot help wondering if the community would be wise to add such countries as Greece, Spain, and Portugal to their number. Still, if the application of Greece is accepted, that might be a signal of the community's inten-tions with respect to the other two countries, and possibly Turkey.

Economic Integration Among Developing Nations
The thrust toward international integration has a different emphasis in the Third World. In Europe, the primary motive, at least in the beginning, was probably the avoidance of war. In the developing world, the primary motive for integration is quite clearly economic. The hope is that by joining together the markets of several small countries, the economic systems of all the countries will benefit from economies of scale. In many cases, each develop-ing country alone, for example, cannot provide a market big enough to make it profitable to set up expensive factories that produce heavy machinery. But if the markets of several small coun-tries are combined, a firm with access to the enlarged market may be able to survive and help the members of the integrating organi-zation develop economically.

Third World political leaders also hope that economic integra-tion will allow them to deal better with what they see as unfair competition from industrialized countries. The United States has often warned Third World countries, especially in Latin America, about the dangers of setting up high tariff walls to protect infant industries. In the American view, such tariffs protect inefficiency and thus result in an overall decrease in productivity, which hurts everyone involved. Most Third World countries have been reluctant to accept this kind of free trade philosophy. They argue that if every country specializes in the production of the goods they produce most efficiently, the result will be a continuation of the present unsatisfactory international division of labor. The industrialized countries will continue to produce the vast majority of processed manufactured goods, while the Third World will be condemned to second-class status, producing agricultural products and raw materials. In order to avoid this fate, most Third World nations feel that they must adopt protective tariffs, even if this does mean, temporarily at least, they will have to pay higher prices for goods manufactured by their own infant, and inefficient, industries. Advocates of integration in the Third World believe that erecting a tariff wall around a larger market than can be provided by most single developing nations will shorten the period of infancy and allow industries in developing countries to reach a level of efficiency competitive with other industries more rapidly than would otherwise be the case.

Obstacles to Integration In theory, the argument for economic integration sounds convincing. In practice, the results of integration efforts in the Third World have been mixed, at best, with no Third World organization even approaching the level of institutional development of the European Community. One reason may be that functionalism does not work as well in less industrialized countries. The economies are less complex, which makes spillover from one technical economic task to another less likely to occur. Even when spillover does occur, the typical integrating organization in the developing countries lacks the necessary administrative and bureaucratic talent to take advantage of the situation. (In contrast, "Eurocrats" are in abundant supply to take advantage of any opportunity to expand the role of the EC.)

These factors are important impediments to integration in the Third World, but there is little doubt that the most serious obstacle arises from the creation of problems inside the integrating organization that are similar to the problems in the outside world that developing countries in such organizations are trying to escape. One of the important motives for integration in the developing world, again, is the hope that free trade areas and/or customs unions will allow industries in these countries a chance to survive in competition with corporations in the developed countries. But when developing countries get together in an integrating organization, they create inside the organizations the kind of market pressures and unfair advantages for relatively developed states that exist in the outside world. For example, industries attracted by the commercial opportunities inside a new customs union will tend to gravitate to the state in the organization that is relatively advanced economically, because the state will probably have a larger supply of workers used to the rigors of industrial labor; in addition, the infrastructure (roads, ports, and so on) will be better equipped to handle the demands of modern business and the consumers in that country will have more money to buy goods produced by the new firm. This does not mean that, necessarily, inside a customs union, where free trade and a free market prevail, the rich get richer and the poor get poorer. It does probably mean, though, that the rich will experience a disproportionate share of some benefits brought about by the integration process.[37] In turn, even if every state in the organization is better off than before integration began, the gap between the richer and poorer states may grow. And the growing gap has produced tensions inside regional economic integration organizations that, almost constantly, threaten to tear them apart.

The East African Community   The strength of these kinds of centrifugal pressures in the developing world is quite obvious in East Africa. There was an East African Common Market as early as 1917 (between Kenya and Uganda), which expanded in 1927 with the inclusion of Tanganyika. As the independence of these countries became imminent in the early 1960s, the value of their common market became a political issue. After Tanganyika (which became known as Tanzania with the addition of Zanzibar in 1964) and Uganda achieved independence (a few months before Kenya became independent), the political leaders of all three countries declared in June 1963 the intention of creating a federation of East Africa within a year. Before the year elapsed, the East African Common Services Organization (EACSO) established in 1961 and providing the basis for the proposed federation, was on the verge of breaking up. The reasons were complex, but clearly one important reason was that Tanzanian and Ugandan political leaders believed that Kenya was receiving an unfair portion of the benefits from the integration process.

[37]See Gunnar Myrdal, *Rich Lands and Poor,* Harper, New York, 1957, for a discussion of spread and backwash effects of free trade between areas of different levels of development.

The statistics which showed that between 1960 and 1964 the gross domestic product as a whole and of each sector of the economy expanded faster in Tanzania and Uganda than in Kenya did not convince them to the contrary. In fact, more attention was paid to the statistics of inter-territorial trade, which showed increasing surpluses for Kenya and deficits for Uganda and Tanzania. . . . These imbalances in trade were taken to demonstrate the unbalanced distribution of benefits.[38]

Despite the tensions, leaders of all three countries apparently perceived sufficient potential benefits from economic integration that they managed to sign, in 1967, the Treaty for East African Cooperation, creating the East African Community (EAC). This treaty was designed to distribute the benefits of integration more equally than they would be if free-market forces were allowed to operate in an untrammeled fashion. For example:

The provisions dealing with trade within the Community authorize states that incur an unfavorable balance of trade within another member of the Community to tax the imports from countries with surpluses up to the amount of the deficits incurred. In effect, Tanzania is permitted to tax goods coming from Uganda and Kenya, and Uganda can tax Kenyan goods. Kenya, however, is not allowed to tax either Tanzanian or Ugandan goods.[39]

Despite such arrangements, by the middle of the 1970s the East African Community was on the brink of dissolution. The rise to power of Idi Amin in Uganda in 1971 was one blow to unity. The socialism of Tanzania, compared to the free-enterprise-oriented economy of Kenya, also led to a certain amount of antagonism. But the basic problem is that both Tanzanian and Ugandan leaders continue to believe that Kenya enjoys a disproportionate share of the benefits of integration, and that unless the rules of the community are structured even more than they are in favor of the relatively poorer countries, they will be economically dominated by Kenya. And they may be right. In any case, the future of economic integration in East Africa is not bright.

[38] Arthur Hazlewood, *Economic Integration: The East African Experience,* Heineman, London, 1975, p. 56.
[39] Dennis L. Dresang and Ira Sharkansky, "Public Corporations in Single-Country and Regional Settings: Kenya and the East African Community," *International Organization,* 27 (Summer 1973), 303–328.

The Latin American Free Trade Association   Regional integration efforts in Latin America have run into strikingly similar problems. In 1960, ten South American countries, later joined by Mexico, formed the Latin American Free Trade Association (LAFTA). The members of this organization are so disparate in character, and spread over such a huge area that the effort may have been doomed to failure from the beginning. Adding to this probability was the severely restrained enthusiasm of the United States for the venture. By the mid-1960s, though, the problem of enthusiasm had solved itself. American investors had learned from their experience in Europe that the creation of regional economic integration organizations need not be inimical to their interests. American-owned subsidiaries set up inside the European Common Market took good advantage of the commercial opportunities there. But for that very reason, many Latin Americans began to fear that LAFTA might benefit North American corporations more than local firms, and they began to doubt the wisdom of strengthening the organization.

But an even more serious problem confronting LAFTA in the late sixties stemmed from the inequalities in the stages of economic development of the member states. That these inequalities could lead to problems was recognized by the founders of the organization, and the realization led to a division of the member states into three categories. Argentina, Brazil, and Mexico were the most developed and comprised the first group. Chile, Colombia, Peru, Uruguay, and Venezuela were categorized as countries with insufficient domestic markets, while Bolivia, Ecuador, and Paraguay qualified as countries of lesser relative development. When LAFTA was founded, the least developed nations were given trade concessions and the right to adopt protective policies for the sake of their few industries. Unfortunately, this foresight has not paid off.

> The trade preferences have not resulted . . . in a significant reduction of Ecuador, Bolivia, and Paraguay's trade deficit with the zone, nor have the middle countries (Chile, Colombia, Peru, Uruguay, and Venezuela) that later asked for special treatment been able to improve their trade positions within the area.[40]

The Andean Common Market   By 1966, six nations in LAFTA became so dissatisfied with what they perceived to be the unequal

[40]Joseph Grunwald, Miguel S. Wionczek, and Martin Carnoy, *Latin American Economic Integration and U.S. Policy,* Brookings Institution, Washington, D.C., 1972, pp. 52–53.

distribution of benefits within the organization that they began to move toward the creation of a separate organization. Within three years Bolivia, Chile, Colombia, Ecuador, and Peru signed the Andean Subregional Integration Agreement, calling for the creation of a common market. (The Andean group was eventually joined by Venezuela.) This organization was later approved by LAFTA, so it is not, strictly speaking, a competitive organization. It is hoped the Andean group will progress to the point where it can rejoin the other LAFTA members and enjoy the benefits of integration on a more equal basis.

The integration agreement appears to be well devised to bring about equal benefits. First, the least developed nations, Bolivia and Ecuador, are given special treatment so that they might receive an equal share of the benefits. And this group has adopted a whole series of stringent rules regarding foreign investment, which, it is hoped, will minimize some of the undesirable effects such investments have brought in the past. For example, there are limits on the amount of money foreign corporations can take out of the member states in the form of repatriated profits. Investments in such sensitive areas as banking are restricted. Within fifteen or twenty years, foreign-owned industries must be transformed into jointly owned firms, with domestic interests having majority control.

Rules for foreign investors have proved difficult to enforce. The multinational corporations have successfully convinced member states to allow exceptions in several cases. In Peru, a modernizing military government that made its reputation by devising apparently strict controls on foreign investment (which served as the inspiration for the controls adopted by the Andean Common Market) appears to be backing away from them. Chile, under the post-Allende regime, has been so desperate to attract foreign investment that it has, temporarily at least, abandoned both the rules controlling foreign investment and active participation in the Andean Common Market. And, predictably, despite the special arrangements on their behalf, Bolivia and Ecuador may not be enjoying a proportionate share of the benefits of the integration process. Political spokesmen for the two countries at least seem to feel this is the case, and doubts about the value of membership in the Andean Common Market are increasingly public and usual in these countries.

The Central American Common Market　　Probably the most successful integration effort in Latin America has been in Central America. A decade of careful preparation resulted in the creation of the Central American Common Market (CACM) in 1960. Guatemala, El

Salvador, Honduras, Nicaragua, and later Costa Rica, agreed to establish a common market by 1966. The founders of the organization were aware of the necessity to take steps to assure an equal distribution of benefits. Plans were made to establish integration industries; these industries would be given incentives to distribute themselves in each of the member countries, instead of congregating in the more developed ones. A Central American Economic Integration bank was created to provide financing for projects in such a way that benefits from integration would be equally distributed.

The CACM made significant progress in its first decade. Intraregional trade increased, and industrial products accounted for a larger portion of the trade than previously. By the middle of the 1960s, intraregional trade was free for all except about 20 percent of the products involved, and uniform external tariffs had been set on more than 80 percent of the goods imported into the region. The common market seemed to be responsible for a significant increase in the flow of foreign investment into the area. The rate of economic growth in Central America increased substantially.[41]

But progress toward integration in Central America came to a crashing halt in 1969 when war broke out between El Salvador and Honduras. Honduras pulled out of the common market as a result of the conflict. Postwar negotiations revealed that Honduras had been dissatisfied with the common market in any case, for the eminently predictable reason. Honduras, along with Nicaragua the least developed country in the area, felt itself the victim of unfair competition. For some time, it appeared that the problem might be insurmountable.

> Agreeing that the problem of unequal participation in the benefits of regional integration was the main obstacle to the revival of CACM, the majority of member countries showed willingness to establish . . . a special fund for financing industrial and agricultural expansion that would give priority to Honduras and Nicaragua. But El Salvador refused to adhere to that fund, nullifying any other progress.[42]

[41]One writer, though, attributes only about 1 % of the increase to the effect of the common market. See Donald H. McClellan, "The Common Market's Contribution to Central American Economic Growth: A First Approximation," in *The Movement Toward Latin American Unity,* ed. Ronald Hilton, Praeger, New York, 1969, pp. 508–536.
[42]Grunwald, Wionzcek, and Carnoy, *Latin American Economic Integration,* p. 49.

By 1976, fortunately, the cold war between El Salvador and Honduras was officially brought to an end, and the CACM seems to be back on the right track. Whether or not the benefits of integration will be distributed in such a way as to satisfy Honduras and Nicaragua remains to be seen.

The Future of Integration   In short, the prospects for economic integration and unification of separate states in the Third World are not very encouraging. About the best that can be said for the probability of integration occurring despite these gloomy prospects is that it may be absolutely necessary if these countries are to develop economically. Certainly many Third World states are too small to entertain realistic hopes of development on their own.[43]

For this reason, the ultimate aim of integration organizations such as those in East Africa and Latin America is the creation of new nation-states, or at least new political entities with statelike characteristics. Unfortunately, the history of nation building in the nineteenth and twentieth centuries suggests that the peaceful emergence of new states is unlikely. The United States, for example, fought a war to gain its independence and engaged in a bloody civil war in the course of its integration process. Italy and Germany, the two most important new states to integrate and emerge in nineteenth-century Europe, did so in a process involving international warfare. Russia was unified forcibly by the czarist regime and then the Bolsheviks. History will not necessarily repeat itself in the Third World, of course, but contemporary events indicate a high probability that nation building, especially when it involves the integration of disparate regions and cultures (as it virtually always does), will be a violent process. Consider the recent civil wars in Pakistan, Nigeria, and Yemen. Can the process of nation building in southern Africa be completed without more violence than has already occurred in Angola, South Africa, and Rhodesia? The emergence of Israel has certainly been violent, as was the integration of North and South Vietnam. The exception to this rule of violence in the Third World is Latin America. The only full scale war in this century in that area was the Chaco War between Bolivia and Paraguay in the 1930s. It is probably not a coincidence that Latin American nations, as Third World nations go, emerged a long time ago, at the beginning of the nineteenth century. They have already gone through the violent upheavals that typically accompany the nation-building process. Generally speaking, though

[43]Not all economists agree with this assessment. See, for example, Simon Kuznets, "Economic Growth of Small Nations," in *The Economic Consequences of the Size of Nations,* ed. Austin Robinson, Macmillan, London, 1960, pp. 14–32.

economic integration might help create new and larger states in the Third World in the years to come, the chances seem good that the process will not be a peaceful one.

Universal Peace-Keeping Organizations

The first serious attempt to establish continuing international institutions to deal with threats to peace was made in the aftermath of the Napoleonic wars at the beginning of the nineteenth century. The Congress of Vienna, a meeting attended only by major powers, dealt with several unsettled political problems and agreed to periodic consultations that became known as the Concert of Europe. This agreement led to a series of international meetings in the next decade that were unprecedented because they occurred during times of peace. But as seen earlier, the grand coalition, which served as the basis for the concert, was prone to disunity, and though the concert did successfully establish the precedent of peacetime consultations, after the first decade of existence it met only in the aftermath of wars to arrange settlements.

International organization on the level of functional organizations made significant advances in the nineteenth century. Various river commissions were created for the purpose of regulating international commerce and transport, and organizations such as the International Telecommunications Organization (1875), the Universal Postal Union (1874), and the International Office of Weights and Measures (1875) were established. These institutions are not directly related to peacekeeping, but according to a form of functionalist theory as applied to economic integration, they may ultimately serve that end. If the tasks that these organizations undertake proliferate, it is possible they will eventually control such a significant portion of international intercourse that they could serve as a basis for some type of world government; at least, a world of states that has become so closely intertwined in a mesh of functional activities, and appreciative of the benefits brought by functional organizations, would be unlikely, according to this functionalist theory, to collapse into international warfare.

International peace conferences at the Hague in 1899 and 1907 were meant to deal more directly with the threat of war by decreasing armament levels. They failed. Still, they began an important trend toward democracy of sorts in international diplomacy because, for the first time at such conferences, small states were invited and given a voice. Only twenty-six states attended the 1899 conference, but forty-four sent delegations to the 1907 meeting.

The latter meeting might be considered the precedent for the establishment of such institutions as the General Assembly of the United Nations.

The League of Nations

The next Hague conference was scheduled for 1915. It was not held, for obvious reasons, but the process leading to the outbreak of the war convinced many leaders that some permanent international organization needed to be established. In retrospect, many political leaders and scholars concluded that the First World War had occurred because the decision makers involved had lost control of a situation that none of them wanted to see culminate in a war. If, this reasoning went, there had been a chance to talk things out, a cooling-off period, none of the conflicts that created the crisis would have proved insoluble. The League of Nations, it was hoped, would provide a place where future crises could be talked over and procedures taken that would institutionalize a cooling-off period. During the First World War, private societies advocating the establishment of the league sprang up in England, France, Italy, and the United States. Wilson included the creation of such an organization as one of his famous fourteen points. A South African, Jan Smuts, published a pamphlet calling for the creation of the league, and it proved to be influential, perhaps because of good timing. (It was published in the month between Wilson's arrival in Europe and the beginning of the peace conference.) In any case, the structure of the league was much like that outlined in Smut's publication. Its three major organs were the Assembly, the Council, and a Secretariat. The Assembly consisted of delegations from all the member states, and its main duties involved the election of new members to the organization, debate and discussion of political and economic questions of international interest, and preparation of the annual budget. The Council was dominated by the great powers, but also contained nonpermanent members whose identity and number varied throughout the history of the league. Its most important duty was the resolution of international disputes. To that end it had the power to advise the member states to institute sanctions against any state committing aggression. The Secretariat was an international civil service that handled administrative details for the league and compiled information relevant to the various problems and issues with which the league was confronted.

The league will always be most famous for its failures, but it was not a total failure. It set precedents, in the establishment of the Secretariat and in the way the entire organization was structured, that provided valuable lessons for those who later established the

United Nations. The league is well remembered for the disputes it did not settle, but it did play a role in the resolution of some conflicts, such as the one between Greece and Bulgaria in 1925.

While the league's covenant provided for potentially effective economic and military sanctions against aggressors, it allowed each member to decide whether aggression had been committed and if sanctions would be applied. These loopholes were not in the covenant as a result of oversight. The founders of the league insisted that they be present. And it seems unlikely that the absence of loopholes would have made any real difference in the behavior of the league members. That is, even if the covenant's articles had made it mandatory for states to apply sanctions, it is unlikely that the states would have been inclined to do so.

Much the same kind of argument can be made about the most notorious flaw in the structure of the league, the absence of the United States. This was brought about by Wilson's unwillingness to consult and compromise with the United States Senate when the covenant was being drafted, by a bitter personal feud between Wilson and Senator Henry Cabot Lodge, and by widespread isolationist sentiment among a significant number of Americans. In any case, after the demise of the league, and the attendant world war, a powerful myth developed that implies the United States' refusal to join the league was a crucial cause of failure. If the United States had not shunned its duty, according to this myth, the league might have been powerful enough to withstand the aggressive policies of Japan, Italy, and Germany.

> This thesis seems dubious, however, when one finds that the desire of the United States in 1931 to avoid any provocation of Japan in order not to aggravate the situation differed very little from the desire of the United Kingdom in 1935 to avoid undue provocation of Italy. One wonders whether membership in the League really would have induced the United States to adopt policies other than those it actually pursued in the Manchurian and Ethiopian crises.[44]

In other words, it does not seem likely that mere formal membership in the league would have changed the foreign policy of the United States very much. If one remembers that the major threats to the league occurred when the United States was in the throes of a

[44]Gerhart Niemeyer, "The Balance-Sheet of the League Experiment," in *The United Nations Political System,* ed. David A. Kay, Wiley, 1967, p. 49.

depression, it seems more likely that the Americans might have withdrawn from the league, if the United States had been a member, rather than energetically pursue obligations under the covenant.

The United Nations: In the beginning

Myth or not, the idea that the failure of the United States to enter the league was a terrible mistake that played a significant role in the process bringing about the Second World War became widely accepted in the United States. The best evidence is the energetic manner in which the American government pushed for the creation of, and became a member of, the league's successor. By October 1943, the governments of the United States, Great Britain, the Soviet Union, and China declared their firm intention to create an international peace-keeping organization after the war. The intention was reaffirmed at several wartime meetings of the allied coalition, and the final charter was hammered out at a meeting in San Francisco in the spring of 1945. The charter was completed in June, and by July the United States Senate had approved it by a vote of 89 to 2. The contrast with the American reaction to the league some twenty-five years earlier could hardly have been more stark. The distinction was made even sharper by the choice of New York as the home of the United Nations.

The structure of the United Nations shares many features with that of the league. The Security Council, according to the charter, has the primary responsibility for international peace and security. The five permanent members, China, France, Great Britain, the Soviet Union, and the United States, have the power of veto in the Security Council. Ten nonpermanent members also serve on the Security Council. The Economic and Social Council (ECOSOC) handles the economic and social programs of the United Nations, serving as a clearing house and central administrative body for the associated functional organizations, such as the International Labor Organization (ILO), the International Monetary Fund (IMF), and the World Health Organization (WHO). The Trusteeship Council monitors the administration of non–self-governing territories transferred from the losers of the world wars, and attempts to assure that administration is carried out in such a way as to speed the independence of such territories. Most of the territories placed under the trusteeship system have achieved independence. The International Court of Justice, composed of fifteen judges elected by the General Assembly and the Security Council, has the twofold function of serving as a tribunal for the final settlement of disputes submitted to it by the parties and acting in an advisory capacity to the General Assembly, the Security Council, and other organs accorded this right of consultation by vote of the General Assembly, on questions of a legal nature which might be referred to it.[45]

Decisions made by the court are binding, but no state can be brought before the court without its consent. The General Assembly is composed of delegations from all of the now-more-than 140 member states and has three principal duties. It determines the budget of the organization; selects (along with the Security Council) the Secretary-General, members of the International Court, and new members of the United Nations; and debates any topic within the scope of the charter. Finally, the Secretariat, headed by the Secretary-General, serves as an international civil service charged with administering the organization. The Secretary-General makes an annual report to the General Assembly and has the right to speak to it at any time, as well as propose resolutions to the committees of the General Assembly. The Secretary-General also has the authority to bring the attention of the Security Council to any matter that, in his or her opinion, threatens the maintenance of international peace and security.

In one important way, the structure of the United Nations is better suited to the maintenance of collective security than was the league's. The United Nations Charter

incorporates more elaborate and ambitious provisions for sanctions. Instead of requiring states to impose economic penalties if and when they unilaterally recognize the existence of aggression, and permitting them the exercise of voluntary participation in military sanctions, the Charter brings all enforcement activity under the aegis of the Security Council, conferring upon that body the authority to identify the aggressor, to order members to engage in non-military coercion, and itself to put into action the military forces presumably to be placed at its permanent disposal by members of the organization.[46]

[45] Leland Goodrich, *The United Nations in a Changing World,* Columbia University Press, New York, 1974, pp. 18–19.
[46] Inis L. Claude. *Swords into Plowshares,* 3d ed., Random House, New York, 1964, p. 242.

The arrangement, though, is not as airtight as it might appear on the surface. First, the military forces, which according to the charter were to be provided to the Security Council, have never materialized. Second, since every permanent member of the Security Council has the right to veto proposals before the council, it is impossible to implement sanctions against one of the major powers.

This latter difficulty led to one of the important modifications of the charter that have occurred since the inception of the organization. When the Korean War began, the Soviet Union was boycotting the Security Council to protest the exclusion of Red China from the U.N. This made it possible for the council to pass a resolution calling on the U.N. to aid South Korea. But the Soviet delegate returned and, in accordance with the regular rotation, became the president of the council. He used that position to block any further action by the U.N. regarding the conflict in Korea. In response, the United States persuaded the General Assembly to pass the Uniting for Peace Resolution, which allowed the General Assembly to assume responsibility for dealing with threats to peace and acts of aggression if the Security Council was prevented from acting by a major-power veto. From the Soviet point of view, the resolution, by authorizing the General Assembly to determine the existence of threats to peace and to recommend collective measures, was completely contrary to the charter, which assigned these responsibilities to the Security Council.[47] In the American view, the resolution did not add to the powers given to the General Assembly in the charter but merely provided a new procedure for rapidly convening the assembly in emergency session on the occasions when the Security Council was immobilized by a veto.[48]

Still, the apparent intent of the United States, in introducing the Uniting for Peace Resolution, was to turn the U.N. into an instrument of collective security that might be used against major powers (especially Communist major powers). This goal was not achieved. The resolution did help the United States to continue military action against North Korea, but when the Chinese intervened in the war, Security Council action was prevented by a Soviet veto. When the Americans tried to get the General Assembly to take action against Communist China, the assembly was very slow to act. It took more than two months before the assembly passed even mild economic sanctions against the Chinese. The

[47]Leland M. Goodrich, "The Maintenance of International Peace and Security," *International Organization,* 19 (Summer 1965), 436.
[48]Lawrence S. Finkelstein, "The United Nations: Then and Now," *International Organization,* 19 (Summer 1965), 385.

Uniting for Peace mechanism has been utilized in such situations as the Suez and Hungarian crises in 1956, the Middle East crisis in 1958, and the Congolese situation in 1960. But it has become quite obvious that the Uniting for Peace plan has not transformed the United Nations into an effective collective security organization.

> Since 1951 it has been clear that the provisions of the Uniting for Peace resolution cannot be used to coerce a major power or to initiate collective measures in situations where a major power—a permanent member of the Council—would feel its vital interests threatened. The principal use of the resolution has been to achieve quicker consideration by the General Assembly, but not the exercise by that body of powers to which a permanent member objects.[49]

Prerequisites for Collective Security

Inability to institute effective sanctions against a major power is only one of the obstacles facing the United Nations in its attempt to establish collective security. Inis Claude, in *Swords into Plowshares,* has pointed out a series of logical and theoretical requirements for a successful collective security system. For example, if any nation that makes aggressive use of force is to be opposed by the combined force of all other nations, there must be some universally agreed definition of *aggression.* Otherwise, it will obviously be impossible for the world community to agree on when the time has come to impose sanctions. There must also be some institution that can make authoritative decisions about disputes and designate aggressors. The states of the world must be so committed to peace and loyal to the world community, they will be willing to forsake their own short-range interests in order to impose sanctions against states in some faraway part of the world, involved in disputes of no immediate concern. Also, if the collective security ideal is to be upheld, the members of a collective security organization must be willing to give up the right to fight to change the status quo and be willing to fight against any state not willing to give up this right. Alliances are, strictly speaking, logically incompatible with the collective security ideal. That ideal implies a willingness by all states to oppose *any* state committing aggression, and alliances involve pre-commitments to avoid military action against certain states. Finally, if collective security is to preserve peace, there should be a diffusion of power in the international system so that one or two

[49]Goodrich, *United Nations,* p. 117.

very powerful states cannot withstand the threat of force by the world community.[50]

Just listing some of the logical requirements for a successful collective security system reveals why the United Nations has had difficulty maintaining such a system. There is no universally accepted definition of *aggression*. International lawyers have tried to devise one, and the General Assembly adopted a resolution in 1969 including such a definition.[51] But agreement on this definition, (or, one suspects, any other) is virtually impossible to maintain when the time comes to apply it to concrete cases. There is no international institution that has the ability and the authority to specify which states should be the target of collective security sanctions. The International Court of Justice can only hear cases willingly brought to it by both sides in a dispute. The Security Council is hamstrung by the veto. The General Assembly is large and unwieldy and in any case does not have (unlike the Security Council), the authority to oblige states to carry out sanctions.

Most political leaders of the member states are quite willing to make verbal commitments to the cause of world peace, but their actions reveal that peace is virtually always second on the list of priorities and usually lower. Leaders are more firmly committed to national security, justice, democracy, socialism, national self-determination, or their own credibility. Commitment to the status quo is much less than universal, and several nations are unwilling to give up the right to fight to change it. Alliances, and the precommitments they involve, are widespread in the present international system. And, for most of the postwar period, the United States and the Soviet Union, with nuclear arsenals, have been so powerful that they cannot be intimidated by any implicit threats made by the United Nations in the name of collective security. When the Soviets invaded Hungary in 1956, and the United States the Dominican Republic in 1965, for example, there was little the United Nations could do to deter the invasions, even if it had been possible for the organization to come to some kind of near-universal agreement on the culpability of either superpower.

Recent Changes in the United Nations

Another problem faced by the United Nations has been brought about, at least in part, by the "explosion" of nation-states in the last twenty-five to thirty years. In 1955, a compromise between the Soviet Union and the United States resulted in the first significant

[50] Claude, *Swords into Plowshares*, pp. 223–260.
[51] Worldmark Press, *The United Nations*, Wiley, New York, 1977, p. 123.

addition to the number of member states, with several East European and Third World countries being the principal beneficiaries. In the years since 1955, ex-colonies have become independent, and the number of members is now nearly three times the original membership.

Increased membership has had an important impact on the U.N. because of a shift of some responsibility for peace keeping from the Security Council to the General Assembly, and because each of the new member states, no matter how small, has one vote. One result is that the United States has lost control of the United Nations. In the early years of its existence, the organization was a fairly dependable instrument of American foreign policy. The addition of several Communist and many Third World nations to the General Assembly has made it impossible for the United States to put together a majority with any consistency. This, by itself, would not necessarily be detrimental to the organization, although it has visibly decreased the enthusiasm for the organization in the country that has consistently contributed one-third to one-quarter of its budget for some time. Perhaps more serious in the long run is the imbalance between political power in the international system and voting power in the General Assembly. Sovereign equality for states in the General Assembly creates the possibility that states representing a very small proportion of the world's population, and contributing an even smaller proportion of the organization's budget, can put together clear majorities in the assembly. (In the mid-seventies, states representing about 10 percent of the world's population and contributing about 5 percent of the annual budget could command a two-thirds majority in the General Assembly.) Situations can arise in which majority votes in the assembly put the credibility and prestige of the organization on the line, but in which there is also a lack of political power behind the measure or proposal for which the majority voted.

The Impact of U.N. Resolutions
The effectiveness of resolutions passed by the U.N. is dubious even when one or more major powers are included in the majority. For example, almost from the birth of the organization, the assembly has attempted to put pressure on Rhodesia and South Africa to reform their domestic political regimes. By the late 1970s, pressure from other quarters, internal and external, seemed to be leading to some modification of the policies of both states, and perhaps even the end of white minority rule in the two countries. But it is difficult to see what good the condemnatory resolutions passed by the General Assembly did before then. And in fact, it is possible to

make a fairly convincing argument that those resolutions did more harm than good. Instead of making the Rhodesians and the South Africans feel guilty about their apartheid policies and inclined to modify them, the U.N. resolutions apparently made many whites, at least, feel persecuted and misunderstood, and more unified behind the status quo. One analysis of both countries concluded that

> the U.N. has been completely ineffective in moving the South African and Rhodesian governments toward a race policy which would be acceptable to most members of the U.N. . . . In both countries the United Nations represented a well-defined external threat which has given extremists one volatile political issue upon which they have partially relied to defeat governments led by prime ministers who were sympathetically compliant with the U.N. or at least compliant in comparison with the defiant prime ministers who have succeeded them.[52]

Israel has been another consistent target of the wrath of the General Assembly. Have the resolutions condemning Israel's foreign policy vis-à-vis its Arab neighbors made Israel more conciliatory or helped alleviate antagonism and conflict in the Middle East? It is difficult to discern such results. In the first place, Israelis, or any other target of condemnation by the General Assembly, can argue convincingly that resolutions passed by the assembly are not an accurate reflection of world opinion. As mentioned earlier, because so many small states have voting power equal to that of larger states, a majority of votes in the assembly may represent only a small portion of the world's population. And even if this happens not to be the case on a particular vote, only a very small proportion of the world's governments is democratic and can claim to have won the right to speak for their nation in a free election.

Perhaps even more important, the resolutions passed by the General Assembly, such as the one passed in 1976 equating

[52]George Alfred Mudge, "Domestic Politics and U.N. Activities: The Cases of Rhodesia and South Africa," *International Organization,* 21, (Winter 1967), 76. In a later piece, having analyzed the impact of U.N. activities in both south African countries, Margaret Doxey concludes that "one must concede that the deterrent and coercive force of sanctions is weak on almost every count: non-legitimacy of the system and its norms, low probability of enforcement, both as regards motivation and capability; serious but not intolerable impact of economic measures; very high values attached to norm-violation by the target regimes and their supporters." In "International Sanctions: A Framework for Analysis with Special Reference to the U.N. and Southern Africa," *International Organization,* 26, (Summer 1972), 547.

Zionism with racism, may simply constitute one more difficulty on the road to solutions for problems that appear nearly insurmountable in any case.

> The decision-making process in the U.N. creates further impediments to peace. Resolutions won in support of national objectives widen differences and harden positions. . . . When Arab states do not want to negotiate with Israel, they go to the U.N. and win resolutions concerning the Palestinian refugees in Jerusalem. Since the resolutions are not part of a negotiating process with Israel, they simply create new obstacles which must somehow be overcome during serious talks.[53]

The Future of the United Nations

All these criticisms do not necessarily imply that the U.N. will be or should be disbanded. One reason this is unlikely to happen is that the vast majority of its members, the Third World nations, find the U.N. convenient for a variety of reasons. Many of them cannot afford to establish embassies in a large number of states. The U.N. provides a place where they can meet and talk with official representatives of states to which they cannot afford to send ambassadors. This kind of contact is valued, especially at a time when Third World leaders generally believe, despite the wide variety of political and economic structures their countries exhibit, that they have many important concerns in common. Also, the U.N. provides a forum and a platform that is probably irreplaceable for most developing nations. If an official from Zaire makes a speech in Zaire, it is likely to go unnoticed in most of the world. But if Zaire's delegate to the U.N. or a visiting dignitary from Zaire delivers a speech in the General Assembly, there is at least a reasonable chance that the speech will be picked up in the *New York Times* or *Le Monde*. Finally, the structure of the U.N. not only allows developing countries to maintain contacts with one another; it also allows them to use those contacts to build a coalition that can exert some political clout in the General Assembly as well as other U.N. institutions and organizations. And if, as mentioned earlier, that coalition creates an imbalance between majority votes in the U.N. and actual political power in the international system, this may not

[53] Abraham Yeselson and Anthony Gaglione, "The Use of the United Nations in World Politics," in *At Issue: Politics in the World Arena,* ed. Steven L. Spiegel, St. Martin's Press, New York, 1977, p. 335.

be such a bad thing. In virtually every other forum and arena of interaction in the global system, the Third World states suffer from a terrible disadvantage in terms of political and economic power vis-à-vis the industrialized world. Perhaps the U.N. can serve the useful purpose of redressing the imbalance. For all these reasons, it seems fairly certain that the U.N. will continue to be supported by most of its members.

Most member states, though, are too poor to make substantial contributions to the operating funds of the organization. The United States continues to contribute a substantial portion of funds. There are several indications that the U.N. is becoming increasingly unpopular among Americans, and the present composition of the U.N. must lead one to believe that the General Assembly will continue to pass resolutions disliked in the United States. Is it possible that this trend will ultimately drive the Americans out of the U.N. or at least result in dramatic reductions in American financial support for the organization? The latter possibility is increasingly real and might conceivably be a death blow to the U.N. On the other hand, to the extent that the U.N.'s activities are disapproved by the Americans, they may very well be increasingly appreciated by Third World and Communist governments. If the United States cuts back its contributions to the organization, the Russians, for example, or the Arabs might very well step in and make up the difference.

And, in the final analysis, the continued existence of the U.N. is desirable. It is possible that debates in the General Assembly and the Security Council serve to exacerbate rather than mollify conflict. Certainly the U.N. cannot enforce effectively the ideals of collective security. But at least a couple of lessons that can be gleaned from the historical record of this century indicate that dismantling the U.N. might be a serious mistake. The crisis that culminated in the First World War might conceivably have been resolved if some institutionalized forum for negotiations among great powers, such as that provided by the Council of the league, and the Security Council of the U.N., had existed. And certainly one of the causes of the Second World War was the failure of the major powers to support the League of Nations. Both of these assertions are, to be sure, debatable. Even the most vigorous dissenter, though, must agree that they are not entirely unreasonable. If there is a reasonable chance that an organization such as the U.N. may help the world avoid catastrophes of the magnitude of the world wars, would it not be prudent to preserve the organization? Targets of the U.N., such as Israel and South Africa, may indeed feel persecuted, but merely the structural biases against them in the organization must allow both states to perceive the votes against them as much less than perfectly reflective of the judgment of mankind, and thus enable them to shrug off the votes with relative ease. Resolutions passed by large majorities against Zionism or racism may make the Arabs and the black Africans feel self-righteous to a degree that is not conducive to fruitful negotiations, but both groups are so convinced of the justice of their causes in any case that it seems unlikely that the increment to these convictions brought about by U.N. resolutions is terribly significant.

And though the U.N. has not, in the years since its birth, preserved perfect peace, it may well deserve credit for keeping relatively minor military conflicts from developing into major conflagrations. Dag Hammerskjold, during his tenure as Secretary-General, developed a strategy of preventive diplomacy, which involved U.N. intervention into various conflicts in order to avoid intrusion by the major powers. As part of this strategy, U.N. peace-keeping forces have been sent into such troubled areas as the Middle East, the Congo, and Lebanon. If the United Nations did not exist, it is possible that peace-keeping forces, typically comprised of troops from a number of small and/or neutral nations, might still be organized and inserted into various trouble spots. But, by definition, time is short when such crises arise, and without the help of the U.N. and the various institutionalized channels of communication it provides, there would be an increased risk that the task of organization, at some future time, will take too long. Meanwhile, one or more major powers will be sorely tempted to send troops to the troubled area to make sure that the situation does not get out of hand from its point of view.

The U.N. can also serve as an institutional focus for the solution of important problems in the area of international law. Two that come most readily to mind are the law of the sea and international terrorism. The U.N. has already attempted to deal with the sticky issue of future exploration of the mineral wealth in, and on the bottom of, the world's oceans, in an evolving series of Law of the Sea conferences. The U.N. has a long way to go before it achieves anything like universal agreement on these issues (see Chapter 7), but

it has achieved wide agreement on a Declaration of Principles Governing the Sea Bed and the Ocean Floor, and the Subsoil Thereof, beyond the Limits of National Jurisdiction. It has assisted in the drafting of, and sponsored a treaty prohibiting, the emplacement of nuclear weapons of mass destruction on the sea bed and ocean floor. Substantial progress in the control of marine pollution by oil has been achieved through the activities of the United Nations and the Inter-Government Maritime Consultative Organization (IMCO).[54]

For many years, the U.N. seemed reluctant to take any steps toward the control of international terrorism, because it was associated so closely with the cause of the Palestinians, who were involved in most incidents. Over the years, it appears to this writer at least, that with terrorism spreading to areas outside the Middle East, involving many conflicts in addition to that between the Arabs and the Israelis, and with the increasing realization that terrorists might soon be capable of causing death and destruction on a massive scale (either by stealing the nuclear materials necessary to make weapons,[55] or by stealing weapons themselves),[56] attitudes in the U.N. seem to be changing. In 1977, for example, when the International Federation of Airline Pilots Associations threatened to go on strike if the U.N. did not do something to combat airborne terrorism, the General Assembly unanimously approved a resolution condemning airline hijacking and calling on all nations to take all necessary actions to stop it.[57] If such attitudes about terrorism prevail in the future, the U.N. might provide an important focal point for solutions to a problem that promises to get worse.

Finally, at a time when positive forces, such as improved communications and transportation, and worldwide problems, such as the depletion of natural resources, pollution, and nuclear proliferation, are making it more necessary for the world community to function as such, to destroy virtually the only existing symbolic and institutional basis for the community would surely be a mistake. On a more practical level, intergovernmental organizations like the International Monetary Fund and the World Health Organization are expanding the scope of their activities and influence; the same can be said for international nongovernmental organizations (NGOs) such as multinational corporations and pro-

[54]Goodrich, *United Nations,* p. 250.

[55]Mason Willrich and Theodore B. Taylor, *Nuclear Theft: Risks and Safeguards,* Ballinger Publishing, Cambridge, Mass., 1974.

[56]Bruce G. Blair and Garry D. Brewer, "The Terrorist Threat to World Nuclear Programs," *Journal of Conflict Resolution,* 21 (September 1977), 379–404.

[57]*Los Angeles Times,* November 4, 1977, p. 1.

fessional societies. What other organization is better suited to the progressively more necessary task of monitoring and coordinating the activities of these international and transnational organizations? The U.N. is not likely to evolve into a world government. It might, though, facilitate the coordination of efforts by the world community to deal with problems that cannot be dealt with effectively by states going their separate ways.

FIVE

Transnational Actors:

A New Possibility

NATION-STATES HAVE BEEN THE PRIMARY FOCUS OF ATTEN-
tion so far. I am not going to ignore them in this chapter, but will
concentrate on actors of a different kind in global politics, all referred to variously as transnational, nongovernmental, or multinational actors. Their distinguishing feature is that, though they are
involved in activities that include people and objects in different
states, they are not formally associated with the governments of
states.

In the last fifteen years or so, these organizations have drawn
considerable attention from political scientists. For one reason, they
have increased rapidly in number (see Table 5.1). For another,
more rapid and inexpensive communications and transportation
have allowed them to organize more effectively and thus make a
bigger impact on the international system. A third reason has to do
with the appearance of many small, poor, and badly integrated

TABLE 5.1 Number of international nongovernmental organizations, 1909–1972

1909	1951	1954	1958	1960	1964	1966	1970	1972
176	832	1008	1073	1268	1718	1935	2296	2470

Source: Union of International Associations, *Yearbook of International Organizations,* 15th ed. Brussels, Belgium, 1974, p. s33. Reprinted with permission.

nation-states in the global political system. These states, compared with at least some international nongovernmental organizations, seem relatively weak and ineffectual. This lack of strength has served to highlight the fact that there are organizations other than states that have an important impact on global politics. Finally, the global political system must deal, in the coming decades, with a growing variety of problems that a state-dominated system seems ill equipped to handle, which has also heightened interest in nongovernmental organizations.

Probably the most important type of nonstate actor to emerge in the last couple of decades is the multinational corporation. This type of organization has, accordingly, received the most attention from political scientists. But other kinds of NGOs have also had an impact. One type discussed in previous chapters is the subnational ethnic group that becomes involved in international politics, usually in order to bring about improvement in conditions for ethnic compatriots. The Palestine Liberation Organization (PLO) may be the most prominent organization in the global system at the moment, although Jewish groups in the United States and elsewhere have also been active, and some radical groups with revolutionary causes based on Marxist ideology, rather than ethnic pride or nationalism, have made headlines in the late 1970s.

The aims of many of these subnational (and increasingly transnational) ethnic groups are quite traditional, in the sense that they are primarily concerned with political issues that have always served as the principal focus of the nation-state system. The major concern of the PLO, for example, is not to transcend the state system. The PLO merely wants to join it.

But in another sense, the impact of these groups might be quite revolutionary. The Palestinians are, as mentioned in Chapter 2, only one of hundreds of ethnic groups seeking "national liberation" in one form or another, and if they attain only a fraction of their goals, they would dismantle the global system based on the nation-states that exist today. Their terrorist tactics, aimed in part at the very transportation linkages (such as those formed by modern airlines) that increase the strength and importance of other transnational organizations, will probably continue to have spectacular, if sporadic, effects on the global political system. Finally, terrorism aimed at corporate officials stationed around the world threatens to be a continuing concern to the first type of transnational organization on which I will focus, multinational corporations.

Multinational Corporations

Corporations that do business in more than one state are not new. Clausen points out that as early as the fifteenth century, the Fuggers operated on a multinational basis in several parts of Europe.[1] Many companies, such as Singer, Herz, Unilever, and Nestle, have been active in several countries for most of this century.[2] The Krupps sold arms to countries in far-off parts of the world before this century began.[3]

There are three basic ways in which multinational corporations are different now. First, in the past, companies that did business in several countries were headquartered in one state and all or most of the production was centered there. This has changed. International commerce is no longer dominated by international trade. Now, if a company wants to sell its products in another country, it may set up a subsidiary for manufacturing there. The extent to which the switch from exporting goods to other countries to direct investments in other states has occurred in the United States is shown in Table 5.2.

Second, there are many of these companies, and the ones involved in business on an international scale have increased dramatically the number of subsidiaries overseas. A combination of opportunities presented by improved and inexpensive communication and transportation, the threat of being closed out of new markets, and a desire to take advantage of cheap labor in some developing countries have led to a rapid proliferation in the number of multinational subsidiaries all over the world, as Table 5.3 demonstrates.

The third reason that multinational corporations have become so visible recently is that they have been spectacularly successful.

[1] A.W. Clausen, "The Internationalized Corporation: An Executive's View," *The Annals*, 403 (September 1972), 21.
[2] David H. Blake and Robert S. Walters, *The Politics of Global Economic Relations*, Prentice-Hall, Englewood Cliffs, N.J., 1976, p. 77.
[3] William Manchester, *The Arms of Krupp*, Little, Brown, Boston, 1968.

TABLE 5.2   American exports compared to direct foreign investment (in billions of dollars)

	1950	1960	1970	1973
Exports	10.3	20.6	43.2	70.3
Investment	11.8	32.0	78.1	107.3

Source: U.S. Congress, Senate Committee on Finance, *Implications of Multinational Firms for World Trade and Investment and for U.S. Trade and Labor,* 93d Cong., 1st sess., 1973, p. 95. Figures for 1973 are from the U.S. Department of Commerce, *Survey of Current Business,* August, 1974, Part II, p. 18, and *Survey of Current Business,* 1974, p. s-3; David H. Blake and Robert S. Walters, *The Politics of Global Economic Relations,* © 1976, p. 78. By permission of Prentice-Hall, Inc., Englewood Cliffs, N.J.

TABLE 5.3   Increase in the number of foreign manufacturing subsidiaries of 187 U.S.-controlled multinational enterprises

Area	1901	1913	1919	1929	1939	1950	1959	1967
Canada	6	30	61	137	169	225	330	443
France	8	12	12	36	52	54	98	223
Germany	10	15	18	43	50	47	97	211
United Kingdom	13	23	28	78	128	146	221	356
Other European	6	22	26	69	105	116	261	648
Latin America	3	10	20	56	114	259	572	950

Source: J. W. Vaupel and J. P. Curhan, *The Making of Multinational Enterprise,* Harvard Business School, Boston, 1969, Chapter 3. By permission of Harvard University Press.

One of the more dramatic ways to demonstrate the degree of success is to compare gross annual sales of corporations with the gross national products of nation-states. As can be seen in Table 5.4, many of the largest economic units in the world are not states, but corporations. In these terms, General Motors is larger than Argentina, the Ford Motor Company out-classes Hungary, and Royal Dutch Shell is more important than Turkey.

In rising to new importance and visibility, MNCs have become controversial partly because most of them are American. About 60 percent of the multinational investment abroad is made by American-based companies, while West European corporations account for 30 percent, and Japanese about 5 percent of such investment. Originating in a country with such immense military and economic power, American MNCs have provoked a certain

TABLE 5.4 The 50 largest economic units in the global system, 1970 (gross national products for countries, and gross annual sales for multinational corporations)

Country or Corporation	Gross National Product, or Gross Annual Sales (Millions of Dollars)
1 United States	974,100
2 Soviet Union	497,000
3 Japan	197,180
4 West Germany	186,300
5 France	147,500
6 United Kingdom	121,000
7 China (PR)	120,000
8 Italy	93,200
9 Canada	84,700
10 India	52,920
11 Poland	39,400
12 Brazil	35,440
13 Mexico	33,000
14 Australia	32,990
15 Sweden	32,600
16 East Germany	32,300
17 Spain	32,300
18 Netherlands	31,200
19 Czechoslovakia	30,500
20 Belgium	25,700
21 *General Motors*	24,300
22 Argentina	23,830
23 Romania	22,300
24 Switzerland	20,500
25 Yugoslavia	19,000
26 Pakistan	17,500
27 South Africa	16,690

amount of suspicion and antagonism in virtually every locale in which they have been active.

Several factors account for the American domination of multinational business. Some American corporations have, for example, been heavily subsidized by the United States government. Aerospace programs and military expenditures have served the purposes of several large American corporations well. One result of subsidizing can be seen in relative amounts spent by American corporations on research and development. Hugh Stephenson reports that in 1970, U.S.-based corporations spent two-and-one-half times as

Table 5.4 *(cont.)*

	Country or Corporation	Gross National Product, or Gross Annual Sales (Millions of Dollars)
28	*Standard Oil* (N.J.)	16,550
29	Denmark	15,600
30	*Ford Motor Company*	14,980
31	Austria	14,300
32	Hungary	14,300
33	Norway	13,400
34	*Royal Dutch Shell*	10,800
35	Venezuela	10,300
36	Philippines	10,230
37	Finland	10,200
38	Iran	10,180
39	Bulgaria	9,800
40	Greece	9,500
41	Turkey	9,000
42	*General Electric*	8,730
43	South Korea	8,213
44	Indonesia	7,600
45	*Mobil Oil*	7,260
46	Colombia	7,070
47	*Chrysler*	7,000
48	*Unilever*	6,880
49	Chile	6,670
50	Egypt	6,580

Source: Marshall R. Singer, "The Foreign Policies of Small Developing States," in *World Politics,* ed. James N. Rosenau, Kenneth W. Thompson, and Gavin Boyd, Free Press, New York, 1976, pp. 265–269. Copyright © 1976 by The Free Press, A Division of Macmillan Publishing Co., Inc. Reprinted with permission.

much on research and development as British, West German, Japanese, and French corporations put together. And 54 percent of this spending was in the form of direct government subsidies. In comparison, only 37 percent of what French corporations spent on research and development, and 32 percent of the amount British corporations spent, was supplied by their respective governments. The areas toward which the money was directed also help account for the superior position of American companies in the international economy. Much of it was focused on electronic technology, and computer technology in particular. Computers are a virtual necessity for the operation of a successful multinational business, and American corporations have made good use of American superiority in this field.[4]

Another significant advantage enjoyed by American corporations involves the opportunity they have to operate within the largest single coordinated economy in the world. The American economy consumes some 30 to 35 percent of the world's economic output every year, even though only about 6 percent of the people in the world live in the United States. The economy is so large that it allows American companies to grow to tremendous size without establishing monopolies. As a result, in market after market, the three largest corporations are American. General Motors, Ford, and Chrysler are all larger than German Volkswagen. Goodyear, Firestone, and General Tire and Rubber are all bigger than Italian Pirelli. And so it goes. What this amounts to is a reinforcing cycle (or a vicious cycle, depending on the point of view). Because they are large, American companies can afford the tremendous costs of research, development and marketing on an international scale; so, they grow larger.[5]

MNCs in Their Home Countries

Interestingly, multinational corporations are viewed as a threat in rich and poor countries. In the industrialized states that serve as their home base, even in the United States out of which most MNCs operate, they are accused of causing a variety of economic problems. American labor unions, for example, are particularly concerned about the contribution of MNCs to unemployment. Repeatedly, MNCs shut down factories in the United States and set up new ones in *export platforms* where labor is cheap, such as Taiwan or Hong Kong. This means, according to labor spokesmen, that jobs Americans could have are lost directly to the laborers in the export platforms, and more jobs are lost indirectly because the foreign subsidiaries monopolize export markets that otherwise could be served by American factories with American workers. Another criticism of MNCs heard in the industrialized countries is based on similar reasoning. By exporting jobs, investing money overseas, and having subsidiaries overseas that make it impossible for products made in the home country to be exported, MNCs exacerbate the balance-of-payment problems for industrialized countries. In addition, more and more of the goods made by American companies are now made by overseas subsidiaries, and

[4]Hugh Stephenson, *The Coming Clash,* Saturday Review Press, New York, 1972, pp. 32–33.

[5]Stephenson, *The Coming Clash,* p. 45.

these products must be imported into the United States, for example, adding again to the deficit in the balance of payments.

According to their opponents, MNCs are also a constant threat to the stability of the international monetary system. They hold such huge amounts of various currency reserves (the currency reserves of corporations may be larger than those held by nation-states) that MNCs can ruin the confidence in and the value of a given currency by irresponsible speculation and manipulation of reserves.

Finally, Barnet and Muller argue, in a chapter entitled "The Latinamericanization of the United States," that the MNCs are causing an increase in the inequality of the distribution of wealth in the industrialized societies (such as the United States) by moving a variety of productive jobs out of the country, leaving nothing but highly specialized occupations, for which only the wealthy and highly educated can qualify, for citizens of those societies.

> The managers of the world corporation are creating, often unconsciously, a global system in which the long-term role assigned to the United States is completely changing what it produces and consequently what its people can do. Production of the traditional industrial goods that have been the mainstay of the U.S. economy is being transferred from $4-an-hour factories in New England to 30-cents-an-hour factories in the "export platforms" of Hong Kong and Taiwan. . . . The effect is to eliminate traditional jobs on the assembly line and thereby reduce the blue collar work force and to replace these jobs with others . . . requiring quite different skills . . . the man who assembles radios cannot easily become a computer programmer or a packaged-food salesman, to name two recent growth occupations. Unemployment and reduced income result.[6]

Multinational corporations, of course, do not take these criticisms lying down, and in some cases their counterarguments are convincing. The contribution of foreign investment activity by MNCs to unemployment is direct and visible, but foreign investment also makes substantial, less direct, and less visible contributions to the number of jobs in an industrialized country like the United States. The wages MNCs pay to workers overseas, for example, create increased demands for American products in the

[6]Richard Barnet and Ronald Muller, *Global Reach,* Simon and Schuster, New York, 1974, p. 216.

countries where the subsidiaries of American corporations operate. And the subsidiaries need parts and capital equipment from the United States, adding again to the number of jobs in the American economy. The fact that television sets can be made for less in Taiwan saves American consumers thousands of dollars a year; if those sets are available to them, this money can be spent on American products.

And in any case, defenders of MNCs argue that if they were somehow prohibited from setting up subsidiaries in export platforms, it would not mean more jobs for Americans. MNCs of other countries could, in that event, utilize the platforms to full advantage. This would mean that production facilities in the United States would not be economically viable, since they could not compete with foreign subsidiaries in places with lower costs, either in the United States or elsewhere. Of course, the United States could forbid American-based corporations from investing overseas (or tax such activity so heavily that it would not be feasible), *and* prevent the import of products made by other companies taking advantage of conditions in Taiwan or Hong Kong. But this would surely be the beginning of an escalatory process involving tariffs and countertariffs, quotas and counterquotas, that would be disastrous for the United States as well as the entire non-Communist world.

It is also unlikely that MNCs add a significant negative pressure to the balance of payments of their home countries. It is true that they invest overseas, pay wages overseas, pay taxes overseas, and have their subsidiaries overseas export goods into the home countries. But apparently careful studies show that the outflow of cash associated with the foreign activities of multinationals is almost certainly offset by the flow of cash they generate into their home base. Thus, overseas investments are consistently smaller than the profits repatriated. Wages paid overseas stimulate demand for American-made products, and the subsidiaries set up overseas also stimulate demand for American technology and capital equipment. In short, taking into account the outflow and the inflow associated with the activities of MNCs, one is led to the conclusion that these corporations make a positive contribution to the balance of payments of home states.[7]

Corporations do wield such tremendous economic power that there is little doubt they can make it more difficult for managers of national economies to accomplish their goals. On the other hand, the accusations against the MNCs, by the Nixon administration

[7]See, for example, Blake and Walters, *Politics,* p. 105.

and others, in the wake of the unhinging of the dollar from gold in 1971, were probably unwarranted. These criticisms implied that the MNCs engaged in an unscrupulous conspiracy against the dollar in order to reap profits when the currency finally succumbed. There may have been some truth in this, but it is difficult to escape the conclusion that both the Johnson and the Nixon administrations mismanaged the war in Vietnam economically. The war was paid for, in large part, by printing dollars faster. If this is true, then the corporations and international banks, in their "attack" on the dollar, were merely protecting themselves against the incompetent managing of the dollar by the United States government.

This does not mean that, generally speaking, the economic power of MNCs is not a problem for managers responsible for national economies. When Ford started Pinto production in Great Britain in 1971, for example, it was faced almost immediately by a strike of workers demanding higher wages. Ford was not inclined to meet this demand, and the British government supported the company, because the wage increase in question would not have been in line with an austerity program it was pursuing at the time. Ford responded by moving its Pinto production to Cologne, Germany (and ultimately, back to the U.S.), thus bringing about more austerity than the British government really had in mind.[8]

It is also possible that the oligopolistic power of many large multinational corporations is a factor in the persistent failure of Keynesian management techniques in the last decade or so. "Stagflation," that is, simultaneous inflation and high unemployment, have plagued most industrialized Western countries in the 1970s. This seems strange to a Keynesian, because inflation is regarded within the Keynesian model as a sign that the economy needs cooling down, while unemployment indicates a need for heating up the economy. One possible cause of this problem is that the MNCs have become so powerful that they have robbed the economies of industrialized states of the modicum of free-market pressures that are necessary for Keynesian techniques to work. When the economy is cooling off and demand decreases, this should put pressure on corporations to lower their prices. But the reaction of corporations to lower sales in the era of "stagflation" is quite often to *raise* prices in order to make up for lost profits. Such a tactic would not be available to corporations if free-market pressures were sufficiently strong. Similarly, one of the classic Keynesian techniques for dealing with inflation is to raise interest rates. Theoretically, this will make it more difficult for corporations to borrow, which in

[8]Stephenson, *The Coming Clash,* p. 113, pp. 157–158.

turn will slow the production and growth of corporations, and the economy will cool off.

> But the pattern of oligopolistic competition for ever-greater shares of the market and its accompanying grow-or-die ideology now mean that corporations will continue to borrow regardless because of their power to "pass on" their cost increases to consumers who have no alternative.[9]

Inflation receives a boost in the form of higher prices charged to the consumer by the corporations, and the tactic of raising interest rates that is supposed to reduce inflation, may end up having the opposite effect.

Perhaps problems of this nature stem not from the multinational nature of corporations, but simply from their large size and the ability of a small number of them to dominate the marketplace. But their multinational base may very well make it more difficult for national governments to deal with the MNCs. The case of Ford in Great Britain may be instructive. Any attempt by a national government to control a corporation, by raising interest rates or by antitrust action, for example, may meet retaliation in the form of shifting bases of operation by the company. In short, large, industrialized states have yet to learn how to deal effectively with MNCs that have devised clever ways to work around, over, and through their borders.

MNCs in Host States
If the MNCs are difficult for wealthy industrialized states to handle, they pose an even greater challenge for developing countries. And the effects of the activities of MNCs on developing states are even more controversial. Despite the fact that the impact of the MNCs is more visible in the smaller economies of the developing states, there is passionate disagreement about whether or not that impact is beneficial.

Criticisms and Counterarguments
Controversy extends to the most basic questions, such as whether or not the multinationals supply needed capital for the poor countries. Some defenders of the corporations argue that they do perform this needed function; that, in addition to the money they bring into poor countries in the form of investments, they also

[9]Barnet and Muller, *Global Reach*, p. 270.

serve to improve the balance of payments of these countries by adding to their exports and manufacturing products locally that would otherwise have to be imported. Corporations can point to the fact that in 1968, for example, 40 percent of all manufactured exports from Latin America were produced by subsidiaries of U.S.-based companies.[10]

One of the most vigorous, and controversial replies to these arguments by critics of MNCs focuses on comparisons of inflows and outflows of capital associated with the activities of MNCs in developing countries. What the comparisons show, year after year and place after place, is that MNCs take more money out of developing countries than they put into them. That this is so is widely agreed on, even by some defenders of the corporations. For example, Raymond Vernon, a professor of international management in the graduate school of business administration at Harvard University, and certainly no rabid critic of MNCs, points out in his well-known book on such corporations, "from 1960 to 1968, when approximately $1 billion of fresh capital was being transferred annually to U.S.-controlled subsidiaries in the less developed areas, approximately $2.5 billion was being withdrawn annually in the form of income alone."[11]

In addition, critics of MNCs point out that these companies do not bring much money into developing countries in the first place. They borrow from local sources, thus depriving local firms access to needed capital. For example, from 1956 to 1965, American-based global corporations financed over 80 percent of their investment in Latin America from local sources, or from reinvestment of earnings generated by subsidiaries in Latin America.[12]

As far as the balance of payments in particular is concerned, there are numerous reasons to expect that MNCs exacerbate problems for developing countries. For example, 79 percent of all MNC subsidiaries are prohibited by their parent companies from exporting products because parent companies do not wish to compete with the output of their own subsidiaries.[13] In addition, MNCs have all sorts of sophisticated ways to sneak money out of a country that make the balance-of-payment problem for developing countries more serious. They can engage in triangular trade. If the parent company in the U.S. has a subsidiary in Argentina and in

[10] Barnet and Muller, *Global Reach*, p. 157.

[11] Raymond Vernon, *Sovereignty at Bay*, Basic Books, New York, 1971, p. 172.

[12] Barnet and Muller, *Global Reach*, p. 153.

[13] Ronald Muller, "The MNC and the Exercise of Power: Latin America," in *The New Sovereigns: Multinational Corporations as World Powers*, ed. Abdul Said and Luiz R. Simmons, Prentice-Hall, Englewood Cliffs, N.J., 1975, p. 65.

Panama, transfer prices among the subentities of the same organization can be arranged in such a way as to maximize profits and minimize taxes. Goods produced by the subsidiary in Argentina can be "sold" to the subsidiary in Panama at a price well below true value. The product can then be forwarded to the parent corporation in the U.S. at a price that will allow the profit to occur in Panama. In this way, no profit, or perhaps even a loss, occurs in Argentina, and the Argentine government has no profits to tax. Meanwhile, on paper at least, since the profits occur in Panama (or the Bahamas), or some other available tax haven, they escape undiminished by taxes. The procedure can be turned around so that the subsidiary in Argentina pays an inflated price for imports from another subsidiary or the parent company in the U.S., thus again resulting in the removal of untaxed money from Argentina, making an additional contribution to a negative balance of payments for Argentina.[14] In any case, even if there are subsidiaries that do not regularly engage in such practices and do replace imports, they also send a large share of their profits to the parent company. Money leaves the host country just as certainly as if it had to be paid for importing those products.

Defenders of MNCs claim that most of these arguments are based on misunderstandings or misinformation or both. Consider first the comparison of inflow of investments and outflow of repatriated profits for a given period of time. It is true, spokesmen for MNCs will concede, that these comparisons typically show that the global companies take more money out of a country than they put into it. But such comparisons are irrelevant or misleading. The fact that corporations took more money out of Country X in 1968 than they put into that country in the same year does not prove that Country X is being "decapitalized," because what comes out of Country X in the form of repatriated profits in that year is not a function of what went into that country in the form of investments during that time. Rather, the profits of 1968 are the result of corporate investments in *several* previous years. Such comparisons also ignore the fact that once capital is invested in a country, it forms the basis of a capital stock, which can grow and produce more with each passing year. Imagine, for example, that a corporation invests $100.00 in Country X in 1978. In that year, the original capital investment produces a profit of 30 percent. Half of that $30.00 is paid to state X in the form of taxes, leaving $15.00 to the corporation. The corporation reinvests $7.50 in Country X and repatriates the remainder of the profit. In 1979, the corporation invests no new

[14]Barnet and Muller, *Global Reach,* pp. 157–159.

capital from the outside, but now the capital stock has grown to $107.50. If the profit rate in 1979 is again 30 percent, and the profit is taxed at the rate of 50 percent that leaves about $16.00 for the company after taxes. If the company sends home $8.00 (and reinvests $8.00), that means the inflow resulting from that company's activities in that year is 0, but the outflow is $8.00. Does this mean that the country is being "decapitalized?" The original $100.00 of capital stock is still growing, and next year's production will be greater, meaning that the corporation will pay even more in taxes.[15]

Finally, the inflow-outflow comparison ignores the multiplier effect of the original investments. Each dollar invested expands the economy by some factor greater than one. A dollar paid in wages is used by the worker to buy groceries, the grocery-store owner buys a pair of shoes, the shoe-store owner invests the dollar in some new furniture, and so on.

As for the contribution of MNCs to balance of payments of developing countries, defenders of the corporations will stress the difficulty of making the relevant calculations. Furthermore, many of the arguments used by critics of MNCs are based on suspicions.

Triangular trade and tricky transfer pricing between entities of the same corporation may take place occasionally. But it is unlikely, according to spokesmen for MNCs, that such deception occurs on a scale sufficiently grand to make any substantial, long-run impact on the balance-of-payment deficits that plague many developing countries. In other words, what critics view as the tip of the iceberg, underneath which there is rampant deception and chicanery, defenders of MNCs view as isolated instances of dishonesty.

This is certainly not the end of the controversies surrounding MNCs. Corporate spokesmen argue that they transfer technology and management techniques to the Third World countries that are needed for economic development. Critics respond that, on the contrary, the technology introduced by MNCs is capital intensive and thus inappropriate for the economies of developing countries for two basic reasons. First, these states have an abundance of labor, and the technologically sophisticated equipment utilized by MNCs is employment displacing. Second,

> in countries where the overall key legal institution governing economic relations is the private ownership of productive

[15] Abdul Said and Luiz R. Simmons, "The Politics of Transition," in *The New Sovereigns: Multinational Corporations as World Powers,* ed. Abdul Said and Luiz R. Simmons, Prentice-Hall, Englewood Cliffs, N.J., 1975, p. 25.

resources . . . it follows that the larger the proportion of total output due to capital-technology resources, the greater the amount of income going to the owners of these resources.[16]

So, in addition to creating unemployment, this capital-intensive technology exacerbates the already unequal distribution of wealth in Third World countries. Supporters of MNCs argue that products are made available to consumers in Third World countries that would otherwise be impossible to purchase there. But, skeptics ask, is it not true that the Coca-Cola MNCs supply to the poor and the large cars they provide the rich are products that a developing country would be better off without? It would be better if the poor invested their meager economic resources in milk for their children, and the rich diverted their wealth from the wasteful conspicuous consumption encouraged by MNCs, toward the creation of domestically owned productive capacities vital to long-term economic development.

Dilemmas Perhaps one of the strongest arguments that can be made in defense of MNCs is that when they invest in developing countries, over the long run they are destined to get caught in dilemmas from which there is no escape. Take, for example, the focus by critics on the enormous profits that they repatriate. How can MNCs respond to this criticism? If they do not send the money to the parent corporation, what can they do with it? The only answer is that they can keep the profits in the country where they were made and reinvest them there. But this tactic is unlikely to boost the popularity of the MNCs, because continuous reinvestment will eventually become very threatening to the host country, as the subsidiary expands into ever greater areas of the country and takes over larger shares of the domestic markets.

And, again, how can MNCs respond to the criticism that they introduce into the Third World inappropriate capital-intensive technology? Obviously, they can use more appropriate labor-intensive technology. But then the cry of the critics is that the MNCs are using the Third World countries as a dumping ground for obsolete technology, producing goods that are, as a result, more expensive for local consumers than need be, and that are not competitive in price on the world market and thus impossible to export.

The longer an MNC stays in a Third World country, the more likely such inescapable dilemmas become. When an operation first

[16]Muller, "MNC and Exercise of Power," pp. 61–62.

starts, it creates jobs, and this is likely to be appreciated. (The net effect, because of the use of inappropriate technology, may be to put more people out of work, but the immediate visible impact of new investment and new factories is the creation of jobs.) But before long the MNC is likely to find that no worker in the country is very happy with it. The workers who cannot get jobs with the MNC will become dissatisfied because, working for local firms, they are not getting paid as well as their peers in the employ of the MNC. (The unrest this dissatisfaction generates is likely to antagonize local entrepreneurs, also, because they will be under constant pressure to pay wages equal to those paid by the foreign-based companies.) The workers who cannot get jobs at all are unlikely to feel any love for the MNC. Meanwhile, are the lucky ones who do have jobs with the MNC grateful? Some undoubtedly are, for a while, but there is no guarantee, because in time they may stop comparing their wages with those of their less fortunate compatriots. Rather, they will begin to compare their wages with those of workers who have similar jobs in the United States, or Western Europe; they will almost certainly discover that they are paid less.

Another factor working against the acceptance of MNCs in developing countries is the decrease, as time passes, in the risk faced by a successful operation. This is especially true for the companies engaged in raw material ventures, but any kind of venture in a foreign country faces a certain risk of failure. At the beginning, the host country is likely to appreciate this fact and the willingness of the MNC to bear the burden of the risk. But after a time, especially if the venture is successful,

> A pronounced change in outlook can be expected to occur. . . . The projects that fail drop out of sight, their cost borne partly by the foreign investor and partly by his tax authorities at home. The projects that succeed take the limelight; what was once a wistful hope becomes a tangible bonanza. The level of risk associated with the enterprise, as perceived by the parties, drops precipitately.[17]

In the view of the host country, then, the MNC is just sitting there raking in enormous profits. The thought that the profits should be going to citizens instead of to some giant, impersonal foreign corporation is bound to occur to the government of the host country.

[17] Vernon, *Sovereignty at Bay,* p. 48.

The thought is even more likely if citizens of the host country feel they are able to run the operation without the help of personnel supplied by the parent corporation. Again the MNC is faced with a dilemma. When it sets up a subsidiary in a developing country, it can be public spirited and place as many qualified local people in management positions as it can find. But the day may be hastened when the local citizens feel they can run the business without the help of the MNC. The alternative, of course, is to keep citizens of the host country out of management positions and provide them only menial jobs. This may lead even more quickly to antagonism on the part of the host country, whose citizens will complain that the MNCs employment policies are designed to keep them in a position of permanent subordination and dependence.

Evaluating the Evidence   That subsidiaries of MNCs in developing countries will become unpopular seems all but inevitable. Their unpopularity, though, is not necessarily deserved. They might serve as engines of development even as they provoke antagonism and opposition. The difficulty of determining whether the economic impact of MNCs on developing countries is positive or negative should not be underestimated. Many of the criticisms of MNCs from developing countries and elsewhere are based on the assumption that the host country could do for itself what the foreign subsidiary is doing. If this is true, then the criticisms are probably valid. If, for example, an MNC moves into a developing country and forces local entrepreneurs out of business, or prevents them from entering markets they would otherwise be able to ser- vice, then the MNC is probably exerting a negative impact on that country's balance of payments. (The MNC will send some of the profits home, and has methods of getting money out of the country and evading taxes that would not be available to a local firm.) But if the same MNC subsidiary produces goods that would otherwise have to be imported, then it may be exerting a positive impact on the balance of payments. Since MNCs have been known to buy out local, ongoing concerns, there is little doubt that in some cases their investment does have the effect of driving domestic firms out of business that could provide the goods and services marketed by the MNC. (Although it is possible that in some of these cases the local firm was on the verge of bankruptcy when it was bought out.) But there have also been cases when MNC subsidiaries have been nationalized by governments that discover they cannot manage the enterprise without the help of the MNC, and thus have had to invite it back. (In how many of these cases was it a coopted elite that invited the MNC back despite the lack of economic necessity to do so?) The answer to the question of whether the economic impact of MNC activity in a developing country is harmful or beneficial often depends heavily on which assumption one makes with regard to the effect of the MNC subsidiary on local businesses. On the level of nations as entities, the question becomes what *percentage* of the goods and services provided by MNC subsidiaries is import substituting and what is not. This is a What would the world by like if X, which did happen, had not happened? kind of question, and the answer will be accordingly controversial.

One way to get around this problem (and, of course, run into new ones) is to compare developing nations that receive large amounts of foreign investment with those that receive smaller amounts. No attempt need be made to trace the exact impact of each investment, and so no assumption need be made about the impact of the intervention of the MNC on local firms. The focus is on the input (the amount of foreign investment) and the output (for example, the growth rate in terms of GNP per capita). Such comparisons are not foolproof, of course. One would expect, for example, that states that are more advanced economically would attract more foreign investment than states experiencing economic difficulties. If, having attracted a larger amount of foreign investment, the more advanced states continue to outperform the less advanced, the superior performance might not be due, even in part, to the impact of foreign investment. It might be that the more developed states have enjoyed this relative success both before and after the investment for other reasons.

There are ways of dealing with this particular problem. One can, statistically, take into account the extent to which a state attracts greater foreign investment because of its higher level of economic development, and then see what impact this investment has on changes in economic development over the succeeding years. Employing such a technique, Chase-Dunn found that states having more foreign investment in 1950 experienced relatively slower growth rates, in terms of GNP per capita, from 1950 to 1970.[18] Ray and Webster, utilizing the same technique but looking only at Latin American states in the 1960s, found that states more penetrated with foreign capital in 1960 experienced slightly faster economic growth over the next decade than other states in the area.[19] In view of the fact that two earlier studies of Latin America

---

[18]Christopher Chase-Dunn, "The Effects of International Economic Dependence on Development and Inequality: A Cross National Study," *American Sociological Review*, 40 (December 1975), 720–738.

[19]James Lee Ray and Thomas Webster, "Dependency and Economic Growth in Latin America," *International Studies Quarterly*, 22 (September 1978).

reported contradictory findings regarding the relationship between foreign investment and economic growth,[20] it is safe to conclude that the controversy regarding the nature of the relationship will continue.

And even if it is resolved in favor of the argument that foreign investment does have a positive impact on a developing country's GNP, the debate over the impact of foreign investment on poor host countries will not be ended. Many critics of multinational corporations are willing to concede that they do speed up growth in terms of GNP but still condemn them because the overall impact, they believe, is detrimental. They will argue, for example, that penetration by MNCs, while it may contribute to the national GNP, concentrates wealth in the hands of a fortunate few in the major cities. The masses in the slums and the peasants in the countryside are not helped. In fact, they are cut off from the economic mainstream of the country and left even further behind.

Opponents of MNCs also worry about the political ramifications of substantial penetration by foreign investment into a developing country. Any developing country that attempts meaningful reforms may find such efforts stifled by the formidable opposition of MNCs. The spectacular example supporting this argument involves the activities of such corporations as International Telephone and Telegraph (ITT) and Kennecott in Chile when the Allende regime was in power in the early 1970s. It is established, for example, that ITT offered funds to the CIA to carry out subversive activities in Chile, and that the CIA later did engage in such activities. (There is no solid evidence, though, that the CIA accepted ITT financial support for these ventures.) One authoritative source on Inter-American relations summarizes the American campaign against Allende this way:

> After Allende's inauguration, the United States encouraged and financed a wide spectrum of opposition groups, including other parties, certain trade and labor organizations, middle class housewives, and right wing terrorist groups; strikes and demonstrations were funded and coordinated through the CIA station in Santiago. In addition, the United States used its influence and voting power in international lending agencies to

[20]Lawrence R. Alschuler, "Satellization and Stagnation in Latin America," *International Studies Quarterly,* 20 (March 1976), 39–82. Robert R. Kaufman, Harry I. Chernotsky, and Daniel S. Geller, "A Preliminary Test of the Theory of Dependency," *Comparative Politics,* 7 (April 1975), 303–330.

put a "credit squeeze" on Chile. . . . Finally, by mid-1973, Chile was in a desperate economic and social situation.[21]

On September 11, 1973, Allende was overthrown by the Chilean military.

Is the Chilean example merely the tip of the iceberg or the exception that proves the rule that MNCs usually do not meddle in the internal political affairs of their hosts? Whatever the answer to that question, the Chilean experiment failed, and the viability of Allende's approach to independence from MNCs is accordingly dubious. It has already been seen that a less radical approach, tried by Peru and the Andean Common Market, may succumb, over time, to the variety of blandishments that MNCs can offer in their persistent attempts to subvert rules and regulations designed to limit their penetration and control of developing economies. The only country in Latin America that has clearly escaped from MNCs altogether is Cuba. And the success of the Cuban experiment is debatable.

Castro has successfully improved the health care and level of education of the average Cuban. But the country continues to be plagued by economic problems, some of which are quite reminiscent of the difficulties Cuba experienced in prerevolutionary days. Perhaps the most spectacular example involves Cuba's heavy reliance on sugar.

Before Castro, Cuba's economy was tied closely to the price of sugar. When the price on the world market was high, the Cuban economy did well. When it fell, Cuba suffered. Furthermore, most of the sugar was sold to the United States. Cuba was extremely dependent on one product and on one country.

This dependency was repugnant to Castro and the rest of the revolutionary leadership, and when they came into power they were determined to do something about it. They had in mind diversification of the Cuban economy, especially in the direction of greater industrialization. After ties with the Russians had been forged, the Cubans relied on them for substantial shipments of heavy equipment and technological assistance necessary to get the industrializing effort off the ground. But by 1963, the Russians were urging the Cubans to concentrate on the production of sugar. Castro announced to the Cubans, on his return from the Soviet

[21]G. Pope Atkins, *Latin America in the International Political System,* Free Press, New York, 1977, p. 234.

Union in 1963, that with Russian help, Cuba would launch a sugar-growing campaign, culminating in the production of 10 million tons in 1970. The campaign failed, the target was not reached, and the effort distorted the Cuban economy.

Cuba recovered from that disaster in the early 1970s and by 1974 came close to achieving the first positive balance of trade since the revolution. But the price of sugar in the world market was very high then, and there was room for skepticism regarding the accomplishments of the Cuban economy. Defenders of Castro thought that his revolution had, perhaps, overcome the earlier economic difficulties. The crucial question became, What will happen to the Cuban economy if the price of sugar falls? The answer was not long in coming. World sugar prices fell from 30 cents a pound in 1974 to 13 cents a pound in 1976, and it soon became apparent that Cuba had not solved the problems associated with a monoculture economy and heavy reliance on one country for its exports. The Cuban economy stumbled badly, and there was a serious shortage of hard-currency reserves brought about by the inability of the Cubans to get a decent price for their sugar on the world market. In 1975, the Soviet Union bought over one-half of Cuba's sugar production and over 50 percent of its other exports. The Russians were still pushing the Cubans to concentrate on sugar production; while the Russians probably did not need the sugar in the 1960s, in the 1970s they were having trouble with their own sugar beet crops and thus had obvious reasons for advocating Cuban efforts in this area.[22]

One example does not necessarily confirm the argument that Castro has merely traded one master for another, or that his revolution will never accomplish economic success. It does, though, cast doubt on any thesis that stipulates that throwing out the MNCs will bring economic independence to any developing country that adopts such a policy. Small, developing countries, and even large ones, are inevitably going to be dependent on some one. Some analysts (discussion follows) still believe they discern a trend toward an increase in the ability of developing countries to handle MNCs through various legal means, despite the experience of Chile and the Andean Common Market. And perhaps it is possible to diversify dependency, allowing a certain amount of activity by MNCs on the one hand, but developing economic contacts with

[22]Mose L. Harvey and Foy D. Kohler, eds., *Soviet World Outlook,* 1 (August 1976), Current Affairs Press, Washington, D.C., pp. 1, 8, 11.

Eastern Europe and the Soviet Union on the other.[23] Diversified dependency is not the same thing as independence, but it might be a step down the road toward interdependence.

MNCs and the Global Political System

There are two major controversies concerning the impact of MNCs on the global political system as a whole. The first focuses on the relationship between the increasing importance of multinational global enterprises and the stability of the global system. In short, is the rise of the MNCs likely to make the global political system more, or less, conflict prone? The second controversy has to do with the relative strength of MNCs and nation-states in the coming decades. Some believe that states have aleady lost their economic sovereignty to the MNCs, and that this trend is likely to continue, while others assert that this thesis, like many before it predicting the demise of the nation-state, is premature at best.

The answer that one provides for the question concerning the impact of MNCs on the degree of conflict in the global system will almost certainly be crucially dependent on one's opinion regarding the effect of MNCs on the distribution of wealth among states. Those who believe that MNCs help developing countries achieve their economic goals are likely to believe also that this equalization of wealth and rationalization of the world's economic system will mollify conflict between rich and poor states. But if it is true that MNCs decapitalize poor states, and that their general impact is to transfer wealth from poor states to rich states, then it seems logical to conclude that MNCs will heighten the levels of tension in the global political system.

At least one author, though, foresees a different relationship between the effect of MNC activities on the distribution of wealth among states on the one hand, and the degree of interstate conflict that MNCs will bring about on the other. C. Fred Bergsten argues that states all over the world, developing states included, are becoming sophisticated enough to assure that MNCs within their boundaries will bring them benefits. Developing countries are, for example, aware of the balance-of-payment problems that MNCs can exacerbate and have taken effective steps to prevent this. Brazil, India, and (as seen earlier) the Andean pact states have passed laws putting limits on the amount of capital that MNCs can repatriate.

[23] David Ray, "The Dependency Model of Latin American Underdevelopment: Three Basic Fallacies," *Journal of Inter-American and World Affairs*, 15 (February 1973), 4– 20.

Mexico insists that MNC subsidiaries be, in part, locally owned, unless they export 100 percent of their output. India requires that foreign-owned firms export 60 percent of their output within three years.[24]

If it is true that developing countries are willing and able to handle MNCs in this manner, then one might reasonably conclude that global enterprises will contribute to a redistribution of wealth and a lessening of tension between rich and poor states. But Bergsten believes otherwise. He asserts that as rich countries, and in particular the United States, become aware of the fact that host countries for MNC subsidiaries are making legal arrangements to ensure that economic benefits are transferred from the rich to the poor countries, the rich countries will retaliate. If host countries pass laws to assure that MNCs within their borders make a positive contribution to their balance of payments, citizens and lawmakers in home countries like the United States are bound to realize, sooner or later, that the subsidiaries will exert a negative impact on *their* balance of payments. If the United States Congress then passes laws forbidding foreign investments that do not have a positive impact on the American balance of payments, then the home country and the host country will have reached an obvious, and perhaps insoluble, impasse. Bergsten points out that

> such measures by home countries could simply lead to a series of retaliatory and counter retaliatory steps between them and

[24]C. Fred Bergsten, "Coming Investment Wars," *Foreign Affairs*, 53, (October 1974), 141. Not all writers are so sanguine about the ability of developing countries to deal with MNCs. James Petras, focusing on Latin America in 1976, asserts that "The Chilean experience has significance far beyond its borders, for the whole of Latin America and the U.S. corporate world, because what has happened in Chile is happening throughout Latin America. Both the economic strategy . . . and the type of political regime — a brutal police state — which the United States helped set up in Chile serves as a model for what U.S. policy-makers and their corporate cohorts would like to see in the rest of Latin America. In Argentina since the March 1976 coup, 3000 workers and students have been assassinated; there have been over a hundred thousand political firings; 30,000 political prisoners; concentration camps. . . . In Bolivia and Uruguay the pattern is similar. A police-state regime reduces wages, increases profits, encourages big business with new concessions and sells off state enterprises. Under the pressure of U.S. multinationals and financial houses, the Peruvians and Ecuadorians, once known as the nationalist regimes in the area, also begin repressing workers and meeting the terms of the bankers and foreign investors. Brazil, of course, continues the same pattern it has adhered to over the past 12 years." See James Petras, "Chile and Latin America," *Monthly Review*, 28, (February 1977), 21–22. For a less ideological, but still rather pessimistic view of how Latin American states (in the Andean Common Market) are dealing with MNCs, see *Latin American Economic Report*, August 13, 1976.

the host countries. Thus international investment wars will be prevented only by the adoption of a truly new international economic order.[25]

In the long run, then, Bergsten believes that MNCs might contribute to the development of a new international economic order and a more peaceful global system. But he also points out that somewhat similar problems involving international economic exchange in the form of international trade resulted in retaliatory and counterretaliatory steps that deepened the worldwide depression in the 1930s, and thus played a role in the process that brought about the Second World War.

The future of MNCs vis-à-vis nation-states is at least as controversial as the impact they have, economically, on home and host countries, and their effect on the stability of the international system. I have already alluded to the opinion of some that MNCs are on the verge of becoming the most important social entity in the global system, replacing nation-states. To varying degrees, this opinion is adhered to by defenders of MNCs as well as critics. The former, of course, believe that the imminent emergence of MNCs will benefit the global system, leading to the rationalization of production and marketing on a worldwide scale, while the latter look forward to the predominance of MNCs with a sense of foreboding.

There are at least two major themes among writers who believe that, on the contrary, MNCs are going to be subordinated to the wishes and control of states. One of these argues that as states become more aware of the modus operandi of MNCs, they will develop effective countermeasures. Writers such as Peter Gabriel note that political support for MNCs in the home countries has declined steadily in the last decade. Further, he asserts that they have never been very popular in the Third World, and Gabriel agrees with Bergsten that less developed states have developed an effective series of controls over MNC activities. Gabriel believes that MNCs will have to learn to accommodate themselves to these controls, and the desires of host country governments, if they are to survive at all as important economic units in the Third World.[26]

Another theme arguing that there are limits to the expansion of power of MNCs is based on the idea that these corporations have

[25]Bergsten, "Coming Investment Wars," p. 152.
[26]Peter Gabriel, "The Multinational Corporation in the World Economy: Problems and Prospects," in *Bargaining Without Boundaries,* ed. Robert J. Flanagan and Arnold R. Weber, University of Chicago Press, Chicago, 1974, p. 9.

flourished only because it has been in the interest of the predominant power in the international system, that is, the United States, to allow them to flourish. According to Robert Gilpin, this has always been the nature of the relationship between transnational actors and nation-states.

> Whether one is talking about the merchant adventurers of the sixteenth century, nineteenth century finance capitalists, or twentieth century multinational corporations, transnational actors have been able to play an important role in world affairs because it has been in the interest of the predominant power(s) for them to do so. . . . From this perspective the multinational corporation exists as a transnational actor because it is consistent with the political interest of the world's dominant power, the United States.[27]

The implication of this argument is that as the United States becomes less predominant in the global system, one can expect to see a decline in the influence of MNCs. (Unless, perhaps, MNCs are in the interests of a successor dominant power.)

Transnational Labor Unions

Logically, as multinational corporations establish themselves worldwide, labor unions might be expected to do the same. Consider, for example, the problems faced by labor unions in a duel with the Ford Motor Company. As mentioned earlier, in 1970 Ford announced it was going to begin production of Pintos in Great Britain, a tactic apparently designed, at least in part, to escape higher American wages. The reader will recall that Ford immediately ran into a strike for higher wages in Great Britain and so moved most of its European-centered Pinto production to a factory in Cologne, Germany. Why did Ford find it wise to do this? Five years earlier, the factory in Cologne had employed mostly Italian workers. But when the Italians began to organize, they were let go and replaced by Turkish workers.[28] So, the Ford Motor Company, an *American* corporation, first moved production to *Great Britain,* and then moved it again to *Germany,* where it had replaced *Italian*

[27]Robert Gilpin, "The Politics of Transnational Economic Relations," in *Transnational Relations and World Politics,* ed. Robert O. Keohane and Joseph S. Nye, Jr. Harvard University Press, Cambridge, 1972, p. 54.
[28]Stephenson, *Coming Clash,* pp. 157–158.

workers with employees from *Turkey*. Obviously, this kind of transnational flexibility is vexatious for labor union leaders, and it is little wonder that many have concluded with Victor Reuther of the United Auto Workers (UAW) that "if it is in the interest of corporations to produce beyond the old nation-state concept, then it's in labor's interest to organize at that level."[29]

And indeed there has been movement in this direction. As early as the 1950s, the International Metal Workers Federation organized world company councils in the automotive industry in order to bring together representatives of unions that dealt with the same auto companies in several different countries.[30] Since then, similar councils have been organized in the electrical, oil, chemical, and rubber industries. In 1969, and again in 1977, the International Federation of Airline Pilots Associations threatened a worldwide boycott to protest the growing number of skyjackings and to urge the United Nations to take action. In neither case did strikes actually occur, but the protest in 1969 did evoke a sympathetic response from Secretary-General U Thant,[31] and (as seen in Chapter 4), in 1977, the General Assembly unanimously passed a resolution condemning airline hijacking. Also, in 1969, one of the most widely publicized transnational labor union activities occurred when the International Federation of Chemical and General Workers coordinated bargaining between a French multinational glass manufacturing company (Compagnie de Saint Gobain) and unions in West Germany, France, Italy, and the United States.[32] Transnational bargaining between American companies such as Continental Can, Bethlehem Steel, and the "Big Three" automakers (General Motors, Ford, and Chrysler) and unions in the United States and Canada has been common for some time now.[33] One (admittedly not unbiased) analyst concludes that

> there are countless instances of international trade union solidarity: actions ranging from the refusal by dockers to unload a

[29]Harry Lenhart, "Labor Fears Loss of Jobs in U.S. as Firms Expand Their Overseas Facilities," *National Journal*, July 17, 1971, pp. 1486–1488. Cited by William J. Curtin, "The Multinational Corporation and Transnational Collective Bargaining," in *American Labor and the Multinational Corporation*, ed. Duane Kujawa, Praeger, New York, 1973, p. 196.

[30]Robert Cox, "Labor and the Multinationals," *Foreign Affairs*, 54, (January 1976), 352–353.

[31]Curtin, "Multinational Corporation," p. 201.

[32]Robert Cox, "Labor and Transnational Relations," *International Organization*, 25 (Summer 1971), 555–556.

[33]John Crispo, "Multinational Corporations and International Unions: Their Impact on Canadian Industrial Relations," in *Bargaining Without Boundaries*, ed. Robert J. Flanagan and Arnold R. Weber, University of Chicago Press, Chicago, 1974, p. 110.

ship sailing under a flag of convenience until the International Transport Workers' Federation has concluded with the shipowners a satisfactory agreement for the crew, to boycotts, fund raising, and work stoppages.[34]

International Labor Organizations

International labor, as it attempts to deal with MNCs, is organized into two basic types of institutions. The first links together unions from all kinds of crafts and industrial activities from different nations. There are three such organizations of major importance. The International Confederation of Free Trade Unions (ICFTU) is composed of social-democratic, or nonpolitical and nonconfessional (nonreligious), labor organizations. The World Federation of Trade Unions (WFTU) has come to be dominated by unions from Communist countries (including the Soviet Union), and Communist-oriented national unions. Finally, there is the World Confederation of Labor (WCL) composed of Catholic-oriented (although often no longer officially Catholic) national unions. The second basic type of international labor organization is the International Trade Secretariat (ITS), which brings together national unions representing workers in the same broad industrial or occupational categories.[35]

International trade secretariats have become particularly important leaders of transnational labor activity in the last decade or so, and certainly one of the most important of these has been the International Metalworkers Federation, supported enthusiastically by the UAW. The automobile industry is well suited for transnational bargaining, since some 80 percent of the world's output of automobiles is accounted for by nine MNCs.[36] That the UAW would become active in this area might also be expected in light of the fact that, while in 1950 80 percent of world auto production occurred in the United States, by 1972 the figure had been reduced to 32 percent.[37]

In order to deal with such multinationalization of production, international trade secretariats like the International Metalworkers

[34]Herbert Maier, "The International Free Trade Union Movement and International Corporations," in *American Labor and the Multinational Corporation,* ed. Duane Kujawa, Praeger, New York, 1973, p. 20. When he wrote this article, Mr. Maier was the director of the Economic, Social, and Political Department of the International Confederation of Free Trade Unions.

[35]Nat Weinberg, "The Multinational Corporation and Labor," in *The New Sovereigns: Multinational Corporations as World Powers,* ed. Abdul Said and Luiz R. Simmons, Prentice-Hall, Englewood Cliffs, N.J., 1974, p. 93.

[36]Curtin, "Multinational Corporation," p. 196.

[37]Cox, "Labor," p. 346.

Federation and the International Federation of Chemical and General Workers have devised a broad range of tactics. First, they have acquired, coordinated, and analyzed data on MNCs; such data are necessary, for example, when a union wants to argue that despite a lack of profits earned by a subsidiary in one particular country, the corporation has earned a profit as a result of its overall activities. (And can thus afford to give *all* its workers a raise.) ITSs have tried to help unions organize in countries where they are weak, or nonexistent, and they have supplemented these efforts by putting pressure on parent corporations in countries where there are strong unions to order their subsidiaries to recognize new unions. International trade secretariats have also tried to coordinate unions in different countries so that, if one of them strikes, the target corporation will not be able to retaliate by shifting production, because unions at sites in other countries will refuse to work over time or cooperate with other increases in work schedules. Finally, ITSs have organized consumer boycotts of products sold by uncooperative MNCs, and have tried to coordinate the terminal dates of collective bargaining agreements in different countries in order to facilitate transnational collective bargaining efforts in the future.[38]

Prospects for Transnational Collective Bargaining

Despite the obvious need on the part of labor for *some* kind of strategy to deal with the MNCs, and despite the considerable effort put into developing transnational bargaining techniques by some union leaders, the emergence of truly transnational, integrated labor unions has not occurred and does not appear probable. First, consider the problems faced by unions in home countries as they attempt to coordinate actions with unions in developing host countries. One problem will likely be that there is no such union in the developing country, or the unions that do exist will be very weak. It is quite probable that the policy of the government of the developing country will aim at oppressing or at least strictly controlling any unions that do exist. That may well be one reason why the MNC moved into the country in the first place. Even if there is a relatively strong and independent union in the developing host country, it may not be inclined to cooperate with the union in the home country. In many cases, the workers for the MNC in the host country will already be receiving higher wages than their compatriots and thus not be inclined to make waves. They may realize that if they do successfully push for wages equal to their American

[38]Cox, "Labor," p. 35.

counterparts, it might cause the MNC to move production again. And the government of the host country is unlikely to favor wage equalization, because such settlements would be inflationary, and because higher wages would restrict the number of employment opportunities that the MNC subsidiary might otherwise create.

Even if labor unions in home countries could develop transnational ties with their counterparts in developing countries, this would not necessarily solve the problems that unions have with MNCs. Most MNC investment is not in the developing countries, but in the industrialized areas of the world. If labor unions in the United States, for example, want to be able to confront the transnational flexibility of MNCs with transnational techniques of their own, they will have to do so in cooperation with their counterparts in other industrialized countries. But this task, too, involves formidable difficulties.

Labor unions, to be sure, exist in Canada, Western Europe, and Japan, as well as the United States. But the philosophies, structures, and functions of these unions differ so greatly from country to country that arranging transnational bargaining among them is difficult. Unions in the United States are relatively decentralized. They typically deal with employers at the plant level. In Great Britain and Europe, the unions are quite centralized, and as a result, collective bargaining is typically conducted on an industry-wide basis. Because breakdowns in such industry-wide negotiations have more disastrous effects for the national economy, government intervention in European labor-management disputes is more common. Obviously, before significant transnational bargaining could take place involving American and European unions, on the one hand, and MNCs, on the other, the American unions would have to become more centralized. If this does happen, and the American government as a result becomes more deeply involved in collective bargaining, then it seems safe to predict that the scope of the confrontation between the MNCs and labor, with national governments also playing a role, would become unwieldy.

Multinational collective bargaining agreements would . . . merely serve to establish levels of compensation that would permit the most marginal employer signatory to the agreement to survive. Meaningful collective bargaining to establish true compensation would continue to occur at the national level. The same disparities in compensation that the union seeks to eliminate would remain as they reflect the realities of the economic posture of each employer, industry, and nation.[39]

While European unions are more centralized and integrated at the national level, American unions are more centralized at the plant level. Typically, the union that wins an election at an American plant represents all the employees at that plant. In Great Britain and most of Western Europe, several unions represent different employees at the same plant and in the same industry.[40] As a result, one labor leader acknowledges that an important obstacle to meaningful transnational collective bargaining is that 'union structures differ widely from country to country. This makes it difficult to identify those units within each country's unions which are the counterparts of those in other countries with which coordination is needed in relation to particular MNCs.'[41]

The structural differences between unions in different countries might be surmountable if it were not for the sharp differences in purpose and philosophy that also exist. The majority trade unions in both France and Italy are Communist, while the American Federation of Labor-Congress of Industrial Organizations (AFL-CIO) is aggressively anti-Communist. West German unions have adopted co-determination goals (labor unions have representation at management levels), and these have yet to provoke much interest in the United States. The Communist, anti-Communist split between labor unions in different countries is reflected also at the international level, with the Communist World Federation of Trade Unions pitted against the International Confederation of Free Trade Unions.[42]

These differences in philosophy and structure of labor union movements have resulted in substantial differences in the issues on which collective bargaining focuses in the various industrialized

[39] Curtin, "Multinational Corporation," pp. 205–207. Curtin bases this argument on an analysis of the process of collective bargaining in states where negotiations are centralized.

[40] Curtin, "Multinational Corporation," p. 207.

[41] Weinberg, "Multinational Corporation and Labor," p. 93.

[42] "The split in the world trade-union movement between a Communist and an aggressively non-Communist federation has also inhibited coordinated discussion and action. As a residual consequence of the Cold War, trade unions affiliated with the International Confederation of Free Trade Unions (ICFTU) have been unable to converse with unions affiliated with the Communist World Federation of Trade Unions (WFTU)." Stephenson, *Coming Clash*, p. 159.

countries. In many European states, legislation provides workers with vacations, limits on hours of work, safety and health measures, and generous severance-pay allowances, while most of these are topics of collective bargaining in the United States. Unions in European countries with relatively comprehensive social legislation are likely to demand housing paid for by the company, nurseries for the children of working mothers, as well as recreation and vacation facilities. Most American unions would not consider making such demands, and American companies would consider them exhorbitant if they were made.[43] Such vast differences in the topics for collective bargaining in the industrialized countries constitute an obvious barrier to comprehensive transnational agreements between MNCs and labor unions.

An Alternative Approach

The combined weight of these obstacles to transnational bargaining has led several scholars, and some influential labor leaders, to conclude that another approach to the problems created by MNCs is likely to be more successful.[44] This approach might appropriately be called the national, as opposed to the transnational strategy. It is exemplified most clearly, and importantly, by the AFL-CIO in the United States. For the most part, the AFL-CIO has not shared the enthusiasm of the UAW for transnational cooperation with foreign counterparts. They have concentrated instead on putting pressure on the American government to institute regulations that would make foreign investment less attractive to American-based MNCs, and also make it more difficult for foreign-based corporations to export their products to the United States. The AFL-CIO objects, for example, to the fact that tax laws are structured in such a way that MNCs get credit for taxes they pay overseas when they pay taxes on their profits (earned overseas and at home) in the United States. In other words, whatever amount they pay in taxes to foreign governments, they subtract from the amount they pay in American taxes. Another provision of the tax laws that the AFL-CIO objects to allows American-based MNCs to defer payment of taxes on profits earned overseas until the profits are returned to the

[43]Curtin, "Multinational Corporation," p. 208.
[44]Kujawa, for example, asserts that "a great variety of circumstances — legal, structural, and so on — particular to each country appears to support the contention that meaningful transnational bargaining resulting in the determination of substantive issues is not to be expected." See "Transnational Industrial Relations: A Collective Bargaining Prospect?" in *International Labor and the Multinational Enterprise,* ed. Duane Kujawa, Praeger, New York, 1975, p. 115.

United States. (And they may never be.)[45] Such laws, according to some American labor leaders, provide unnecessary and economically artificial incentives for American corporations to transfer production overseas, thus depriving American workers of job opportunities.

The AFL-CIO has been trying to abolish such provisions of the tax laws through a proposal known as the Burke-Hartke bill. This bill also contains provisions that would restrict imports into the United States, according to quotas based on import quantities from 1965 to 1969. At this writing, such a bill has not passed, but there seems little doubt that the AFL-CIO will continue to push for legislation similar in intent to the Burke-Hartke bill, so it is worth considering what the impact of such a law might be.

That a measure like the Burke-Hartke bill would save some jobs in the United States seems clear. But it would also destroy other jobs, and what the net impact would be is a matter of great dispute that was touched on earlier.[46] I will not continue the discussion here but will point out that the AFL-CIO does not represent all American workers. It is perfectly understandable that the AFL-CIO would respond to members thrown out of work by MNC production strategies, and it is equally clear that something should be done to help these people. But a decision on whether help should be based on suggestions by the AFL-CIO must take into account the fact that the interests of U.S. workers who are hurt by foreign operations of American-based MNCs conflict directly with those of workers whose jobs are created by such operations. In addition, one analysis of this problem concludes that "the actually or potentially harmed workers tend to be unionized and members of international unions that are dominant in the AFL-CIO. . . . Those whose interests are directly related to expansion of foreign operations are less organized and more diffused throughout the economy."[47]

It is also important to remember that while the import restrictions that are part of the Burke-Hartke bill would also save some American jobs (and destroy others), there would be a cost to the United States in the form of higher prices for products that could no longer be bought from foreign producers (or subsidiaries of

[45] Elizabeth R. Jager, "U.S. Labor and Multinationals," in *International Labor and the Multinational Enterprise,* ed. Duane Kujawa, Praeger, New York, 1975, p. 38.

[46] For a more detailed discussion of the dispute, see Robert G. Hawkins and Michael Jay Jedel, "U.S. Jobs and Foreign Investment," in *International Labor and the Multinational Enterprise,* ed. Duane Kujawa, Praeger, New York, 1975, pp. 47–93.

[47] Hawkins and Jedel, "U.S. Jobs," p. 79.

American corporations). One writer estimates that this would amount to $28 billion in the first fifteen years after a Burke-Hartke type of bill was passed.[48]

An expansion of the present trade-adjustment program to cover dislocations brought about by the creation of overseas subsidiaries might be preferable to protectionist measures that restrict the freedom of American-based MNCs to compete with their counterparts overseas and restrict access to the American market by foreign concerns.[49] Despite the fact that there *are* significant differences between the international economic system of the 1930s and that system in the 1970s, this writer, at least, is reluctant to see protectionist measures adopted on a large scale in the United States, because of the inevitable countermeasures they will provoke and the possibility that the conditions leading to the economic disaster of the 1930s will be re-created.

In any case, it seems clear that to the extent political alternatives to protectionism can be devised, the pressure for such measures on the part of labor in the industrialized countries will be reduced. If pressure is not reduced, if the AFL-CIO, for example, does successfully get a Burke-Hartke type of bill passed, it will be another blow to transnational cooperation among labor unions. For the transnational strategy of unions like the UAW and the national strategy of the AFL-CIO are obviously incompatible. Political barriers in the United States to imports from other industrialized countries will hurt the workers in those other states. And the corporations in those states will be sorely tempted to transfer production to the United States in order to avoid the barriers as well as obtain access to the vitally important American market. In the process of transferring production, they will be exporting jobs from, say, Europe to the United States. European workers, then, will no longer be able to find employment producing goods for export to the U.S. because of a Burke-Hartke bill, and they would also be less likely to find employment with American subsidiaries operating in Europe because of the same type of bill. Faced with such a situation, how long would it be before European countries (and Japan, Canada, and so on) would pass Burke-Hartke bills of their own?[50] The lack of countervailing power available to labor unions

[48]Stephen P. Magee, "The Welfare Effects of Restrictions on U.S. Trade," *Brookings Papers on Economic Activity,* Brookings Institution, Washington, D.C., 1973, pp. 689– 690, 701.

[49]Raymond Vernon, Foreword, in *International Labor and the Multinational Enterprise,* ed. Duane Kujawa, Praeger, New York, 1975, xi– xii.

[50]This rhetorical question should not be interpreted as a total condemnation of Burke-Hartke types of measures. At least some of the tax breaks that American corporations receive for overseas activities might well be modified in such a way as to discourage irresponsible (however defined) transfers of production overseas.

as they confront MNCs is a problem, and one can hope that unions find ways to deal wth this problem, even if one is skeptical of the ways some of them are approaching it now.

Other Transnational Organizations

Deciding which types of transnational organizations, other than multinational corporations, are most important in terms of impact on global politics is not easy. One criterion might be the number of members in such an organization; another could be the size of annual budgets. But these data are not readily available for all transnational organizations and if they were, comparability would still be a problem. For example, some transnational groups have only individuals as members, while others have affiliated national organizations as official members. Which transnational organization is more important: one with 20,000 individual members or one that, counting all individual members of affiliated national organizations, has 1 million members? The people who are counted in the latter organization may not even be aware of its existence, since their membership is the result of a decision by the national leadership to join a transnational entity.

*Ten Important Transnational
Organizations*
Another method of gauging the relative impact of different transnational organizations would be based on the frequency with which they are recognized (for example, given consultative status) by intergovernmental organizations, such as the United Nations Educational, Scientific, and Cultural Organization (UNESCO) or the OAS. The ten transnational organizations that receive the highest scores on this criterion are:

1 International Confederation of Free Trade Unions
2 World Confederation of Labor
3 International Organization for Standardization
4 International Chamber of Commerce
5 International Cooperative Alliance
6 World Federation of United Nations Associations
7 World Federation of Trade Unions
8 International Federation of Agricultural Producers
9 International Union for Conservation of Nature and Natural Resources
10 World Veterans Federation

These data were compiled by the Union of International Associations and published in *Yearbook of International Organizations.*[51] A nongovernmental organization, according to the criteria used by the union, must operate actively in at least three countries, be independent, have a constitution giving members the right to elect governing officers, have officers of more than one nationality (perhaps on a rotating basis), and be able to supply evidence of current activity.

As the list indicates, many of the most important transnational organizations are involved primarily in economic issues; the three transnational labor union organizations discussed in the previous section are among the top ten, and organizations such as the International Chamber of Commerce and the International Federation of Agricultural Producers are somewhat analogous to the economic pressure groups that operate within domestic political systems. The International Organization for Standardization is not really a pressure group, but it does aim to facilitate international economic intercourse by promoting the development of common measurement and quality standards for goods and services exchanged across international boundaries.[52] The International Union for Conservation of Nature and Natural Resources is also involved in economic issues as they relate to the "promotion of international cooperation in the application of ecological concepts to the conservation and management of nature and natural resources."[53]

Three of the organizations listed have as a stated purpose the promotion of international peace and cooperation, although they approach this goal from different angles. The World Federation of United Nations Associations acts as a "people's movement" for the United Nations, cooperating with other organizations whose objects include support of the United Nations and promoting research and education about the various aspects of the U.N. It conducts regional seminars for educators who teach about the U.N. and arranges travel and lodging grants for young people who wish to learn about the U.N. by attending one of the annual summer schools sponsored by the federation.[54] The World Veterans Federation, made up of some 160 national veterans' organizations in 48 countries totaling 20 million members, is dedicated to the defense of the interests of all war veterans and war victims through legal and constitutional means, which means that it does function as a

[51]*Yearbook of International Organizations,* 15th ed., Union of International Associations, Brussels, Belgium, 1974, p. s25.
[52]*Yearbook,* pp. 418–419.
[53]*Yearbook,* pp. 481–482.
[54]*Yearbook,* pp. 642–643.

pressure group. But it also has more grandiose and altruistic aims, such as to "maintain international peace and security by application of the U.N. Charter and the implementation of the Universal Declaration of Human Rights."[55] Finally, the International Cooperative Alliance joins together 542,948 cooperative societies, with a total membership of 280 million individuals in almost 60 countries. The aims of this mammoth organization are to be the universal representative of cooperative organizations of all types, to propagate cooperative principles throughout the world, promote cooperation in all countries, safeguard the interests of the cooperative movement in all its forms, and to maintain good relations between all its affiliated organizations.[56]

Transnational Religion

Another kind of transnational entity that, some argue, is becoming more important in terms of political impact is based on religion. For example, Gerald and Patricia Mische assert that "religion networks, church-related organizations and religious institutions that encircle the earth constitute a unique global social fibre. They can be major actors in the construction of a more human world order."[57] The Mische's admit that the history of the Christian church, marred by religious wars and intolerance symbolized most dramatically, perhaps, by the Inquisition, makes it seem unlikely that the church could play such a role. But they also believe that adherence to true religious values will make it possible for the Christian church to help in the construction of a global society.

The best-organized, longest-lasting arm of Christianity, of course, is the Roman Catholic church. This transnational organization claims some 560 million members, with a professional staff of about 1.6 million. Strictly speaking, though, it is not a transnational organization, since its center is the sovereign state of the Vatican City. It has a diplomatic corps, and even (an admittedly insignificant) military force. In the nineteenth century it seemed for a time that the entire Italian state might be united under the papacy. But the papal states were conquered by a military force, and in time the pope withdrew to the Vatican. Finally, in the Lateran Treaty of 1929, the Italian government recognized the sovereignty of the Vatican City, and since that time several states have chosen to recognize it in the time-honored fashion of nation-states with an

[55]*Yearbook*, p. 659.
[56]*Yearbook*, pp. 307–308.
[57]Gerald and Patricia Mische, *Toward a Human World Order*, Paulist Press, New York, 1977, p. 303.

exchange of ambassadors.[58] "No other religious institution in the modern world functions as both a church and a political organization that exchanges diplomatic representatives and claims total recognition as an independent member of the community of nations."[59]

The Vatican City, though, is obviously not an ordinary territorial state, since it claims the loyalty, through the Roman Catholic church, of individuals scattered in virtually every part of the globe. This brings Vatican City into an interesting relationship with the international system and member territorial governments. In some cases, such as Colombia, the state government and the Catholic church are very close allies. Catholicism is the official state religion of Colombia, the state is officially committed to protect the church, the church is given "complete liberty and independence of civil power," it can acquire property, it is given a central role in all types of public education, religious instruction is obligatory in all schools, and the Vatican is given the right to make appointments within the hierarchy of the Colombian church.[60] On the other hand, many Communist countries try to deny the Vatican any access to their citizens. (There are, though, an estimated 8 million Catholics in the Soviet Union and 3 million in mainland China.)

Perhaps the most interesting confrontation today between the Catholic church and national government is taking place in Latin America. The conflict between church and government there represents a sharp break with tradition, since the two have historically formed an effective coalition in favor of the status quo in that part of the world. Recently, at least a few members of the Catholic hierarchy have spoken out against the more reactionary and oppressive policies of some of the Latin American military governments. Helder Camora, for example, the archbishop of Olinda and Recife in Brazil, has been a prominent critic of the Brazilian regime. Some priests have argued for the relevance of Marxism to Christian social change, expressed admiration for Che Guevara, and even joined guerrilla bands in violent protests against the status quo.[61]

The Catholic church has, in recent years, shown an increasing interest in formal ties with the World Council of Churches, consist-

---

[58]G. Pope Atkins, *Latin America in the International Political System,* Free Press, New York, 1977, p. 123.

[59]Francis X. Murphy, "Vatican Politics: Structure and Function," *World Politics,* 26 (July 1974), 542.

[60]Ivan Vallier, "The Roman Catholic Church: A Transnational Actor," *Latin national Organization,* 25 (Summer 1971), 486.

[61]Atkins, *Latin America,* pp. 127–128. See also, P. E. Sigmund, "Latin American Catholicism's Opening to the Left," *Review of Politics,* 35 (January 1973), 61–76.

Jorge Videla of Argentina, one of the Latin American dictators criticized by the Catholic clergy in the 1970s. UPI Photo.

ing of national organizations of Protestant denominations. Also, in 1970 and 1974, leaders of virtually all the world's major religions — Buddhism, Christianity, Confucianism, Hinduism, Islam, Jainism, Judaism, Shintoism, Sikhism, and Zoroastrianism, met in two world conferences on religion and peace.[62] If indeed the ecumenical movement is successful, it is conceivable that religion networks may form the basis for significant transnational activity in the coming decades.

Amnesty International

One of the more intriguing transnational groups to appear in the last two decades is Amnesty International (AI). This organization dedicates itself to the release of political prisoners all over the world,[63] as well as to securing humane treatment for political prisoners that it cannot get released. The time is ripe for such a group,

---

[62]Mische, *Toward a Human World,* pp. 314–315.

[63]The organization works for the release of such prisoners "provided they have neither used nor advocated violence." This has proved to be one of the more controversial aspects of the modus operandi of AI, but as of this writing the group continues to adhere to that principle.

for there is little doubt that governments in modern times have more sophisticated methods for apprehending political dissidents and abusing them when they are in custody. Miniaturized electronic surveillance equipment to gather information, and computerized systems to process information, make it difficult for dissidents to escape the clutches of repressive governments. Injections, tranquilizers, cattle prods, electroshock, sleep deprivation, noise bombardment, psychosurgery, and sensory deprivation chambers are among the instruments available to governments bent on torture and behavior modification.[64]

Amnesty International's drive to curb the use of these "modern" techniques began in 1961. A London lawyer, Peter Benenson, noticed while reading a newspaper in the subway that Portuguese students had been imprisoned for taking part in a peaceful demonstration. Benenson organized some friends and acquaintances to agitate for the release of these students. It was presumed to be a temporary campaign, but by the end of the year, the need for a continuing organization had become evident. In 1962, the movement adopted the name Amnesty International, and in 1963, an international secretariat was set up in London. The group today claims a membership of about a hundred thousand.[65]

Amnesty International maintains a scrupulous neutrality with respect to international ideological conflicts. It selects prisoners of the month toward which it directs letter-writing campaigns of individual members; the prisoners are selected from one free-world, one Communist, and one Third-World state. The organization also sets up adoption groups (there are now about 1600) of ten to twenty people to work in a concerted way to obtain the release of three prisoners (again from the free, Communist, and Third worlds), none of which is located in the home country of the group. Amnesty International originated in Great Britain, but that has not prevented it from pointing out mistreatment of prisoners in Northern Ireland or reporting alleged torture of detainees by British interrogators in Aden. And there are now more adoption groups in West Germany and Sweden than there are in Great Britain. The Soviet Union welcomed the activities of Amnesty International, as long as it highlighted repression in non-Communist countries, but has become considerably less enthusiastic about the organization since it published a report entitled *Prisoners of Conscience in the*

[64]Harry Scoble and Laurie S. Wiseberg, "Human Rights and Amnesty International," *The Annals,* 413 (May 1974), 15.
[65]*The Amnesty International Report,* Amnesty International Publications, London, 1976, p. 13.

An elderly woman in Belfast watches as a British sharpshooter takes a position on her doorstep. Wide World Photo.

U.S.S.R.: Their Treatment and Condition. [66] The United States government did not view with favor the agitation by Swiss citizens (members of Amnesty International) for the release of Americans in

[66] "Clearly the KGB has been authorized to treat Amnesty just like any other dissident group and put it down" "No Amnesty," *The Economist,* April 26, 1975, 68.

jail for refusing military service during the Vietnam War, nor the AI reports on the status of political prisoners in South Vietnam. One can readily guess the reaction of the Brazilian military government to an AI publication, *Report on Allegations of Torture in Brazil.*[67]

The ideological neutrality of AI undoubtedly strengthens its hand when it attempts to secure the release of political prisoners, canceling the credibility of any charge by target governments that AI agitation is politically motivated. But the neutrality is certainly no guarantee of success. How successful has AI been? It has achieved consultative status with the United Nations (ECOSOC and UNESCO) and the Council of Europe, has cooperative relations with the Inter-American Commission on Human Rights of the Organization of American States, and observer status with the Organization of African Unity. But the point of the organization is to obtain the release of political prisoners and success here is difficult to gauge. It has become involved in over 15,000 cases and claims to have helped secure the release of some 8,500. How many of these prisoners would have been released without the intervention of AI? And in how many cases did AI intervention provoke a backlash on the part of an embarrassed government, leading to prolonged imprisonment of people a government might have otherwise released?

Even given the difficulty of answering such questions, one can logically argue that the global political system needs to have an organization that operates outside the nation-state framework to put pressure on states to respect human rights. States will always resist and resent intrusions in internal affairs by other states. Intergovernmental organizations (IGOs) are often the creatures of the strongest national governments within them. Also, "the personnel who staff IGOs — human rights or general purpose — are in the main, permanent civil servants, including former foreign service officers . . . international lawyers, and professional economists."[68] Since these people owe their jobs to particular national governments, or groups of national governments who make up IGOs, the independence and zeal with which they will expose human rights violations by governments is dubious. In any case, Amnesty International offers an encouraging example in favor of the argument that one private citizen with a good idea can have a visible impact on global

[67] Another interesting indication of the ability of Amnesty International to appeal to (and antagonize) people from a broad ideological spectrum is the membership of AI's National Advisory Council in the United States. Among the members of the council in the middle 1970s were Joan Baez, Leonard Bernstein, William Buckley, and Zbigniew Brzezinski.

[68] Scoble and Wiseberg, "Human Rights," p. 16.

politics. And the Nobel Peace Prize that AI received in 1977 may serve to increase its visibility and impact.

The Red Cross

Amnesty International, of course, is not the only transnational organization working in the area of human rights. Others include the World Moslem Congress, the International Movement for Fraternal Union among Races and Peoples, the Law Association for Asia and the Western Pacific, the Committee on Society, Development and Peace, the Confederation Mondiale, the International Commission of Jurists, the International League for the Rights of Man, and the International Committee of the Red Cross.[69] The last-named organization is, perhaps, particularly deserving of further comment.

The Red Cross was started by Swiss persons in the 1860s, and at present is comprised of more than 120 national Red Cross societies. The original Red Cross agency later became known as the International Committee of the Red Cross (ICRC); it is still entirely Swiss in composition, but it recognizes new national societies on behalf of the organization. After the First World War, the ICRC was joined by the League of Red Cross Societies, which has a secretariat in Geneva, and is charged with the coordination of assistance in natural disasters and promoting the development of national societies.[70]

In addition to providing relief in case of natural disaster, the Red Cross has carved out a role for itself in disasters such as war and conflict short of war that results in administrative detention, summary executions, secret military trials, and so on. Since the beginning, the organization has helped bring into existence a series of multilateral treaties designed to "humanize" war and political conflict; these treaties have dealt with the rights and treatment of sick and wounded military personnel, prisoners of war, civilians in a war zone or occupied territory, and persons affected by internal war.[71]

Like Amnesty International, the ICRC has achieved a respectable status of ideological neutrality, which enhances its ability to influence governments in the direction of respecting human rights. Unlike Amnesty International, the ICRC has chosen to work

[69]Harry Scoble and Laurie S. Wiseberg, "Amnesty International: Evaluating Effectiveness in the Human Rights Arena," *Intellect,* 105, (September–October 1976), 80.

[70]David P. Forsythe, "The Red Cross as a Transnational Movement: Conserving and Changing the Nation-State System," *International Organization,* 30 (Autumn 1976), 610.

[71]Forsythe, "Red Cross," p. 626.

within the nation-state system, taking care not to violate the sovereignty of states, and typically avoiding actions that will embarrass national governments. "The ICRC has treated even flagrant violations of the law of armed conflict or widely recognized humanitarian principles without publication of details."[72] Of course, this allows the Red Cross access to situations and prisoners from which organizations such as Amnesty International would be barred. Though the Red Cross is open to the charge of lending respectability to governments that do not deserve it, the activities of the Red Cross may complement those of organizations like Amnesty International in a useful way that no organization more independent of sovereign states could accomplish.

Scientific and Educational Organizations
Scientists and educators have joined in the transnational wave of the sixties and the seventies, for a variety of reasons. The scientific community has always had a certain element of transnationality, partly because the goals and methods of science serve as a kind of internationally accepted language. In recent decades, several hundred scientific international nongovernmental organizations have been created, for the purpose of standardizing data and techniques and organizing international conferences.[73] One positive pressure behind this phenomenon has been less expensive and more efficient communications and transportation. An important negative pressure has been the accelerating costs of high-level scientific research. Costs have reached the point where the scientists of many nations feel they must pool their resources in common efforts. This has proved to be easier in basic research than in applied science and technology; in the latter area, international competitive suspicions tend to assert themselves.

At the apex of transnational scientific efforts stands the International Council of Scientific Unions (ICSU). The council is an unusual combination of nongovernmental and intergovernmental organizations, having both governments and international professional associations as members. The ICSU is financed by subscriptions from its members and funds supplied by UNESCO.[74]

---

[72]Forsythe, "Red Cross," p. 613. The ICRC refused to risk embarrassing the government of Nazi Germany; it visited allied prisoners of war there even though the Nazi government refused the Red Cross access to concentration camps. See Forsythe, "Red Cross," p. 620.

[73]"It has been estimated that each year 2,000 American scientists join 10,000 scientists from other countries at such meetings." See Diana Crane, "Transnational Networks in Basic Science," *International Organization,* 25 (Summer 1971), 585–586.

[74]Crane, "Transnational Networks," p. 591.

Most of the professional organizations in the ICSU have as their main goal the progress of a particular scientific field. But scientists, scholars, educators, and even industrialists, have shown a propensity in recent years to form transnational organizations for the purpose of analyzing, and proposing solutions for, global problems. For example, in 1973, the International Political Science Association authorized the creation of a Research Committee on Peace and Conflict. Serving on the committee are specialists in international conflict from such countries as the United States, Sweden, West Germany, Norway, Poland, Japan, and Brazil. The committee organizes international conferences focusing on the problem of war, and it attempts to stimulate and organize transnational research and educational efforts aimed at understanding international conflict and preserving peace.

The World Order Models Project

Another transnational organization with similar goals is the World Order Models Project (WOMP). WOMP was started in the 1960s by a few Americans whose main concern was to increase the attention given in formal academic programs to the matter of war prevention. They eventually decided to engage the energies of the academic community outside the United States and invited scholars in various parts of the world to participate in regionally based inquiries into the problem of war prevention; in the process they discovered that their academic colleagues overseas wished to broaden the focus of the group's efforts to include such problems as poverty and social injustice.

The first meeting of the World Order Models Project was held in New Delhi, India, in 1968. By that time research groups had been organized in West Germany, Latin America, Japan, India, and North America. Since then, groups representing Africa, the Middle East, China, the Soviet Union, and a nonterritorial perspective have joined the project. WOMP has dedicated itself to the delineation of *preferred worlds* for the 1990s. Preferred worlds have been described in a series of books by scholars from various parts of the world. WOMP has also decided to publish a transnational journal called *Alternatives* and issues an annual *State of the Globe* message. It has launched a series of transnational seminars, educational programs, and a mass public education movement on a global basis.[75] The suggestions and programs of WOMP will be discussed in Chapter 7.

[75]Saul Mendlovitz, ed. *On the Creation of a Just World Order,* Free Press, New York, 1975, pp. vii–xviii.

The Club of Rome

Another interesting transnational scientific approach to the world's problems has been inspired by an organization known as the Club of Rome. In 1968, an Italian industrialist named Aurelio Peccei called together in Rome a group of thirty individuals from ten countries — scientists, educators, economists, international civil servants. From this meeting arose the club, which decided to do what it could to foster an understanding of the interdependent components — economic, political, natural, and social — that make up the global system, and to bring this new understanding to the attention of policymakers and the public.[76]

The group searched for scholars who had a methodology appropriate to the study of the global system and came across Jay Forrester at the Massachusetts Institute of Technology (M.I.T.), a specialist in system dynamics based on computer simulation. A group headed by Donella and Dennis Meadows was eventually organized at M.I.T., and using Forrester's methods, the Meadows devised a computer simulation of the global system. They described the results of their work in a report to the Club of Rome entitled "The Limits to Growth."

The basic thrust of the report, which will be analyzed more closely in Chapter 7, was that the global system can no longer tolerate exponential economic growth, and that solutions for the world's problems must be based on no-growth policies. The impact of the book, which was published in twenty-seven languages and sold over 3 million copies, was indubitably beyond the most optimistic hopes of its instigator, the Club of Rome. In Italy, England, and France, the report was the subject of lengthy television programs. In the Netherlands, the queen, in the presence of the prime minister and cabinet members, presented copies of the Dutch version to high-school students. The Club of Rome was awarded the German Peace Prize in 1973.[77] *The Limits to Growth* has been discussed in the United Nations and has provoked lively controversy throughout the Third World. "Publication of . . . *The Limits to Growth* in 1972 stimulated worldwide interest in dynamic computer simulation models as aids to forecasting and resolution of world problems. . . . There are now over 30 institutions around

[76]Donnella H. Meadows, Dennis L. Meadows, Jorgen Randers, and William W. Behrens, III, *The Limits to Growth: A Report for the Club of Rome's Project on the Predicament of Mankind,* Universal Books, New York, 1972, p. 9.

[77]Alexander King, "The Club of Rome — Setting the Record Straight," *The Center Magazine,* 7 (September 1974), 16–17.

the world, where major projects both on world models and world issue modelling are underway."[78]

In the meantime, the Club of Rome has become a significant transnational actor. In the Netherlands, the sole Dutch member of the club has created an information center to deal with the intense interest generated by *The Limits to Growth* there. Japanese members of the club are sponsoring several studies, including one based on a Meadows type of model of the Japanese economy. The prime minister of Canada has recently been instrumental in the formation of a Canadian Association for the Club of Rome. Members of the club's executive committee have visited Moscow as guests of the Soviet government to take part in lengthy discussions of the problems of growth.[79] The club has also inspired the formation of the International Federation of Institutes of Advanced Study, a body comprised of twenty of the outstanding research institutes of the world aimed at providing specialist skills for a multidisciplinary attack on world problems.[80]

Aurelio Peccei, the founder of the club, has visited more than twenty prime ministers and heads of state. The Club of Rome, like Amnesty International, is a testimony to the potential impact on global politics of one person with a timely idea.

The Future of Transnational Organizations

Do groups like the Club of Rome and Amnesty International represent the wave of the future, or are they aberrations and exceptions that prove the rule that nation-states are the primary actors in the global political system? Ideologically, this writer is frankly inclined to hope that transnational organizations do become increasingly important. Certainly one of the points of this chapter is to highlight the extent to which they are already having an impact. But I am still moved to end the chapter with a note of caution for readers who are inclined to bury the state-centric approach to global politics. First, I believe it is important to point out that much of present-day transnational activity is, at best, only marginally important for global politics. Such groups as the International Association of Lagopedics and Phoniatrics, the International Society of Money Box Collectors, and the International Organization for the Study of the Endurance of Wire Ropes seem unlikely to transform global politics,

[78]Sam Cole, "World Models, Their Progress and Applicability," *Futures*, 6 (June 1974), 201.

[79] King, "Club of Rome," p. 24.

[80] King, "Club of Rome," p. 20.

even in the aggregate. Second, I believe it is also important to remember that passionately committed people have been trying to bury the state-dominated global system almost from the time of its emergence in 1648. "Transnational relations . . . fits neatly into the anti–State centric position. . . . This position thus contains elements of anti–State integrative functionalism of the 1930s, which in turn owed much of its anti–State strain to 19th century economic liberalism."[81] Finally, it is important to realize that the rise of transnational organizations does not necessarily imply the demise of nation-states.

> Transnational relations play a counter role to the State-centric approach only as long as the submerged nation-centric position is ignored. The attempt to avoid development of such a position . . . results in considerable confusion. This confusion can be solved by accepting that while transnational relations do not necessarily pass through State foreign policy machinery they are, nonetheless, expressions of national power and influence and can thus be considered within the framework of the power of a nation and State.[82]

In short, transnational organizations, like intergovernmental organizations, are not immune to the possibility of being used by states for national political purposes.

As was mentioned before and will be discussed in detail in Chapter 7, the global political system is faced today with numerous problems that a state-dominated system may find impossible to resolve. Transnational organizations have become increasingly visible in recent decades, and they can conceivably play a key role in the resolution of such problems. Whatever the outcome of the current contest for influence between states and transnational organizations, it is unlikely that the latter will lose out entirely; they will probably win an increasingly important place in the global political system, even if it is not the predominant position.

[81]Jeffrey Harrod, "Transnational Power," in *The Year Book of World Affairs 1976,* ed. George W. Keeton and Georg Schwarzenberger, Stevens, London, 1976, p. 103.

[82]Harrod, "Transnational Power," pp. 106–107.

SIX

The International System and War

BY NOW THE ALERT READER IS AWARE THAT THE PRECEDING chapters have adopted progressively more comprehensive viewpoints, starting with a focus on individuals and groups inside states (Chapter 2), looking at states as entities (Chapter 3), analyzing the interaction between groups of states, (Chapter 4), and finally considering the impact of transnational entities with members scattered all over the globe (Chapter 5). This chapter concentrates on the international system as a whole. Until the earthbound system begins to interact with systems on other planets, that viewpoint is the most comprehensive that scholars of international politics are likely to consider. Analyses on the system level have their own special virtues as well as peculiar shortcomings.

The Levels-of-Analysis Problem

Both the virtues and the difficulties involved in system-level analyses are analyzed most frequently within the context of the *levels-of-analysis problem.* [1] An intelligible discussion of this problem must be prefaced by a few crucial definitions. First, it is important to understand that the levels-of-analysis problem involves the relationship among analyses of different social entities. *Social entities* are individuals or collections of individuals. There are two basic types of collections of individuals that qualify as social entities. The most loosely integrated kind of social entity is an *aggregation*. This is a collection of individuals who share certain attributes in common but who need not necessarily be interdependent. A *system,* on the other hand, is a collection of individuals or groups who may not share common attributes, but who, by definition, must be interdependent in such a way that the actions of some consistently affect the behavior and fate of the rest. [2] A *unit of analysis* is the social entity whose attributes, relations, or behavior one seeks to describe, predict, or explain. Finally, a *level of analysis* is that point on the vertical scale of increasing size and complexity at which one finds the social entity that serves as the unit of analysis.

Despite appearances to the contrary, distinctions among analyses on different levels do not amount to silly games with words amusing only to pedantic academicians. Studies on different levels of analysis are not distinct only in the sense that they utilize different words to talk about the same things. Voting studies, for example, are particularly prone to levels-of-analysis errors based on this assumption. Before the days of national surveys of individuals, it was common practice to infer the voting habits of individuals from data on precincts. If precincts with large percentages of labor union members gave large majorities to Democratic candidates, it was assumed this meant that individual labor union members favored Democratic candidates. Such assumptions are not entirely misleading most of the time, but they do involve inferences across different levels of analysis (from the precinct level to the individual level in this case) that can be dangerous. In the days when George Wallace ran for governor of Alabama, he did quite well in counties with high percentages of black individuals. It is unlikely that this pattern was brought about by large portions of blacks voting for

[1] J. David Singer, "The Level of Analysis Problem in International Relations," in *The International System,* ed. Klaus Knorr and Sidney Verba, Princeton University Press, Princeton, 1961, 77–92. See also, William B. Moul, "The Levels of Analysis Problem Revisited," *Canadian Journal of Political Science,* 6 (September 1973), 494–513; Ronald J. Yalem, "The Level of Analysis Problem Reconsidered," *The Yearbook of World Affairs,* 31 (1977), 306–326.

[2] Bruce Bueno de Mesquita and J. David Singer, "Alliances, Capabilities, and War: A Review and a Synthesis," in *Political Science Annual,* vol. 4 (1973), ed. Cornelius P. Cotter, Bobbs-Merrill, Indianapolis, 1973, pp. 239–240; Donald Campbell, "Common Fate, Similarity, and Other Indices of the Status of Aggregates of Persons as Social Entities," *Behavioral Science,* 3 (January 1958), 14–25.

Wallace (especially in the days when most blacks did not vote). It is more likely that white voters in counties with many blacks found Wallace's rhetoric appealing.

In one important respect, levels-of-analysis problems in studies of world politics are less serious than they are in voting behavior studies. Often, students of voting behavior do not have access to individual level data, and thus have no choice but to make the best inferences they can from data pertaining to a higher level of analysis. In world politics, if nations are the basic unit of analysis, the available data are likely to pertain to the national level and can be used to construct indices and carry out analyses on the level of the international system. But even in the study of world politics, it may be a type of levels-of-analysis error to infer that national decisions are a perfect reflection of decisions made by individual decision-makers (about whom there is often no data). (For example, if it is inferred from a national decision to start a war that the national leaders preferred that option to others, the inference might be wrong. Possibly no one of the leaders wanted to start war, but war was the only decision that, collectively, they could agree on. It is possible that each decision-maker involved had a preferred option.) And it is also possible to fall into levels-of-analysis errors even when data for all relevant levels *are* available.

Imagine, for example, the relationship between military expenditures and war. Imagine further, for the sake of simplicity, that there are only three states in a hypothetical international system being investigated. Looking at Nation A and considering three successive time periods (t_0, t_1, and t_2), it is found that when Nation A's military expenditures go up, it experiences more war, and when expenditures go down, it has less war.

Inferring causality from the covariation would be extremely risky. First, only three time periods have been considered; the covariation might well have occurred by chance alone. Second, it might well be that war is causing the military expenditures and not vice versa. Finally, there might be some third factor, such as the amount of internal unrest in the state, that has an impact on both military expenditures and war and causes them to covary. But suppose, for the sake of this example, that after investigating all the possibilities, it is discovered that none apply. For Nation A, the positive correlation between military expenditures and war indicates that the former causes the latter. Suppose further that an analysis of Nations B and C in the hypothetical system reveals the same pattern between expenditures and war.

Since it has been found for each state in the system that the higher its military expenditures, the more war it experiences, can the assumption be made that the higher the military expenditures in the system, the greater will be the amount of war? It might seem logical to conclude this, but to do so would constitute a levels-of-analysis error. Consider Table 6.1, showing the relationship between military expenditures and war experience of the three states, Nations A, B, and C, discussed in the previous paragraph. Notice that as the figures for military expenditures across the three time periods for each state go up, the figures representing the amount of war experienced go up, too. Similarly, as military expenditures go down (for example, in the case of Nation A from t_1 to t_2), so the amount of war experienced does, too. For every state there is a positive relationship between military expenditures and war. But consider the figures pertaining to the entire system, obtained by simply adding up the military expenditures and the war experiences of every state. On the systemic level of analysis there is a negative relationship between military expenditures and war. As military expenditures go up from t_0 to t_1, the amount of war in the system decreases. From t_1 to t_2, the military expenditures in the system decrease, but the amount of war increases substantially.

This system-level negative correlation may or may not be causal; the point is that one cannot safely infer that a pattern that exists on a lower level of analysis necessarily exists on a higher level and vice versa. That is, it would be just as disastrous a mistake, if one analyzed the imaginary system depicted in Table 6.1, to focus

TABLE 6.1 An imaginary systemwide profile showing national and system-level relationships

	t_0	t_1	t_2
Nation A			
Military expenditures	10	40	20
War	5	10	5
Nation B			
Military expenditures	15	10	20
War	20	15	40
Nation C			
Military expenditures	30	15	20
War	40	10	30
Total System			
Military expenditures	55	65	60
War	65	35	75

on the system-level relationship between military expenditures and war and conclude that states in the system with higher military expenditures were likely to experience less war, as it would be to infer the higher-level relationship from the lower-level patterns.

Finally, levels-of-analysis problems can occur in verbal as well as statistical analyses of issues relevant to the global political system. Often, as will be seen, historical analyses of the relationship among various systemic attributes become confused because scholars engaged in debate implicitly focus on different lower-level units of analysis. Such confusion will be endless and inevitable unless the debaters are aware of the necessity to limit discussion to the relationships among social entities on *one* level of analysis, or unless they make transitions from one level to another clear and explicit.

The Balance of Power

For example, confusion can arise in the discussion of one of the most venerable concepts in the literature of international relations, that is, the balance of power. Despite its longevity, there is considerable controversy over its exact definition. Ernst Haas, for example, discerns the following meaning of the balance of power in his analysis of scholarly writings on the subject: (1) *distribution of power,* (2) *equilibrium,* (3) *hegemony,* (4) *stability and peace,* (5) *instability and war,* (6) *universal law of history,* (7) *system and guide to policy making.*[3]

Out of this plentiful supply of definitions, it is possible to pick two or three that are the most important. The balance of power theory is quite complex,[4] but as a concept describing a characteristic of the international system, balance of power usually serves simply to describe the distribution of power among states or among coalitions of states. It may refer to an equal distribution among states, but perhaps more usually it denotes an equal distribution of power among coalitions of states.[5] These two definitions (applying to social entities on different levels of analysis) are sufficiently similar, yet distinct enough, to lead to confusion.

[3] Ernst Haas, "The Balance of Power: Prescription, Concept, and Propaganda," *World Politics,* 5 (July 1953), 442–477.

[4] Edward V. Gulick, *Europe's Classical Balance of Power,* Norton, New York, 1955.

[5] It is this writer's impression that when leaders and politicians speak approvingly of the balance of power, they are usually referring to the existing distribution of power (among states or coalitions), and that they approve of it because it favors them and their friends.

For example, A. F. K. Organski, discussing the balance of power, concludes that

> In the nineteenth century, after the Napoleonic Wars, there was almost continuous peace. The balance of power is usually given a good share of the credit for this peaceful century, but . . . there was no balance at all, but rather a vast preponderance of power in the hands of England and France.[6]

Hans Morgenthau, on the other hand, looks at the nineteenth century and asserts that

> of the temperateness and indecisiveness of the political contests . . . from 1815 to 1914, the balance of power is not only the cause but also the metaphorical and symbolic expression as well as the technique of realization.[7]

How could two well-known scholars of international politics look at the same century and come to such contrasting conclusions about whether a balance of power existed? One reason certainly involves ambiguity in the concept of *power*. But another may well involve the difference between the balance as a distribution of power among individual states, on the one hand, and a distribution of power among coalitions of states, on the other. In terms of the former definition, the nineteenth century international system was not balanced. Great Britain was predominant, certainly in terms of the military-industrial indicators considered in Chapter 3, until nearly the end of that century. But looking instead at the distribution of power among coalitions of states, the picture is much less clear. Despite England's preponderance, it was not always a member of an overwhelmingly powerful coalition. In the 1880s, for example, Austria, Germany, and Russia were allied to one another, as were Austria, Germany, and Italy. In the face of such coalitions, England may still have been the most powerful actor in the system, but its superiority was certainly not overwhelming, and one could plausibly argue that a balance of power existed in the 1880s and throughout much of the nineteenth century.

[6]A. F. K. Organski, *World Politics,* 2d ed., Knopf, New York, 1968, p. 294.
[7]Hans J. Morgenthau, 4th ed., *Politics Among Nations,* Knopf, New York, 1967, p. 213.

Even more basic to the dispute about the relationship of the balance of power and the stability of the international system than the levels of analysis confusion is a debate about the conditions under which states are more likely to go to war. Some scholars, such as Organski, believe that states are unlikely to go to war unless they have a good chance of winning, and that this in turn is not probable unless there is a balance of power between them. Thus, from Organski's point of view, such a balance is dangerous, since it increases the probability that two or more states will decide that they have a chance to win a war against one another. But if there is a preponderance of power in the system, then the stronger states will be able to get their way without fighting a war, because the weaker states will know better than to offer resistance in a battle they must lose.[8]

Defenders of the stability of balance of power will, of course, disagree. They will argue that as long as a balance is maintained, no state will feel confident that it can win a war, and so all states will be reluctant to start one.[9] On the other hand, if there is a preponderance of power in the system, the stronger states will be constantly tempted to take advantage of their superiority, and wars are the likely outcome.

An Analysis of Empirical Evidence

Both arguments are reasonable, and it would be interesting to know which one turns out to be more accurate. One trio of authors decided to find out.[10] They collected data on the "power" of all the major powers in the international system from 1820 to 1965, utilizing the same indicators discussed in Chapter 3. They obtained these data for every fifth year in the time span, and then calculated an index of concentration that reflected the extent to which power, or military-industrial capability was unequally distributed at each fifth year observation point. The higher this index score, called CON,[11] the more unequal the distribution of capabilities among the major powers. These concentration scores were then used to predict (in a statistical sense; some would prefer the term *post-dict.*) the amount of war experienced by the major powers in the five year periods

[8] Organski, *World Politics*, p. 294.

[9] Ernst B. Haas and Allen S. Whiting, *Dynamics of International Relations*, McGraw-Hill, New York, 1956, p. 50.

[10] J. David Singer, Stuart Bremer, and John Stuckey, "Capability Distribution, Uncertainty, and Major Power War, 1820–1965," in *Peace, War, and Numbers*, ed. Bruce M. Russett, Sage Publications, Beverly Hills, 1972, pp. 19–48.

[11] James Lee Ray and J. David Singer, "Measuring the Concentration of Power in the International System," *Sociological Methods and Research*, 1 (May 1973), 403–436.

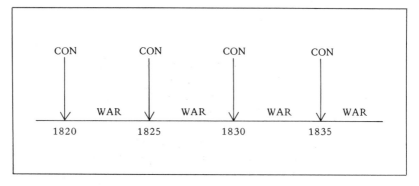

FIGURE 6.1 Structure for the study of the relationship between concentration of power and war

subsequent to each point at which the concentration of power was observed (see Figure 6.1). War was measured in terms of nation-months; for example, if two major powers fought against each other for five months, that was counted as a contribution of ten nation-months of war to the major power subsystem for that time period. To count as a war, for the purposes of this study, a conflict had to have resulted in at least 1,000 battle deaths.[12]

The preliminary results of this study are presented in Table 6.2. The table shows that throughout the time period being analyzed, the concentration of military-industrial capabilities among the major powers did not make much difference with respect to the amount of war they experienced. This can be seen most easily by concentrating on the differences in the amount of war experienced, in terms of percentages, between the times when concentration was low, and the times when it was high. When concentration was low, that is, when military-industrial capability was evenly distributed throughout the major power subsystem, the major powers experienced a relatively large amount of war 50 percent of the time. When power was unevenly distributed (when concentration was high), they experienced a large amount of war 46 percent of the time. In short, the probability of extensive warfare involving the major powers was almost the same whether concentration of power was low or high.

But initial appearances in this case may be deceiving. One might suspect that the relationship between power distribution and

[12]J. David Singer and Melvin Small, *The Wages of War, 1816–1965: A Statistical Handbook,* Wiley, New York, 1972.

war is different in this century than it was in the nineteenth century. In the earlier century, the system was definitely Euro-centered; the great powers of Europe consciously pursued balance-of-power policies, and the relative lack of democratic pressures on the elites in Europe allowed them to pursue such policies unencumbered by the necessity to explain the intricacies to the people. In the twentieth century, non-European states (the United States and Japan) complicated the major power subsystem, and the combination of more rapid communication and transportation and perhaps a better informed public made it more difficult for diplomats to ply their trade in the manner to which they had been accustomed in the nineteenth century. For these kinds of reasons, Singer, Bremer, and Stuckey decided to observe the centuries separately (actually 1895 was chosen as the dividing point), to see whether they might be different with respect to the relationship between concentration of power and occurrence of war. The results of such an analysis are given in Tables 6.3 and 6.4.

Obviously, the relationship in question is not the same in the two centuries. In the nineteenth century, greater amounts of war were more likely when the concentration of power among the major powers was higher. But in the twentieth century, greater amounts of war occurred when concentration was lower. Because

---

TABLE 6.2   The relationship between concentration of power in the major power subsystem and war experienced by major powers, 1820–1965[a]

Amount of War Experienced by Major Powers (Average Annual Nation-Months Under way)	Concentration of Power	
	Low	High
Low	8 (50%)	7 (54%)
High	8 (50%)	6 (46%)

[a]The observations are sorted into Low and High categories using the median scores for both Concentration and war as the dividing lines. (Observations falling exactly on the median were placed in the Low category.)
Source: This table adapted from "Capability Distribution, Uncertainty, and Major Power War, 1820–1965" by J. David Singer, Stuart Bremer, and John Stuckey is reprinted from *Peace, War, and Numbers,* edited by Bruce M. Russett © 1972, p. 29 by permission of the Publisher, Sage Publications, Inc. (Beverly Hills/London).

TABLE 6.3 The relationship between concentration of power in the major power subsystem and war experienced by major powers, 1820–1894

Amount of War Experienced by Major Powers (Average Annual Nation–Months Under way)	Concentration of Power	
	Low	High
Low	6 (75%)	2 (29%)
High	2 (25%)	5 (71%)

Source: This table adapted from "Capability Distribution, Uncertainty, and Major Power War, 1820–1965" by J. David Singer, Stuart Bremer, and John Stuckey is reprinted from *Peace, War, and Numbers,* edited by Bruce M. Russett © 1972, p. 29 by permission of the Publisher, Sage Publications, Inc. (Beverly Hills/London).

the number of cases analyzed is small, the possibility that the relationships occurred by chance should be kept in mind.[13] Even so, the pattern in both centuries is reasonably clear, and the difference between the centuries is quite striking.

These findings shed interesting light on the equality-leads-to-peace versus the equality-leads-to-war controversy, but it would be a mistake to conclude that they settle it. The most important reason for avoiding conclusions involves the failure of Singer, Bremer, and Stuckey to consider the effect of alliances on the distribution of power among the major powers. This failure was not the result of oversight; rather, the difficulty of dealing with alliances and coalitions in the context of a study such as this persuaded the researchers to postpone their consideration and focus on individual states. The difficulty stems from the fact that not all formal alliances are "real," and not all "real" coalitions are formalized. That is, on several occasions in the time span analyzed by Singer, Bremer and Stuckey, there were states that were formally allied with one another but that were actually quite antagonistic and unlikely to cooperate in time of crisis. Also, there were states that had not signed formal alliances but were so closely tied by informal bonds that cooperation between them in time of war was quite probable. This means

[13] A chi-square test applied to the tables reveals that the nineteenth century relationship is significant only at the .10 level, and the twentieth century relationship only at the .20 level. Utilizing Pearson's *r,* Singer, Bremer, and Stuckey found that the nineteenth century relationship was considerably stronger than the twentieth century relationship.

TABLE 6.4 The relationship between concentration of power in the major power subsystem and war experienced by major powers, 1895–1965[a]

Amount of War Experienced by Major Powers (Average Annual Nation–Months Under way)	Concentration of Power	
	Low	High
Low	2 (29%)	5 (71%)
High	5 (71%)	2 (29%)

[a]The entries in the analogous cells of Tables 6.3 and 6.4 will not, if added together, reproduce exactly the cell entries in Table 6.2, because the median scores used as dividing lines for the former tables, which focus on the nineteenth and twentieth centuries separately, do not always coincide exactly with the median scores for the same variables when the centuries are analyzed together, as they are in Table 6.2.
Source: This table adapted from "Capability Distribution, Uncertainty, and Major Power War, 1820–1965" by J. David Singer, Stuart Bremer, and John Stuckey is reprinted from *Peace, War, and Numbers,* edited by Bruce M. Russett © 1972, p. 29 by permission of the Publisher, Sage Publications, Inc. (Beverly Hills/London).

that defenders of both the equality-leads-to-peace and the equality-leads-to-war schools of thought are difficult to pin down. If a war occurs when power is very unevenly distributed among the states in the system, an equality-leads-to-war advocate can point to the existence of a coalition, formalized or not, that actually made the distribution of power in the system quite equal. And equality-leads-to-peace advocates could utilize the same technique to save their particular idea from embarrassment. Whether or not operational rules for identifying formal alliances that are not actually in effect, and informal coalitions that are strong enough to be taken into account, can be devised and implemented in a way satisfactory to advocates of both ideas is a question still to be answered.

Bipolarity Versus Multipolarity

The post–Second World War international system was unusual in many respects; one of its more important characteristics involved domination by two superpowers, the United States and the Soviet Union. Not only were these two states far superior to all others in terms of orthodox economic and military indicators of power; they also possessed (after 1949, when the American nuclear monopoly was broken by the Soviets) by far the largest stockpiles of nuclear weapons, and to this day far outrank any other state in the size and range of the delivery systems necessary to transport weapons to targets.

The Advantages of Multipolarity

Naturally, this "bipolarity" of the system, marked not only by the pre-eminence of the superpowers but also by the tendency of the other states in the world to align themselves on one side or the other, provoked extensive commentary among scholars of international politics. Most concluded that such a system is inherently unstable and prone to disastrous collapse, and that any trend toward multipolarity was desirable. Karl Deutsch and J. David Singer, for example, argued that a multipolar system, in which there are several important independent actors, is likely to be more stable than a bipolar system, because the former type of system allows each actor a larger number of normal interaction opportunities. If there are only two important actors, and the two disagree with one another on every important issue, *and* virtually every state in the system lines up with one of the two major actors, conflict among states is likely to be exacerbated. Every cleavage in the system reinforces all other cleavages. But if there are several important actors in the system, each state has an increased number of normal-interaction opportunities with other states, and the result is likely to be a number of cross-cutting cleavages that will serve to stabilize the system. Issue A will be unlikely to divide the system into two groups of states unremittingly hostile to one another, because some states on one side of that issue will agree with a number of states on the opposing side when issue B arises.[14]

Deutsch and Singer also argued that a multipolar system is more stable than a bipolar one because actors in a multipolar system are able to pay less attention to one another. The assumption is that states must devote considerable attention to one another to become so hostile as to start a war. In a bipolar system, this is likely to happen. In a multipolar system, State A cannot devote full energy to concentration on the dastardly deeds of State B, because it must also worry about states C, D, and E. Thus, according to this reasoning, State A is unlikely to become involved in a war with State B.

[14]Karl W. Deutsch and J. David Singer, "Multipolar Power Systems and International Stability," in *International Politics and Foreign Policy,* 2d ed., ed. James N. Rosenau, Free Press, New York, 1969, pp. 317–318.

This idea is particularly interesting when it is applied to the development of arms races. In a bipolar system, every time one of the major actors increases its arms level, the other actor has little choice but to reciprocate. Arms races are likely. But in a multipolar system, an increase in the armaments by one of the major actors need not have such a destabilizing impact. The potential enemies of the arms-increasing state need not increase their arms levels by an equal amount. They can either calculate, since there are several important actors in the system, that only a portion of the original arms increase was aimed at them and react with an accordingly reduced increment in their armaments, or they can simply form an alliance with another of the major actors in the system and not increase their arms levels at all. Arms races, this argument concludes, are much less likely in a multipolar system.[15]

This does not mean, of course, that multipolarity is a panacea, as Deutsch and Singer realize full well. They point out that the same reasoning that supports the argument that multipolarity may serve to slow down arms races also leads to the conclusion that arms control will be more difficult in a multipolar system. Just as other states might be less likely to react to an arms increase by one nation in a multipolar system, they will also be less likely to react to an arms decrease. They may reason that only a small portion of arms were aimed at them in the first place. And since they have so many other potential enemies to worry about, an arms reduction by one state may have little impact on the other states in the system in any case. This is a difficulty of exceptional importance in the age of nuclear weapons. It might well be easier, for example, for the United States and the Soviet Union to conclude agreements to reduce their stockpiles of nuclear weapons and ballistic missiles if the Soviet Union in particular did not have the Chinese to worry about. Finally, Deutsch and Singer point out that, in the long run,

[15] Deutsch and Singer, "Multipolar Power," pp. 321–322. This is a plausible argument, but the Middle East provides an interesting counterexample. One analysis of arms races between Arab states and Israel points out that the multipolar nature of the Middle Eastern subsystem, brought about by a combination of Arab-Israeli hostility and rivalries among Arab states, added urgency to the arms accumulation efforts of all concerned. "What has been going on has been essentially a primary contest between Egypt and Israel that has tended to spill over on the Egyptian side and induce higher levels of armament among other Arab countries; this in turn has tended to induce Israel to try for an extra margin of safety in its competition with Egypt, which in turn has driven Egypt to raise its own level again, and so on . . . while Israel has tended to add the forces of other Arab countries to Egypt in its reckoning, Egypt has considered that it could not count much if at all on the accretion of power to other Arab countries in connection with its contest with Israel, and has therefore sought to achieve a favorable balance with Israel all by itself." See Nadav Safran, *From War to War*, Pegasus, New York, 1969, pp. 144–145.

as states compete with one another and align themselves in coalitions, a multipolar system is likely to evolve into a bipolar one. Thus, a multipolar system provides at best a temporarily preferable alternative to bipolarity, which "might bring mankind some valuable time to seek some more dependable bases for world order."[16]

The Advantages of Bipolarity

Kenneth Waltz disagrees. He believes that the bipolar system since the Second World War has been quite stable, especially in comparison with the multipolar system of the past. He says that

> in a world of three or more powers the possibility of making and breaking alliances exists. . . . Flexibility of alignment then makes for rigidity of national strategies: a state's strategy must satisfy its partner lest that partner defect from the alliance. . . . The alliance diplomacy of Europe in the years before the First World War is rich in examples of this. Because the defection or defeat of a major state would have shaken the balance of power, each state was constrained to adjust its strategy, and the deployment of its forces to the aims and fears of its partners.[17]

In short, Waltz argues that the multipolar system of the early 1900s resulted in the First World War, whereas the bipolar system since the Second World War has been relatively stable.

The alert reader will note a sleight of hand involving a type of levels of analysis switch. It is true that, if the focus is on relationships among nations, the pre-First World War system was multipolar. But if the focus is on relationships among coalitions instead, the system was clearly bipolar, with two major alliances confronting one another. Thus the First World War can be attributed to bipolarity *or* multipolarity, depending on which kind of social entity one chooses to concentrate on and which particular ax one has in mind of grinding.

Still, Waltz's point is clear. Whether there are two very powerful states or several, there is likely to be a tendency toward bipolarity in the international system, among coalitions at least. If this is so, Waltz argues, it is better to have two opposing coalitions led by two clearly predominating states than to have those coalitions made

---

[16] Deutsch and Singer, "Multipolar Power," pp. 323–324.

[17] Kenneth Waltz, "International Structure, National Force, and the Balance of World Power," in *International Politics and Foreign Policy,* 2d ed., ed. James N. Rosenau, Free Press, New York, 1969, p. 306.

up of nearly equal partners. In the latter type of system, any change is likely to be resisted on the grounds that it will allow one side or the other a crucial advantage. The result will be the kind of rigidity that contributed so strongly to the start of the First World War. In contrast, since the Second World War, both the United States and the Soviet Union have been so powerful in comparison to every other state that they have been able to accept major changes in the international system with relative equanimity. For example, both superpowers have "lost" China since the Second World War, and even a change in the balance of power of that magnitude did not lead either superpower to panic or to launch a Third World War in order to resist it.[18]

A Golden Mean?

Richard Rosecrance finds good and bad points in both arguments concerning bipolarity and multipolarity. On the one hand, he agrees that bipolarity may increase the stability of the international system, since each superpower in such a system is able to keep its allies in line and out of conflict with one another. But, on the other hand, a bipolar system also has rigid aspects, with the superpowers eyeing each other suspiciously and every change in the system creating a crisis based on the fears of each superpower that any change might result in some crucial advantage for its counterpart. Multipolarity, Rosecrance agrees, adds flexibility to the system; conflicts are diffused in such a system, and thus any single conflict will probably be less serious than the focused battles likely to occur in a bipolar system. But Rosecrance believes that multipolarity also entails important deficiencies (in addition to a tendency toward bipolarity). The most crucial involves the uncertainty it engenders in the members of such a system. Every change that occurs in a multipolar system is of unpredictable impact. No state is quite sure which state is on whose side. Conflicts *are* diffused in such a system, but there are more of them, and the increased number of conflicts added to the uncertainty that multipolarity generates might well be a deadly combination, especially in an era of nuclear proliferation.

Rosecrance concludes that the most desirable type of international system would exhibit both bipolar and multipolar characteristics. The two superpowers would be antagonistic enough to compete with one another and motivated to make some attempt to

[18]Kenneth Waltz, "The Stability of a Bipolar World," *Daedalus,* 93 (Summer 1964), 887.

keep their respective allies in line. A minimum amount of antagonism would also be necessary in order to allow the superpowers to convince the smaller powers on each side that they need the protection of a superpower. If the superpowers become too friendly, the smaller powers may decide that they do not need protection from either one, (or, perhaps, that they need protection from both), and the present bipolar conflict might be replaced by a more dangerous one between the rich and the poor or among the races.

But, in this ideal system that Rosecrance describes, the superpowers must avoid total antagonism, and there should be a degree of multipolarity. The smaller powers on both sides should be sufficiently independent and influential to be able to mediate and mollify conflicts between the superpowers. In Rosecrance's own words: "The two major states would act as regulators for conflict in external areas; but multipolar states would act as mediators and buffers for conflict between the bipolar powers. In neither case would conflict be eliminated, but it might be held in check."[19] Such a system, Rosecrance concludes, might best be described as a system of "bi-multipolarity."

Levels Versus Changes in Polarity

To some extent, debates about the relative stability of bipolar and multipolar systems must be dealt with philosophically, because there is an insufficient number of cases to settle the argument empirically. Defenders of bipolarity, such as Waltz, depend essentially on one example, the bipolar post–Second World War system, and their case stands or falls on the application of logic, intuition, and rhetoric to that example. Rosecrance, of course, speculates about the stability of a kind of system that had never existed up to the time he wrote the article. (And which, I would gather from his article, has yet to exist.)

But the polarity of the international system need not necessarily be treated as a categorical variable, with only a few values (for example, bipolar, multipolar, and bimultipolar). One might instead focus on formal-alliance ties in the international system and concentrate on the number of poles, or groups of states, that are based on such ties, as well as the clarity with which these groups are defined. This kind of approach would allow one to measure different degrees of polarity in the system, and to determine empirically the relationship between polarity and interstate conflict.

[19] Richard Rosecrance, "Bipolarity, Multipolarity, and The Future," *Journal of Conflict Resolution,* 10 (September 1966), 314–327.

Such an approach has been adopted by Bruce Bueno de Mesquita. He devised a measure of the polarity of the international system, based on formal alliances, and providing index scores for three different aspects of polarity. The first of these was a *tightness* score, reflecting the extent to which states in the same group are bonded to each other. For example, if each state in a group is allied to every other state in the group, then the tightness score for that group, or pole, would be maximized. Every pair of states in a given group that is not allied to one another would decrease that score. The second index score devised by Bueno de Mesquita focused on the *discreteness* of the groups or poles in the system. If the poles are entirely distinct, with no between-group ties, then the discreteness score would be high. Any alliance ties between states in different poles make the discreteness score lower. Finally, Bueno de Mesquita utilized another index score that was simply a function of the number of poles, or groups of states, emerging from an analysis of the alliances in the international system.[20]

These three indices of systemic polarity were then used to predict (or postdict) the occurrence of interstate war, and the duration of wars, in both the nineteenth and twentieth centuries. Bueno de Mesquita found that virtually none of these indices correlated with the occurrence or the duration of wars in either century. That is, whether or not the system was polarized seems to have made little difference in the probability that wars would occur or how long they have lasted over the last 150 years.

In light of these results, Bueno de Mesquita hypothesized that the occurrence and duration of wars might be related to *changes* in the polarity of the system, rather than to *levels* of polarity. Furthermore, he argued that it is certain kinds of changes, those that increase the clarity of the system structure, that can be expected to make wars more likely and of longer duration. The greater the increases in clarity, the more likely it will be that potential initiators of war will feel confident about their calculations of relative costs and benefits that are likely to result if they actually do carry out their plans. The increases in clarity, for example, will help the potential initiating state determine from which other states it and the intended opponent will receive aid. Finally, Bueno de Mesquita argued that increases in the clarity of the system structure (for example, increases in the tightness of existing groups of states) will help opponents of initiators identify and attract supporters, thus prolonging any wars that do occur.

[20] Bruce Bueno de Mesquita, "Measuring Systemic Polarity," *Journal of Conflict Resolution,* 19 (June 1975), 187–216.

Basically, what Bueno de Mesquita finds, in his empirical test of these arguments, is that increases in structural clarity over five-year periods are related to the probability and the duration of interstate wars from 1900 to 1965 but not in the nineteenth century. In other words, in this century, war has been more probable in a given year, and a war was likely to last longer if that year or the war were preceded by substantial increases in the clarity of the system's structure. Changes in the tightness of the groups, or poles, in the system were particularly important. Wars occurring after five years of substantial increases in tightness have been significantly longer in this century. Furthermore,

> *War almost never occurs during periods of declining tightness.* Eighty-nine percent of the twentieth century periods of declining tightness preceded years in which no war began, while eighty-four percent of the wars in the twentieth century began in years following a five year rise in systemic tightness.[21]

The tenuous nature of the link between Bueno de Mesquita's study and the previous discussion of the merits of bipolarity and multipolarity should be emphasized at this point. The measure of polarity utilized by Bueno de Mesquita is quite complex, and while the operations on which it is based seem sensible enough, the results obtained are somewhat surprising. According to this measure, for example, the international system during the 1950s and the early 1960s was not bipolar at all but quite multipolar.[22] This certainly does not mean that Bueno de Mesquita's measure is inaccurate or invalid, but it may well indicate that Bueno de Mesquita's conception of polarity and that of writers such as Deutsch and Singer, or Waltz, are quite different.

And even if it is assumed that Bueno de Mesquita's measures are valid, the logic of his arguments is at times less than compelling. For example, he argues that decision makers can better calculate the potential costs and benefits of a war after periods of increasing tightness. But why should increases in the clarity of system structure rather than high levels of structural clarity make it easier for a potential initiator of war to calculate possible benefits?

Finally, it should be emphasized that Bueno de Mesquita does not argue that increases in the tightness of poles are a direct cause of war, but rather they serve as a catalyst, making it more likely that

[21] Bruce Bueno de Mesquita, "Systemic Polarization and the Occurrence and Duration of War." *Journal of Conflict Resolution* (Forthcoming).
[22] Bueno de Mesquita, "Measuring Systemic Polarity," 215–216.

whatever disputes arise (for other reasons) will result in war. Even keeping in mind the limitations of Bueno de Mesquita's findings, though, one can in these days when the tightness of the Communist and the free-world poles seems to be on the wane, be encouraged by Bueno de Mesquita's conclusion that "decreases in systemic tightness . . . signal both a reduction in the occurrence of war and in the duration of wars in the twentieth century."[23]

Deterrence, Arms Races, and Arms Control

At least as important in its implications for the stability of the international system as the distribution of power among the states is the level of power in the form of military weapons and military personnel. Despite the apparent prevalence of the argument that war is obsolete in today's world,[24] states are spending increasingly large amounts on defense. By 1975, the world's military budgets totaled some $300 billion a year,[25] and states have accumulated firepower equivalent to 15 tons of TNT for every man, woman, and child on the earth.[26]

The United States and the Soviet Union possess most of this military might, spending about one-half as much as the rest of the world put together in frantic efforts to deter one another. In view of the clear fact that each superpower commands enough firepower to obliterate the other's citizens several times over, a couple of obvious questions come to mind. Does it all make sense? Are there *any* good reasons why both the Russians and the Americans continue to accumulate fantastically destructive weapons, or does the process continue willynilly because both sides have succumbed to madness or foolish pride or both?

Thinking the Unthinkable
At bottom, perhaps the most important question would be, Is nuclear war possible? Considering that millions of people on both

[23] Bueno de Mesquita, "Systemic Polarization" (Forthcoming).

[24] One's confidence in this assertion might be tempered somewhat in light of the following quotation from a British newspaper editorial (in the *Manchester Examiner*) in 1853: "Statesmen shrink from war now, not only on account of its risks, its cost, its possible unpopularity, but from a new borne sense of the tremendous moral responsibility which lies on those who . . . bring upon humanity such an awful curse." See F. H. Hinsley, *Power and the Pursuit of Peace*, Cambridge University Press, London, 1967, p. 114.

[25] Ruth Sivard, *World Military and Social Expenditures 1976*, WMSE Publications, 1976, p. 5.

[26] Gerald and Patricia Mische, *Toward a Human World Order*, Paulist Press, Ramsey, N. J., 1977, p. 12.

sides would die in such a conflict, it might seem reasonable to conclude that a nuclear war is unthinkable and virtually certain not to occur. But that would be an overly optimistic conclusion. The problem would be much less serious and intractable than it is if the truth were that the probability of a nuclear war were near zero. It is pertinent to recall that before the First World War it was rather commonly believed that the destructive power of modern weapons, and the complex, interwoven nature of the world's economy, made international war too horrible to contemplate and obviously irrational for all concerned.[27] On the one hand, such arguments were well founded. International war in the second decade of the twentieth century did turn out to involve death, destruction, and suffering on an unprecedented and intolerable scale, and almost all the participants were worse off after the carnage was over, winners as well as losers. Yet the war occurred. The mere fact that nuclear war would be madness does not mean that it will not occur, as the First World War should make clear.

A Possible Dilemma

And to conclude that nuclear war would be madness is, perhaps, also an overly optimistic conclusion. Under certain conditions, it might be rational for one or both sides to initiate a nuclear war. It is possible that the two superpowers will one day find themselves in what has become known in the realm of game theory as the prisoners' dilemma. The structure of such a game is presented in Figure 6.2. The prisoners in the game depicted have been arrested by a sheriff with a problem. The sheriff admits there is not enough evidence to convict either one if they both refuse to confess. That outcome of the game is represented in the upper left-hand cell of the matrix, and each player would win 10 points. But the sheriff further informs the prisoners that if one of them does confess, the confessor will go free and get a large reward (that is, win 20 points), while the other will be hanged (that is, lose 20 points). If, finally, both prisoners confess on the same day, they will each receive long prison sentences (both will lose 10 points, as the lower right-hand cell of Figure 6.2 indicates).

Each prisoner has two possible strategies; each can confess or not confess. Which is the rational strategy from their individual points of view? Social scientists have debated the definition of rationality at some length, but in the context of games such as this,

[27]Norman Angell, *The Great Illusion,* Heinemann, London, 1914. Angell is unjustly blamed on occasion for predicting (before the First World War) that international war was impossible. He did no such thing. He merely argued that it was not economically rational, which is not the same as predicting that it would not occur.

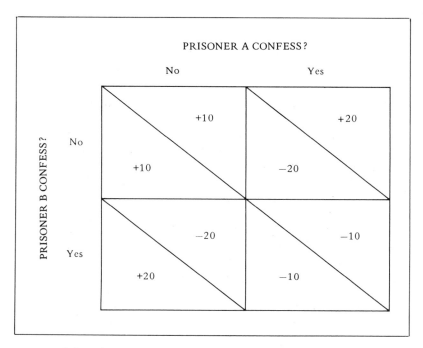

FIGURE 6.2   The prisoners' dilemma game

game theorists specify the minimax strategy as the rational selection for each player. A *minimax* strategy is one that assures a player he or she will minimize the maximum possible loss. If the prisoners decide *not* to confess, the maximum possible loss that each would suffer (if the other chose to confess) would be death; the nonconfessor would be hanged. But if both prisoners confess, the maximum possible loss for each would involve a substantial prison sentence. Thus, the minimax strategy for each prisoner is to confess. So, despite the fact that both prisoners would be better off if they did not confess, each prisoner, making rational calculations, will opt for the strategy that will lead to many years of prison.

Could the United States and the Soviet Union find themselves confronted with a similar dilemma? It is conceivable, as Figure 6.3 suggests. The structure of the confrontation depicted is clearly such that both sides would be better off if a nuclear war did not occur. (Both sides, in that case, win 10 points.) But it is also clear that both sides have an incentive to start a war, because if they get their attack under way first, they wipe out their opponent, inflicting, say, 100 million deaths, while suffering none themselves. In addition, they are free of the menace posed by the other side. Finally, if they both launch a nuclear war simultaneously, they both suffer substantial

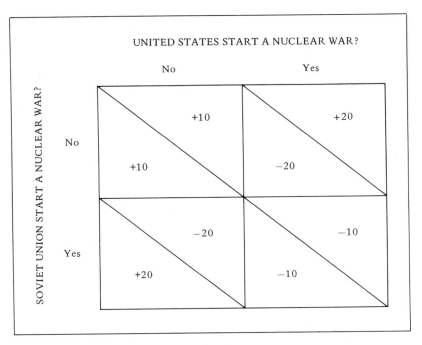

UNITED STATES START A NUCLEAR WAR?

	No	Yes
No	+10 / +10	+20 / −20
Yes	−20 / +20	−10 / −10

SOVIET UNION START A NUCLEAR WAR?

FIGURE 6.3 A potential dilemma for the superpowers

losses (for example, 50 million people), but they do catch at least some of their opponent's missiles on the ground (thus saving the lives of some of their citizens), and they avoid total defeat. Each side suffers grievous losses, but neither state emerges clearly superior in strength.

What is the rational strategy for states engaged in such a confrontation? If the decision makers of both states decide that the minimax strategy is rational, they will both decide to send their missiles hurtling toward one another. If they opt for such a strategy, they might lose 50 million citizens, but so will their opponent. If they avoid the minimax strategy, they risk losing everything: 100 million people and any ability to resist domination by their opponent in the postwar world. Confronted with such a situation, leaders on both sides might reason as follows: Our side, of course, would not dream of committing such a horrifying and repugnant act as launching a first strike. We are too honorable and humanitarian to do such a thing. But I am not sure about the Russians (Americans). Being Communists (Capitalists), they are inherently imperialistic. And they know that if they strike first, they will win. Worse, they know that we know that if they strike first, they will win. Since they know that we know that they will win if they strike first, they might well conclude that we will strike first to avoid catastrophe. Considering this, they are sure to attack. Thus, we must launch a nuclear attack. We may lose 50 million people, but if we do not strike first we will lose 100 million. So, by striking first, we are saving ourselves from possible domination in the postwar world *and* the lives of 50 million people!

The Prisoners' Dilemma and the Real World

Fortunately, there are important differences between the structure of the game presented in Figure 6.3 and the structure of the actual nuclear confrontation between the Soviet Union and the United States today. One of these differences involves the difficulty of making calculations in the real world as accurately as they are made in the game just described. No one really knows how many Russians would be killed by a successful American first strike, and contamination in the form of fallout might come back to haunt the Americans even if the Russians could not retaliate. Furthermore, while the game is a one-shot affair between two players,[28] the real-world nuclear confrontation is a continuing game with more than two players. This adds to the complexity of calculations. Even if the Russians, for example, do convince themselves that they can, at worst, come out of a nuclear war with "only" 50 million deaths and on a par with the United States, they must then think about how the Chinese would react to such a situation. Would they take advantage of it to launch a nuclear or conventional attack of their own?

But by far the most important difference between the structure of the prisoners' dilemma game and that of the nuclear confrontation between the United States and the Soviet Union has to do with the probability of a successful first strike. In the game, the success of a first strike is certain. In actuality, a successful first strike seems highly unlikely. Land-based missiles are, for the most part, underground in "hardened" silos, and the probability that either side could wipe out virtually all of the opponent's missiles on land is very low. Both sides now have missiles that can be launched from submarines, and these could almost certainly launch a deadly retaliatory blow even if the unlikely happened and one side successfully destroyed the land-based missiles of the other. Finally, the early-warning systems of the Americans and the Russians are sufficiently effective that it seems improbable that either would lose all

---

[28] Prisoners' dilemma games *can* be played on a continuing basis, and it is interesting to note that when they are, the players tend to adopt the cooperative strategy after several plays.

of its missiles and nuclear weapons in a first strike by the opponent, even assuming that one side or the other could somehow develop the technology necessary to locate and destroy missiles on land and sea. By the time the missiles of the first striker arrived at their targets, the early-warning system of the opponent would have already triggered a retaliatory response, and the first striking missiles would blow up empty holes and missile-less submarines. If one keeps in mind that any attempt to overcome all these barriers to a successful first strike must be very close to totally effective, lest a few of the enemy's missiles slip through and wipe out several million people, then one must conclude that the Russians and the Americans have successfully achieved what has become known in the United States as a position of mutual assured destruction (with its interesting acronym MAD). That is, both the Americans and the Russians can be serenely confident that if they are the victim of a first strike killing tens of millions of people, their second strike capability will allow them to return the favor.[29]

Technology and Stability
Returning to the original question, Is a nuclear war possible? Under present conditions, one might reasonably conclude that such a war between the United States and the Soviet Union is highly unlikely, since it would lead to disaster for both. Even so, an accidental war is possible. Normally sane men might succumb to the extreme pressure of a crisis, or normally irrational people might somehow get access to a missile or two. But if this were the only kind of nuclear war that seemed possible, much of the tension might be removed from the nuclear confrontation between the United States and the Soviet Union, and much of the steam might be taken out of the arms race. The more serious uncertainty that subverts the comforting conclusion that a nuclear war between the superpowers is highly unlikely stems from the possibly ephemeral nature of the premise for that conclusion, that is, under present conditions. Given the present state of American and Russian technology, it may be highly unlikely that either side will decide to launch a first strike. But how confident can one be that the present relationship

[29] This statement should not be taken to mean, necessarily, that the United States or the Soviet Union are now, or will be in the future, satisfied with a strategy based on MAD or on the idea that the principal role of the military is to deter nuclear war. There are, for example, American strategic theorists who insist that the Russians are basing their strategy on a doctrine that stipulates that a nuclear war can be fought and won. See Richard Pipes, "Why the Soviet Union Thinks It Could Fight and Win a Nuclear War," *Commentary*, 64 (July 1977). Since Americans are so obviously debating the value of the MAD strategy, the Soviets must suspect that the Americans have, or will soon adopt, similar ideas about the "winnability" of a nuclear war.

between American and Russian technology will remain stable for the foreseeable future? With both sides making frantic efforts to achieve various kinds of breakthroughs, does it not seem probable that sooner or later one side or the other will succeed, thus creating a credible first-strike capability?

If, given all the barriers just discussed, a successful first strike seems implausible, consider the following possible technological developments. The Americans have already developed a cruise missile that flies so low it is virtually undetectable by radar. It is also extremely accurate. Such a missile might undermine quite effectively the early-warning system of the Soviets, and the accuracy of the cruise missile combined with satellite-based spy-in-the-sky devices to locate land-based missiles, might conceivably give the Americans the ability to knock out such missiles. The Soviets would still have their submarine-based missiles, but both sides are working on various techniques that may enable them to search out and destroy submarines. Such a development may well be unlikely, but it hardly seems inconceivable. For a final example, consider the following revelation from a 1977 issue of *Aviation Week and Space Technology*:

> The Soviet Union is developing a charged-particle beam device designed to destroy U.S. intercontinental and submarine launched ballistic missile nuclear warheads. . . . A charged-particle beam weapon focuses and projects atomic particles at the speed of light which could be directed from ground-based sites into space to intercept and neutralize reentry vehicles . . . In increasing numbers, U.S. officials are coming to a conclusion that a decisive turn in the balance of strategic power is in the making, which would tip that balance heavily in the Soviet's favor through charged-particle beam development.[30]

The importance of this development may well be exaggerated. (President Carter immediately denied that the Soviets had achieved such a breakthrough or were about to.)[31] Even so, the point about the instability of the nuclear confrontation created by the possibility

[30] Clarence A. Robinson, Jr., "Soviets Push for Beam Weapon," *Aviation Week and Space Technology,* 106 (May 2, 1977), 16–17.

[31] In defense of its position, *Aviation Week and Space Technology* published the following statement delivered in testimony by Dr. Vannevar Bush to a Senate committee in 1945: "There has been a great deal said about a 3000-mi. high angle rocket. . . . In my opinion, such a thing is impossible. . . . I say technically I don't think anybody in the world knows how to do such a thing and I feel confident it will not be done for a very long period of time to come." See *Aviation Week and Space Technology,* 106 (May 2, 1977), 17.

of technological developments by one side or the other remains valid. Such developments may occur, and for that reason alone, a nuclear war between the Soviet Union and the United States may also occur, not because of an accident or insanity, but because one side or the other will find itself in a position where nuclear war is, by some calculations, a logical option.

The possibility adds significantly to the urgency of the arms race between the United States and the Soviet Union. Foolish pride on both sides, and the economic interests of the military-industrial complexes in both countries, are partially responsible for the continued accumulation of weapons, but again, to deny that there is a stubborn element of logic in the arms race is to oversimplify it and to underestimate the dimensions of the problem. That both the Americans and the Russians have overkill in great abundance does not eliminate the possibility that a technological breakthrough might allow one side or the other to destroy or neutralize such a great portion of its opponent's weapons that the opponent will find that it needs more weapons than it has in order to launch an effective second strike. In addition, at least some policymakers worry that if the Soviet Union, for example, develops a significant advantage in the numbers game, it might successfully exploit that advantage politically, even if the numerical advantage it enjoys is meaningless in strict military terms. One pair of analysts argues that "national images are important . . . strategic nuclear forces play a significant role in the projection of these images, and . . . there is some risk of Soviet attempts to exploit a situation of perceived strategic superiority."[32] One can confidently predict that the Russians worry about the possibility that Americans would similarly exploit a perceived strategic superiority.

None of this is meant to imply that, from the American or Russian point of view, the reasons for accumulation of missiles and nuclear weapons are so compelling that there is no choice but to continue. The points considered here are designed to demonstrate that the nuclear confrontation and the arms race between the United States and the Soviet Union are more serious and deep rooted than they might seem if one focuses too closely on the overkill capacity at the command of both sides and the resulting madness or unthinkable nature of nuclear war.

Arms Races

Of course, the arms race between the Russians and the Americans since the Second World War is an unprecedented phenomenon only

[32] Ted Greenwood and Michael C. Nacht, "The New Nuclear Debate: Sense or Nonsense?" *Foreign Affairs,* 52 (July 1974), 780.

Participants	Duration	Outcome
1 *France vs. England*	1840–1866	Peace
2 *France vs. Germany*	1874–1894	Peace
3 *England vs. France and Russia*	1884–1904	Peace
4 *Argentina vs. Chile*	1890–1902	Peace
5 *England vs. Germany*	1898–1912	Peace
6 *France vs. Germany*	1911–1914	War
7 *England vs. U.S.*	1916–1930	Peace
8 *Japan vs. U.S.*	1916–1922	Peace
9 *France vs. Germany*	1934–1939	War
10 *U.S.S.R. vs. Germany*	1934–1941	War
11 *Germany vs. England*	1934–1939	War
12 *U.S. vs. Japan*	1934–1941	War
13 *U.S.S.R. vs. U.S.*	1946–	Expensive?

Source: Samuel P. Huntington, "Arms Races: Prerequisites and Results," in *The Use of Force,* ed. Robert J. Art and Kenneth N. Waltz, Little, Brown, Boston, 1971, p. 367. Reprinted by permission of John Wiley & Sons, Inc.

in the sense that it involves ballistic missiles and nuclear weapons. There have been several arms races in this century and the last, and it would be a mistake to assume that they all ended disastrously. Consider for a moment a list of arms races compiled by Samuel Huntington, presented in Table 6.5. Notice that only five of these thirteen arms races ended in war, and four of the five were associated with the Second World War. With respect to those latter cases, one can reasonably argue that

> in the case of the origins of the second world war, the autonomous arms race cannot be regarded as having been important. On the contrary, we should say that the military factor which was most important in bringing it about was the failure of Britain, France, and the Soviet Union to engage in the arms race with sufficient vigor, their insufficient response to the rearmament of Germany.[33]

[33] Hedley Bull, "The Objectives of Arms Control," in *The Use of Force,* ed. Robert J. Art and Kenneth N. Waltz, Little, Brown, Boston, 1971, p. 352.

Arms Races and Peace

In the light of these data, then, it might be tempting to conclude that arms races are actually a force for peace, provided that both sides engage in them with sufficient vigor. This, indeed, is what Samuel Huntington concludes about the present arms race between the United States and the Soviet Union.

> The great problem of international politics now is to develop forms of international competition to replace the total wars of the first half of the twentieth century. One such alternative is . . . the qualitative arms race. . . . Until fundamental changes take place in the structure of world politics, a qualitative arms race may well be a most desirable form of competition between the Soviet Union and the United States.[34]

By *qualitative* arms race Huntington means a competition that centers on developing new forms of military force and the discovery of technological breakthroughs, as opposed to a *quantitative* arms race, based on competition in the expansion of existing forms of military force.[35] As long as the Russian–American arms race is of the former (qualitative) type, Huntington feels that it "may well be a most desirable form of competition." He further warns that "the likelihood of war increases just prior to a change in military superiority from one side to another."[36]

Dangers in the Present Arms Race

In short, what this writer seems to be arguing is that the accumulation of more deadly weapons by the Russians and the Americans is actually a good thing (at least given the present structure of world politics), and that it is a good thing partly because both sides are concentrating on making their weapons as destructive as possible! I am moved to disagree with Huntington, on several grounds. First, there is some question about the quality of the data base on which he builds his conclusions. Although he never says so explicitly, it seems clear that the list of arms races he presents is supposed to be a more or less complete one for the time period he analyzes. (And he argues that arms races are essentially a modern phenomenon.) But his list is not complete. One scholar, C. B. Joynt, asserts that

[34] Samuel P. Huntington, "Arms Races: Prerequisites and Results," in *The Use of Force,* ed. Robert J. Art and Kenneth N. Waltz, Little, Brown, Boston, 1971, p. 401.
[35] Huntington, "Arms Races," pp. 370–371.
[36] Huntington, "Arms Races," p. 381.

Huntington does not include all the arms races from the twenties and thirties or all those that occurred since 1946 and before 1840.[37] (This disagreement might stem, obviously, from differences in the definition of arms race, but Huntington discusses at least one arms race in the text of his article, that between Israel and Egypt in the middle 1950s, which he does not include in his list.) If the sample of arms races on which Huntington focuses is somehow a biased subset of the phenomenon, then the validity of his conclusions is clearly suspect. One can also quarrel with the delimitation of the time spans for the arms races that Huntington does include in his list. Most important, Huntington specifies that the naval arms race between Germany and England that began in 1898 ended in 1912. As John Mueller points out, "If that arms race is seen to end, not in 1912 . . . , but rather in 1914, it would form a damaging example of a long, qualitative arms race which led to war."[38]

What is perhaps most disturbing about Huntington's argument is its complacency in the face of possible technological breakthroughs on the part of the Americans or the Russians. He is undisturbed by the possibility that one of the nuclear contenders may make some terribly destabilizing discovery. He does consider the problem. But he argues that, historically, "the tendency toward simultaneity of innovation is overwhelming," and that "the logic of scientific development is such that separate groups of men working in separate laboratories on the same problem are likely to arrive at the same answer to the problem at the same time."[39] Historically, Huntington may be correct, although it is worth remembering (as Huntington admits) that the Americans developed the atom bomb four years before the Soviets were able to duplicate the feat.[40] Generally speaking, a consideration of historical parallels as a basis for appraising the present and future is to be highly recommended, and there is a constant temptation to conclude that contemporary problems are unique in character and in potential for disaster. Even so, it is possible that the nuclear confrontation is

[37] "Arms Races and the Problem of Equilibrium," *The Yearbook of World Affairs 1964,* Stevens, 1964, 23– 40. Cited by Patrick M. Morgan, *Theories and Approaches to International Politics,* Page-Ficklin, Palo Alto, 1975, p. 277.

[38] *Approaches to Measurement in International Relations,* Appleton-Century Crofts, New York, 1969, p. 12. To his credit, Huntington is not unaware of the problem. See "Arms Race," p. 384.

[39] Huntington, "Arms Race," pp. 391– 392.

[40] One might take some comfort from this fact, arguing that a substantial advantage for one side in the nuclear contest does not necessarily lead to catastrophe. But during those four years (1945– 1949), because the Russians did not have atomic weapons, the Americans did not have to deal with the possibility that the Russians, knowing that an American first strike could be successful, would launch a first strike themselves.

uniquely susceptible to destabilization by technological breakthroughs. In prenuclear days, a state with a new and better battleship or a machine gun could not take immediate advantage of its good luck. It would first have to drum up a crisis, issue an ultimatum, and then fight a war that was certain to last a matter of weeks, if not months or years. By that time, it is true, as Huntington argues, the opponent was likely to have incorporated the technological innovation into its own military organization or have developed some manner of dealing with it. None of this applies, necessarily, to a nuclear confrontation. Huntington is correct when he argues that it takes several years to get a modern weapons system off the drawing board and into quantity production, and that during that time the other side will probably acquire access to the knowledge necessary to develop the new system for itself. But what if those two processes are not perfectly synchronized, so that one side will have some overwhelming advantage for two weeks or a month, and both sides are aware of the impending imbalance? That two weeks, or perhaps even two days, would be plenty of time to take advantage of a technological breakthrough in the nuclear age and the tensions on both sides might become unbearable. The side about to enjoy the advantage could not look forward to the prospect with confidence, for fear that the opponent would do something desperate before the time arrives. The about-to-be technologically outclassed opponent would have to deal not only with that unpleasant thought but also with the fear that its opponent would do something desperate in order to pre-empt its own desperation move.

Arms Control

What steps can be taken to avoid such a situation? One step involves arms control (efforts to slow down the accumulation and development of new weapons) and disarmament (efforts to lower arms levels on both sides). There is a great deal of skepticism about arms control and disarmament in the literature of international relations, and at least part of this skepticism is based on a simplistic argument that seems to strike some writers as terribly profound. Consider, for example, these assertions from a currently popular introductory text in international politics:

> To attribute wars to arms is to confuse cause and effect. . . .
> An arms race reflects political tensions between nations; it does
> not cause these tensions. . . . Nations do not fight because they
> possess arms. Rather, they possess arms because they believe it

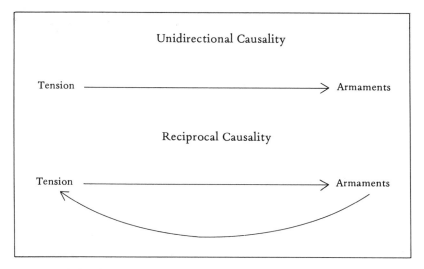

FIGURE 6.4 Two views of the relationship between armaments and tension

might someday be necessary to fight. . . . Since arms are a *symptom* of interstate political conflict, it is an illusion to expect states to disarm as long as conflict persists.[41]

Arms Control and Tension

The basic problem with all these statements is that they are based on a rather simplistic view of the world in which causality is unidirectional. One can agree that an "arms race reflects political tensions between nations" without discounting the possibility that an arms race also adds to the tensions (see Figure 6.4). This is especially so in the nuclear era. There are several reasons for tension in the Soviet-American relationship, but certainly one of those is the tremendous firepower that each state has aimed at the other and which can be delivered at a moment's notice (or, for that matter, without a moment's notice). That the *other* reasons for tension came first is, at this point, nearly irrelevant. What is presently in place is a vicious circle, and the important question is, where best to break into that circle? It is true that the arms race problem might take care of itself if all the other reasons for tension are removed. But that will probably never happen, and it makes at least as much sense to

[41] John Spanier, *Games Nations Play,* 2d ed., Praeger, New York, 1975, pp. 263–264.

attempt to break the vicious circle by reducing arms levels as it does to try to resolve all the other issues that lead to conflict. If it is true that resolving the other issues will make arms control and disarmament easier, it is also true that reducing arms levels will, by reducing tensions, make it easier to resolve the other issues.[42]

The History of Arms Control

The preceding argument is essentially a logical one, designed to counter such assertions as "an arms race reflects political tensions between nations; it does not cause these tensions." However compelling that logical argument may be, it does not establish the case in favor of arms control and disarmament. More important to an evaluation of that case is the historical record involving arms control and disarmament agreements. Here, the critics and the skeptics are on stronger ground. The record reveals some fairly spectacular failures.

As one evaluates this record, though, one must keep in mind that the most important successes for arms control and disarmament agreements are, virtually by definition, not empirically identifiable. These successes are instances of agreements the absence of which would have led to war between the signatories. It is logically possible that every arms control and disarmament agreement has resulted in the elimination of at least one war that would have otherwise occurred. (Even in cases where agreements broke down and war resulted, the war might have occurred sooner in the absence of an agreement.) Since history cannot be replayed it will never be known for sure.

It is known that agreements to control or reduce arms levels do not always end in failure and armed conflict. The Rush-Bagot Treaty of 1817 led the British and the Americans to reduce their naval armaments on the Great Lakes and "made an important contribution to the development of confidence between these powers."[43] The Pactos de Mayo between Argentina and Chile brought about a peaceful demise to the 1890–1902 arms race between those two states that is listed in Table 6.4. The Washington Naval Treaty of 1922 served as the basis of a ten-year naval holiday during which the British Empire, the United States, Japan, France, and Italy limited the expansion of their navies. By means of the London Naval Treaty of 1930, the British, the Americans, and the Japanese

[42] J. David Singer, *Deterrence, Arms Control, and Disarmament,* Ohio State University Press, Columbus, 1962, pp. 179–180.
[43] Bull, "Objectives," p. 354.

A trident missile takes off from Cape Canaveral. UPI Photo.

extended this naval holiday until 1936. In the post–Second World War, the Soviets and the Americans have adhered to a test ban treaty signed in 1963. In 1972, the superpowers signed a strategic arms limitation talk, SALT I, which restricted the deployment of antiballistic missile systems, put limits on expansion of the number of intercontinental ballistic missile systems, and contained a commitment to continue talks that may result in an agreement on SALT II.

The Desirability of Total Disarmament

Assume for the moment that SALT II does become a reality. (At this writing, negotiations are under way.) President Carter has announced that his ultimate goal is to rid the world completely of nuclear weapons. Should disarmament be carried to that extreme? Even assuming that such a goal is feasible, it may not be desirable. A world in which states have the knowledge necessary to produce nuclear weapons, but possess none, might be extremely unstable. Every state would necessarily fear the consequences of even a little successful atomic cheating by others; rumors that one state had hidden away ten or twenty bombs would inevitably arise, placing every other state with nuclear knowledge in the "we had better attack now because they think we are going to attack, and therefore they surely will" position. One way to avoid this and still denuclearize states completely, would be to transfer some nuclear weapons from states to storage depots managed by an international organization such as the United Nations.[44] If some responsible international organization possessed nuclear weapons, minimally successful cheating by an irresponsible state would not be so dire in its consequences, and thus the fear of it need not be so destabilizing. Of course, no major state, and perhaps in this era especially the United States, seems inclined to entrust the United Nations with such a mission. Until that day arrives, it might be more reasonable to allow each nuclear state to retain a (minimal) level of nuclear weapons to protect it from minor violations of disarmament agreements, than to aim for total nuclear disarmament.

"If You Want Peace, Prepare for War"

If some nuclear weapons in the hands of the major powers will create a more stable system than no nuclear weapons, is it not true that vast numbers of weapons will make it even more stable? There are those, in the United States and the Soviet Union, for example, who take to heart the old saying, "If you want peace, prepare for war," and conclude that safety lies in the direction of an ever greater accumulation of weapons. Any kind of arms control and disarmament agreement, if it is to be successful, will entail some amount of trust among the parties to that agreement. Why, an American might ask, should the Russians be trusted? Let us play it safe; build up the strongest defense that can possibly be mustered and not take any of the risks involved in the implementation of arms control or disarmament agreements.

---

[44] Singer, *Deterrence*, p. 234.

The answer to this argument, of course, is that the Americans and the Russians (as well as the other nuclear powers) are not faced with a choice of playing it safe or taking risks. Arms accumulation and arms control both involve risks. Escalating arms accumulation may provoke nuclear catastrophe. Arms control and disarmament agreements may be violated, leading to a confrontation in which the cheater will take advantage of superiority. Perhaps the most reasonable argument can be made for a mix of adequate armaments and limitations of the armaments. Weapons levels can be high enough to deter but not so high as to provoke panic in the opponent. Arms control agreements can be ambitious enough to reduce weapons levels significantly but not so stringent as to create conditions powerfully tempting to cheaters.

Nuclear Proliferation

One kind of arms control effort that the Soviet Union and the United States have agreed upon is nonproliferation. The superpowers collaborated in the drafting of a treaty on the nonproliferation of nuclear weapons in the late sixties, and it went into effect in 1970. Since that time over a hundred nations have signed it.

Pressures Toward Proliferation

But any hope that the Non-Proliferation Treaty would restrict the nuclear club to a membership of five was crushed in May 1974, when India exploded a "peaceful" nuclear device. There were several pressures that pushed India in this direction, and unfortunately the same pressures operate in many Third World countries. India was in a position to benefit militarily from the development of nuclear weapons. Relations with China had been rather uneasy ever since the border clash in 1962, and China exploded a nuclear weapon in 1964. India had also had a series of wars with Pakistan, and Indian leaders may well have thought that an atomic weapon in Indian hands would discourage Pakistan from any effort to recoup losses.[45] In any case, "India manufactures her own rockets and solid fuel propellants, and plans to launch rockets by 1979 capable of putting a 1,200 kilogram payload into orbit, or of delivering nuclear warheads anywhere in Asia."[46] It is clear that though India's nuclear device may have been, as diplomats insisted, intended

[45] Of course, Pakistan announced its intention to acquire a nuclear weapons capability immediately after the Indian explosion.

[46] Norman Gall, "Atoms for Brazil, Dangers for All," *Foreign Policy,* 23 (Summer 1976), 175.

for peaceful purposes, that country was not unaware of the military implications.

The other major pressure pushing India in the direction of experimentation with and reliance on nuclear power was economic. The tremendous increase in the price of oil brought about by the Organization of Petroleum Exporting Nations (OPEC) in 1973 gave a tremendous boost to interest in nuclear power, not only in India but around the world. Of course, not every nation that develops nuclear energy will necessarily develop an atomic weapon. But if the technology and expertise are present, combined with perceived military advantages as in the case of India, how many states will pass up the opportunity to join the nuclear weapons club?

This question will be answered, one way or the other, several times in the next decade. "India's example has not been lost on other ascendant powers,"[47] and one such ascendant power is Brazil. Like India, Brazil was hit hard by the increase in the price of oil in 1973. So was West Germany, and the two nations got together in 1975, with West Germany promising to supply Brazil with nuclear technology and expertise in the coming years. West Germany wanted to sell nuclear technology and obtain access to supplies of uranium, on the assumption that the Germans will have to rely more heavily on nuclear power in the future. Brazil is also planning to rely heavily on nuclear power, thus was interested in buying the West German technological expertise and equipment, and might be able to supply West Germany with uranium in the future. The Brazilians, with the help of West German geologists, intend to find out.

Another reason that Brazil is interested in nuclear power involves the activities of one of its neighbors to the south. Argentina has uranium, a fuel fabricating facility, and a reprocessing plant;[48] it is also generally considered to be more advanced in terms of nuclear technological expertise than Brazil. The Brazilians have announced an interest in the development of peaceful nuclear explosives (PNEs). If they go ahead with plans in this area, it seems probable that Argentina will not be far behind. And if either Argentina or Brazil go nuclear, it is possible that Chile and Venezuela will follow.[49]

There are a number of additional nuclear "hot spots" throughout the Third World. Taiwan and South Korea, confronted with

[47] Gall, "Atoms for Brazil," p. 175.
[48] William Epstein, "Nuclear Proliferation in the Third World," *Journal of International Affairs,* 29 (Fall 1975), 185–202.
[49] Epstein, "Nuclear Proliferation," p. 194.

China and a conceivable weakening of the commitment on their behalf by the United States, may both be on the path toward the development of nuclear weapons. Israel almost certainly has them already, which has sparked Egyptian interest. Iran and Libya, and probably several other oil-rich Middle Eastern states, could join the nuclear club. South Africa's technological abilities may well be more advanced in the nuclear area than India's and, if pressed, that country might certainly develop an atomic weapon. Indonesia could be added to the list, as might, in the long run at least, Nigeria and Turkey.

The Joys of Proliferation

The possible proliferation of nuclear weapons in the Third World is not necessarily a bad thing. Is it not arrogant and hypocritical of the superpowers to continue to accumulate nuclear weapons at a fantastic rate and yet worry self-righteously about a few weapons falling into the wrong hands in the Third World? It is plain to any reasonable person that the present global system needs a redistribution of wealth and power. Nuclear weapons in the Third World would certainly help bring about a redistribution of power, and this in turn could encourage a redistribution of wealth. "The frustration and anger of the Third World can . . . be assuaged by using their nuclear capability as a protective shield behind which they can manipulate the prices of their raw materials with less fear of threats from the nuclear powers."[50] The impact of nuclear proliferation on relations among Third World nations may also be beneficial. The presence of nuclear weapons on both sides of the Soviet-American conflict has helped preserve the peace between the superpowers for over a quarter of a century. Might it not, by making war unthinkable, have the same effect on Third World conflicts?[51]

The Disadvantages of Proliferation

From the point of view of many in the Third World, one can see how persuasive these arguments might be. It is certainly true that the arguments by the nuclear powers against proliferation would be strengthened if they would take more effective steps to slow down their own acquisition of such weapons. But even if we accept the argument that the nuclear powers have put themselves in the embarrassing position of saying to Third World leaders, Do as I say, not as I do, it does not necessarily follow that proliferation would have a beneficial impact on the global political system in general or

[50] Epstein, "Nuclear Proliferation," p. 190.
[51] Hedley Bull, "Rethinking Non-Proliferation," *International Affairs,* 51 (April 1975), 178.

the Third World in particular. If some Third World nations did acquire nuclear weapons, it would not significantly increase the strength of their bargaining position vis-á-vis industrialized buyers of raw materials. They would still lack the delivery systems (not to mention any means to protect themselves from retaliation) to make a nuclear threat credible. And while it may be true that nuclear weapons have helped to stabilize American-Russian relations, there is no guarantee that they would have the same effect on tense relationships in the Third World. Proliferation in the Third World would be likely to lead to nuclear monopolies or great superiority on one side of conflicts.[52] If both sides of a Third World conflict obtained nuclear weapons at about the same time, then this stalemate would face the same dangers of destabilization by way of technological breakthroughs that exist in the American-Soviet confrontation.

Nuclear weapons might also introduce an unhealthy measure of rigidity into several important Third World conflicts. The relationship between mainland China and Taiwan is complex and dangerous enough without the addition of Taiwanese nuclear weapons to the equation. Compromise between the Arabs and the Israelis may be impossible to achieve in any case, but threats of nuclear war made by either side can hardly help the situation. South Africa, buttressed by nuclear weapons, could be even more intransigent in its defense of the status quo.

Though it may smack of condescension to say it, one must also consider the possibility that new nuclear powers may have several characteristics that would intensify the risks of nuclear war. The governments of new nuclear states may be exceptionally unstable, or they may come under the control of irrational individuals.[53] They might employ less reliable safeguards against unauthorized or accidental firings of nuclear weapons than those used by the superpowers. They might also fail to secure their nuclear retaliatory forces to the extent achieved by the superpowers, thus creating conditions inviting first strike attacks.

Hope for the Future
And there is an increased probability that terrorists would obtain either a bomb or the materials necessary to make one if several additional states develop nuclear weapons. With this, and the other considerations in mind, one would argue that the nuclear powers should do what they can to stop, or at least slow down, nuclear

[52] Bull, "Rethinking Non-Proliferation," p. 179.
[53] Imagine for a moment nuclear weapons in the hands of a leader like Idi Amin.

proliferation. In the mid-1970s, the suppliers of nuclear technology were so eager to sell their wares to Third World countries that they were reluctant to insist on adequate safeguards for the equipment and materials they sell. One observer noted that "competition among the United States, the Soviet Union, France, West Germany, Canada . . . to supply nuclear energy to the Third World has begun to mirror competition in conventional arms sales—with even more disastrous implications."[54] But in 1975, seven of the leading suppliers of nuclear technology (the United States, the Soviet Union, France, West Germany, Canada, Great Britain, and Japan) held a secret meeting in London, at which they apparently agreed to apply International Atomic Energy Agency safeguards to all exports of nuclear technology.[55] In the first few months of his administration, President Carter seemed to have some success in discouraging the export of various kinds of nuclear technology by other suppliers to Third World customers. In 1977, fifteen nations reached an agreement that tightened guidelines on the transfer of technology.[56] These developments, plus the fact that several years have passed since India's "peaceful device" exploded, without additions to the nuclear club, allows some hope that nuclear proliferation may be brought under control.

Imperialism

One of the most popular and influential explanations of the origins of war in this century relies on the *redistribution* of power in the international system as a major causal factor. As mentioned in Chapter 1, Lenin argued in his book on imperialism that wars in the modern era are the result of the uneven rates of growth among the great capitalist powers. Uneven growth leads to wars because "there can be *no* other conceivable basis under capitalism for the division of spheres of influence, of interests, of colonies, etc., than a calculation of the *strength* of the participants in the division, their general economic, financial, military strength."[57] When this basis for division changes, according to Lenin, then there must be a redivision of spheres of influence, interests, and colonies, and typically this process involves international war among the capitalist states.

[54] Steven J. Baker, "Monopoly or Cartel," *Foreign Policy,* 23 (Summer 1976), 211.
[55] Baker, "Monopoly or Cartel," p. 205.
[56] *Albuquerque Tribune,* September 22, 1977, p. A-7.
[57] V. I. Lenin, *Imperialism: The Highest Stage of Capitalism,* International Publishers, New York, 1917 (reprint 1939), p. 119.

The Relationship Between
Capitalism and Imperialism

The most famous Leninist arguments specify the reasons that capitalist powers must acquire spheres of influence, interests, and colonies. By his own admission, Lenin relied heavily on the earlier writings of an English economist, John Hobson. Hobson had observed firsthand the machinations of British entrepreneurs that played an important role in the crisis leading to the Boer War in southern Africa at the end of the nineteenth century, and he generalized from that experience in order to develop an explanation for capitalist imperialism. According to Hobson, capitalism in Britain, and elsewhere, labored under a great difficulty as long as it was confined to its home base. Great wealth was concentrated in the hands of a few, while the vast majority of workers were very poor. Because the workers were poor, capitalist economic systems suffered from underconsumption; consumers could not buy what the capitalists could produce. Thus, capitalists needed outlets to provide investment opportunities for their surplus capital. Opportunities were created by imperialism. Colonies were acquired to provide the capitalists the opportunities for profitable investment that were not present at home because of underconsumption.[58]

This explanation made sense to many people at the time it appeared, partly because there was a current phenomenon that cried out for explanation. Starting about 1870, virtually every large state in the world indulged in an imperialistic binge. Britain, France, and Germany were very active in Africa and Asia. Japan defeated China in 1895 and Russia in 1905, acquiring territory in both cases. Russia expanded over land to the east. The United States took on Spain in the war of 1898 and acquired the Philippines, Puerto Rico, and Cuba. Why was this happening? Hobson thought he had the answer.

And so, to some extent, did Lenin. Writing during the First World War, he argued that free competition in capitalist societies ultimately results in the establishment of monopolies as losers in the competition are eliminated. Lenin was particularly impressed by the tendency of capital and power to become concentrated in the hands of banks, creating finance capital.[59] Once monopolies emerge, according to Lenin, they extend their tentacles worldwide in order to acquire "sources of raw materials, for the export of capital, for spheres of influence, i.e., for spheres of profitable deals,

---

[58]John Hobson, *Imperialism: A Study,* Allen and Unwin, London, 1902.
[59]Lenin, *Imperialism,* p. 124.

Lenin. SOVFOTO.

concessions, monopolist profits, and so on; in fine, for economic territory in general."[60]

Lenin, unlike Hobson, was also concerned with the task of modifying Marxist theory in order to account for a couple of disturbing (to a Marxist) contemporary phenomena. (Hobson was not concerned with "saving" Marxism, because he was not a Marxist.) Marx had argued that workers in capitalist countries would become progressively more impoverished, until they reached the point of rising up and overthrowing their capitalist masters. Ultimately, proletarian solidarity would overwhelm national boundaries, and states—with their boundaries and their wars—would wither away.

[60] Lenin, *Imperialism,* p. 124.

Uncooperative Facts

But, in the decades before the First World War, things had not been developing in the manner a Marxist might expect. The workers in the capitalist states were not becoming progressively more impoverished. By modern standards, to be sure, working conditions and wages were atrocious, but there was a nearly universal trend toward improvement in both. Even so, as the First World War approached, most socialists apparently believed that the common interests of the working classes in the opposing capitalist states would prevail in case of armed conflict, that the workers would join hands across national boundaries in opposition to the capitalists, who wished to lead them into war against each other. Instead, the workers and their leaders in the socialist parties proved, in the hour of crisis in August 1914, to be steadfastly patriotic. Lenin was among those socialists who found this difficult to accept. He

> would not at first believe that Social Democrats had decided to support the war effort of the German government. . . . When informed of the event, he could explain it only as a plot of the capitalist press. It had, with obvious intent, wrongly reported the stand of the German socialists.[61]

Lenin's Revision of Marxism

This explanation, Lenin soon discovered, was wrong. He ingeniously devised another, which survives in the minds of many adherents to this day. At least some workers, Lenin said, were not becoming impoverished and were actually loyal to the bourgeois class because they were being bribed. And these bribes were financed by imperialism.

> The receipt of high monopoly profits by the capitalists . . . makes it economically possible for them to corrupt certain sections of the working class, and for a time a fairly considerable minority, and win them to the side of the bourgeoisie of a given industry or nation against all the others.[62]

In other words, capitalism must exploit to survive, but the exploitation does not necessarily result in the impoverishment of all

[61] Kenneth N. Waltz, *Man, the State, and War,* Columbia University Press, New York, 1954, p. 137.

[62] Lenin, *Imperialism,* p. 126.

workers in a capitalist society, because modern capitalists have colonies to exploit, and this makes it possible to bribe members of the working class at home. These bribes ruin working-class solidarity and postpone the revolution based on the solidarity Marx had predicted.

With some variations, Lenin's theory of war, and the relationship between capitalism and imperialism, regained popularity in the Western world in the wake of the war waged in Vietnam by the United States.[63] Basically, the argument is the same now as it was in Lenin's day, that capitalist societies will be imperialistic in order to acquire fields of profitable investment, sure access to needed raw materials, and markets for exports.

The Leninist Theory and the Evidence

How persuasive are these arguments, as they apply either to pre–First World War imperialism or to American foreign policy after the Second World War? In both eras, it must be admitted, there is evidence to support a Leninist interpretation of the history of global politics. During the earlier era, the major capitalist states did export huge amounts of capital overseas, and they became dependent on foreign investments in the sense that the resulting profits were substantial. In the later era, the United States also increased dramatically the level of its foreign investments and is becoming increasingly reliant on foreign sources of raw materials. And if the United States has not been imperialistic in the sense of establishing formal control over new colonies or attacking its capitalist rivals, it has engaged in an updated form of neoimperialism. In addition to obvious activities such as the war in Vietnam, the United States has consistently and energetically supported the status quo, often a reactionary status quo, in developing countries throughout the Third World. In Syria, Iran, Guatemala, and Chile, to name only a few of the more well-known cases, the CIA has helped to subvert governments that were not sufficiently friendly to the American government or American economic interests. Elsewhere, reactionary governments have been sustained by foreign aid, military aid, and private sources of financial support. According to some critics of American foreign policy, the plain pattern of support for the status quo throughout the Third World is motivated primarily by a desire to make the world safe for capitalism.

Critics of Lenin's ideas, as they apply to either era being discussed, have relied mainly on an argument that demonstrates a

[63] See Harry Magdoff, *The Age of Imperialism,* Monthly Review Press, New York, 1969, and Gabriel Kolko, *The Roots of American Foreign Policy,* Beacon Press, Boston, 1969.

weakness in the link between the foreign economic activities and political imperialistic policies of capitalist states. It is true that, in the latter part of the nineteenth century, the great capitalist powers did invest heavily overseas, and they did grab a substantial number of new colonies. But the two activities were not necessarily causally connected, and in fact very little of the foreign investment that occurred in that era went to the newly acquired colonies. By 1913, for example, less than half of the foreign investment originating in Great Britain went to its empire; the British had more money invested in the United States than in any colony or other foreign country, and most of the capital invested in the empire was not located in the new colonies added in the previous decades. Most French capital, as Lenin knew, [64] was invested in Russia and other European countries. In 1914, Germany had invested some 25 billion marks abroad, but only 3 percent of that was in Asia or Africa, and only a small part of that was in its colonies. The United States never had significant colonial holdings, in the formal sense, and what was sent to its colonies in the way of foreign investment was inconsequential. Briefly, in no case did a capitalist state rely heavily on its newly acquired colonies as outlets for foreign investment during the era that Lenin analyzed.[65]

Very similar arguments can be made with regard to the modern relationship between the United States and the Third World, which it allegedly treats in a neoimperialistic manner. American economic reliance on the Third World, at least in terms of foreign investment and international trade, is simply not very substantial. In 1972, for example, only 27 percent of American foreign investment was directed to developing states; by far the greatest part of investment went to other developed economies. Also, the extent to which the United States relies on developing states as outlets for investments is decreasing. In 1960, 35 percent (as opposed to 27 percent in 1972) of American foreign investment went to less developed countries. And American earnings from foreign investments in developing states in 1972 accounted for an extremely small part of the GNP.[66] American trade with developing countries is also not very important. In 1968, only 31.4 percent of American exports went to developing states, and only about 3 percent of the

[64]Lenin, *Imperialism,* p. 64.

[65]William Langer, "A Critique of Imperialism," *Foreign Affairs,* 14 (October 1935), 102–119. For similar arguments, see D. K. Fieldhouse, "Imperialism: A Historiographical Revision," and Mark Blaug, "Economic Imperialism Revisited," both in *Economic Imperialism,* eds. Kenneth Boulding and Tapan Mukerjee, University of Michigan Press, Ann Arbor, 1972, pp. 95–123, 142–155.

[66]Joan Edelman Spero, *The Politics of International Economic Relations,* St. Martin's Press, New York, 1977, pp. 126–127.

output of American industry went to low-income countries. Again, the United States trades most heavily with other developed economies, and in any case, total exports constitute only about 4 percent of the American GNP.[67] It does not seem likely, at least according to critics of neo-Leninist interpretations of American foreign policy, that such relatively insignificant American economic interests in the Third World can account for the shape of American foreign policy vis-à-vis those nations.

But what about raw materials? It is true that the United States is becoming increasingly dependent on overseas sources of raw materials, and such important resources as copper, iron ore, lead, manganese, phosphate, tin, and petroleum are located primarily in Third World countries.[68] Could this be the explanation for neoimperialistic foreign policies? Perhaps, but there is room for doubt in view of the contemporary relationship between the United States and the Third World suppliers of a most critical natural resource, oil. Despite efforts to stem the tide, the United States became increasingly reliant on Middle Eastern oil throughout most of the 1970s. Yet, the United States did not abandon Israel, and it did not attack any Middle Eastern country. Such attacks may still occur, of course, and the CIA may be busily subverting the recalcitrant government of an oil-rich Middle Eastern state. But to date the record supports the argument that increased reliance by the United States on Third World sources of raw materials will not strengthen the neoimperialist tendencies of the former, but rather will improve the bargaining power and relative economic standing of the latter.

A Defense of Leninism

Defenders of Leninism as it applies to the earlier era of imperialism have had to acknowledge that the newly-acquired colonies of the late nineteenth and early twentieth centuries did not, as a matter of fact, serve as crucially important outlets for foreign investment or exports, or as particularly valuable sources of raw materials.[69] Some have argued that the colonies were nevertheless acquired for economic reasons, because the imperialists thought the colonies were going to *become* important economically. And there is plenty

[67] S. M. Miller, Roy Bennett, and Cyril Alapatt, "Does the U.S. Economy Require Imperialism?" *Social Policy,* 1 (September–October 1970), 13–19.

[68] U.S. Council on International Economic Policy, *Critical Imported Raw Materials,* Government Printing Office, Washington, D.C., 1974, pp. 24, 43, 45, 46. Cited by Spero, *Politics,* p. 127.

[69] Some colonies did supply raw materials, but not necessarily to the mother country. "The great industrial countries got but a fraction of their raw materials from the colonies, and the colonies themselves continued to sell their products in the best market." Langer, "Critique," p. 106.

of evidence in the form of statements by leading politicians in the earlier imperialist era to support this assertion.[70] Proponents of a Leninist critique of American foreign policy vis-à-vis Third World countries have several things to say about the kinds of figures cited earlier to demonstrate the weakness of the link between the American economy and the Third World. Harry Magdoff, for example, argues that comparisons of earnings on overseas investments in developing countries with the total American GNP is misleading. The total GNP reflects several facets of economic activity that are not very important, such as various kinds of services (as opposed to goods), perfume production, and earnings by major league baseball teams. (These are my examples, not Magdoff's.) Magdoff asserts that concentrating on crucial sectors of the economy, such as the capital goods industries, reveals that foreign economic activity does play a crucial role in the American economy. Appreciation of this role is further enhanced when it is understood that the small percentage figures that are cited to demonstrate a lack of dependence by the United States on the Third World focus on annual flow of foreign investment abroad, and do not take into account the accumulated levels of capital equipment abroad to which the annual flows contribute.[71] A final argument points out that, even though foreign economic activity may not constitute an overwhelming portion of the total American economy, the activity is crucial to a few corporations, and these corporations are typically the largest and most influential, capable of pushing American foreign policy in a neoimperialist direction.

An Alternative Thesis

The alternative explanations of pre–First World War imperialism and post–Second World War American foreign policy offered by critics of Leninist ideas emphasize the role of national security considerations in the activities of capitalist states. In this view, Britain obtained new colonies in self-defense because Germany and France were doing the same, and all the great imperial powers of that era

---

[70]Joseph Chamberlain, for example, a leading British proponent of imperialism, said in 1888 that "if tomorrow it were possible . . . to reduce by a stroke of the pen the British Empire to the dimensions of the United Kingdom, half at least of our population would be starved." See William Langer, *The Diplomacy of Imperialism,* 2d ed., Knopf, New York, 1951, p. 77.

[71]Magdoff, *Age of Imperialism,* pp. 9–16. Robert Tucker claims the Magdoff exaggerates the importance of foreign earnings as compared to domestic earnings in the American economy because he calculates the two differently. When calculating foreign earnings, Magdoff includes the earnings of financial corporations (banks) and quotes profits *before* taxes. Magdoff minimizes domestic earnings by excluding the profits of financial corporations and by quoting profits *after* taxes. See Robert Tucker, *The Radical Left and American Foreign Policy,* Johns Hopkins Press, Baltimore, 1971, p. 128.

were sure that these colonies would be strategically valuable in any future conflict.[72] Similarly, the important reason for United States resistance to a Communist regime in South Vietnam, and anti-American governments throughout the Third World, is not economic but strategic. American policy makers genuinely fear the strategic consequences of hostile political control of countries in Asia, Africa, and Latin America, and any economic losses that radical regimes in these areas might cause Americans is clearly secondary in importance to policy makers.

The controversy, then, boils down to a question of motives. Why do policy makers in capitalist states behave in the way they do? Are they primarily motivated by the economic interests of capitalists, or by national security? Since motives are invisible, this is a difficult question. It is easy to find statements by policy makers implying that their primary motives are economic, but it is even easier to find statements indicating that decision makers are motivated entirely by national security considerations. And, of course, it is possible that both motives play a role in some decisions, or that each plays the principal role in different decisions.

Some Crucial Comparisons

One way to sort out the arguments is left open, though, by the fact that Leninist theorists insist that capitalism as an economic system leads to imperialism. One apparent weakness in this argument stems from the fact that imperialism existed long before the appearance of capitalism. Lenin was aware of this problem. He asserts in *Imperialism* that

> colonial policy and imperialism existed before this latest stage of capitalism, and even before capitalism. Rome, founded on slavery, pursued a colonial policy and achieved imperialism. But "general" arguments about imperialism, which ignore or put into the background the fundamental difference of social-economic systems, inevitably degenerate into absolutely empty banalities. . . . Even the colonial policy of capitalism in its previous stages is essentially different from the colonial policy of finance capital.[73]

Lenin emphasizes the unique aspects of capitalist imperialism. Imperialism did exist before capitalism, but imperialism in the capitalist era is somehow different, and its causal origins are special.

[72] George Quester, *Offense and Defense in the International System,* Wiley, New York, 1977, p. 88.
[73] Lenin, *Imperialism,* pp. 81–82.

A skeptic might reasonably ask why one should believe that something that has been occurring for centuries (such as imperialism) should suddenly acquire entirely new causes. Still, logically speaking at least, Leninists could be right when they argue that if capitalism is destroyed, imperialism will disappear. But at least one important available test case is not very encouraging. Capitalism was destroyed in Russia in 1917. Since then the Communist government of the Soviet Union has been quite imperialistic in its relations with the non-Russian people of that country, signed a treaty with Nazi Germany one aim of which was to dismember Poland, and has since the Second World War treated its East European neighbors in an imperialistic manner. "The Soviet Union probably extracted more goods from East Germany in the ten years after the Second World War than Britain did in two hundred years from India, and this was pure tribute."[74] Since then, Soviet troops invaded Hungary in 1956 and Czechoslovakia in 1968 when these states threatened to step out of line. Add the Chinese takeover in Tibet, and one could conclude that capitalism is not a crucial ingredient in the recipe for imperialism, or that it will not necessarily disappear in a postcapitalist era.

The controversy, though, will not be buried so easily. Defenders of the Soviet Union will argue that the policy of the Russian Communists toward non-Russians was necessary in order to modernize their state. Before the Second World War, the Russians merely took back (for example, from Poland) what was wrongfully taken from them in the aftermath of the First World War. The Soviets, it is true, did exact tribute from East European states after the Second World War, but especially in the case of East Germany, the tribute was in the form of war reparations, not the fruits of ordinary aggressive imperialism. As for the Hungarian and Czechoslovakian incidents, the Russians were merely protecting themselves and their fellow socialists in Eastern Europe from capitalist subversion. And the Chinese actions in Tibet were justified on grounds of historical Chinese ties to that area.

Some theorists, sympathetic to Marxist-Leninist ideas, will not buy all these arguments, especially those regarding the Soviet Union, but will still insist that the destruction of capitalism will end imperialism. They acknowledge that the Soviet Union has been imperialistic but assert that this is only because (1) it is surrounded by hostile capitalist states; once all capitalist states are destroyed, this argument continues, there will be no need for defensive imperialism such as that perpetrated by the Soviets in Eastern Europe,

[74]Kenneth Boulding, Introduction, in *Economic Imperialism*, University of Michigan Press, Ann Arbor, 1972, p. xv.

or (2) the Soviet Union is not truly socialist. It has degenerated into a form of state capitalism.[75] Truly socialist states will not be imperialistic.

An Empirical Analysis of the
Law of Uneven Development

For a final look at the Leninist theory of imperialism, consider an empirical test of the law of uneven development. Recall that Lenin argues that war occurs because some capitalist states grow faster than others, and those that grow stronger will insist on a redistribution of spheres of influence, colonies, and so forth. From this argument one can logically conclude that a more rapid redistribution of power among the most important states in the system will make war more likely. Singer, Bremer, and Stuckey, in the article discussed earlier, calculated for every five-year period from 1820 to 1965, an index score that reflected the extent to which "power" (measured as stipulated in Chapter 3) was redistributed among the major powers during those periods. They then analyzed the relationship between this redistribution of power and the amount of major-power war that occurred in the subsequent five-year periods, to see if it has been true that more war occurs as a result of periods of greater redistribution. They found, for the entire time period, a very weak pattern. The pattern does not hold at all for the nineteenth century and is so weak in the twentieth century that one must conclude, on the basis of evidence available now, that uneven rates of change in the power of major states has, at best, a very small impact on the amount of war they experience.[76]

Human Nature and International War

A firm body of popular and scholarly opinion rests on the idea that all the causes of war considered in this chapter so far are only superficially relevant to the problem. The most basic cause, in this view, lies in the nature of the elemental constituent units of the international system, human beings. The human animal is greedy, suspicious, bigoted, in short, "naturally" evil. As long as man's

[75] For example, Bernard Chavance, in the socialist periodical *Monthly Review,* says that "the Soviet Union is clearly a society in which the *capitalist mode of production* predominates. Consequently, the dominant class is in fact a capitalist class, a bourgeoisie." See Bernard Chavance, "On the Relations of Production in the U.S.S.R.," *Monthly Review,* 29 (May 1977), 5.

[76] J. David Singer, Stuart Bremer, and John Stuckey, "Capability Distribution, Uncertainty, and Major Power War, 1820–1965," in *Peace, War, and Numbers,* ed. Bruce M. Russett, Sage Publications, Beverly Hills, 1972, p. 33.

nature is evil, no matter what changes occur in the more superficial aspects of the international system, war, or at least intergroup violence, is going to be present.

The Evil-Nature Theory of War

In the most general philosophical sense, it is possible that this argument has merit. If the question at hand is, Why is this the kind of world in which wars periodically occur? one possible answer is, Because human beings are naturally evil. That is, if one is comparing this world with another, imaginary world in which wars would not occur, it is at least arguable that the one single change that might transform this world into a warless one would involve a change in human nature. If human beings were "naturally" altruistic, honorable, and trustworthy, perhaps wars would disappear.

But as an answer to empirical questions about the causes of war, the argument that points to man's evil nature as the most crucial causal factor is virtually useless. Empirical questions are addressed to variations in war across space and time. An example would be, Why was the international system relatively free of warfare in 1910 but extremely war prone in 1914? References to the evil nature of humanity cannot help to answer such questions. Human nature certainly remained the same from 1910 to 1914, and the war-proneness of the system obviously changed between the first year and the last. If the evil nature of humanity accounts for the outbreak of the First World War in 1914, what accounts for the peace in 1910?

And even on the most speculative philosophical level, the assertion that the evil nature of humanity is the crucial cause of war is unsatisfying. First, the argument is circular. How does one know that humans have an evil nature? Because they do evil things, like fight wars. Why do they fight wars? Because they have an evil nature. Second, the argument that war is a product of the most admirable qualities of human beings makes as much sense. If humans were by nature totally selfish, then war might not be such an intractable problem. No one would willingly risk his or her life for country, political beliefs, or even family. It is just because many soldiers on both sides of a conflict are altruistic, honorable, and trustworthy that wars are so intensely fought.

The Aggressive Instinct and War

A somewhat more sophisticated explanation of international war traces its origins to the fact that human beings are naturally aggressive. Konrad Lorenz is, perhaps, most prominently associated with this idea. Lorenz believes that the ever-recurrent phenomena of history do not have reasonable causes. . . . Unreasoning and unreasonable human nature causes two nations to compete, though no economic necessity compels them to do so. . . . It impels an Alexander or a Napoleon to sacrifice millions of lives in his attempt to unite the world under his system.[77]

Why, Lorenz asks rhetorically, do reasonable human beings act in such an unreasonable manner?

All these amazing paradoxes . . . find an unconstrained explanation, falling into place like the pieces of a jigsaw puzzle, if one assumes that human behavior, and particularly human social behavior, far from being determined by reason and cultural tradition alone, is still subject to all the laws prevailing in all phylogenetically adapted instinctive behavior.[78]

Human beings, according to Lorenz, are instinctively aggressive. Evolution has been honing this aggressive instinct for eons, because it aids in the survival of the individual and the species. In the animal world, intraspecific aggression is only rarely dangerous, because most animals have instinctively developed ritualized, inhibitory mechanisms that prevent conflicts from becoming too violent. But the human species is in a precarious position, because the strength of these inhibitory mechanisms is a function of the efficiency with which one member of a species can kill another. One wolf, for example, can kill another with a single bite on the jugular vein, and so wolves have developed effective inhibitory rituals. Doves, on the other hand, have no such killing ability, and their inhibitory mechanisms are accordingly weak. In human evolution, no inhibitory mechanisms developed, because it is comparatively difficult for one person, unaided by tools, to kill another. Now human beings have access to artificial weapons, such as atom bombs, that give great killing power, and the natural equilibrium between killing potential and inhibitory mechanisms has been grievously upset.[79]

Lorenz's theory leaves no doubt about measures that would be most effective in eliminating war. He believes that it would be a

[77] Konrad Lorenz, *On Aggression,* Harcourt Brace, New York, 1966, pp. 236–237.

[78] Lorenz, *On Aggression,* p. 237.

[79] Lorenz, *On Aggression,* pp. 240–241.

mistake to try to eliminate aggression. Aggressive behavior is instinctive, and the longer it is repressed, the more powerful the drive behind it becomes. Aggression must be discharged, and the trick is to discharge it in ways other than warfare. Lorenz is particularly in favor of competitive sports, especially in the form of the Olympic games, as one way to redirect aggression. Lorenzians also typically favor other forms of sublimation, such as academic and artistic endeavors, and other kinds of cultural activities. Eibl-Eibesfeldt, for example, suggests that one can discharge aggression by watching a film with aggressive content.[80]

Criticism of the Lorenzian Thesis

The Lorenzian theory of war is vulnerable to the same criticism directed at the human-nature-is-evil theory. There is no variation in Lorenz's major causal factor. The aggressive instinct on which Lorenz relies so heavily varies only, if at all, over several eons. Thus, the aggressive instinct cannot explain variations in violence and war, that is, why some people are more aggressive than others, why some states are more war prone than others, or why the international system is more war prone at some times than at others.

The ideas of Lorenz, though, are not necessarily irrelevant to an understanding of international war. Conceivably, Lorenz is right, and the aggressive instinct of human beings is the crucial causal factor behind all interpersonal and interstate violence, while other factors cause violence to vary across space and time. If this is true, it is vital information, because knowing that aggression is the result of an instinct honed in the evolutionary process would presumably be important in the proper selection of the other factors that bring the instinct to the fore in some instances (and so lead to violence), and cause it to be suppressed or redirected in others. For example, relying on his theory, Lorenz cites overpopulation and crowding as a key factor in the process that leads to violence.[81] If his theory about aggression is correct, then crowding should account for variation in violence.

But unfortunately for the Lorenzian thesis, there is very little evidence to support his idea that aggressive behavior is instinctive. There is, on the contrary, considerable evidence to indicate that

[80]I. Eibl-Eibesfeldt, *Love and Hate,* Holt, Rinehart, & Winston, New York, 1972, p. 77.
[81]F. De Towanicki, "A Talk with Konrad Lorenz," *New York Times Magazine,* July 5, 1970, 29.

aggressive behavior is a learned response to environment (and heredity) rather than instinctive.[82]

> Apparently even "instinctive" behaviors operate against a complex tangle of interaction which includes other genes as well as the influence of the external environment. Hence the concept of instinct has now become passé as more and more students of behavior have abandoned use of the concept as outmoded.[83]

The Lorenzian idea that aggressive behavior is normal and healthy, and that expressing aggression will have a beneficial impact on future behavior, is also contradicted by experimentation. "Expression of aggression tends to strengthen the subsequent aggressive response."[84] Exposure to aggressive behavior does not serve to blow off steam, making a person less aggressive. Experiments with children show that exposure to live and filmed models exhibiting aggressive behavior makes them *more* aggressive.[85] And adults who watch filmed violence are more likely to behave aggressively after the experience.[86] Finally, Goldstein and Arms conclude in an experiment involving spectators of a football game that watching an aggressive sport increases hostility.[87]

That Lorenzian ideas are not supported by scientific evidence is not surprising, since his methods lack even rudimentary scientific characteristics. It is no exaggeration to say that Lorenz bases his theory on war, for example, on some insightful observations of greylag geese and random observations of human beings, such as his aunt.[88] Even if his conclusions about animals were impeccable

---

[82]See, for example, Leonard Berkowitz, *Aggression*, McGraw-Hill, New York, 1962, and S. D. Nelson, "Nature/Nurture Revisited," *Journal of Conflict Resolution*, 18 (June 1974), 285–335.

[83]Samuel S. Kim, "The Lorenzian Theory of Aggression and Peace Research: A Critique," *Journal of Peace Research*, 13, No. 4 (1976), 257.

[84]Kim, "Lorenzian Theory," p. 268.

[85]A. Bandura, D. Ross, and S. A. Ross, "Transmission of Aggression Through Imitation of Aggressive Models," *Journal of Abnormal and Social Psychology*, 63, No. 2 (1961), 575–582.

[86]Leonard Berkowitz and Edna Rawlings, "Effects of Film Violence on Inhibition Against Subsequent Aggression," *Journal of Abnormal and Social Psychology*, 66, No. 5 (1963), 405–412.

[87]J. H. Goldstein and R. L. Arms, "Effects of Observing Athletic Contests on Hostility," *Sociometry*, 34 (March 1971), 83–94. This, and the previously cited experiments, are also cited by S. Kim in "Lorenzian Theory," on which the anti-Lorenzian arguments here rely heavily.

[88]Lorenz, *Aggression*, p. 55.

(and they may not be), to extrapolate from them in drawing conclusions about human behavior would be dangerous. And even if his extremely dubious assertions about individual human beings were, in fact, supported by scientific evidence, it would be foolhardy to leap onto higher levels of analysis, such as the national or international systemic level, and make conclusions about international war. Lorenz pays little, if any, attention to research conducted on higher levels of analyses. "In all the writings of Lorenz . . . there is little reference to the growing literature of peace research. . . . Instead, sources of 'evidence' or 'proof' of his observations of human aggression come exclusively from casual anecdotes."[89]

There is little wonder then, that when Lorenz does venture to offer a hypothesis on a higher level of analysis, such as his assertion that crowding leads to war, the evidence does not bear him out. Haas[90] as well as Bremer, Singer, and Luterbacher[91] report that there is no positive correlation between population density and foreign conflict or war. These findings are not conclusive, but they are considerably more persuasive than Lorenzian assertions based almost entirely on observations of crowded rats, even when that proof is buttressed by further observations of human behavior at the bus terminal on Forty-second Street in New York City, another source of evidence for Lorenz.[92]

Individuals and World Politics

The first occasion that reservations were expressed about the relevance of the study of individuals qua individuals to an understanding of global politics involved a discussion of Great-Man theories of history in Chapter 2. To drop the subject there would be misleading. Grandiose Lorenzian assertions about the nature of all human beings are probably of limited utility. Overemphasizing the impact of idiosyncratic characteristics of particular individuals can be dangerous. But developing generalizations about individuals, specifying how certain types of individuals will behave under varying environmental conditions, for example, can lead to valuable

[89] Kim, "Lorenzian Theory," 260.

[90] Michael Haas, "Societal Approaches to the Study of War," *Journal of Peace Research,*" 2, No. 4 (1965), 307–323.

[91] Stuart A. Bremer, J. David Singer, and Urs Luterbacher, "The Population Density and War Proneness of European Nations, 1816–1965," *Comparative Political Studies,* 6 (October 1973), 329–348.

[92] R. I. Evans, "Lorenz Warns," *Psychology Today,* 8 (November 1974), 82–93.

knowledge about global politics. Ole Holsti formulates the following hypothesis about individual national leaders: "As stress increases decision-makers will tend to perceive the range of alternatives open to themselves as becoming narrower." He goes on to find evidence to support the hypothesis, utilizing data on decision makers involved in the crisis leading to the First World War.[93] Joseph De Rivera discusses evidence that individuals with a high need for achievement are likely to choose tasks with intermediate risks, while those with a lower need for achievement will select options involving either extremely high or very low risks. He then uses that evidence to explain the behavior of General Douglas MacArthur in the Korean War.[94] Evidence from psychological studies, then, derived from scientific observations of individual human beings (or human beings in small groups), and which can thus be applied to individual decision-makers in more than one time and place, should not be ignored by serious students of global politics. Individual foreign-policy decision-makers are indeed subject to powerful constraints, operating as they do within the structure of the global political system as well as that of their own state and government. But psychological analysis can illuminate the manner in which these constraints operate, and the effects they have on the psychological processes out of which foreign policy decisions emerge (including, of course, those that result in international war).[95]

[93]Ole Holsti, *Crisis Escalation War,* McGill-Queen's University Press, Montreal, 1972, pp. 104, 145.

[94]Joseph De Rivera, *The Psychological Dimensions of Foreign Policy,* Merrill, Columbus, O., 1968, pp. 165–206.

[95]Herbert Kelman, "The Role of the Individual in International Relations: Some Conceptual and Methodological Considerations," *Journal of International Affairs,* 24, No. 1 (1970), 5.

SEVEN

Limits to Growth

Versus Dreams of Development

IN THE INTRODUCTION TO THE LAST CHAPTER I SAID THAT THE
international system level of analysis is the most comprehensive
level that is utilized by students of global politics. That is true, but
in recent years some scholars have begun to analyze global politics
from a viewpoint that is different from the international systemic
level in the sense that it emphasizes the extent to which a global
community exists, as opposed to a set of interrelated but still separate nation-states. Such a viewpoint has become increasingly
relevant partly because better methods of communication and
transportation have led some individuals from different states to
interact so intensively as to blur national boundaries. This kind of
interaction is perhaps of special importance in the realm of economics, in which multinational corporations discussed in Chapter 5
have tried to treat the globe as a single market rather than a set of
distinct national markets. It has been seen that there is lively con-

troversy about the good and bad effects of these corporations, but most would agree that they have served to unify the international marketplace, transforming it into a nascent global market. Finally, the global community has emerged as a real entity in the minds of scholars over the last decade or so because of a set of interrelated problems, constantly threatening to reach crisis proportions, that has served to highlight the extent to which individuals everywhere, of whatever nationality, are passengers on the spaceship earth. The population explosion, the energy crisis, pollution, and the widening rich-poor gap all seem to be problems that cannot be solved on a state-by-state basis, and they all make the common fate of individuals in the global community dramatically visible.

This chapter will focus on the future of the global community. I will describe some of the most important problems faced by the community and analyze the now-raging controversy of how to deal best with these problems. The controversy rages, in large part, because of widely disparate estimates of how serious the problems will become in the next few decades. I will consider starkly different predictions and analyze their bases in such a way as to allow, it is hoped, at least tentative decisions about which predictions are most likely to prove accurate, and in what direction the most promising solutions lie.

Four Crises

Poverty, Starvation, and Increasing Inequality

Certainly one of the most dismal facts about the global system today is that so many people are poor and starving. The Food and Agricultural Organization estimates that between one-third and one-half of the world's population is consistently undernourished. Lester Brown points out that the average calorie intake in countries containing close to two-thirds of the world's population is below the minimum required for normal growth.[1] Others surmise that 10 to 20 million people die every year from malnutrition or diseases brought on by it.

Figures like this are so large, and involve phenomena so remote from the experience of the average citizen in most industrialized countries, that they make very little impression. On a per capita basis, the figures may become somewhat more comprehensible. Consider, for example, that in Zambia, 260 of every

[1] Lester Brown, *World Without Borders*, Vintage, New York, 1972, p. 89.

thousand babies die before they reach their first birthday. In India and Pakistan, the figure is 190 out of every thousand.[2]

Anecdotes may help to illustrate. In the summer of 1968, India held Olympic trials to select a track and field team to send to the games in Mexico City. India then had a population of 535 million, but not one of the entrants to the trials could meet even the minimum qualifying standards for any of the thirty-two track and field events. Lester Brown concludes that "widespread under-nourishment undoubtedly contributed to this poor showing."[3]

But perhaps nothing more effectively communicates the meaning of poverty and starvation than a picture of one starving child.

Equally distressing is the lack of progress over the last few years in solving this problem and the unencouraging prospects for progress in the future. In the last two decades, developing countries have increased agricultural output about 2.8 percent a year, but the increase in most places has just barely kept up with the average 2.5 percent increase in population. The result: per capita food production in the poor countries as of the middle 1970s is just about the same as in 1955.[4] As for the future, one must be discouraged by estimates that approximately half of the world's arable land, and the richest, most accessible half at that, is already under cultivation. Even if it is estimated optimistically that by the year 2000 all of the world's available land will be utilized, if population growth continues at its present pace, there will still be a desperate land shortage.[5] In other words, if the population of the world is about 6.5 billion by the year 2000, a widely accepted estimate, the increase in the world's food-producing capacity over the next thirty years would have to equal that accomplished from the time agriculture originated to the present day.[6]

In many Third World countries, even when increases in food production occur, for example, as a result of the Green Revolution involving new high-yield cereals, the starving are not helped very much because they cannot afford to buy the food that is available. Rampant unemployment is a serious problem in most developing countries. The economies of the developing countries, in terms of the GNP, have been growing at an average of about 5 percent a year. New jobs are becoming available, but the population of most

[2] Lester Brown, *Seeds of Change,* Praeger, New York, 1974, p. 135.
[3] Brown, *World Without Borders,* p. 89.
[4] David J. Finlay and Thomas Hovet, Jr., *7304: International Relations on the Planet Earth,* Harper & Row, New York, 1975, p. 166.
[5] Donella H. Meadows, Dennis L. Meadows, Jorgen Randers, and William W. Behrens, III, *The Limits to Growth: A Report for the Club of Rome's Project on the Predicament of Mankind,* Universe Books, New York, 1972, pp. 48–51.
[6] Brown, *World Without Borders,* p. 95.

developing countries is growing so fast that unemployment and poverty are only marginally affected by the 5 percent growth rate. During the 1960s, the growth rates of the developed and developing world were about the same, but population grew twice as fast in the latter. The result was that per capita incomes during that decade rose only $10 in the poor countries, while they rose $300 in the rich countries, thus further increasing the gap between the two. In 1970, the income per person in the United States was $4,100, while in India it was $90. If present trends continue (an admittedly dangerous assumption), by the end of this century the income per person in the United States will be about $10,000 a year, while in India it will be $215 a year. An annual increase of 5 percent a year in the United States represents an increment in goods and services produced equal to the entire annual production of goods and services in India.[7]

The Population Explosion

Closely associated with the problems of poverty and starvation, or so it seems, is the so-called population explosion. There is lively controversy over the relationship of population growth to other problems, but no one can deny that in the middle decades of the twentieth century, the population of the world has been growing at an unprecedented rate. It took from the beginning of the human race until 1830 for the world's population to reach 1 billion. The second billion was added in only a hundred years (1930), and the third billion took only thirty years (1960). In 1970, the population of the world was an estimated 3.6 billion, and as already pointed out, it is widely anticipated that the world's population will be about 6.5 billion by the end of the century. In other words, the present level of population was achieved during the entire life of the human race on this planet, yet that level may be just about doubled in the next thirty years alone.

There seems to be some agreement among those who analyze the phenomenon that it is brought about by two major factors. One is the success of medical science. In 1650, the average lifetime of most people was only about thirty years. Now, the world average life expectancy is about fifty-three years and is still rising.[8] People are being born at about the same rate per thousand as they have been for several centuries, but they are dying at a significantly lower rate.

Children, though, still die in great numbers at an early age, and this too adds pressure to the upward trend in population. Large

[7] Brown, *World Without Borders*, p. 43.
[8] Meadows, et al., *Limits to Growth*, p. 8.

families serve as a form of social security in many developing countries. Parents want to have several children around to support them in their old age. And since the infant mortality rate is so high in much of the Third World, they are likely to want to play it safe, adding more children to the family in anticipation of the early loss of several of them. Also, in some rural settings especially, children can be economic assets as agricultural laborers even before the parents reach old age, providing an added incentive for large families.[9]

Whatever the causes, it is likely that the world's population will continue to grow until the end of this century at least. "Most of the prospective parents of the year 2000 have already been born"[10] There is a long lag before the time when fertility rates reach an equilibrium level and the population stops growing. One study concludes that if a fully effective population policy had been implemented throughout the Third World in 1975, it would have taken seventy-five years for that policy to achieve its goal of zero population growth, and by that time the population of the Third World will have doubled. A delay of twenty years in the implementation of such a policy will, according to these projections, add 4 billion to the population in the Third World alone, by the time an equilibrium is achieved.[11] Some parts of the world are overcrowded now. They will become even more heavily populated by the end of the century.

Shrinking Natural Resources
The view that the world is about to run out of several important natural resources is gaining wide acceptance.[12] In the industrialized world, the most visible impact of this depletion of natural resources involves the energy crisis. In the United States, for example, the Carter administration has made the energy crisis its top domestic priority, and at this writing is trying to get a program aimed at energy conservation through Congress. The price of gasoline has increased considerably in the United States in the 1970s, but it has yet to approach the much higher prices in most Western European countries. The winter of 1976–1977 was especially harsh in the

[9] Barry Commoner, "How Poverty Breeds Overpopulation," in *An Issue: Politics in the World Arena,* ed. Steven C. Spiegel, St. Martin's Press, New York, 1977, pp. 392–402.

[10] Meadows et al., *Limits to Growth,* p. 37.

[11] Mihajlo D. Mesarovic and Eduard C. Pestel, *Mankind at the Turning Point,* New American Library, New York, 1974, p. 78.

[12] See the results of a Harris poll cited in Herman Kahn, William Brown, and Leon Martel, *The Next 200 Years,* Morrow, New York, 1976, p. 84.

eastern part of the United States, creating an extra demand for natural gas, which, it turned out, was in short supply.

It would be a mistake, though, to conclude that only energy resources are running low. Consider Table 7.1. The results of a computerized analysis of the rates of depletion of nineteen important natural resources are summarized. In the first column after the name of the resource is the estimate of how long the resource will last if current rates of consumption continue. But, of course, current rates of consumption will *not* continue. The usage rate of virtually all of these natural resources is growing exponentially. Usage is increasing by a constant percentage amount in a constant time period. Exponential growth accumulates speed in the manner of a snowball rolling down a hill and leaves ordinary growth behind. For example, if one starts out with a savings account of $100, and adds $5 to it every year, it will take twenty years before the savings are doubled. But if one adds 5 percent to the account every year, it will have doubled in only fourteen years.

Column 3 in Table 7.1 gives the estimate of the number of years that the resource will last if the current exponential growth rate in the use of the resource continues. Finally, column 4 shows how many years the resource will last if actual reserves are 5 times the amount of known reserves. Notice that multiplying known reserves by a factor of 5 does not delay the depletion of any of the resources for very long, because exponential growth consumes so much in a short time. If current rates of growth continue, known reserves of petroleum will, according to this study, be entirely consumed in twenty years. If there is actually 5 times more petroleum than is known now, all petroleum will still be consumed within fifty years.

But, again, it is not only energy resources that are becoming more scarce. Known reserves of mercury will, at current rates of growth, be consumed in less than thirteen years. This is reflected in the price of mercury, which increased 500 percent in the twenty years before 1967.[13] Known reserves of lead can last only about twenty-one years, and the price of lead increased about 300 percent in the thirty years before 1971.[14] The clear implication of the data presented in Table 7.1 is that if the exponential increase in the consumption of natural resources should continue, most currently important resources will be extremely costly a hundred years from now.

[13] United States Bureau of Mines, *Minerals Yearbook,* Government Printing Office, Washington, D.C., 1967, p. 724, and United States Bureau of Mines, *Commodity Data Summary*, Government Printing Office, Washington, D.C., 1971, p. 9.
[14] Meadows et al., *Limits to Growth,* p. 66.

TABLE 7.1   Depletion rates of important natural resources

Resource	At Current Consumption Rates, Number of Years Resource Will Last	If Usage Increases at Present Rate, Number of Years Resource Will Last	If Actual Reserves Are 5 Times Known Reserves, Number of Years Resource Will Last
Aluminum	100	31	55
Chromium	420	95	154
Coal	2300	111	150
Cobalt	110	60	148
Copper	36	21	48
Gold	11	9	29
Iron	240	93	173
Lead	26	21	64
Manganese	97	46	94
Mercury	13	13	41
Molybdenum	79	34	65
Natural gas	38	22	49
Nickel	150	53	96
Petroleum	31	20	50
Platinum	130	47	85
Silver	16	13	42
Tin	17	15	61
Tungsten	40	28	72
Zinc	23	18	50

Source: The Limits to Growth: A Report for The Club of Rome's Project on the Predicament of Mankind, by Donella H. Meadows, Dennis L. Meadows, Jørgen Randers, William W. Behrens III. A Potomac Associates book published by Universe Books, New York, 1972. Graphics by Potomac Associates. Reprinted with permission.

Pollution

Starvation is not new. Thomas Malthus worried about a population explosion in the nineteenth century, and fears that one or more natural resources will be entirely depleted have occurred before. The only crisis of the present era that seems new involves the extent to which human beings are polluting the environment. Perhaps the most notorious pollution results from the world's present reliance on fossil fuels (coal, oil and natural gas) to generate about 97 percent of its industrial energy.[15] Burning these fuels causes carbon dioxide to be released into the atmosphere. Currently about 20 billion tons of carbon dioxide are released into the atmosphere every year as a result of fossil fuel combustion.[16] The amount of carbon dioxide in the air is increasing at an exponential rate of .02 percent a year.[17]

Another infamous form of pollution is the insecticide DDT. Richer countries have banned its use, but poorer countries have been reluctant to do so because of its ability to control malaria and help expand food output. The spread of DDT throughout the ecosystem has been insidious. It has been found in the tissues of penguins in Antarctica, in the bodies of Alaskan eskimos, and in mothers' milk in Indiana. In fact, the level of DDT in mothers' milk throughout the United States is above the safe level permitted by the Food and Drug Administration (FDA); mothers' milk in containers could not legally be permitted to cross state boundaries.[18]

Americans tend to think of pollution as a peculiarly American problem, because the United States is so industrialized. But tributaries of the Rhine River in Germany and the Mediterranean Sea have been subjected to serious pollution. The problem is not restricted to capitalist industrialized countries, either. The Cuyahoga River in Ohio has achieved an honored place in the annals of pollution horror stories, because it became so polluted that it caught fire. The same thing happened, though, to the Volga River in the Soviet Union.[19] Nor is pollution strictly the result of industrial activity. Pressure for more food has led to dramatic increases in the use of fertilizer, in the Third World for example, and the chemicals in the fertilizer end up in lakes, rivers, and streams, destroying fish and turning lakes into swamps.

The frightening aspect of the pollution problem is that it confronts humankind with unprecedented dangers, the dimensions of which are unknown. It is not known, for example, how much carbon dioxide can be released into the atmosphere without causing irreversible changes in the earth's climate. The thin envelope of air around this planet may have already been adversely affected. Climatological data show that from about 1880 to 1940 the earth's

[15] United Nations Department of Economic and Social Affairs, *Statistical Yearbook 1969*, United Nations, New York, 1970, p. 40.
[16] Bert Bolin, "The Carbon Cycle," *Scientific American*, 223, (September 1970), 131.
[17] Meadows et al., *Limits to Growth*, p. 73.
[18] Brown, *World Without Borders*, p. 26.
[19] Brown, *World Without Borders*, p. 30.

average temperature rose about 1 degree Fahrenheit. One explanation for this at the time was that the tremendous increase in industrial activity in the world was causing heat to be poured into the atmosphere at such an alarming rate as to increase the earth's temperature. But since 1940, the earth's average temperature has declined .5 degrees Fahrenheit. Now it is hypothesized that industrial activity is resulting in the release of such a tremendous amount of particulate matter into the atmosphere that it is, in effect, blocking out the sun's rays. The point is that no one really knows why the earth's average temperature has changed. It is at least possible that humankind will cause irreparable damage to the earth's environment, leading to a new ice age or melting the polar ice caps. And because there is so little past history to go on in this area, the cause of the damage might not be discovered until it is too late to do anything about it.

A Computer Simulation of the World

The crises that have been discussed are familiar to most people. Over the last decade the news media have brought attention to the population explosion, resource depletions, the energy crisis, starvation, and pollution. The media have also, in the last decade, given a considerable amount of attention to an analysis of all these problems based on a computer simulation of the world. The results of this simulation were published in a report to the Club of Rome, an organization discussed in Chapter 5. The report was entitled *The Limits to Growth,* and its publication in 1972 has provoked a torrent of praise, criticism, books, articles, newspaper stories, and political speeches that continues today.

What Is Computer Simulation?

Part of the controversy surrounding *The Limits to Growth* has focused on the methodology from which its findings were derived, that is, computer simulation. Some critics may have given the report more credibility than it deserves on the assumption that if a computer says it, it must be true. Others, perhaps, are skeptical that even a computer can handle problems on a scale as grand as the world system.

It is important to understand, of course, that what a computer "says" is not necessarily so. In fact, even in a complex simulation of the world, the computer will only say exactly what the designers of the simulation tell it to say (even if the designers may turn out to be surprised by what they told it to say). The *Limits to Growth* simulation does nothing that a human being could not do with a paper and pencil, given enough time.

Still, computer simulations provide social scientists with a powerful tool. While the computer only makes calculations that could be accomplished by hand, it performs them with incredible speed and accuracy. This allows a simulation to be based on a large number of factors and take into account the impact of literally hundreds of interrelationships. The simulator can analyze the world system, for example, bit by bit, and incorporate into the simulation information about the relationships between pollution levels and life expectancy, industrial output and birth rates, crowding and death rates, resource depletion and economic growth, and so on. Once the information about the important relationships on which the system is based has been put into a language that the computer understands, the machine can calculate the "relationships among all the relationships" and thus inform the simulator about the implications of all the initial assumptions and information that serve as the basis of the simulation.

How can one tell, when the simulation is functioning, whether it bears any relationship to the simulated real world? One criterion is *face validity;* the results of the simulation must seem reasonable to scientists who have some knowledge of the workings of the simulated system. But there are other criteria. The *Limits to Growth* simulation, for example, can be judged on the accuracy of its "post-dictions." Information about the state of the world in 1900 is used to set all the initial values of the parameters of the simulation, and then it is allowed to simulate the next sixty to seventy years. Obviously, if the relationships among the factors included in the simulation have been correctly specified, the simulation should be able to make postdictions about the state of the system in 1970 that can be checked against real-world data. The *Limits to Growth* model is able to make accurate postdictions, which increases the chances that if the simulation is allowed to run for a hundred simulated years past 1970, its predictions will be reasonable.

One of the advantages of simulations of social systems is that they can be more complicated and realistic than other kinds of mental or mathematical models, the implications of which must be worked out by hand or with mathematical, statistical techniques that necessitate more simplifying assumptions. They also allow social scientists a form of experimentation with social systems that would not otherwise be possible. Once the simulation is operational, the social scientist can ask a multitude of What-would-happen-if-the-world-were-this-way questions. If the simulation is based on the assumption that a 5 percent increase in a state's GNP increases carbon monoxide pollution by 10 percent, and the social scientist suspects that actually pollution increases 15 percent for every 5 percent increase in the GNP, he or she can run the simulation under both assumptions and see what impact the different assumptions have on the operation of the system.

This kind of *sensitivity analysis,* according to exponents of system dynamics, based on computer simulation, is especially important for policy makers. Social systems, these exponents argue, operate in a counterintuitive manner. Policies that seem, logically, to be designed to solve problems, actually will have no effect or make the problem worse. Armed with a computer simulation of the social system whose problems are being addressed, the policy maker can experiment with various policy options, that is, run the simulation under different sets of assumptions and discover at which points the relevant system is sensitive to outside influence. Such experimentation will allow the policy maker to avoid errors resulting from the counterintuitive operation of social systems.

For example, Jay Forrester, a pioneer in system dynamics, designed a simulation of urban centers, which, he argues, demonstrates that the American approach to urban blight has actually worsened the blight. Planners see human suffering in the cities, accompanied by inadequate housing. So, they build low-cost housing. But, Forrester argues, the simulation shows that "the fundamental cause of depressed areas in cities comes from *excess* housing in the low-income category."[20] The low-cost housing attracts low-income people to the inner city until their numbers far exceed the available job opportunities. Soon unemployed poor can no longer afford even the lost-cost housing, and it falls into disrepair. A policy designed to improve the inner city actually creates a downward spiral to even worse problems.

The world system, according to the designers of the *Limits to Growth* simulation, operates in a similarly counterintuitive fashion. Measures that seem designed to alleviate problems actually make them worse, or have an impact on other parts of the system that creates even worse problems. The interrelationships among these problems can be understood only if the system is analyzed as a whole. The *Limits to Growth* simulation focuses on four basic problems as they affect the entire global system: (1) food production and

---

[20] Jay Forrester, "Counterintuitive Behavior of Social Systems," in *Collected Papers of Jay W. Forrester,* Wright-Allen Press, Cambridge, Mass., 1975, pp. 216–217.

industrialization,[21] (2) consumption of nonrenewable natural resources, (3) population growth, and (4) pollution. The simulation allows one to determine the impact of different solutions, not only on the problems to which they are addressed, but on the global system as a whole.

The Impact of Increased Food Production
and Economic Development

For example, given the rampant poverty and starvation in the global system, a logical solution would involve substantially increased food production and economic development. But the *Limits to Growth* simulation shows that the ultimate result of accelerated food production and economic development on a global basis would be disaster. Increased economic growth would of course help alleviate poverty and starvation in the short run, but in the long run (over the next hundred years or so), it exacerbates all the other problems in the system. Since more food is available, the population grows faster. In time, increases in GNP per capita levels help bring the population under control ("In general, as GNP rises, the birth rate falls."[22]) but the same rising GNP results in an accelerating depletion of natural resources and dramatic increases in levels of pollution. So it is clear that if present trends continue, the world system is headed for catastrophe. But it is also clear that if the only solution to the world's problems concentrates on increasing food production and speeding economic growth, this too will bring disaster.

The Effect of Conservation

Part of the problem with the economic growth solution is that it depletes the earth's natural resources. What if, through intensified exploration, the amount of available natural resources is doubled? The result of this solution, according to the *Limits to Growth* simulation, is disastrous. A rise in available resources allows industrialization to accelerate until pollution reaches dangerous levels. And even though the amount of natural resources is doubled, growth is so rapid that the reserves are used up in a few years.[23] If one becomes more optimistic and assumes that nuclear energy will satisfy the world's energy needs, and if one allows recycling programs to

[21] These problems are listed separately by Meadows et al., but for the purpose of this discussion I believe they can be dealt with together, under the common rubric of economic growth.

[22] Meadows et al., *Limits to Growth*, p. 113.

[23] Meadows et al., *Limits to Growth*, pp. 126–127.

conserve supplies of natural resources effectively, the world's population is still doomed to a sad end. Pollution, again, leads the system to collapse within a hundred years.[24] So, it is clear that, to avoid disaster the world must discover new sources of energy and additional reserves of crucial natural resources. But if it does, disaster is still imminent.

Is Population Control the Answer?

At the root of many of these dilemmas, it seems, is the population explosion. If it could be brought under control, perhaps the other problems would solve themselves. With the *Limits to Growth* simulated world at hand, the hypothesis can be tested. This simulated world can be fixed so that births automatically equal deaths. To institute a policy having the same effect in the real world would clearly be impossible, but assume that tomorrow the U.N. passes a resolution calling for a worldwide program of zero population growth and by next Friday the program is in place. What happens? By now the reader can guess that the ultimate impact of zero population growth is disastrous. Industrial growth accelerates as capital accumulation is facilitated by the decreased pressure of the population explosion. "Eventual depletion of nonrenewable resources brings a sudden collapse of the industrial system."[25] The world's population cannot continue to grow at its present rate without precipitating disaster. But zero population growth will, according to Meadows et al., bring catastrophe just as certainly.

How About Pollution Control?

What are do-gooders to do? Every solution makes things worse. There is just one problem left unattacked. Surely, pollution control can have only good results. Imagine again that the U.N. passes a resolution exhorting the world to institute effective pollution control measures, and by next Saturday the world has successfully reduced pollution by a factor of 4. This is a highly unrealistic assumption, but an effective pollution control program can be instituted in the simulated world without difficulty. Would such a program make the world a better place to live in? Only temporarily. Pollution controls would allow industrialization levels to reach new heights unattainable in a world that would have choked to death. But people no longer die of emphysema, cancer, lead poisoning, birth defects, and other pollution-related diseases, and so population growth continues. Ultimately food production cannot keep up with the population growth, arable land is depleted, and within

[24]Meadows et al., *Limits to Growth*, pp. 132–133.
[25]Meadows et al., *Limits to Growth*, p. 160.

the next hundred years, the system collapses.[26] Foiled again. Pollution obviously cannot continue unabated because disaster surely results. But if pollution levels are reduced 75 percent, if the world embarks on an incredibly effective program of pollution control, its reward will be catastrophe.

The End of Growth

Is there no escape? There is, according to Meadows et al., but the path entails a drastically new and comprehensive approach to the world's problems. Pollution controls must be implemented. Population control is necessary. Natural resources should be conserved. But even if all these measures together are successfully implemented, ultimately "industrial growth is halted, and the death rate rises as resources are depleted, pollution accumulates, and food production declines."[27] If the world is to avoid disaster, conservation, population control, and pollution control *must be combined with a halt in economic growth.* There are limits to growth, and the world is on the verge of reaching those limits. If economic growth is not checked in time, disaster is inevitable.

Criticisms of The Limits to Growth Theory

Bad Data and Insufficient Knowledge

The Limits to Growth has been a tremendous journalistic success; it has been adopted as gospel by scores of intelligent, concerned people all over the (mostly the developed) world. On the other hand, *Limits* has also provoked considerable criticism. Some of it is technical. The simulators, it is argued, have underestimated the supplies of natural resources that exist. The knowledge on which the simulation is based, according to another argument, is too weak to allow the kinds of forecasts that Meadows et al. attempt. The history of demographic predictions, for example, must make one wary of present population forecasts. The predictions of Thomas Malthus in the nineteenth century have proved to be, at best, extremely premature. But twentieth-century demographers have not done much better. In 1932, noted American demographer P. K. Whelpton pointed out that the annual rate of population increase in the United States had fallen to only 9.1 per 1,000. He predicted that the birth rate in the United States would continue to fall and on that

[26] Meadows et al., *Limits to Growth,* pp. 136–137.
[27] Meadows et al., *Limits to Growth,* p. 140.

assumption made forecasts about the size of the American population for 1960 and 1970. He turned out to be off by 20 percent in 1960, and by almost 30 percent for 1970.[28] "The methodology of current extrapolative forecasts is not significantly different from those of the past, and so one does not have a sound basis for expecting present day exercises to prove superior."[29] And demography is only one of many areas where Meadows et al. had to rely on seat-of-the-pants projections, the quality of which cannot be significantly improved by being run through a computer. Present-day knowledge, this argument concludes, is simply not sufficient for the task of making predictions of the kind Meadows et al. attempt.

The Role of Technological Advances

Even if contemporary knowledge about the operation of the global system were better than it is, critics of *Limits* contend, the predictions by Meadows et al. would be of dubious validity, because they underestimate the role of technological advances. Meadows et al. simply cannot anticipate the form of these advances, and all their projections are likely to go awry if only for this reason. If computers had been available a hundred years ago, world simulators attempting to assess future availability of energy resources would not have included oil, natural gas, and uranium in their inventory; they would have focused instead on known reserves of coal, peat, and wood.[30] A similar point is made by those who argue that a "computer freak" of the nineteenth century might have extrapolated the growth rate of the horse population from data available in 1880 and predicted on that basis that by 1980, the world would be covered by one-half foot of horse manure.

The Use of Worldwide Averages

The Limits to Growth has also sparked its own levels of analysis dispute. Critics point out that the world averages on which the *Limits* simulation is based are misleading. The simulation implies that population growth and food production will stage a worldwide race, until some day the population growth will win, and starvation will be rampant all over the globe. Similarly, in the simulated world of Meadows et al., pollution levels build up all

[28] William Page, "Population Forecasting," in *Models of Doom,* ed. H. S. D. Cole, Christopher Freeman, Marie Jahoda, and K. L. R. Pavitt. Universe Books, New York, 1973, pp. 166–167.

[29] Page, "Population Forecasting," p. 172.

[30] A. J. Surrey and A. J. Bromley, "Energy Resources," in *Models of Doom,* ed. H. S. D. Cole, Christopher Freeman, Marie Jahoda, and K. L. R. Pavitt, Universe Books, New York, 1973, p. 105.

over the earth, and suddenly one morning the world's population wakes up to find that it can no longer breathe. Actually, of course, such crises, if they occur at all, will not unfold in this manner. The crises will be localized, and the global system will be able to adapt to them without the characteristic collapse of the Meadows' simulated world. Population will outrun food supplies in specific areas (such as sub-Saharan Africa), and literally millions of people in those areas may die. This is tragic, but the problem will work itself out on a local basis, if only because the death rate will reach such a high level that local food supplies will once again become adequate. Pollution levels will reach crisis proportions in specific, industrialized areas, like Lost Angeles, Pittsburgh, or London, and the results will be very unpleasant. (Thousands may even die, as did happen in a pollution crisis in London in the early fifties.) But smog in Los Angeles and worldwide catastrophe are two different things, and the former can be handled with relative ease. Local measures will resolve pollution crises as they arise on a local basis.

Pseudoscience and the Status Quo
Perhaps the most passionate criticism of *The Limits to Growth* has been ideological in character. Speakers for the Third World, in rich and poor states, for example, have condemned Meadows et al. for their conclusion that economic growth must stop now before the poor countries have a chance to improve their lot. One critic draws an interesting parallel between the work of Meadows et al. and the nineteenth-century economist Thomas Malthus. In *A Summary View of the Principle of Population,* published in 1830, Malthus predicted that population growth would soon outrun food production. In addition, Malthus argued that economic growth (or steps to encourage economic growth, such as a redistribution of wealth) would just make things worse in the long run, because it would spur population levels to new heights. K. L. R. Pavitt points out that this theory conveniently served the interests of the class to which Malthus belonged, the landed gentry. Malthus was trying to make a case against the capitalist bourgeois class that was, in England especially, muscling in on the territory of the landed interests. He asserted, in effect, that if capitalists had their way, the economic growth that they fostered would lead to disaster.[31]

Now, in the 1970s, Pavitt asserts, "the movement hostile to economic growth can be seen as supporting the interests of the materially well-off, who find that life is less pleasant for them when

[31] K. L. R. Pavitt, "Malthus and Other Economists," in *Models of Doom,* ed. H. S. D. Cole, Christopher Freeman, Marie Jahoda, and K. L. R. Pavitt, Universe Books, New York, 1973, p. 142.

an ever larger number of people begin to approach the same living standards as their own"[32] In this view, Meadows et al. have, unwittingly or not, provided a pseudoscientific defense of the status quo, which favors rich people and rich states. No-growth debates also serve to distract attention and energy from the important problems of the poor. "The young people who 10 years ago spent their time and energy working for the alleviation of gross poverty, at home, as well as in poor countries, are more concerning themselves with traffic congestion, smoke pollution, and clean bathing water in their own backyards."[33] In short, some opponents of The Limits to Growth argue that it is basically a political document, masquerading as ideologically neutral science, using the computer as a device to disguise the reactionary bias of its conclusions.

The Meadows et al. Respond

Meadows et al., and the Club of Rome, must have been surprised by the passion behind much of the criticism of The Limits of Growth, but they have stuck by most of their conclusions. Defenders of the simulation admit that human knowledge concerning many of the relationships incorporated into the simulation is fallible, and that much of the data on which it relies is of questionable accuracy. But, they argue, Meadows et al. have utilized the best knowledge and the best data available, and there is no time to wait for perfect knowledge and data to appear. Many of the impending crises must be dealt with *now:* "We suspect on the basis of present knowledge . . . that the growth phase cannot continue for another one hundred years. . . . Because of delays in the system, if the global society waits until those constraints are unmistakenly apparent, it will have waited too long."[34]

Defenders of the Limits simulation also point out the lack of importance of even gross errors in the data base. Exponential growth consumes resources so rapidly, as already seen, that even if the Limits estimates of reserves are off by a factor of 5, (probably a foolishly optimistic assumption), it does not change the essential conclusions of the report. Similarly, it is probable that some of the relationships in the simulation are misspecified; the simulation does not reflect accurately the operation of the real-world global system. But no one of these errors is likely to have such an impact on the

[32] Pavitt, "Malthus," p. 154.
[33] IDS Bulletin, 4 (December 1971), p. 34.
[34] Meadows et al., Limits to Growth, p. 183.

simulation as to invalidate it. Even several errors combined might cause only minor variations in the outcome of the different runs of the simulation, as long as the essential dynamics of the global system have been described accurately.

Meadows et al., and their defenders, must admit that it is possible that technological innovations in the coming years will solve all the problems they foretell. It would have been possible to design the simulation in such a way that every time a problem in the simulated world reaches crisis proportions, some technological solution is devised, and the problem disappears. It would, of course, have been silly to design the simulation this way, and it is equally silly, Meadows et al. argue, to plan the future of the global system on the assumption that every time a problem becomes serious, somebody will think of something. Somebody always has, might seem a convincing retort, but it will not stand scrutiny. When the Black Death hit Europe in the 1300s, for example, nobody was able to think of anything (that worked), and 25 million people, or about one-half the population of Europe, died as a result.

Perhaps the most ambiguous response to critics of *Limits to Growth* involves the reaction by Meadows et al. and their defenders to the argument that the worldwide averages on which the *Limits* simulation is based are misleading. Meadows et al., in response to this point, assert that "aggregated models . . . are often employed by system dynamics modelers . . . because of our feeling that a system should first be approached from its most general aggregated properties. Only when these are understood should details be introduced."[35] The Executive Committee of the Club of Rome has acknowledged that in practice, crises are likely to occur sporadically at points of stress, rather than generally or simultaneously throughout the world. But, they argue,

> it is probably no less true that these crises would have repercussions worldwide and that many nations and people, by taking hasty remedial action or retreating into isolationism and attempting self-sufficiency, would but aggravate the conditions operating in the system as a whole. The interdependence of the various components of the world system would make such measures futile in the end.[36]

[35] Donella H. Meadows, Dennis L. Meadows, Jorgen Randers, and William W. Behrens, III, "A Response to Sussex," in *Models of Doom,* ed. H. S. D. Cole, Christopher Freeman, Marie Jahoda, and K. L. R. Pavitt, Universe Books, New York, 1973, p. 238.
[36] Meadows et al., *Limits to Growth,* pp. 188–189.

Neither the comment by Meadows et al. nor the statement by the executive committee, it seems to this writer, address the criticism directly or clearly. If the world is substantially less interdependent with respect to the phenomena analyzed in *Limits* than the worldwide averages on which it is based imply, then the global system might react differently than the simulated *Limits* world to the crises predicted by Meadows et al. In a way, the Club of Rome (if not, necessarily, Meadows et al.) has acknowledged the validity of this particular criticism of *Limits* by sponsoring a second report, also based on a simulation of the world, but one that treats the system as composed of ten separate if interdependent regions.[37] (This report emphasizes the possibility of organic growth, rather than the necessity of no growth and is in general more sensitive to the aspirations of the Third World.)

The ideological criticism of *The Limits to Growth* has been fascinating, because it has come from such widely separated points of the political spectrum. The outcry from the left, accusing the Meadows et al. of being pseudoscientific defenders of the reactionary status quo, has been mentioned. But the political right has not been happy with *Limits,* either. In particular, defenders of the free enterprise system have been highly suspicious of the no-growth idea, viewing it as a subversion of the raison d'etre of capitalism. In 1972, Sicco Mansholt, who was then acting head of the Commission of the European community, made a public statement in favor of the conclusions of *The Limits to Growth.* Within two weeks after the speech, he was attacked by the French Communist party, and the Confederation of French Industry (the French counterpart of the American National Association of Manufacturers), for his views.

That *The Limits to Growth* has had a political impact there can be little doubt, but this writer, at least, is quite confident that Meadows et al. did not set out to serve the interests of either the left or the right. They may have some qualms about capitalism as it operates now, but socialism (at least in the Soviet Union) is equally dedicated to economic growth and just as opposed to the no-growth ideas in *Limits.* And the no-growth ideas do not necessarily imply a defense of the present highly unequal distribution of wealth in the world. In fact, Meadows et al. will argue the opposite. If economic growth can continue into the foreseeable future, then redistribution of wealth in the global system is not such an urgent need, since everyone in the system will have a chance to improve his or her economic lot even if inequality does persist. But if eco-

---

[37] Mihajlo D. Mesarovic and Eduard C. Pestel, *Mankind at the Turning Point: The Second Report to the CLub of Rome,* New American Library, New York, 1974.

nomic growth must be halted, if the pie cannot be enlarged, then obviously redistribution of wealth does become an urgent priority. So, Meadows et al. argue that the implications of their no-growth ideas, far from being defensive of the status quo, are actually radical.

The Author Assesses . . .

Any attempt to assess the relative merits of the arguments on both sides of the complicated dispute between the Meadows et al. and their critics must be based on a healthy measure of humility. Ideally, the arbiter of this debate would have advanced degrees in demography, economics, political science, chemistry, biology, history, computer science, mathematics, geology, and physics. Holding only one of these requisite degrees, I must admit my credentials are less than complete. Still, in my judgment, the arguments and evidence that have come to light since *The Limits of Growth* was published in 1972 provide the critics of Meadows et al. with the more convincing case.

Population Projections
Consider first the dire warnings by Meadows et al. concerning the population explosion. The effects of this explosion have always been debatable. The richer countries have long insisted that rapid population growth constitutes one of the major obstacles to economic development in the Third World. Lately, no-growth advocates have blamed the explosion for adding intolerable pressures on the earth's supplies of natural resources. Some spokesmen for poor countries, on the other hand, argue that poverty leads to population growth, not vice versa, and the really disastrous pressure on natural-resource supplies stems from the tremendous affluence in the richer countries.[38] Radical economists typically have been suspicious of efforts by rich countries to persuade poor countries to institute programs of population control. Howard Sherman, for example, argues, the "racist solution is that the poor, mostly black, should be pressured into having less [sic] babies . . . The primary problem of these countries is not population, but imperialism."[39] Other radicals have asserted that the real motive

[38] Lester Brown, "Rich Countries and Poor in a Finite, Interdependent World," *Daedalus*, 102 (Fall 1973), 153–165.
[39] Howard Sherman, *Radical Political Economy*, Basic Books, New York, 1972, p. 80.

behind the push by rich countries for population control is not a concern for the welfare of poor states, but a fear that the status quo in the global system will be overwhelmed by yellow (or black, or brown) hordes. In this view, birth control efforts are designed to "kill guerrillas in the womb."

It is beginning to appear that this entire debate may soon acquire a rather quaint air. Almost from the moment Meadows et al. published their pessimistic predictions about population growth, demographers have been revising their projections about future population levels. In 1972 (the year, recall, that *The Limits* appeared), the World Bank published a report that concluded, "most demographers are agreed by now that the 1970s will see the population growth rate reach a plateau so that by 1980 population growth rates will tend to decline, slowly at first and rapidly thereafter."[40] Basing its conclusions on data from the following year (1973), the United Nations Population Division, for the first time in its history, revised *downward* its estimate of future population growth. Previously, it had predicted that by the year 2000, the world's population would be almost 6.5 billion. In 1975, it pointed out that recent trends indicated that the figure would be closer to 6.3 billion.[41] Then, in 1976, Lester Brown published a report noting that the world's population-growth rate had fallen from 1.9 percent a year in 1970 to 1.64 percent a year in 1975.[42] This may not seem like a significant drop, but the result of the lower growth rate is a projected world population of only 5.4 billion by the year 2000. The figure is 900 million short of the population projected in 1973 by the United Nations Population Division, or equivalent to the population of North America, Latin America, and Western Europe combined. And evidence indicates that the rate of growth of the world's population is continuing to fall. In 1976, the population director of the U.S. Agency for International Development predicted that the growth rate for the world will fall below 1 percent by 1985.[43]

Several factors account for this apparent demise of the population explosion. One of the most significant has been the tremendous success of the family planning program in China, the home of

[40]International Bank for Reconstruction and Development, *Report on Limits to Growth,* Washington, D.C., 1972, pp. 8–9.
[41]United Nations Population Division, "World Population Prospects, 1970–2000, as assessed in 1973," ESA/P/WP.53, March 1975.
[42]Lester Brown, *World Population Trends: Signs of Hope, Signs of Stress,* Worldwatch Institute, Washington, D.C., 1976, p. 7.
[43]Charles Panati and Mary Lord, "Population Implosion," *Newsweek,* December 6, 1976, 58.

one-fourth of the world's population. AID estimates that China successfully lowered its birth rate from 35.5 per thousand in 1964 to 14.0 per thousand in 1975.[44] But China has not been the only country to institute effective birth control programs. A variety of contraceptive devices have had widespread impact; in addition, Lester Brown notes that the early 1970s saw a dramatic increase in legalized abortion. In 1971, only 38 percent of the world's population lived in countries where abortions were legal. By 1976, that figure was 64 percent.[45]

The drop in the population-growth rate brought about by birth control programs has surprised most demographers, who previously assumed that such programs would not be successful in poor countries until those states reached much higher levels of GNP per capita and average education. Since wealth and education levels will probably rise in most poor countries in the coming decades, the downward trend in population levels might receive important reinforcement.

None of the recent data on population growth necessarily implies that all population control programs are outmoded. One of the reasons that the growth rate slowed so dramatically in the early 1970s was that hundreds of thousands of people died of starvation. And in certain countries (such as Mexico), rapid population growth continues; bringing it under control is almost certainly a desirable goal. It should also be pointed out that if demographers can change their minds so drastically in the few short years from 1970 to 1975, it is conceivable that they will be surprised again in the years from 1975 to 1980. But, as of this writing, most evidence seems to indicate that the predictions by Meadows et al. (and to be fair, almost everyone else who tried to predict world population growth in the early 1970s) concerning the future disastrous impact of exponential population growth were unduly alarmist.

Reserves of Natural Resources
Assuming it is true, though, that predictions about population growth are alarmist, would not warrant the conclusion that all the warnings in *The Limits to Growth* may be safely ignored. Recall that they instituted zero population growth in their simulated world, and it did not allow the system to escape disaster. Controlling population growth, for example, can actually speed up depletion of natural resources by facilitating economic expansion.

[44] Panati and Lord, "Population Implosion," 58.
[45] Brown, *World Population Trends,* p. 8.

But the warnings about natural resource depletion in *Limits* are at least as suspect as the predictions about population growth. The estimates by Meadows et al. about future recoverable resources are almost certainly mistaken. Consider first the most visible aspect of this particular problem, the energy crisis. When OPEC successfully quadrupled the price of oil in the winter of 1973–1974, this cost rise was seized on by no-growth advocates as proof that the world's supply of energy resources was running low. But it proved no such thing. The Arabs were not running out of oil; they were just charging more for it. Their costs of production were still about 10 cents a barrel, even though they were asking $10 a barrel in the international marketplace. Total world production of oil actually increased by 8 percent in 1973. And the flow of oil from the Middle East gave no indication of oil wells drying up. "Total oil tanker loadings from six major Middle East oil terminals during the last quarter of 1973 were 31 percent higher than the same quarter of 1972. Some exhaustion of supplies!"[46] Even the conservative estimate by Meadows et al. projects that the world's reserves of petroleum will last twenty years, and that estimate probably errs in the direction of pessimism. In Alberta, Canada, alone, tar sands and oil-containing shale rock are estimated to contain more oil than the reserve figure given by *The Limits to Growth* for the entire world.[47]

It is possible that technological developments necessary to allow access to oil in sources such as tar sands and shale rock will not be completed in time to avoid disaster. But, in the long run at least, it is important to realize that oil is not the only source of energy. Coal, another fossil fuel, is abundant on a global basis. Again, even Meadows et al. estimate that, given only known reserves and the present exponential rate of growth in the use of coal, the world will not run out of this energy resource for 111 years. Development of techniques for conversion of coal to liquid and gaseous fuels is taking place in several countries today, and if oil does become more scarce and/or more expensive, this development will certainly be expedited.

And there is no reason for the world to maintain reliance on fossil fuels indefinitely. Nuclear power, through fission or fusion, provides one alternative. If the environmental impact of nuclear power proves to be so detrimental as to preclude its use (and nuclear fusion seems much less problematical in this regard), solar and

[46] Wilfred Beckerman, *In Defence of Economic Growth,* Jonathan Cape, London, 1974, p. 250.

[47] Alberta Oil and Gas Conservation Board, *A Description and Reserve Estimate of Oil Sands of Alberta,* Calgary, 1962.

TABLE 7.2 Changes in known reserves, 1950–1970

Ore	Known Reserves 1950	Known Reserves 1970	Percentage Increase
Iron	19,000,000	251,000,000	1,321
Manganese	500,000	635,000	27
Chromite	100,000	775,000	675
Copper	100,000	279,000	179
Lead	40,000	86,000	115
Zinc	70,000	113,000	61
Tin	6,000	6,600	10
Bauxite	1,400,000	5,300,000	279
Potash	5,000,000	118,000,000	2,360
Phosphates	26,000,000	1,178,000,000	4,430

Source: Council on International Economic Policy, Executive Office of the President, Special Report, Critical Imported Materials, Washington, D.C., U.S. Government Printing Office, December, 1974. Reprinted by permission of William Morrow & Co., Inc. from *The Next 200 Years* by Herman Kahn, William Brown and Leon Martel. Copyright © 1976 by The Hudson Institute.

geothermal energy resources promise essentially infinite supplies in the long run.[48]

Contrary to the predictions of Meadows et al., the world also seems unlikely to deplete its reserves of nonenergy resources, such as iron, copper, lead, and tin. The *Limits* predictions are based on known reserves of the various resources, but these reserves, historically, have always understated substantially actual reserves. Consider Table 7.2, showing reserves of several key resources in 1950 and in 1970. Consumption of all these materials increased during twenty years, and yet at the end of the two decades, known reserves were dramatically higher in virtually every case.

Why does this happen? Perhaps the most important reason involves the economic incentives operating on those who gather data on known reserves. Usually, the original sources of such data are companies interested in the commercial exploitation of a given resource. Once a company has located reserves that are projected to last, say, thirty years, there are at least two important reasons why it is unlikely even to attempt to find additional reserves. First, since it will not be able to sell those reserves for thirty years, there is little

[48] Kahn, Brown, and Martel, *Next 200 Years,* pp. 58–83.

incentive to spend time and energy to locate them. Second, if known reserves become too abundant, they exert a strong downward pressure on the price of the resource in question.

So, time after time, for resource after resource, dire predictions emanate from various quarters about an imminent depletion. But when the time period passes, typically, the resource is not depleted; rather, known reserves have become larger than at the time of the prediction. Table 7.3 shows an interesting series of predictions about the depletion of oil in the United States. The gloomy predictions of the 1970s, as the table shows, are only the latest in a string of similar prophesies extending back in time for over a century. Given this demonstrated track record, who would bet on the accuracy of current predictions of disastrous energy shortages in the United States?

The situation is not drastically different on the global level. Despite dramatic increases in consumption, and all the publicity given the energy crisis of the 1970s, it is important to remember that,

> without even allowing for all the recent increases in prospective reserves . . . whereas proven world oil reserves were only about 15 times annual oil production before the war, they had risen to 25 times annual production by the 1950s (when demand was already twice the pre-war level) and now stand at about 35 times world production in spite of the demand having trebled again.[49]

Another reason that pessimistic predictions by Meadows et al. concerning depletion of natural resources are unlikely to prove accurate is that they overlook probable technological developments that will allow the exploitation of new untapped reserves. The *Limits* estimates are largely based on the assumption, for example, that the only available supplies of resources will be ore of a quality that is economically profitable to mine at the present time. But, historically, technological developments have allowed the successful exploitation of ores of increasingly lower quality. In the nineteenth century, copper ores were not mined unless they contained from 4 to 6 percent copper. In the 1970s, ores containing only .4 percent copper are mined profitably, and this trend seems likely to continue. If one adds to the additional supplies of resources in the earth's crust that might become available the reserves on the

[49] Beckerman, *Economic Growth,* p. 256.

TABLE 7.3   A short history of predictions about American oil supplies, 1866–1949

Date	Prediction	What Actually Happened
1866	Synthetics available if oil production should end (U.S. Revenue Commission)	In next 82 years the U.S. produced 37 billion barrels with no need for synthetics
1885	Little or no chance of oil in California (U.S. Geological Survey)	8 billion barrels produced in California since that date with important new findings in 1948
1891	Little or no chance of oil in Kansas or Texas (U.S. Geological Survey)	14 billion barrels produced in these two states since 1891
1908	Maximum future supply of 22.5 billion barrels (officials of Geological Survey)	35 billion barrels produced since 1908, with 26.8 billion reserve proven and available on January 1, 1949
1914	Total future production only 5.7 billion barrels (official of U.S. Bureau of Mines)	34 billion barrels produced since 1914, or six times this prediction
1920	U.S. needs foreign oil and synthetics: peak domestic production almost reached (director of U.S. Geological Survey)	1948 U.S. production in excess of U.S. consumption and more than four times 1920 output
1931	Must import as much foreign oil as possible to save domestic supply (secretary of interior)	During the next 8 years imports were discouraged and 14 billion barrels were found in the U.S.
1939	U.S. oil supplies will last only 13 years (radio broadcasts by Department of Interior)	New oil found since 1939 exceeds the 13 years supply known at that time
1947	Sufficient oil cannot be found in United States (chief of Petroleum Division, State Department)	4.3 billion barrels found in 1948, the largest volume in history and twice our consumption
1949	End of oil supply almost in sight (Secretary of the Interior)	Petroleum industry demonstrated ability to increase U.S. production by more than a million barrels daily in the next 5 years

Source: Presidential Energy Program, Hearings before the Subcommittee on Energy and Power of the Committee on Interstate and Foreign Commerce, House of Representatives. First sessions on the implication of the President's proposals on the Energy Independence Act of 1975. Serial no. 94–20, p. 643. U.S. Government Printing Office, Washington, D.C. February 17, 18, 20, 21, 1975. Reprinted by permission of William Morrow & Co., Inc. from The Next 200 Years by Herman Kahn, William Brown and Leon Martel. Copyright © 1976 by The Hudson Institute.

TABLE 7.4 Comparative estimates of some natural resource reserves (in tons)

	Meadows[a]	In Ocean Nodules[b]	In Sea Water[c]	In the Earth's Crust[d]
Aluminum	3.6 billion	— — —	18 billion	80,000 trillion
Chromium	8.9 billion	— — —	80 million	110 trillion
Cobalt	11 million	3 billion	800 million	25 trillion
Copper	1.06 billion	3 billion	6 billion	63 trillion
Gold	50,000	— — —	8 million	3.5 billion
Iron	710 billion	130 billion	18 billion	58,000 trillion
Lead	1.8 billion	4 billion	60 million	12 trillion
Manganese	24 billion	160 billion	4 billion	1,300 trillion
Mercury	920,000	— — —	60 million	9 billion
Uranium	29 million	— — —	6 billion	180 billion

[a]Dennis Meadows, *Dynamics of Growth in a Finite World,* Wright-Allen Press, Cambridge, Mass, 1974.
[b]Kahn et al, *Next 200 Years,* p. 104.
[c]National Research Council, *Resources and Man,* W. H. Freeman, San Francisco, 1969.
[d]U.S. Mineral Resources, 1973.
Source: Reprinted by permission of William Morrow & Co., Inc. from *The Next 200 Years* by Herman Kahn, William Brown and Leon Martel. Copyright © 1976 by The Hudson Institute.

floor of the ocean in the form of nodules, and in the sea water itself, the world's supplies of resources look very different from the picture painted by Meadows et al. As Table 7.4 shows, when Meadows et al. assume, for the sake of argument, that actual reserves are five times greater than known reserves, what appears to be magnanimous optimism on their part often amounts instead to gloomy, unwarranted pessimism. Even if the potential reserves in the ocean are ignored, natural concentrations of key resources in the top mile of the earth's crust are estimated to be about a million times known reserves. These supplies should last approximately 100 million years.[50]

Even if, in some instances, the earth's supply of a natural resource does become depleted, the *Limits* simulation probably overestimates the impact of such an occurrence. The end of supplies will occur gradually, with higher prices decreasing demand and

[50]Beckerman, *Economic Growth,* p. 219.

stimulating the search for alternative materials. When copper becomes too expensive as a conductor of electricity, aluminum can be used instead. If aluminum in turn becomes scarce, glass fibers can be substituted. If substitutes are unsatisfactory or unavailable, recycling may extend the use of resource X into the indefinite future. In short, the prediction by Meadows et al. that the world faces imminent disaster sparked by the total exhaustion of several crucial natural resources can be rejected with some confidence.

Pollution and Economic Growth

The conclusions of *The Limits to Growth* concerning the future dangers of pollution are, paradoxically, the weakest and the strongest in the report. They are weak because the evidence on which they are based is extremely scanty. Pollution is a relatively recent concern, and data on the relevant problems rarely go back more than ten to twenty years. But this same scanty evidence makes it difficult to discount entirely even the gloomiest predictions by Meadows et al. Dealing with possible crises without precedent, the predictions *could* turn out to be true, and there simply is no hard evidence to prove otherwise.

Still, there are good reasons to believe that Meadows et al. have based their predictions about future environmental catastrophes on a confused idea of the relationship between pollution and economic growth. Their basic proposition is that growth unavoidably adds to the pollution burden on the earth's environment. The proposition is dubious at best.

There is a widespread assumption that Meadows et al. are right, that as economic growth in the developed countries, for example, continues, pollution inexorably becomes an increasingly serious problem. Barry Commoner, a noted American environmentalist, writes that "a rather striking picture does emerge from the data that are available; most pollution problems made their first appearance, or became very much worse in the years following World War II."[51] But Wilfred Beckerman points out several exceptions to this alleged trend. Total smoke produced in Britain fell from 2.3 million tons in 1953 to 0.9 million in 1968. The total quantity of sulfur oxides emitted into the air in Britain has been falling since 1962. Air quality improvement has been especially dramatic in the urban areas. The decrease in the output of smoke per unit of industrial output was about 85 percent in the 1960s.

[51] Barry Commoner, *The Closing Circle,* Knopf, New York, 1971, p. 128. As will be seen, Commoner does not argue that this has occurred as a result of economic growth per se.

Partly as a result of this success, average visibility in London, which was only one mile in 1958, is now up to four miles. Similar successes have been enjoyed in the fight against water pollution in Britain. The mileage of completely unpolluted rivers rose slightly from 1958 to 1972, and the percentage of grossly polluted rivers fell from 6.4 percent in 1958 to 3.7 percent in 1972. In 1958 there were virtually no fish in the Thames in London. By 1972, fifty-five different species were thriving, along with several species of water birds.[52]

The United States, while continuing to grow economically, has also achieved some notable environmental improvement. Lake Erie was once thought to be "dead" because of eutrophication, but recently there have been dramatic increases in the fish catch. The highest fish catch on record took place in 1972.[53] The air in steel-producing Pittsburgh is undeniably cleaner than in previous decades, and Los Angeles has made significant progress in the battle against its infamous pollution. Overall, smoke concentrations in American urban areas declined slightly between 1957 and 1970, and recent legislation, such as the Air Quality Act of 1967 (as amended in 1970) and the Federal Water Quality Act of 1972, seems destined to reinforce the trend toward improving environmental quality. The Environmental Protection Agency (EPA) reported in the mid-1970s that the standards of the Air Quality Act were generally being met throughout the United States. While the standards of the Water Quality Act for 1983 and 1985 may be impossible to meet, successes such as those experienced in Lake Erie and the Willamette River basin are encouraging.[54]

These are relatively short-term trends that must make one doubt that economic growth necessarily causes a deterioration of the environment. Long-term trends reinforce the doubt. Industrial, urban societies have not obviously become progressively more burdened by pollution problems with the passing of time and continuing economic growth. Admittedly, it is difficult to prove that things were worse in the "good old days," since there are virtually no precise measures of pollution from the last century. But there are sources that make it clear that pollution was a serious problem then. Charles Dickens, for example, in his novel *Hard Times,* describes a nineteenth century Coketown (actually Preston) in these terms:

[52] Beckerman, *Economic Growth,* pp. 123–124.
[53] Beckerman, *Economic Growth,* p. 122.
[54] Kahn, Brown, and Martel, *Next 200 Years,* p. 141.

It was a town of machinery and tall chimneys, out of which interminable serpents of smoke trailed themselves for ever and ever, and never got uncoiled. It had a black canal in it, and a river that ran purple with ill-smelling dye, and vast piles of building full of windows, where there was a rattling and a trembling all day long.[55]

Nineteenth century Manchester, in northern England, was, apparently, not much more attractive.

A sort of black smoke covers the city. The sun seen through it is a disc without rays. Under this half-daylight, 300,000 human beings are ceaselessly at work. A thousand noises disturb this dark, damp labyrinth.[56]

Meanwhile, things were also rather unpleasant in another budding nineteenth-century industrial power, the United States. The largest industrial center there was New York City, with some 300 foundries and machine shops, and a printing industry powered by 125 steam engines, bone mills, refineries, and tanneries.

The crux of New York's filthy air was Hunter's point, on the rim of the Bronx. Grievous odors from the Point poured over Manhattan, affecting all who lived there regardless of rank or address. . . . By 1881 even the doggedly patient New Yorkers had coughed enough, and angrily compelled the State Board of Health to investigate the origin of their misery. During the inquiry ninety witnesses specified the ingredients that gave the city air its rich flavor: sulfur, ammonia gases, offal rendering, bone boiling, manure heaps, putrid animal wastes, fish scrap, kerosene, acid fumes, phosphate fertilizer, and sludge.[57]

There apparently was a lively controversy in that day about whether New York or Chicago was more grievously afflicted with

[55] Cited by T. C. Sinclair, "Environmentalism," in *Models of Doom*, ed. H. S. D. Cole, Christopher Freeman, Marie Jahoda, and K. L. R. Pavitt, Universe Books, New York, 1973, p. 182.
[56] *Industrialisation and Culture, 1830–1914*, Oxford University Press, 1970. Cited by T. C. Sinclair, "Environmentalism," p. 186.
[57] Otto L. Bettman, *The Good Old Days—They Were Terrible*, Random House, New York, 1974, pp. 5–6.

Pittsburgh in the 1890s. The Bettmann archive.

pollution. The Chicago River was reportedly polluted with "grease so thick on its surface it seemed a liquid rainbow." An Italian visitor noted that

> During my stay of one week, I did not see in Chicago anything but darkness, smoke, clouds of dirt. . . . One morning when I happened to be on a high railroad viaduct, the city seemed to smolder, a vast unyielding conflagration.[58]

And nineteenth-century Chicago and New York could not have been worse than Pittsburgh, with its 14,000 chimneys (belonging mostly to iron and steel mills) bombarding the city with smoke and

[58] Bettman, *Good Old Days,* p. 14.

soot twenty-four hours a day, "a noisome vomit, killing everything that grows—trees, grass, and flowers."[59]

As is true today, the major form of transportation in the nineteenth century was a source of serious pollution. Of the 3 million horses in American cities, about 150,000 lived and worked in New York City, producing some twenty to twenty-five pounds of manure a day.

> These dumplings were numerous on every street, attracting swarms of flies and radiating a powerful stench. The ambiance was further debased by the presence on almost every block of stables filled with urine-saturated hay. During dry spells, the pounding traffic refined the manure to dirt, which blew "from the pavement as a sharp, piercing power, to cover our clothes, ruin our furniture and blow up into our nostrils."[60]

This last example illustrates nicely the principle that economic growth and progress do not necessarily bring increased pollution. The automobile is unquestionably a serious polluter, but, as Elliot Montrol has pointed out, a car emits only 6 grams of pollutant per mile, while a horse emits about 600 grams of solid pollutant and 300 grams of liquid pollutant over the same distance.[61]

A comparison of contemporary developing societies with industrialized countries provides additional support for the assertion that economic growth and environmental deterioration do not necessarily go hand in hand. Developing states typically have water pollution problems, for example, brought about by poor sanitation systems, that are more serious than those of industrialized societies. Fatal illnesses related to the consumption of impure water are extremely rare in richer countries; dysentery and more serious diseases are commonplace in most poor states. And the crowding in the slums of major cities in many poor countries is creating additional serious pollution problems. Economic growth may exacerbate some pollution problems for poor countries in the short run,

[59] Bettman, *Good Old Days*, p. 16.

[60] Bettman, *Good Old Days*, p. 3.

[61] Cited by Beckerman, *Economic Growth*, p. 120. This last argument is partially facetious, since automobiles facilitate travel over much greater distances than did horses, and if only for that reason, probably constitute a more serious pollution problem. Even so, it is not obvious that pollution is a more serious problem today than in the last century, though it is clear that it is attracting more attention. The American Food and Drug Administration recently warned against eating swordfish because of a high mercury content. It was soon discovered that swordfish (as well as tuna) that had been dead a hundred years contained equally large amounts of mercury. See Beckerman, *Economic Growth*, p. 121.

but ultimately such growth is likely to be a necessary condition for the alleviation of pollution. Generally speaking, pollution only becomes a high priority problem for individuals and states whose more fundamental problems, such as obtaining sufficient food, clothing and shelter, have been solved. The countries that have devoted substantial resources to environmental improvement are relatively rich, such as Britain, the United States, and Sweden. Present trends indicate clearly that developing countries are unlikely to devote resources to pollution abatement until they achieve significantly higher standards of living.

The point, then, is that economic growth per se is not the villain in the story of pollution. Unfortunately, the no-growth debate has taken the spotlight away from a more important topic for debate with respect to pollution, that is the kind of economic growth a society should strive for. Growth and pollution control can complement one another. For example, a decrease in pollution in an industrialized society might increase the GNP by decreasing the number of work days lost owing to pollution-induced illnesses in the work force. Barry Commoner points out that the economic growth of the 1930s improved the environment of the United States because it was based in part on a soil conservation program.[62] He also argues persuasively that the post-Second World War pollution problems of the United States on which he focuses have not been the result of increases in the population or affluence but rather certain qualitative characteristics of the economic growth. Nonreturnable soda bottles, synthetic, nonbiodegradable fibers and plastics, detergents, and high-powered automobiles have added tremendously to the burden on the American environment, without adding significantly to the welfare of the population. Returnable bottles, cotton clothes, wood and steel products, soap, and more efficient automobiles were not replaced because of economic necessity, and certainly not because their continued use posed insuperable barriers to economic growth. They were shoved aside because the American economic system (with the help of Madison Avenue) rewards innovation for its own sake and does not impose the cost of pollution on the polluters. If polluters were taxed according to the amount of damage they did to the environment, then such products as detergents and plastics would be more costly, reflecting the greater burden they impose on society. Soap would once again become marketable, without any loss of cleaning power to American consumers.[63] And such taxes need not impose an intolerable burden on the economy. It is true that taxes on pollution

[62] Commoner, *Closing Circle,* p. 141.
[63] Commoner, *Closing Circle,* p. 156.

would make some products cost more, resulting in decreased sales and lost jobs. But if the government uses these taxes to stimulate demand in other sectors of the economy, the overall impact need not be a slowing of economic growth or an increase in unemployment.[64]

In short, environmentalists would aid their cause if they called a halt to the attack on economic growth per se and concentrated instead on certain kinds of economic growth. There are environmentalists, happily, who are quite aware of this. As Barry Commoner points out, some environmentalists

> reason—erroneously, as we have seen—that pollution is caused by excessive consumption of goods and resources by the United States population. Since the wastes generated by this intense consumption pollute our environment, the eco-activist is advised to "consume less." In the absence of the added statistic that in the United States per capita consumption by blacks is much less than that of the white population, such observations are not likely to make much sense to blacks or to anyone who is concerned with social justice.[65]

The same point is valid on the international level. Leaders and citizens of poor countries are understandably concerned that the recent discovery of the environment in rich countries will serve as an excuse to let the poor states continue to suffer in the name of pollution abatement. Even if economic growth clearly and inevitably led to a deterioration of the earth's environment, the damage to the environment would have to be grievous indeed to justify the condemnation of so many millions to the misery they suffer now. Since economic growth may lead to or at least allow significant improvements in the environment, there is no convincing justification for the pursuit of no-growth policies for the sake of pollution control.

Population Control, Conservation,
and Pollution Control
None of these criticisms of no-growth policies, or of the conclusions of Meadows et al. in *The Limits to Growth,* should be interpreted as a condemnation of efforts aimed at population control, conservation of natural resources, or pollution control. All three are desirable goals, even if not exactly for the reasons suggested by Meadows et al. In purely physical terms, the world, in the coming

[64] Beckerman, *Economic Growth,* p. 272.
[65] Commoner, *Closing Circle,* p. 208.

decades, will probably be able to produce enough food for the population. But

> the problem of providing the world's population with adequate food is made much more complex by the fact that over half the world's population is confined to less than one-seventh of the world's agricultural land, while one-sixth of the population occupies more than one-half of the productive soil.[66]

Getting food to the people who need it may be difficult, to say the least. Population control in India, Pakistan, Bangladesh, Indonesia, and Mexico may not, as some economists argue, provide an important stimulant to economic growth and may not even be a necessary condition for such growth. Still, barring a series of unlikely economic miracles, these countries will not be able to feed themselves in the coming years, and disasters that loom there can only be made worse if the populations continue to grow at the present pace.

Similarly, in purely physical terms, the earth's supply of natural resources may be much further from exhaustion than Meadows et al. suggest. But disaster sparked by natural resource depletion could still occur. The world at this point seems particularly prone to catastrophe as a result of oil shortages brought about by depletion of resources in countries that need it (such as the United States), or by the kind of political activities OPEC engaged in after the 1973 Arab-Israeli War. Finding alternative sources of energy may well be the easy part of the problem to solve. The more difficult aspect of the energy crisis may involve bringing about the political, technological, and economic transitions that are necessary to end heavy dependence on oil with sufficient speed. This problem is quite apparent in the United States. Even if there is only a small probability that oil supplies will be exhausted in the next twenty to fifty years, logic would dictate that the Americans should take steps to end heavy reliance on oil. But the political lobby formed by oil companies and automobile manufacturers, among others, forms a powerful force for the status quo.[67] On the global level, even if

[66] Finlay and Hovet, *7304: International Relations,* p. 165.

[67] Carl Solberg points out that after the Second World War, Americans made a serious effort to duplicate the German process for producing synthetic gasoline by the hydrogenation of coal. "The U.S. Bureau of Mines founded a Consolidation Coal Co. test plant in West Virginia to exploit and improve the German process. Few doubted in those confident years that what the Germans could do the Americans would do better. But a little-noticed decision changed everything . . . oil interests successfully pressured the Eisenhower administration into cutting off funds. It was, John F. O'Leary . . . said later, 'the most serious error in energy policy made in the postwar years.' " See Solberg, *Oil Power,* New American Library, New York, 1976, p. 248.

energy resources are plentiful, there is still considerable doubt whether the changes necessary to shift from oil to alternative sources of energy can be made in time. If conservation can buy time for these changes to be made (in the United States, as well as the rest of the world), then conservation is a highly laudable goal.

Economic growth may not, logically, lead to a deterioration of the environment. Even so, economic and political pressures can push economic growth in that direction. Here again, automobile manufacturers in the United States provide a convenient illustrative example. They have fought against legal measures aimed at decreasing the polluting power of American automobiles virtually every step of the way. When they threaten to shut down rather than meet new standards, they acquire the strong support of labor unions and many congressmen. On a worldwide basis, nation-states are caught in a kind of prisoners' dilemma with respect to pollution. All states would be better off if pollution-creating activities were curbed; but if one nation insists on manufacturing product A in a manner unrestricted by expensive pollution controls and thus can put the product on the international market at a low price, pressure to forgo the luxury of pollution controls is put on any other country wishing to sell product A. In short, economic growth need not necessarily be associated with increased pollution. Actually, though, economic growth may have exactly that result unless environmentalists and their supporters are successful in the attempts to divert adequate resources toward pollution control.

So, it is only when Meadows et al. suggest that steps aimed directly at slowing economic growth are necessary in order to avoid worldwide disasters that this writer believes they are mistaken. Conservation, and pollution control in particular, may, as a more or less *unintended* consequence, result in slower economic growth. But this does not mean that the most effective way of attaining those goals involves actions *intended* to slow growth; and it certainly does not imply that no growth is a necessary condition for the achievement of conservation and pollution control.

The Political Future

There is an obvious omission in the discussion of *The Limits to Growth* so far. Meadows et al. imply that the present political structure of the world must be altered in order to avoid the disasters they predict. But they are not explicit about how the world should be organized politically. And, of course, Meadows et al. specifically exclude from their discussion the political problem that might bring disaster to the world even if none of the catastrophes they predict ever occur, that is, international war.

One important reason that Meadows et al. do not discuss such political problems in any detail involves their reliance on data-based computer simulated forecasts. A computer may help one predict how the world *will* be if present trends continue or under varying sets of assumptions. But a computer can only be an indirect help, at best, in any effort to determine how the world *should* be. That, of course, is a question of values, and only human beings can decide which values should be maximized.

The World Order Models Project (discussed in Chapter 5) is dedicated to the proposition that the world as it is presently structured will not result in the maximization of values its members hold most dear. They have agreed that the most important values are: (1) peace, (2) economic well being, (3) social justice, (4) ecological stability, and (5) positive identity. Scholars participating in the project (from West Germany, Latin America, Japan, India, Africa, North America, the Soviet Union, China, the Middle East, and a nonterritorial group) have also agreed to cooperate in a modelling effort that produces *diagnoses* of current problems, *prognoses* concerning the future development of those problems, and viable *strategies of transition* designed to bring about a world in which the five central values of the project can be most fully realized.[68] And these strategies of transition are not focused on a time period so far off into the future as to be of only academic interest. Rather, meaningful transitions are expected to occur within the next twenty years, with the decade of the 1990s assumed to be of critical importance.

What changes would the WOMPers like to see occur in the next twenty years? To this writer, at least, a reading of the essays produced by the project so far leaves a more vivid impression of diversity than a feeling of coherence. But there is some visible agreement that the domination of the present system by states (or, at least, the states that dominate it now) must be ended. Richard Falk[69] and Johan Galtung[70] both stress their preference for increasing the influence of various nonterritorial actors. Rajni Kothari believes that the domination of the present system by a few large

---

[68] Saul Mendlovitz, ed., Introduction, in *On the Creation of a Just World Order,* Free Press, New York, 1975, pp. vii–xvii. For more discussion of the methodology utilized by WOMP and others in the design of future alternative worlds, see Louis René Beres and Harry R. Targ, *Reordering the Planet: Constructing Alternative World Futures,* Allyn and Bacon, Boston, 1974, and several articles in *Planning Alternative World Futures: Values, Methods, and Models,* ed. Louis René Beres and Harry R. Targ, Praeger, New York, 1975.

[69] Richard Falk, "Toward a New World Order: Modest Methods and Drastic Visions," in *On the Creation of a Just World Order,* ed. Saul Mendlovitz, pp. 211–258.

[70] Johan Galtung, "Nonterritorial Actors and the Problem of Peace," in *Creation of Just World,* pp. 151–188.

states might best be remedied by a reduction in the number of sovereign units from the present 140 or so to 20 to 25 more or less equal states.[71] Ali Mazrui is particularly concerned about the extent to which the powerful states dominate the contemporary system culturally. To deal with this problem, Mazrui proposes that five world-languages (English, French, Russian, Arabic, and Chinese) be adopted on a global basis, and that every child in the world learn three languages: (1) a world language, (2) a regional language, and (3) a national or a subnational language.[72]

But aside from this antistate theme, the project, so far at least, has created more confusion than credibility. Peace is supposedly one of the five major values agreed on by the project members, yet Paul T. K. Lin clearly advocates a kind of "just war" doctrine.[73] The project does not see itself as an instrument to be used by one great power as a political weapon against others in the global political system, but Lin is the only participant from a major power who stresses the relevance of the political, economic, and social institutions of his country (China) to the creation of a preferred world. Readers can hardly be blamed if they get the impression that the project as a whole is advocating Chinese approaches to global problems, as opposed to Russian, American, or, say, Brazilian approaches. Such an impression might be strengthened by the fact that one of the American participants (Richard Falk) is clearly not enamored of the institutions of his country, nor does he advocate their relevance for the rest of the world. (In fact, he makes quite the opposite argument.) Can WOMP realistically expect an organized worldwide movement based on Professor Lin's philosophy to gain anything like the necessary support to bring about global changes? (Since the death of Mao, does Lin even represent the views of the present Chinese leadership?)

Of course, it is possible (even probable) that the project does not mean to officially endorse Chinese solutions to the world's problems. More probably, its leaders simply felt, given that one-quarter of the world's population is Chinese, a Chinese point of view ought to be included among the essays presented. But concessions of this nature have served, in my view at least, to eliminate any coherence the project might have achieved. Add to the diversity among the participants the obvious lack of agreement in WOMP on the methods, goals, and future course of the project,

[71] Rajni Kothari, "World Politics and World Order: The Issue of Autonomy," in *Creation of Just World*, p. 56.

[72] Ali A. Mazrui, "World Culture and a Search for Human Consensus," in *Creation of Just World*, pp. 23–26.

[73] Paul T. K. Lin, "Development Guided by Values: Comments on China's Road and Its Implications," in *Creation of Just World*, pp. 281–283.

and the result is confusion that even a sympathetic reader must find disturbing. Mendlovitz, director of the project, states at one point:

> it is my considered judgment that there is no longer a question of whether or not there will be a world government by the year 2000. As I see it, the questions we should be addressing to ourselves are: how will it come into being—by cataclysm, drift, more or less rational design—and whether it will be totalitarian, benignly elitist, or participatory.[74]

Yet Richard Falk, in his essay in the same volume, concedes that the present state-dominated system may well survive for another fifty to a hundred years.[75] Mendlovitz stresses that the project participants were urged to come up with "coherent and viable" strategies of transition.[76] But many of the proposals made by WOMPers so far can only be considered fantastic, and even an obviously sympathetic reviewer of the project's progress to date warns that "the most important insight into the role of inventive thinking in reference to world organization is that many proposals are not to be taken literally."[77] Other reviewers express essentially the same point in less diplomatic language. David Wilkinson concludes:

> Had Mendlovitz and his original associates . . . actually produced their intended diagnoses, prognoses, and strategies with due attention to descriptive precision and strategic common sense, they might well have made advances in peace theory. . . . But they chose to do otherwise; and this choice has altered and impaired their contribution.[78]

Tom Farer, in a similar vein, argues that "what we actually get is a hodge-podge of essays related, higgledy piggledy, by a collective judgment that the existing world order is rotting away."[79]

[74] Mendlovitz, Introduction, p. xvi.

[75] Falk, "Toward New World Order," p. 246.

[76] Mendlovitz, Introduction, p. xii.

[77] Harold D. Lasswell, "The Promise of the World Order Modelling Movement," *World Politics,* 29 (April 1977), 434.

[78] David Wilkinson, "World Order Models Project: First Fruits," *Political Science Quarterly,* 91 (Summer 1976), 331.

[79] Tom J. Farer, "The Greening of the Globe: A Preliminary Appraisal of the World Order Models Project (WOMP)," *International Organization,* 31 (Winter 1977), 130.

If, as seems to be generally supposed, the globe is shrinking, and as a result the world's political entities and their problems are becoming increasingly interdependent, then it makes sense to conclude that the political entities must come up with cooperative strategies and solutions to their common problems. It is also true that present global institutions are poorly suited to such cooperation. Thus, the need for institutions such as WOMP seems clearly established. If the first fruits of the project are disappointing to many, this can hardly be surprising. The globe may be in the process of shrinking, but in many ways this has served merely to make people in the various parts of the globe more aware of their differences. Intellectuals in the same country rarely, if ever, come to any consensus about the best solutions to their country's problems. Little wonder that scholars from all over the world have sharp disagreements about global problems and solutions.

But communication facilitated by WOMP-like projects may lead, in the future, to some shared ideas and ideals; it may also lead to timely awareness of problems only dimly perceived in more orthodox political circles. To put it another way, many of the changes predicted by the WOMPers seem far-fetched. But given the history of the past fifty years or so, one must conclude that many seemingly far-fetched changes are almost certain to occur in the next fifty years. If the scholars in WOMP (or similar projects) can help the world perceive and predict unexpected changes so that their potentially disastrous effects can be anticipated and dealt with, they will have performed a valuable service. Harold Lasswell suggests that WOMP will undergo a basic revision about every ten years.[80] Such conscious and repeated efforts at self-improvement could provide a basis for collective learning and maturation, and WOMP may well come to fulfill an important role in the global political system.

Economic Development

Until the 1970s, and the onset of the *Limits to Growth* controversy, there was little interest in the question of whether economic growth was a desirable goal. Its desirability was assumed, and the debate focused instead on how to achieve that goal. The debate continues, and the experience of Third World countries in the three

[80] Lasswell, "Promise," 427.

decades since the Second World War has demolished one theory another concerning the most effective ways to speed economic development.

"Democracy" and Economic Growth

In the 1950s, the United States was predominant economically, and Americans tended to dominate the discussion about economic development in academic circles as well as international forums. Even among Americans, of course, there was a variety of ideas about how the emerging new countries could best attain economic growth, but there were a few basic themes and assumptions that were widely shared. One implicit assumption was that England, the United States, and the other industrialized Western countries served as a historical model that the new countries should try to emulate in their efforts to develop politically and economically. Related to this assumption was the idea that new countries were more likely to develop economically under a system of political democracy. Development theories in the 1950s stressed the importance of internal changes in the new states as the crucial steps toward economic development. The people would have to be educated and socialized in order to give up their old-fashioned ideas. Urbanization was considered desirable for its impact on the education and socialization process, and industrialization, with attendant concentration in the cities and capital-intensive activities, was presumed to be the primary goal of developing countries. All these processes would be aided by a maximum amount of contact between rich countries and poor countries. The poor countries would need foreign aid, they should trade extensively with rich countries, and they should attract as much private foreign investment as possible. Eventually, such policies would allow a poor country to reach a take-off stage, and it would be on its way toward self-sustaining growth and the affluent society.

Things have turned out very differently. "Democracy," in the American and West European sense of the word, is very rare in the Third World. There are so many convincing explanations for this that it is difficult to decide which one is most important. One involves a certain amount of condescension; it is argued that the peoples of poor countries are not ready for democracy, because they are insufficiently educated or not mature enough to run their own governments. If this idea were espoused entirely by Western intellectuals, it might arouse more indignation in the Third World than it actually does. But, in fact, Third World political leaders often make similar assertions when defending their own undemocratic regimes. "Democracy" is also associated with the old colonial powers, and that has served to discredit it in many poor countries. In addition, political leaders who have struggled through wars of national liberation, or perhaps simply long political battles to obtain national independence, have been understandably reluctant to give up their positions of power for the sake of free elections. Most modernizing elites realize that sacrifices of present consumption are necessary to accumulate capital, which can serve as a basis for sustained growth. In a democracy, it would be difficult, if not impossible, to impose this kind of discipline on the populace. Demagogues would always be willing to promise increases in present consumption for the sake of winning votes, and leaders interested in limiting that consumption for the sake of future development would not be able to stay in power. Finally, it seems likely that a relatively high level of economic well-being is necessary to the existence of a Western-style democracy. Otherwise the economic struggles become too desperate to be resolved through the ballot box. In any case, although there are certain interesting exceptions (such as India), the vast majority of Third World countries are not democratic, and this seems unlikely to change very soon.

Foreign Aid and Development
Americans have been disappointed by this; they, as well as the alleged benefactors, have also become progressively more disillusioned with foreign aid. Some of the problems involved in the aid-giving process were discussed in Chapter 2. The United States and West European countries have indulged in the practice of tying aid to enforced purchases of their goods and services. The ultimate impact of the aid, then, often seemed to benefit certain interests in the donor state more than the recipient country. Also, over the years, many recipients of foreign aid have built up such vast debts that now, in a typical year, they pay out more in interest on past aid than they receive in new aid.

While avarice and unintelligent planning on the part of the donor countries have helped considerably to give foreign aid a bad name, it must also be admitted that dealing with Third World countries would not be easy for the most altruistic and wise donor state. Critics of the aid in Third World countries often point out that the funds are used by governments in developing countries, not to foster economic development, but to oppress domestic political opponents or to line the pockets of corrupt government bureaucrats. Such charges are well founded in many cases. But what can the donor country do about it? It can refuse to dispense any aid at all, but that makes very few happy. Or it can give aid to organizations and political groups outside the government. This alternative, though, smacks of interference in the domestic affairs of another country. Another strategy involves sending, along with the aid, responsible officials to ensure that the money is used properly. But then the donor country is open to the charge of being arrogant enough to feel that it knows how to solve the problems of the recipient country better than its citizens.

International Trade and Development

Trade between rich and poor countries has also failed to have the beneficial impact on economic development in the latter that some theorists of development in the 1950s had predicted. This problem was touched on earlier, when economic integration in the Third World was discussed (Chapter 4). Basically, with the United States in the lead, the richer countries persist in the belief that free trade, and the operation of market forces in the international system, will lead to the greatest possible efficiency and productivity and thus the greatest benefits for all. The poor countries, on the contrary, suspect that free trade will only perpetuate the present division of labor, which confines them to the marketing of commodities and raw materials.

This is hardly a new controversy in the history of international politics.

> Both in the history of past experience and in the current international debate, one is struck by the differences in perception of countries in different positions. To the dominant countries—Britain in the 19th century and the industrialized world today—political barriers to market forces reduce global economic efficiency and threaten to disrupt economic relationships. . . . To the contenders, exposure to unrestricted market forces entails acceptance of existing economic and political subordination in the guise of immutable economic law. Economics is when I have it; politics is when you want it.[81]

[81] Fred Hirsch, "Is There a New International Economic Order?" *International Organization,* 30 (Summer 1976), 527–528.

The Third World countries seem to have several legitimate complaints about the operation of the international trading system in the fifties and sixties. Their share of the world's trade fell, as compared to that of the richer countries, throughout both decades. The terms of trade for the developing countries were highly unstable. Many of the developing countries depend heavily on the export of one or two raw materials or commodities. While it is apparently not true (even though many Third World economists insist it is)[82] that the prices of primary products have suffered steady deterioration vis-à-vis the prices of the manufactured goods that must be imported, the prices of raw materials and commodities have fluctuated in a notorious fashion. Occasionally, the prices of exports from developing countries, such as copper, coffee, or sugar, have been very high, and the producers have experienced temporary windfalls. But in the next year, the prices of the same products will have dropped precipitously, and the developing countries that export them have suffered grievous balance-of-trade deficits and other painful dislocations in their highly vulnerable economies.

In addition, the rich countries refused to abide by the free trade doctrine when it did not suit their purposes. They erected high tariff-barriers or adopted quotas in order to protect domestic economic interests from competition of cheap labor in poor countries, especially in labor-intensive industries, such as textiles and shoes, where the comparative advantage of the poor countries is greatest. When the poor countries attempted to retaliate by adopting policies aimed at import substitution, the system still worked against them. They would, for example, erect tariff barriers to protect a domestic manufacturer of refrigerators. In time, they would find that they did not have to import refrigerators. But they would also find that their protected manufacturer could not produce refrigerators that were competitive in price on the international market. So, no refrigerators could be exported, local consumers had to pay higher prices for refrigerators, and the import-substituting country ultimately found that it had become reliant on rich countries for imports of expensive capital equipment (and spare parts) necessary to manufacture refrigerators. Importing expensive equipment exerted an important negative pressure on their balance of trade, and the import-substitution policies often seemed to have effects contrary to their purpose.

[82]John P. Powelson argues persuasively that "with close to thirty years of post-war data available, the evidence is *overwhelming* that terms of trade do *not*, generally and over long periods, move against the producers of primary products." See "The Strange Persistence of the 'Terms of Trade,'" *Inter-American Economic Affairs,* 30 (Spring 1977), 17.

Foreign Investment and Growth

Reliance on foreign investment also seemed to work badly, in most instances, or so critics in the Third World claimed. The critique of foreign investment in Third World countries was discussed in some detail in Chapter 5, dealing with multinational corporations. Suffice it to say here that as the sixties came to an end, economists in the Third World were becoming increasingly skeptical about the impact of foreign investment in poor countries, and they called for stricter controls on the flow of such investment.

A New International Economic Order

In fact, politicians and economists throughout the Third World, in the early 1970s, were increasingly vocal in their criticism of the entire structure of the international economic order, for the reasons just discussed. These arguments were cogently summarized in what became known as dependency theory, developed largely by Latin American economists. Inspired by such ideas, Third World countries formed a loose coalition that pressed for changes in the international economic system.

One of their first concrete demands, in the early 1960s, was for a worldwide conference on problems involving international trade and economic development. The richer countries at first opposed the idea, but they could no longer control the General Assembly of the United Nations, and so in 1962 the first United Nations Conference on Trade and Development (UNCTAD) was held. At about the same time, the coalition of poor southern states became known as the Group of 77, a name it retains today even though it is much larger. This coalition held periodic summit meetings, and at the fourth meeting, it outlined the basic framework for what has become known as a new international economic order (NIEO). At first, the reaction to these demands by political leaders in the rich countries ranged from apathy to antagonism. By the time of the Seventh Special Session of the United Nations in 1975, though, the rich nations, including most prominently the United States, had become more conciliatory. The motivating factor behind this dramatic change of attitude, it seems clear, was the success of the Organization of Petroleum Exporting Countries. "The Group of 77 is using OPEC as its major political instrument in negotiations with the Western industrialized countries for a new international economic order. . . . OPEC, for its part, is using the 77 in very much the same manner."[83]

Revisions in the Aid Process

What does the Group of 77 want? How can the current global economic system be transformed into a new international economic order? Despite their bitter criticism of aid over the last ten years, the developing nations still insist that the richer states should help the poor by transferring resources to the south. They want the process through which such transfers take place changed. Instead of country-to-country aid, the developing states would generally prefer funds to be dispensed through multilateral agencies like the International Bank for Reconstruction and Development (the World Bank), and the International Monetary Fund. This, by itself, though, will not necessarily solve the problems associated with unilateral aid programs. Some critics of the World Bank and the IMF argue that, in the past at least, those two organizations have been so dominated by the United States (and a few like-minded countries) that the aid dispensed through them has had as many strings attached to it as funds originating from the United States directly. The same kind of conservative austerity programs favored by the United States government and American corporations have been demanded by the IMF and the World Bank as conditions for loans.[84] In order to avoid this unwelcome pressure, the developing countries want a greater voice in the governing bodies of the IMF and the World Bank.[85] They also argue that the debt burden resulting from past foreign aid loans is so great for many Third World countries that they can never realistically hope to meet their obligations. In such cases, the Group of 77 would like to see these debts renegotiated, and if possible, canceled altogether.

The Third World countries would also like to see the creation of a new international currency to replace the dollar, and that would be more available to them. The special drawing rights (SDRs), created by the IMF in 1968, would do nicely, in their view.

[83] Branislav Gosovic and John Gerard Ruggie, "On the Creation of a New International Economic Order," *International Organization,* 30 (Spring 1976), 313.

[84] Teresa Hayter, *Aid as Imperialism,* Penguin, Baltimore, Maryland, 1971.

[85] Pierre Uri makes the interesting suggestion that the aid process be multilateralized on both sides of the fence, with the poor countries joining together in regional associations to receive and dispense aid from the richer countries. This would remove the developing countries one step further from the pressure of rich countries, and allow rich countries to distribute funds to poor countries without implying approval of specific governments in the Third World. See *Development Without Dependence,* Praeger, New York, 1976, p. 57.

If the IMF would simply create new SDRs in abundance and transfer them to developing countries, this would be an easy way for the richer countries to meet their responsibilities to provide foreign aid and to help the poor states meet their liquidity problems. The richer nations, have, so far, been reluctant to do this, on the grounds that it would transform the IMF, whose primary responsibility is to ensure currency stability, into an aid-giving agency; the rich countries also fear that creating new SDRs would exacerbate inflation throughout the world's economy. It seems unlikely that SDRs will become the new international currency, or be created in great numbers, until the rich countries are convinced that there is no longer an excess of liquidity in the system, especially in the form of dollars.[86]

Transforming the International Trade System
The Group of 77 has three basic transformations in the international trading system that they would like to see in the New International Economic Order. First, they would like to have freer access to the markets of the rich countries. Present tariff barriers and quotas imposed on their goods should be dismantled. Second, they would like to see at least two important steps taken toward the stabilization of prices for the commodities on which so many of them rely as exports. They advocate the formation of commodity agreements, in which the richer countries would promise ahead of time to buy set amounts of a given commodity at a predetermined price. Part of these arrangements would involve the creation of buffer stocks of commodities, financed by international institutions, in order to smooth out the cycles of boom and bust experienced by most sellers of commodities. In times of great demand, surpluses could be drawn from these buffer stocks in order to satisfy the demand and prevent the agreed-on prices from being subverted by a black market. When demand falls, the surplus commodities could be purchased for addition to the buffer stocks, so that they would be available when needed, and to provide support for the guaranteed price. Details of such arrangements have yet to be worked out, and doing so will not be easy; still, the Carter administration seems amenable to the creation of such buffer stocks, in principle at least

Finally, the Group of 77 has expressed a desire for indexing commodity prices in the world market. This would involve fixing the relationship between the prices of commodities and the prices of manufactured goods, to avoid deterioration of the terms of trade that Third World countries claim they have experienced in the past.

[86] Robert Russell, "Governing the World's Money: Don't Just Do Something, Stand There!" *International Organization,* 31 (Winter 1977), 111–119.

(But see footnote 82.) It seems unlikely, at this point, that the rich countries will go along with the particular kind of interference with free-market processes, though. It also seems possible, given recent trends in the prices of several raw materials (such as oil) that Third World countries may lose interest in this particular aspect of the new international economic order.

Controlling Foreign Investment

With respect to international investments and MNCs, the Group of 77 has two major demands. They insist on the right of sovereignty over natural resources within their boundaries (even if they are owned by foreign investors) and the complementary prerogative to nationalize corporations that interfere with this right. They also would like to institute the international regulation and supervision of MNCs (probably through an organ of the UN). These demands seem likely to serve as bones of contention between north and south for some time to come.[87]

The Future of the Oceans

Another key issue in the current debate between the north and the south concerning the international economic order concerns the disposition of the riches at the bottom of the world's vast oceans. Some oil is at stake, perhaps, but most attention has been focused on the nodules on the ocean floor, containing manganese, nickel, copper, cobalt, and other minerals. The value of the minerals in those nodules is estimated to be several trillion dollars.[88]

If the poor countries have their way, this wealth will serve as a base for important new efforts aimed at their economic development. In the United Nations General Assembly, the Political Committee has adopted a resolution (by a vote of 90 to 0) "placing the seabed beyond the reach of national sovereignties, linking benefits from peaceful use to the needs of developing countries.[89] Pushing the exploitation of the riches of the sea in the opposite direction is the fact that most of the mineral-bearing nodules are under more than 5,000 meters of water.[90] This means that mining

[87] For a formal presentation of the structure of the new international economic order, see "Declaration and Action Programme on the Establishment of a New International Economic Order," in *Beyond Dependency,* ed. Guy F. Erb and Valeriana Kallab, Overseas Development Council, Washington, D.C., 1975, pp. 185–202.

[88] Robert L. Friedham and William J. Durch, "The International Seabed Resources Agency Negotiations and the New International Economic Order," *International Organization,* 31 (Spring 1977), 351.

[89] Brown, *World Without Borders,* p. 306.

[90] Friedham and Durch, "International Seabed," p. 351.

the nodules is going to require sophisticated technology, and that technologically advanced nations, such as the United States, will be in the best position, barring political regulations, to take advantage of the seabed resources. The future of the nodules has been the major topic of debate at a series of United Nations Law of the Sea conferences. The Group of 77 advocates the establishment of an International Seabed Resources Agency, with extensive powers and in which the poor nations have an important voice, to ensure that the benefits of the seabed resources are directed primarily to the developing nations. The rich nations want the powers of that agency more limited, and they do not want to turn political control of the agency over to the more numerous Group of 77. From the viewpoint of the rich nations, the Group of 77 is trying to get them coming and going. On the one hand, the poor nations want to limit the access by rich nations to raw materials in the poor nations through nationalization of the resources and through the formation of cartels like OPEC. On the other hand, if rich nations try to reduce their dependence on poor nations for raw materials by exploiting seabed resources, the Group of 77 would utilize the International Seabed Resources Agency to block the escape route.

NIEO and Economic Development

One impression created by the demands associated with the new international economic order is that the Third World nations have rejected totally the 1950s thesis that the major obstacles to their economic development are internal. They cleave fervently now to the idea that it is the international system that must be altered and not their internal social, political and economic arrangements.[91] Some Third World thinkers are willing to admit that changes in archaic internal political and social structures will have to come, along with changes in the structure of the international system. But many will also argue that these internal changes will be impossible until the international system, especially the international economic system, is radically revised. Until that happens, dependency theorists, for example, will assert that elites in poor states that

[91] In the meantime, many economists have changed their minds about what kinds of internal changes should be made to spur economic development. "The discussions of the late sixties appear now to have led to a fairly wide consensus among economists. It began with dissatisfaction over the outcome of the strategy pursued in the 1950s, which stressed industrialization, rural to urban migration, urbanization, import substitution, capital formation, etc. . . . The talk now is about integrated rural development, agricultural intensification, intermediate technology, appropriate education . . . small industry and export promotions." See Harry T. Oshima, "New Directions in Development Strategies," *Economic Development and Cultural Change,* 25 (April 1977), 555.

benefit from the present international economic order will be in a very strong position to prevent any meaningful internal reforms.

*NIEO and the Future of the
Global Political System*

Another strong impression that is nearly inescapable as one analyzes the list of demands made by the Group of 77 is the similarity between the contest taking shape now in the global system and an earlier conflict between social classes in industrialized Western societies. In the United States, for example, until the Great Depression, the predominant political philosophy rested heavily on the idea that free-market pressures should be allowed to operate to the greatest extent possible. Franklin D. Roosevelt instituted a kind of philosophical revolution, which has also occurred in most industrialized Western societies, based on the notion that the central government should intervene to ameliorate the worst effects of free-market machinations. Now, the poorer nations of the global system, supported by the nouveau riche in the Middle East, are making demands concerning the operation of the international economic system that are reminiscent of the demands to which Roosevelt responded in the 1930s. If they have their way, the Third World nations will not tolerate the untrammeled operation of free-market pressures. They demand, in effect, redistributive taxes on rich countries. They want the right to form cartels like OPEC. They demand a kind of unemployment insurance in the form of buffer stocks and guaranteed prices for their products. This phenomenon, the success that the Third World nations are having in obtaining for their demands a high place on the international political agenda, and the logical similarity of their demands to earlier ones made by lower classes in industrialized Western societies, is the clearest evidence, in my view, in favor of the argument that there really is a community evolving out of the global political system. It is arguable that, if the Third World meets with significant success in its attempt to create a new international economic order, the effect of that success on the structure of the global system will be similar to the effect of successful equivalent demands by lower classes in domestic political systems. Centralized political institutions will become more powerful.

But there are attitudes pushing in the opposite direction. Some Third World intellectuals are prone to ridicule the old-fashioned notion of national sovereignty and to call for strengthened internation institutions. A close analysis of their arguments, though, often reveals that they are interested in international institutions that control and dilute the sovereignty of *rich* nations so that Third World nations can be *more* sovereign. Rajni Kothari, for example, is an Indian scholar who has contributed significantly to the World Order Models Project. Saul Mendlovitz, the director of the project, asserts that the scholars associated with WOMP are in general agreement that there is a need to go beyond the nation-state system.[92] Kothari fits this description in that he calls for the eventual creation of twenty-five states to replace the multitude of sovereign units in the contemporary system. But for the present, Kothari seems as concerned about sovereignty (at least for Third World states) as any eighteenth-century monarch. At one point he argues that "progress towards world peace and a stable world order is closely linked with the struggle for national autonomy and equality among states." Then, again, in his discussion of the problems of Third World societies, he asserts that "the autonomy and self-regulation of the individual in those societies vitally depends on the autonomy of the state in which he lives." And "to achieve both the autonomy of men and satisfactory states of community and fellow feeling among them it is necessary to provide greater autonomy to individual states." And finally, Kothari acknowledges that "the chief concern that has guided us . . . is the realization of the dignity and autonomy of man, and hence of states."[93]

I would argue that Kothari, and his ideas, are rather typical in the Third World. The new states, generally, have acquired independence too recently to be interested in moving immediately beyond the concept of national sovereignty. Another indication of the new states' attitude toward intenational institutions is the amount these states spend on military hardware to defend their sovereignty.

> By 1973 India's federal budget allocated twice as much on military as on education; and health care was allocated only one-fourth as much as defense. . . . Bangla Desh, a country facing grave starvation, spends more on military security than on feeding its hungry. Indonesia, with only one physician per 24,000 population, spends twenty-five times more on military than on health programs. Pakistan, with an illiteracy rate of 84 percent, spends four times as much on military as on education.[94]

Certainly, such extravagant military expenditures constitute a barrier to economic development that does not seem to be ad-

---

[92] Saul H. Mendlovitz, Introduction, in *Creation of Just World*, p. xiii.
[93] Rajni Kothari, "World Politics and World Order," pp. 39–69.
[94] Gerald and Patricia Mische, *Toward a Human World Order*, Paulist Press, New York, 1977, pp. 88, 93.

dressed by the measures to be incorporated into the new international economic order. Even so, there are many obstacles that would be dealt with if the demands by the Group of 77 were met, and any measures that would alleviate poverty in the Third World and lead to a redistribution of wealth in the global society must be welcomed by concerned citizens of the society. In any case, there seems little doubt that there *will be* a new international economic order, even if it does not meet exactly the specifications of the Group of 77, because the old order relied so heavily on the economic superiority and domination of the United States.

Conclusion

THREE THEMES HAVE BEEN EMPHASIZED IN THIS BOOK: (1) THE history, (2) the scientific study, and (3) the future, of global politics.

The historical theme was included for two basic reasons. First, the most important and influential individuals involved in global politics are generally familiar with the history of the global system, and their actions and decisions often bear the impact of this familiarity. Ignorance of history will necessarily detract from an understanding of those actions and decisions.

The Lessons of History

The impact of history on important decision-makers emerges nicely from an analysis of the extent to which world leaders "learn from history to make the opposite mistakes."[1] This aphorism applies neatly, I believe, to relationships among the successive wars

---

[1] I believe historian A. J. P. Taylor uses this phrase, but I do not know if he coined it.

involving major powers. I have already discussed, for example, how the Franco-Prussian War in 1870 may have helped convince decision makers that it is vital to line up firmly committed allies before a crisis occurs. France did not do this before the clash with Prussia, and the absence of help from potential allies like Austria and Italy contributed to the disaster that befell France then. As a result, in the years leading up to the First World War, decision makers made the "opposite mistake," and set up a series of rigid alliances that helped turn the war into such a catastrophe. Another lesson learned from the Franco-Prussian war that helped precipitate the First World War stemmed from the rapidity with which Prussia mobilized for the prior war. Compared to those of France, Prussia's mobilization procedures were fantastically efficient, and Prussia went on to score a quick victory. This is certainly one of the reasons that all the major powers, in August 1914, were so intent on rapid mobilization. They thought that the most rapid mobilizer would emerge victorious in short order. They were wrong, of course, but that lesson learned from the Franco-Prussian War provoked another "opposite mistake" that sparked the First World War.

There was a whole series of lessons learned from the First World War that led to "opposite mistakes," culminating in the Second World War. Again, we have already mentioned that alliances acquired a bad reputation in the First World War. This may account, in part, for the reluctance of the Allied powers to form a meaningful alliance with the Russians, and a similar reluctance to rely on and honor the alliance treaties they did have. (For example, the French did not honor their commitment to Czechoslovakia in 1938.) Similarly, many historians and decision makers came out of the First World War convinced that the conflict was a result, in large measure, of an arms race, especially between Great Britain and Germany. This may explain why the British, in the 1930s, were determined not to get involved in another arms race with Germany and failed to meet the challenge posed by Hitler's rapid rearmament program. In a similar fashion, the French learned that the offensive strategies they tried at the beginning of the First World War were tragically unsuccessful, while the defenses in that war had proved quite impenetrable. So, they decided to rely on a quintessentially defensive strategy as the Second World War approached, based on the Maginot Line. Perhaps most important, as mentioned in Chapter 1, a lesson learned from the First World War was that patience in the face of provocation is an important virtue for political leaders in time of international crisis. If only those leaders, in July and August 1914, had been more patient, according to this lesson, the war might have been averted. So, the leaders in the Allied states patiently allowed the Japanese to take over in Manchuria, the Italians to annex Ethiopia, and Hitler to rearm in violation of the Versailles treaty, send troops into the Rhineland, annex Austria, take over the Sudetenland, and obliterate Czechoslovakia.

If one assumes that the North Koreans launched the Korean War with an unprovoked attack on South Korea, then it is difficult to argue that the American decision to enter that war was a mistake. It is much less difficult, though, to argue that the British and French attack on Nasser in 1956 was a mistake, and it is clear that the mistake was based on a lesson culled from the British and French experience in the Second World War. Leaders in both countries perceived Nasser to be another Hitler, and they made the "opposite mistake" with respect to Nasser. They stood up to his first aggressive move immediately and forcefully. If they had done that to Hitler, chances are that he might have been forced to retire in disgrace. But when they did it to Nasser, they made him a hero in the Arab states and throughout most of the Third World.

And it is equally clear that the American stand in Vietnam was based, in part, on the lesson of Munich, in spite of the fact that Ho Chi Minh bore no more resemblance to Hitler than did Nasser. What lesson will the Americans learn from the war in Vietnam that will lead them into an "opposite mistake"? Will they retreat into isolationism? Or will they decide that prolonged wars in the Third World must be avoided and move in with reckless abandon to bring the next war there to a quick end?

Historical Generalizations

The second reason for the historical theme in *Global Politics* is that the historical record provides a kind of laboratory within which generalizations about world politics can be tested. "Grand coalitions fall apart" is an example of such a generalization that was tested by analyzing the experience of grand coalitions in the global system since the Napoleonic wars.

History, used in this way, blends into the scientific theme in *Global Politics*. The scientific method and analysis of the historical record can both be used to develop and test generalizations about world politics. Traditional, intuitive historical analysis, without question, cannot provide as rigorous a test for generalizations as the scientific method. But if the generalization lacks specificity (such as the one that asserts that world leaders "learn from history to make the opposite mistakes"), the scientific method is inapplicable. And there are statements about global politics that are not specific enough to be tested scientifically, that may still provide valuable insights, and that can be tested with a logical, intuitive, and philosophical analysis of the historical record. In other cases, the generalization in question may be sufficiently specific to be tested scientifically, ("Grand coalitions fall apart" is reasonably specific), but the number of cases to which it applies may be too small to allow a rigorous application of the scientific method. If so, an analysis of the historical record provides a useful alternative.

Scientific Generalizations

There are many occasions, though, when the scientific method is applicable to generalizations and hypotheses about world politics, as, I hope, the scientific theme in *Global Politics* has demonstrated. By scientific method I mean a logical method of testing hypotheses (or generalizations) based on reproducible, controlled comparisons. An implication of this definition is that scientific tests of generalizations must include all relevant cases or a representative sample of those cases. Once the data on the cases have been assembled, they can be subjected to reproducible comparisons. Such comparisons (as in Chapter 1) are based on procedures so clearly defined that any qualified scientist, in addition to the original researcher, can carry them out.

I have discussed the results of such comparisons several times in *Global Politics*. Recall, for example, that (in 1963 at least) no relationship was found between a constituency's attitudes about foreign affairs and the voting record of the respective member of Congress on issues involving foreign policy. Similarly no relationship was found between the amount of military spending in a senator's state and the senator's votes on defense budgets.

Recall also that I looked, scientifically, at the relationship between a state's characteristics and its foreign policy and found that large states, for example, are more active participants in the internation system than small states. I also discussed the finding that personalist regimes exhibit more conflictful behavior than polyarchic regimes, and that, generally speaking, states with more internal conflict do not become involved in more foreign conflict. But, if states are divided into categories based on type of political regime, it is found that certain types of internal conflict are associated with specific kinds of external foreign conflict. States with centrist regimes, for example, do tend to experience more foreign conflict during periods of extensive revolutionary domestic conflict.

In addition, I discussed findings of scientific analyses of the relationships between alliances and war. I found, further, that concentration of power in the international system is associated with greater amounts of international war, but only in the nineteenth century. In the twentieth century, changes in the polarity of the system are related to the probability, and the duration of wars. Redistribution of power in the system (uneven development) does not seem to be associated with amount of war in either century.

Scientific Control

In at least one important way, the discussion of all these analyses has been misleading. For the sake of simplicity, I have restricted the discussion to relationships involving only two variables, and the evidence I have analyzed has been based on bivariate correlations. Correlation, the old saying goes, does not prove causation. This is true because a correlation between variables A and B may be brought about entirely by variable C. For example, there is, in most societies, a positive correlation between an individual's level of education (variable A) and yearly income (variable B). Is that correlation brought about because a higher education causes increased earning power? Perhaps, but the correlation, at least in part, is probably brought about because the social class of an individual's parents (variable C) is causally connected to both the educational level and yearly income of the individual. That is, the higher the social class of a person's parents, the more likely he or she is to attain a higher educational level and to earn a higher salary later in life.

A similar criticism could be directed at the bivariate relationships discussed in this book. It is at least possible that each relationship has been brought about by some third factor, and that none of them is evidence of causal relationships. It is important to understand, though, that the scientific methods utilized by social scientists do not ignore this problem. In fact, a crucial part of those methods, that is, control, is designed specifically to meet the problem of a third factor. *Control,* in this context, can be defined as the elimination of the effect of confounding variables. Confounding variables are variables that can lead to confusion; for example, if variable C (such as parents' social class) causes a correlation between variables A (level of education) and B (yearly income), thus leading to the confusing notion that variable A causes variable B, then variable C is a confounding variable.

Some scientists deal with confounding variables with experimental controls in a laboratory. Social scientists, usually, must rely on other kinds of control, that is, statistical control. For example, if a social scientist suspects that the correlation between educational level and yearly income is not causal but is brought about by the confounding variable of parents' social class, he or she can control the third variable (that is, eliminate its effect) in the manner

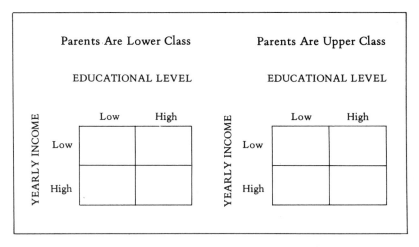

FIGURE C.1   The relationship between educational level and yearly income, parents' social class controlled

demonstrated in Figure C.1. The representative sample of individuals, say, from the American society can be divided into two groups. One will include only individuals with lower-class parents, and the other, individuals with higher-class parents. If it is discovered, even among individuals all of whom have lower-class parents (or all of whom have upper-class parents), that those with higher levels of education have higher yearly incomes, then one can argue convincingly that education levels are causally connected to income levels. Controlling the confounding variable of parents' social class provides evidence that the correlation between the other two variables is causal. Of course, some other variable may be causing the original correlation, but the other variables can be controlled, too. The more often this is done, the more confidence one can have that the original correlation is causal.

The same kind of procedures are applicable, of course, to variables of interest to scholars of global politics. I discussed in Chapter 6, for example, the correlation between changes in polarity of the international system and the duration of wars. This correlation might not be causal but brought about instead by some prior third factor, that is, a confounding variable. It might be hypothesized that high levels of military expenditures cause both changes in polarity and prolonged duration of wars. This hypothesis can be tested using scientific control. That is, time periods can be divided into those when military expenditures were high and those when

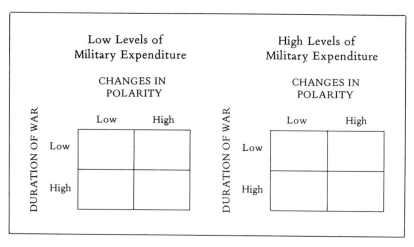

FIGURE C. 2   The relationship between changes in polarity of the international system and duration of war, levels of military expenditure controlled

expenditures were low (see Figure C.2). If it turns out that, in both groups, wars tended to be longer during periods marked by greater changes in polarity, then again evidence will have been uncovered that the original correlation is a reflection of a causal relationship. Additional hypotheses to the contrary can be disposed of in a similar fashion.

Now, the kind of statistical control demonstrated in Figures C.1 and C.2 is only one type that is available to social scientists. Other types such as those associated with a technique known as multiple regression, are more amenable to controlling three, four, and five variables at the same time. And there are other reasons in addition to a desire for control for analyzing more than two variables at a time. Most phenomena in global politics have, of course, more than one cause. If the discussion of bivariate relationships created an impression that social scientists are unaware of this fact, then that is another way in which the discussion has been misleading. Multiple causes certainly can be dealt with by social scientific methods.

In short, the discussion of scientific analyses of global politics has been a preliminary one. Students who want to know more about these analyses should acquire the knowledge about the scientific method and analytical techniques (such as statistics) that is necessary to understand them fully.

History, Science, Values,
and the Future

Serious students of global politics will want to develop several tools in addition to a competence in statistics. The discussion of the history of global politics in this book has been as preliminary as that dealing with the scientific study, and there are numerous excellent historical sources that can be used to increase one's knowledge about the past of the global political system. *A Diplomatic History of Europe Since the Congress of Vienna* by René Albrecht-Carrie (Harper & Row, New York, 1958) is a good source of information about the Euro-centered international system up to the post–Second World War era. *International Politics Since World War II* by Charles L. Robertson (John Wiley and Sons, New York, 1975) covers more contemporary events in a competent manner. For analyses of current events in more depth than one can usually find in newspapers or weekly magazines, the journal *Foreign Affairs* is a widely respected and influential source.

Of the numerous additional scholarly journals with which serious students of global politics will want to become familiar, *World Politics, International Studies Quarterly, International Organization,* and *Journal of Conflict Resolution* are certainly among the most important. Those who would like a more complete list of journals, plus a compilation of other useful sources, such as edited volumes, textbooks, and abstracts, would do well to consult *The Study of International Politics* by Dorothy F. LaBarr and J. David Singer (Clio Books, Santa Barbara, California, 1976). More information about sources, as well as instructions on how to locate sources in libraries, can be found in *A Handbook of Library Research for International Relations* by Merry Coplin (Learning Package Series Number 4, The ISA Consortium for International Studies Education, 1974).

As students become familiar with these and other sources, they should become aware that historical and scientific analyses must be combined in any fruitful attempt to anticipate, or predict, the future of the global political system or any of its constituent elements. Conceptually, future occurrences can be divided into the unique and the recurrent. Historical intuitive analyses are well suited for understanding the former, while scientific studies are primarily aimed at the comprehension of the latter.

For example, imagine predicting the future foreign policies of Great Britain. To some extent, Great Britain shares similarities with other states, and scientific generalizations about states like Great Britain (such as those about open societies) should help in formulating accurate predictions about its foreign policy. But in some ways, Great Britain is unique, having combinations of characteristics not shared by any other state in the global system, and these combinations of characteristics will probably have an important impact on Britain's foreign policy.

It is important to understand that scientific methods are not useless in the face of unique characteristics. Unique does not necessarily imply incomparable. Britain is the only state in the world that was the most powerful in the global system throughout most of the nineteenth century, and this characteristic could conceivably have an impact on its current and future foreign policies. But Britain's uniqueness in this regard, from a scientific point of view, merely places it at the extreme end of a continuum, and thus Britain, even with respect to this unique characteristic, is comparable. The impact of this characteristic might be studied scientifically, with scientific methods being applied to a form of hypothesis: The more powerful a state was in the nineteenth century, the more _____ its foreign policies will be in the future.

But the combinations of characteristics found in the British case may well make that country, to some extent, both unique and incomparable. Britain is the only modern, industrialized democracy on an island that was the most powerful state in the world in the nineteenth century and that evolved from a monarchy to its present democratic status. If the uniquely British constellation of characteristics will have an impact on Britain's future foreign policy, probably the only way to gain an appreciation of the impact will be to analyze British history in a traditional, intuitive, philosophical manner. Reproducible comparisons will not be possible, because the various combinations of characteristics exhibited by British make it (as well as every other country in the world) incomparable.

Similarly, the future of the global system can be divided into sectors consisting of recurrent phenomena and unique events. Scientific analyses allow one to identify relationships among recurrent phenomena (such as those between concentration of power and amounts of war, or economic growth and polluting levels) and make predictions about the future of the global system. But, in some ways, the global system of today is unique; it exhibits some characteristics (and combinations of characteristics) that did not exist in 1950 or 1900 or 1815. These characteristics (and combinations of characteristics), too, as well as relationships among recurrent phenomena, will make their mark on the future of the global political system. Without knowledge of the history of the global system, it would be impossible even to identify these unprecedented characteristics, much less apply one's logical and analytical abilities to the task of calculating what impact they may have on the future of global politics.

Finally, of course, students of global politics (whether they are college freshmen or full professors) will be interested not only in ways the global system will change, but in those ways it should change. The two questions are obviously not unrelated. Changes that may be very desirable but are highly unlikely are necessarily less interesting than changes that combine some optimum amounts of desirability and feasibility. The ability to identify these latter kinds of changes, and to formulate strategies that might bring them about, must rest not only on a knowledge of the history of the global political system, and scientific evidence, but also on one's values. In order to make coherent predictions about preferred worlds of the future, students must combine their historical and scientific knowledge about global politics with an understanding of their own values as well as difficult decisions concerning the relative importance of those values.

Bibliography

Alberta Oil and Gas Conservation Board. *A Description and Reserve Estimate of Oil Sands of Alberta.* Calgary, 1962.

Allen, Richard. *Imperialism and Nationalism in the Fertile Crescent.* Oxford University Press, New York, 1974.

Allison, Graham T. *Essence of Decision.* Little, Brown, Boston, 1971.

Al-Marayati, Abid A. et al. *The Middle East: Its Governments and Politics.* Duxbury Press, Belmont, California, 1972.

Almond, Gabriel. *The American People and Foreign Policy.* Harcourt Brace Jovanovich, New York, 1950.

Almond, Gabriel, and Sidney Verba. *The Civic Culture.* Princeton University Press, Princeton, 1963.

Alperovitz, Gar. *Atomic Diplomacy.* Vintage, New York, 1965.

Alschuler, Lawrence R. "Satellization and Stagnation in Latin America." *International Studies Quarterly,* 20 (March 1976), 39–82.

The Amnesty International Report. Amnesty International Publications, London, 1976.

Angell, Norman. *The Great Illusion.* Heinemann, London, 1914.

Aron, Raymond. *Peace and War.* Doubleday, Garden City, N.Y., 1966.

Aspaturian, Vernon A. "The Foreign Policy of the Soviet Union." In *World Politics,* edited by James N. Rosenau, Kenneth W. Thompson, and Gavin Boyd. Free Press, New York, 1976.

Aspaturian, Vernon A. "The Soviet Military-Industrial Complex —Does It Exist?" *Journal of International Affairs,* 26, No. 1 (1972), 1–28.

Atkins, G. Pope. *Latin America in the International Political System.* Free Press, New York, 1977.

Axelrod, Robert. *Conflict of Interest.* Markham Publishing, Chicago, 1970.

Axline, Andrew. *European Community Law and Organizational Development.* Oceana, Dobbs Ferry, New York, 1968.

Baker, Stephen J. "Monopoly or Cartel?" *Foreign Policy,* 23 (Summer 1976), 202–220.

Balassa, Bela. *The Theory of Economic Integration.* Richard B. Irwin, Homewood, Ill., 1961.

Bandura, A., D. Ross, and S. A. Ross. "Transmission of Aggression Through Imitation of Agressive Models." *Journal of Abnormal and Social Psychology,* 63, No. 2 (1961), 575–582.

Barnet, Richard J. *The Roots of War.* Penguin, Baltimore, 1971.

Barnet, Richard, and Ronald Muller. *Global Reach.* Simon and Schuster, New York, 1974.

Barnett, Correlli. *The Collapse of British Power.* Morrow, New York, 1972.

Bean, Richard. "War and the Birth of States." *Journal of Economic History,* 33 (March 1973), 203–221.

Beckerman, Wilfred. *In Defence of Economic Growth.* Jonathan Cape, London, 1974.

Bell, Coral. "China: The Communists and the World." In *The Foreign Policies of the Powers,* edited by F. S. Northedge. Free Press, New York, 1974.

Beres, Louis René, and Harry R. Targ. *Reordering the Planet: Constructing Alternative World Futures.* Allyn and Bacon, Boston, 1974.

Beres, Louis René, and Harry R. Targ, eds. *Planning Alternative World Futures: Values, Methods, and Models.* Praeger, New York, 1975.

Bergsten, C. Fred. "Coming Investment Wars." *Foreign Affairs,* 53 (October 1974), 135–152.

Berkowitz, Leonard. *Aggression.* McGraw-Hill, New York, 1962.

Berkowitz, Leonard, and Edna Rawlings. "Effects of Film Violence on Inhibition Against Subsequent Aggression." *Journal of Abnormal and Social Psychology,* 66, No. 5 (1963), 405–412.

Bettmann, Otto L. *The Good Old Days — They Were Terrible.* Random House, New York, 1974.

Blair, Bruce G., and Garry D. Brewer. "The Terrorist Threat to World Nuclear Programs." *Journal of Conflict Resolution,* 21 (September 1977), 379–404.

Blake, David H., and Robert S. Walters. *The Politics of Global Economic Relations.* Prentice-Hall, Englewood Cliffs, N.J., 1976.

Blaug, Mark. "Economic Imperialism Revisited." In *Economic Imperialism,* edited by Kenneth Boulding and Tapan Mukerjee. University of Michigan Press, Ann Arbor, 1972.

Bolin, Bert. "The Carbon Cycle." *Scientific American,* 223 (September 1970), 124–135.

Boulding, Kenneth. Introduction. In *Economic Imperialism,* edited by Kenneth Boulding and Tapan Mukerjee. University of Michigan Press, Ann Arbor, 1972.

Bowden, Witt, Michael Karpovich, and Abbot P. Usher. *Economic History of Europe Since 1750,* American Book, New York, 1937.

Brams, Steven J. *Game Theory and Politics.* Free Press, New York, 1975.

Bremer, Stuart A., J. David Singer, and Urs Luterbacher. "The Population Density and War Proneness of European Nations, 1816–1965." *Comparative Political Studies,* 6 (October 1973), 329–348.

Brierly, James L. *The Law of Nations.* 2d ed. Oxford University Press, New York, 1936.

Brinton, Clarence Crane. *The Lives of Talleyrand.* Norton, New York, 1963.

Brown, Lester, "Rich Countries and Poor in a Finite, Interdependent World." *Daedalus,* 102 (Fall 1973), 153–165.

Brown, Lester. *Seeds of Change.* Praeger, New York, 1974.

Brown, Lester. *World Without Borders.* Vintage, New York, 1973.

Brown, Lester. *World Population Trends: Signs of Hope, Signs of Stress.* Worldwatch Institute, Washington, D.C., 1976.

Bueno de Mesquita, Bruce. "Measuring Systemic Polarity." *Journal of Conflict Resolution,* 19 (June 1975), 187–216.

Bueno de Mesquita, Bruce. "Systemic Polarization and the Occurrence and Duration of War." *Journal of Conflict Resolution* (Forthcoming).

Bueno de Mesquita, Bruce, and J. David Singer. "Alliances, Capabilities, and War: A Review and Synthesis." In *Political Science Annual,* vol. 4, edited by Cornelius P. Cotter, 1973.

Bull, Hedley. "The Objectives of Arms Control." In *The Use of Force,* edited by Robert J. Art and Kenneth N. Waltz. Little, Brown, Boston, 1971.

Bull, Hedley. "Rethinking Non-Proliferation." *International Affairs,* 51 (April 1975), 175–189.

Bury, J. P. T. *France 1814–1940.* Barnes, New York, 1962.

Campbell, Donald. "Common Fate, Similarity, and Other Indices of the Status of Aggregates of Persons as Social Entities." *Behavioral Science,* 3 (January 1958), 14–25.

Carr, Edward Hallet. *The Twenty Years' Crisis, 1919 – 1939*. Macmillan, London, 1939.

Caspary, William. "The 'Mood Theory': A Study of Public Opinion and Foreign Policy." *American Political Science Review*, 64 (June 1970), 536 – 547.

Cerami, Charles. *Crisis: The Loss of Europe*, Harcourt Brace Jovanovich, New York, 1975.

Chase-Dunn, Christopher. "The Effects of International Economic Dependence on Development and Inequality: A Cross National Study." *American Sociological Review*, 40 (December 1975), 720 – 738.

Chavance, Bernard. "On the Relations of Production in the U.S.S.R." *Monthly Review*, 29 (May 1977), 1 – 13.

Chertkoff, Jerome. "A Revision of Caplow's Coalition Theory." *Journal of Experimental Psychology*, 3 (April 1967), 172 – 177.

Claude, Inis L. *Swords into Plowshares*. 3d ed. Random House, New York, 1964.

Claude, Inis L. *The Impact of Public Opinion upon Foreign Policy and Diplomacy*. Humanities Press, Atlantic Highlands, N.J., 1965.

Clausen, A. W. "The International Corporation: An Executive's View." *The Annals*, 403 (September 1972), 12 – 21.

Cobb, Stephen. "The Impact of Defense Spending on Senatorial Voting Behavior." In *Sage International Yearbook of Foreign Policy Studies*, vol. 1, edited by Patrick J. McGowan, 1973.

Cole, Sam. "World Models, Their Progress and Applicability." *Futures*, 6 (June 1974), 201 – 218.

Commoner, Barry. *The Closing Circle*. Knopf, New York, 1971.

Commoner, Barry. "How Poverty Breeds Overpopulation." In *At Issue: Politics in the World Arena*, edited by Steven C. Spiegel, St. Martin's Press, New York, 1977.

Connor, Walker. "The Politics of Ethnonationalism." *Journal of International Affairs*, 27, No. 1 (1973), 1 – 21.

Connor, Walker. "The Political Significance of Ethnonationalism Within Western Europe." In *Ethnicity in an International Context*, edited by Abdul Said and Luiz R. Simmons. Transaction Books, New Brunswick, New Jersey, 1976.

Cooper, Duff. *Talleyrand*. Jonathan Cape, London, 1964.

Cox, Robert. "Labor and the Multinationals." *Foreign Affairs*, 54 (January 1976), 344 – 365.

Cox, Robert. "Labor and Transnational Relations." *International Organization*, 25 (Summer 1971), 554 – 584.

Crane, Diana. "Transnational Networks in Basic Science." *International Organization*, 25 (Summer 1971), 585 – 601.

Crispo, John. "Multinational Corporations and International Unions: Their Impact on Canadian Industrial Relations." In *Bargaining Without Boundaries*, edited by Robert J. Flanagan and Arnold R. Weber, University of Chicago Press, Chicago, 1974.

Current, Richard N., T. Harry Williams, and Frank Friedel. *American History: A Survey,* 3d ed. Knopf, New York, 1971.

Curtin, William J. "The Multinational Corporation and Transnational Collective Bargaining." In *American Labor and the Multinational Corporation,* edited by Duane Kujawa. Praeger, New York, 1973.

De Conde, Alexander. *A History of American Foreign Policy.* Scribner's, New York, 1963.

De Rivera, Joseph. *The Psychological Dimensions of Foreign Policy.* Merrill, Columbus, O., 1968.

De Towanicki, F. "A Talk with Konrad Lorenz." *New York Times Magazine,* July 5, 1970.

Deutsch, Karl W. *The Analysis of International Relations.* Prentice-Hall, Englewood Cliffs, N.J., 1968.

Deutsch, Karl W., and J. David Singer. "Multipolar Power Systems and International Stability." In *International Politics and Foreign Policy,* 2d ed., edited by James N. Rosenau, Free Press, New York, 1969.

Dougherty, James, and Robert Pfaltzgraff. *Contending Theories of International Relations.* Lippincott, Philadelphia, 1971.

Doxey, Margaret. "International Sanctions: A Framework for Analysis with Special Reference to the U.N. and Southern Africa." *International Organization,* 26 (Summer 1972), 527–550.

Dresang, Dennis L., and Ira Sharkansky. "Public Corporations in Single-Country and Regional Settings: Kenya and the East African Community." *International Organization,* 27 (Summer 1973), 303–328.

Dror, Yehezkel. *Public Policymaking Re-examined.* Chandler, San Francisco, 1968.

Dugan, James, and Laurence Lafore. *Days of Emperor and Clown.* Doubleday, Garden City, N.Y., 1973.

Dunn, Frederick S. *Peaceful Change: A Study of International Procedures.* Council on Foreign Relations, New York, 1937.

Dye, Thomas. *Understanding Public Policy.* Prentice-Hall, Englewood Cliffs, N.J., 1975.

Eagleton, Clyde. *International Government.* Ronald Press, New York, 1932.

East, Maurice A., and Charles F. Hermann. "Do Nation-Types Account for Foreign Policy Behavior?" In *Comparing Foreign Policies,* edited by James N. Rosenau. Wiley, New York, 1974.

Eibl-Eibesfeldt, I. *Love and Hate.* Holt, Rinehart, and Winston, New York, 1972.

Epstein, Leon D. "British Foreign Policy." In *Foreign Policy and World Politics,* 5th ed., edited by Roy C. Macridis. Prentice-Hall, Englewood Cliffs, N.J., 1976.

Epstein, William. "Nuclear Proliferation in the Third World." *Journal of International Affairs,* 29 (Fall 1975), 185–202.

Erb, Guy F., and Valeriana Kallab, eds. *Beyond Dependency*. Overseas Development Council, Washington, D.C., 1975.

Erikson, Robert L., and Norman R. Luttbeg. *American Public Opinion*. Wiley, New York, 1973.

Evans, R. I. "Lorenz Warns." *Psychology Today,* 8 (November 1974), 82–93.

Falk, Richard. "Toward a New World Order: Modest Methods and Drastic Visions." In *On the Creation of a Just World Order,* edited by Saul Mendlovitz, Free Press, New York, 1975.

Fann, K. T., and Donald C. Hodges, eds. *Readings in U.S. Imperialism*. P. Sargent, Boston, 1971.

Farer, Tom J. "The Greening of the Globe: A Preliminary Appraisal of the World Order Models Project (WOMP)." *International Organization,* 31 (Winter 1977), 129–148.

Farley, Miriam S. *United States Relations with Southeast Asia with Special Reference to Indochina*. Institute of Pacific Relations, New York, 1955.

Fay, Sidney B. *The Origins of the World War*. Macmillan, New York, 1928.

Feis, Herbert. *Churchill, Roosevelt, and Stalin*. Princeton University Press, Princeton, 1957.

Fieldhouse, D. K. "Imperialism: A Historiographical Revision." In *Economic Imperialism,* edited by Kenneth Boulding and Tapan Mukerjee. University of Michigan Press, Ann Arbor, 1972.

Finkelstein, Lawrence S. "The United Nations: Then and Now." *International Organization,* 19 (Summer 1965), 367–393.

Finlay, David J., and Thomas Hovet, Jr. *7304: International Relations on the Planet Earth*. Harper and Row, New York, 1975.

Floyd, David. *Mao Against Khrushchev*. Praeger, New York, 1963.

Fontaine, André. *History of the Cold War*. Pantheon, New York, 1969.

Forrester, Jay. "Counterintuitive Behavior of Social Systems." In *Collected Papers of Jay W. Forrester*. Wright-Allen Press, Cambridge, Mass., 1975.

Forsythe, David P. "The Red Cross as a Transnational Movement: Conserving and Changing the Nation-State System." *International Organization,* 30 (Autumn 1976), 607–630.

Frankel, Joseph. "Britain's Changing Role." *International Affairs,* 50, No. 4 (1974), 574–583.

Friedham, Robert L., and William J. Durch. "The International Seabed Resources Agency Negotiations and the New International Economic Order." *International Organization,* 31 (Spring 1977), 343–384.

Gabriel, Peter. "The Multinational Corporation in the World Economy: Problems and Prospects." In *Bargaining Without Boundaries,* edited by Robert J. Flanagan and Arnold R. Weber. University of Chicago Press, Chicago, 1974.

Galbraith, John Kenneth. "Foreign Policy: The Plain Lessons of a Bad Decade." *Foreign Policy,* 1 (Winter 1970), 31–45.

Gall, Norman. "Atoms for Brazil, Dangers for All." *Foreign Policy,* 23 (Summer 1976), 155–201.

Galtung, Johan. "Nonterritorial Actors and the Problem of Peace." In *On the Creation of a Just World Order,* edited by Saul Mendlovitz. Free Press, New York, 1975.

Garson, G. David. "On the Origins of Interest-Group Theory: A Critique of a Process." *American Political Science Review,* 68 (December 1974), 1505–1519.

Gettleman, Marvin E., ed. *Vietnam.* Fawcett, New York, 1965.

Gilpin, Robert. "The Politics of Transnational Economic Relations." In *Transnational Relations and World Politics,* edited by Robert O. Keohane and Joseph S. Nye, Jr. Harvard University Press, Cambridge, 1972.

Goldstein, J. H., and R. L. Arms. "Effects of Observing Athletic Contests on Hostility." *Sociometry,* 34 (March 1971), 83–94.

Goodrich, Leland M. "The Maintenance of International Peace and Security." *International Organization,* 19 (Summer 1965), 429–443.

Goodrich, Leland. *The United Nations in a Changing World.* Columbia University Press, New York, 1974.

Gosovic, Branislav, and John Gerard Ruggie. "On the Creation of a New International Economic Order." *International Organization,* 30 (Spring 1976), 309–346.

Greenwood, Ted, and Michael C. Nacht. "The New Nuclear Debate: Sense or Nonsense?" *Foreign Affairs,* 52 (July 1974), 761–780.

Groennings, Sven. "Patterns, Strategies, and Payoffs in Norwegian Coalition Formation." In *The Study of Coalition Behavior,* edited by Sven Groennings, E. W. Kelley, and Michael Leiserson. Holt, Rinehart, and Winston, New York, 1970.

Grunwald, Joseph, Miguel S. Wionczek and Martin Carnoy. *Latin American Economic Integration and U.S. Policy.* Brookings Institution, Washington, D.C., 1972.

Gulick, Edward. *Europe's Classical Balance of Power.* Norton, New York, 1955.

Haas, Ernst. "The Balance of Power: Prescription, Concept, or Propaganda." *World Politics,* 5 (July 1953), 442–477.

Haas, Ernst. *The Uniting of Europe.* Stanford University Press, Stanford, 1958.

Haas, Ernst B., and Allen S. Whiting. *Dynamics of International Relations.* McGraw-Hill, New York, 1956.

Haas, Michael. "Societal Approaches to the Study of War." *Journal of Peace Research,* 2, No. 4 (1965), 307–323.

Haigh, Anthony. *Congress of Vienna to Common Market.* Harrap, London, 1973.

Halberstam, David. *The Best and the Brightest.* Random House, New York, 1972.

Haley, P. Edward. "Britain and the Middle East." In *The Middle East in World Politics,* edited by Tareq Y. Ismael. Syracuse University Press, Syracuse, 1974.

Halperin, Morton H. "Why Bureaucrats Play Games." *Foreign Policy,* 2 (Spring 1971), 70–90.

Hammer, Ellen J. *The Struggle for Indochina.* Stanford University Press, Stanford, 1954.

Harrod, Jeffrey. "Transnational Power." In *The Yearbook of World Affairs 1976,* edited by George W. Keeton and Georg Schwarzenberger. Stevens, London, 1976.

Hartmann, Frederick H. *The Relations of Nations,* 6th ed. Macmillan, New York, 1957.

Harvey, Mose L., and Foy P. Kohler, eds. *Soviet World Outlook,* 1 (August 1976), Current Affairs Press, Washington, D.C.

Hawkins, Robert G., and Michael Jay Jedel. "U.S. Jobs and Foreign Investment." In *International Labor and the Multinational Enterprise,* edited by Duane Kujawa, Praeger, New York, 1975.

Hayes, Carlton J. H. *Essays on Nationalism.* Macmillan, New York, 1920.

Hayes, Carlton J. H. *A Political and Social History of Modern Europe.* Macmillan, New York, 1921.

Hayter, Teresa. *Aid as Imperialism.* Penguin, Baltimore, 1971.

Hazlewood, Arthur. *Economic Integration: The East African Experience.* Heinemann, London, 1975.

Hazlewood, Leo. "Diversion Mechanisms and Encapsulation Processes: The Domestic Conflict–Foreign Conflict Hypothesis Reconsidered." In *Sage International Yearbook of Foreign Policy Studies,* vol. 3, edited by Patrick J. McGowan. Sage Publications, Beverly Hills, 1975.

Hermann, Charles. "Policy Classification: A Key to the Study of Foreign Policy." In *The Analysis of International Politics,* edited by James N. Rosenau, Vincent Davis, and Maurice East. Free Press, New York, 1972.

Hermann, Margaret G. "When Leader Personality Will Affect Foreign Policy: Some Propositions." In *In Search of Global Patterns,* edited by James N. Rosenau. Free Press, New York, 1976.

Herz, John. *International Politics in the Atomic Age.* Columbia University Press, New York, 1959.

Hinsley, F. H. *Power and the Pursuit of Peace.* Cambridge University Press, London, 1967.

Hinton, Harold C. *Communist China in World Politics.* Houghton Mifflin, Boston, 1966.

Hirsch, Fred. "Is There a New International Economic Order?" *International Organization,* 30 (Summer 1976), 521–531.

Hobson, John. *Imperialism: A Study.* Allen and Unwin, London, 1902.

Hoepli, Nancy. Editor's Introduction. In *The Common Market,* edited by Nancy L. Hoepli. Wilson, New York, 1975.

Hoggard, Gary. "Differential Source Coverage in Foreign Policy Analysis." In *Comparing Foreign Policies,* edited by James N. Rosenau. Wiley, New York, 1974.

Holsti, K. J. *International Politics,* 2 ed. Prentice-Hall, Englewood Cliffs, N.J., 1972.

Holsti, Ole. *Crisis Escalation War.* McGill-Queen's University Press, Montreal, 1972.

Horowitz, David. *The Free World Colossus.* Wang and Hill, New York, 1965.

Horvath, William J., and Caxton C. Foster. "Stochastic Models of War Alliances." *Journal of Conflict Resolution,* 7 (June 1963), 110–116.

Howard, Michael. *The Franco-Prussian War.* Rupert Hart Davis, London, 1961.

Hudson, Michael. *Super Imperialism.* Holt, Rinehart, and Winston, New York, 1972.

Huntington, Samuel P. *Political Order in Changing Societies.* Yale University Press, New Haven, 1968.

Huntington, Samuel P. "Arms Races: Prerequisites and Results." In *The Use of Force,* edited by Robert J. Art and Kenneth N. Waltz. Little, Brown, Boston, 1971.

IDS Bulletin, 4 (December 1971).

International Bank for Reconstruction and Development. *Report on Limits to Growth.* Washington, D.C., 1972.

Jager, Elizabeth R. "U.S. Labor and Multinationals." In *International Labor and the Multinational Enterprise,* edited by Duane Kujawa. Praeger, New York, 1975.

Johnson, Haynes. *The Bay of Pigs.* Norton, New York, 1964.

Kahn, Herman, William Brown, and Leon Martel. *The Next 200 Years.* Morrow, New York, 1976.

Kaufman, Robert R., Harry I. Chernotsky, and Daniel S. Geller. "A Preliminary Test of the Theory of Dependency." *Comparative Politics,* 7 (April 1975), 303–330.

Kelman, Herbert. "The Role of the Individual in International Relations: Some Conceptual and Methodological Considerations." *Journal of International Affairs,* 24, No. 1 (1970), 1–17.

Keohane, Robert O., and Joseph S. Nye, Jr., eds. *Transnational Relations and World Politics.* Special edition of *International Organization,* 25 (Summer 1971).

Keynes, John Maynard. *The Economic Consequences of the Peace.* Harcourt, Brace, and Howe, New York, 1920.

Khouri, Fred J. *The Arab-Israeli Dilemma.* Syracuse University Press, Syracuse, 1968.

Kim, Samuel S. "The Lorenzian Theory of Aggression and Peace Research: A Critique." *Journal of Peace Research,* 13, No. 4 (1976), 253–276.

King, Alexander. "The Club of Rome — Setting the Record Straight." *The Center Magazine,* 7 (September 1974), 15–24.

Kingdon, John. *Congressmen's Voting Decisions.* Harper and Row, New York, 1973.

Kissinger, Henry. *A World Restored.* Grossett and Dunlap, New York, 1964.

Kissinger, Henry. "Domestic Sources of Foreign Policy." In *Politics and the International System,* edited by Robert L. Pfaltzgraff. Lippincott, Philadelphia, 1972.

Kissinger, Henry A. *American Foreign Policy.* Expanded ed. Norton, New York, 1974.

Knapton, Ernest John. *France.* Scribner's, New York, 1971.

Koenig, Louis, ed. *The Truman Administration: Its Principles and Practice.* New York University Press, New York, 1956.

Kolko, Gabriel. *The Roots of American Foreign Policy.* Beacon Press, Boston, 1969.

Kolko, Gabriel, and Joyce Kolko. *The Limits of Power.* Harper and Row, New York, 1972.

Kothari, Rajni. "World Politics and World Order: The Issue of Autonomy." In *On the Creation of a Just World Order,* edited by Saul Mendlovitz. Free Press, New York, 1975.

Kujawa, Duane, ed. "Transnational Industrial Relations: A Collective Bargaining Prospect?" In *International Labor and the Multinational Enterprise,* Praeger, New York, 1975.

Kuznets, Simon. "Economic Growth of Small Nations." In *The Economic Consequences of the Size of Nations,* edited by Austin Robinson. Macmillan, London, 1966.

Langer, William. "A Critique of Imperialism." *Foreign Affairs,* 14 (October 1935), 102–119.

Langer, William. *The Diplomacy of Imperialism,* 2d ed. Knopf, New York, 1951.

Lasswell, Harold D. "The Promise of the World Order Modelling Movement." *World Politics,* 29 (April 1977), 425–437.

Latin American Economic Report, August 13, 1976.

Lauterpacht, Hersch. *The Function of Law in the International Community.* Oxford University Press, New York, 1933.

Lenhart, Harry. "Labor Fears Loss of Jobs in U.S. as Firms Expand Their Overseas Facilities." *National Journal,* July 17, 1971.

Lenin, V. I. *Imperialism: The Highest Stage of Capitalism.* International Publishers, New York, (1917), 1939.

Levinson, Jerome, and Juan de Onis. *The Alliance that Lost Its Way.* Quadrangle Books, Chicago, 1970.

Lin, Paul T. K. "Development Guided by Values: Comments on China's Road and Its Implications." In *On the Creation of a Just World Order,* edited by Saul Mendlovitz, Free Press, New York, 1975.

Lindblom, Charles. "The 'Science' of Muddling Through." *Public Administration Review,* 19 (Spring 1959), 79–88.

Lipset, Seymour Martin. *Political Man*. Anchor Books, Garden City, N.Y., 1959.

Lorenz, Konrad. *On Aggression*. Harcourt Brace Jovanovich, New York, 1966.

Lowenthal, Abraham. *The Dominican Intervention*. Harvard University Press, Cambridge, Mass., 1972.

McClellan, Donald H. "The Common Market's Contribution to Central American Economic Growth: A First Approximation." In *The Movement Toward Latin American Unity*, edited by Ronald Hilton. Praeger, New York, 1969.

McClelland, Charles, and Gary Hoggard. "Conflict Patterns in the Interaction Among Nations." In *International Politics and Foreign Policy*, revised ed., edited by James N. Rosenau. Free Press, New York, 1969.

Magdoff, Harry. *The Age of Imperialism*. Monthly Review Press, New York, 1969.

Magee, Stephen P. "The Welfare Effects of Restrictions on U.S. Trade." *Brookings Papers on Economic Activity*. Brookings Institution, Washington, D.C., 1973.

Maier, Herbert. "The International Free Trade Union Movement and International Corporations." In *American Labor and the Multinational Corporation*, edited by Duane Kujawa. Praeger, New York, 1973.

Manchester, William. *The Arms of Krupp*. Little, Brown, Boston, 1968.

Mansbach, Richard W., Yale H. Ferguson, and Donald E. Lampert. *The Web of World Politics*. Prentice-Hall, Englewood Cliffs, N.J., 1976.

Mantoux, Étienne. *The Carthaginian Peace*. University of Pittsburgh Press, Pittsburgh, 1952.

March, James G. "The Power of Power." In *Varieties of Political Theory*, edited by David Easton. Prentice-Hall, Englewood Cliffs, N.J., 1966.

Mazrui, Ali A. "World Culture and a Search for Human Consensus." In *On the Creation of a Just World Order*, edited by Saul Mendlovitz. Free Press, New York, 1975.

Meadows, Donella H., Dennis L. Meadows, Jorgen Randers, and William W. Behrens, III. *The Limits to Growth: A Report for the Club of Rome's Project on the Predicament of Mankind*. Universe Books, New York, 1972.

Meadows, Donella H., Dennis L. Meadows, Jorgen Randers, and William W. Behrens, Ill. "A Response to Sussex." In *Models of Doom*, edited by H. S. D. Cole, Christopher Freeman, Marie Jahoda, and K. L. R. Pavitt. Universe Books, New York, 1973.

Mendlovitz, Saul, *On the Creation of a Just World Order*. Free Press, New York, 1975.

Mesarovic, Mihajlo D., and Eduard C. Pestel. *Mankind at the Turn-*

ing Point: The Second Report to the Club of Rome. New American Library, New York, 1974.

Miller, S. M., Roy Bennett, and Cyril Alapatt. "Does the U.S. Economy Require Imperialism?" *Social Policy,* 1 (September-October 1970), 13–19.

Miller, Warren E., and Donald E. Stokes. "Constituency Influence in Congress." *American Political Science Review,* 57 (March 1963), 45–56.

Mills, Lennox, and Charles H. McLaughlin. *World Politics in Transition.* Holt, Rinehart, and Winston, New York, 1956.

Mische, Gerald and Patricia. *Toward a Human World Order.* Paulist Press, New York, 1977.

Mitrany, David. *A Working Peace System.* Royal Institute of International Affairs, London, 1943.

Moore, David. "National Attributes and Nation Typologies: A Look at the Rosenau Genotypes." In *Comparing Foreign Policies,* edited by James N. Rosenau. Wiley, New York, 1974.

Morgan, Patrick M. *Theories and Approaches to International Politics,* 2d ed. Page-Ficklin, Palo Alto, 1975.

Morgenthau, Hans J. *Politics Among Nations,* 4th ed. Knopf, New York, 1967.

Morse, Edward. *Modernization in the Transformation of International Relations.* Free Press, New York, 1976.

Moul, William B. "The Levels of Analysis Problem Revisited." *Canadian Journal of Political Science,* 6 (September 1973), 494–513.

Moyer, Wayne. "Congress and Defense Policy, 1937–1972." Ph. D. Dissertation, Yale University (Forthcoming).

Mudge, George Alfred. "Domestic Politics and U.N. Activities: The Cases of Rhodesia and South Africa." *International Organization,* 21 (Winter 1967), 55–78.

Mueller, John, ed. *Approaches to Measurement in International Relations.* Appleton-Century Crofts, New York, 1969.

Mueller, John. *War, Presidents, and Public Opinion.* Wiley, New York, 1973.

Muller, Ronald. "The MNC and the Exercise of Power: Latin America." In *The New Sovereigns: Multinational Corporations as World Powers,* edited by Abdul Said and Luiz R. Simmons. Prentice-Hall, Englewood Cliffs, N.J., 1975.

Murphy, Francis X. "Vatican Politics: Structure and Function." *World Politics,* 26 (July 1974), 542–559.

Myrdal, Gunnar. *Rich Lands and Poor,* Harper, New York, 1957.

Nathan, James A. "The Missile Crisis: His Finest Hour Now." *World Politics,* 27 (January 1975), 256–281.

Nathan, James A., and James K. Oliver. *United States Foreign Policy and World Order.* Little, Brown, Boston, 1976.

Neal, Fred Warner, and Bruce P. Hamlett. "The Never-Never Land of International Relations." *International Studies Quarterly,* 13 (September 1969), 281–305.

Nelson, S. D. "Nature/Nurture Revisited." *Journal of Conflict Resolution,* 18 (June 1974), 285–335.

Nicolson, Harold. *The Congress of Vienna.* Methuen, London, 1961.

Niemeyer, Gerhart. "The Balance-Sheet of the League Experiment." In *The United Nations Political System,* edited by David A. Kay. Wiley, 1967.

"No Amnesty." *The Economist,* April 26, 1975.

Northedge, F. S. "The Adjustment of British Policy." In *The Foreign Policies of the Powers,* edited by F. S. Northedge. Free Press, New York, 1974.

Northedge, F. S., and M. J. Grieve. *A Hundred Years of International Relations.* Praeger, New York, 1971.

Olson, Mancur. *The Logic of Collective Action.* Schocken Books, New York, 1968.

Organski, A. F. K. *World Politics,* 2d ed., Knopf, New York, 1968.

Oshima, Harry T. "New Directions in Development Strategies." *Economic Development and Cultural Change,* 25 (April 1977), 555–579.

Page, William. "Population Forecasting." In *Models of Doom,* edited by H. S. D. Cole, Christopher Freeman, Marie Jahoda, and K. L. R. Pavitt. Universe Books, New York, 1973.

Panati, Charles, and Mary Lord. "Population Implosion." *Newsweek,* December 6, 1976, 58.

Pavitt, K. L. R., "Malthus and other Economists." In *Models of Doom,* edited by H. S. D. Cole, Christopher Freeman, Marie Jahoda, and K. L. R. Pavitt. Universe Books, New York, 1973.

Petras, James. "Chile and Latin America." *Monthly Review,* 28 (February 1977), 13–24.

Pettman, Ralph. *Human Behavior and World Politics.* St. Martin's Press, New York, 1975.

Pickles, Dorothy. "France: Tradition and Change." In *The Foreign Policies of the Powers,* edited by F. S. Northedge. Free Press, New York, 1974.

Pickles, Dorothy. "The Decline of Gaullist Foreign Policy." *International Affairs,* 51, No. 2, (1975), 220–235.

Pierce, John C., and Douglas D. Rose. "Nonattitudes and American Public Opinion." *American Political Science Review,* 68 (June 1974), 626–649.

Pipes, Richard. "Why the Soviet Union Thinks It Could Fight and Win a Nuclear War." *Commentary,* 64 (July 1977), 21–34.

Potter, Pitman B. *An Introduction to the Study of International Organization,* 3d ed. D. Appleton-Century, New York, 1928.

Powelson, John P. "The Strange Persistence of the 'Terms of Trade.'" *Inter-American Economic Affairs,* 30 (Spring 1977), 17–28.

Pye, Lucian, *China.* Little, Brown, Boston, 1972.

Quester, George H. *The Continuing Problem of International Politics.* Dryden Press, New York, 1974.

Quester, George. *Offense and Defense in the International System.* Wiley, New York, 1977.

Rapoport, Anatol. "Various Meanings of 'Theory.'" In *International Politics and Foreign Policy,* edited by James N. Rosenau. Free Press, New York, 1961.

Ray, David. "The Dependency Model of Latin American Underdevelopment: Three Basic Fallacies." *Journal of Inter-American and World Affairs,* 15 (February 1977), 4–20.

Ray, James Lee, and J. David Singer. "Measuring the Concentration of Power in the International System." *Sociological Methods and Research,* 1 (May 1973), 403–436.

Ray, James Lee, and Thomas Webster. "Dependency and Economic Growth in Latin America." *International Studies Quarterly,* 22 (September 1978).

Reischauer, Edwin O. *Japan: Past and Present.* Knopf, New York, 1964.

"Review of U.N. and U.S. Action to Restore Peace." *Department of State Bulletin,* 23 (July 10, 1950), 46.

Riencourt, Amaury de. *The American Empire.* Dial Press, New York, 1968.

Riker, William. *The Theory of Political Coalitions.* Yale University Press, New Haven, 1962.

Ripley, Randall B., and Grace A. Franklin. *Congress, the Bureaucracy, and Public Policy.* Dorsey Press, Homewood, Ill., 1976.

Robinson, Clarence A. Jr. "Soviets Push for Beam Weapon." *Aviation Week and Space Technology,* 106 (May 2, 1977).

Robinson, John P. *Public Information About World Affairs.* Institute for Social Research, Ann Arbor, 1967.

Rosecrance, Richard. *Action and Reaction in World Politics.* Little, Brown, Boston, 1963.

Rosecrance, Richard. "Bipolarity, Multipolarity, and the Future." *Journal of Conflict Resolution,* 10 (September 1966), 314–327.

Rosenau, James N. "Pre-theories and Theories of Foreign Policy." In *Approaches to Comparative and International Politics,* edited by R. Barry Farrel. Northwestern University Press, Evanston, 1966.

Rosenau, James N. "Private Preferences and Political Responsibilities." In *Quantitative International Politics,* edited by J. David Singer. Free Press, New York, 1968.

Rosenberg, Milton, Sidney Verba, and Philip Converse. *Vietnam and the Silent Majority.* Harper and Row, New York, 1971.

Rummel, Rudolph J. "Dimensions of Conflict Behavior Within and Between Nations." *General Systems Yearbook,* 8 (1963), 1–50.

Rummel, Rudolph J. "Testing Some Possible Predictors of Conflict Behavior Within and Between Nations." *Peace Research Society (International) Papers,* 1 (1964), 79–111.

Rummel, Rudolph J. "Understanding Factor Analysis." *Journal of Conflict Resolution,* 11 (December 1967), 444–480.

Rummel, Rudolph J. "Indicators of Cross-National and International Patterns." *American Political Science Review,* 63 (March 1969), 127–147.

Russell, Robert. "Governing the World's Money: Don't Just Do Something, Stand There." *International Organization,* 31 (Winter 1977), 111–119.

Russett, Bruce M. *International Regions and the International System.* Rand McNally, Chicago, 1967.

Russett, Bruce M. "Components of an Operational Theory of Alliance Formation." *Journal of Conflict Resolution,* 12 (September 1968), 285–301.

Russett, Bruce M. *What Price Vigilance?* Yale University Press, New Haven, 1970.

Russett, Bruce M. "Apologia pro Vita Sua." In *In Search of Global Patterns,* edited by James Rosenau. Free Press, New York, 1976.

Safran, Nadav. *From War to War.* Pegasus, New York, 1969.

Said, Abdul, and Luiz R. Simmons. "The Politics of Transition." In *The New Sovereigns: Multinational Corporations as World Powers,* edited by Abdul Said and Luiz R. Simmons. Prentice-Hall, Englewood Cliffs, N.J., 1975.

Said, Abdul, and Luiz R. Simmons, eds. "The Ethnic Factor in World Politics." In *Ethnicity in an International Context.* Transaction Books, New Brunswick, N.J., 1976.

Said, Abdul, and Luiz R. Simmons, eds. Introduction. In *Ethnicity in an International Context.* Transaction Books, New Brunswick, N.J., 1976.

Sawyer, Jack. "Dimensions of Nations: Size, Wealth, and Politics." *American Journal of Sociology,* 73 (September 1967), 145–172.

Scammon, Richard M., and Ben J. Wattenberg. *The Real Majority.* Berkeley Publishing, New York, 1970.

Schattschneider, E. E. *The Semisovereign People.* Holt, Rinehart, and Winston, New York, 1960.

Schram, Stuart. *Mao Tse-tung.* Penguin, Baltimore, 1968.

Schuman, Frederick L. *International Politics: An Introduction to the Western State System.* McGraw-Hill, New York, 1973.

Scoble, Harry, and Laurie S. Wiseberg. "Human Rights and Amnesty International." *The Annals,* 413 (May 1974), 11–26.

Scoble, Harry, and Laurie S. Wiseberg. "Amnesty International:

Evaluating Effectiveness in the Human Rights Arena." *Intellect,* 105 (September-October 1976), 79– 82.

Servan-Schreiber, Jean Jacques. *The American Challenge.* Atheneum, New York, 1968.

Sherman, Howard. *Radical Political Economy.* Basic Books, New York, 1972.

Shirer, William L. *The Rise and Fall of the Third Reich.* Simon and Schuster, New York, 1960.

Shirer, William L. *The Collapse of the Third Republic.* Simon and Schuster, New York, 1969.

Sigmund, P. E. "Latin American Catholicism's Opening to the Left." *Review of Politics,* 35 (January 1973), 61– 76.

Simon, Herbert. *Administrative Behavior,* 2d ed. Free Press, New York, 1957.

Simon, Herbert. *Models of Man.* Wiley, New York, 1957.

Sinclair, T. C. "Environmentalism." In *Models of Doom,* edited by H. S. D. Cole, Christopher Freeman, Marie Jahoda, and K. L. R. Pavitt, Universe Books, New York, 1973.

Singer, J. David. "The Level of Analysis Problem in International Relations." In *The International System,* edited by Klaus Knorr and Sidney Verba. Princeton University Press, Princeton, 1961.

Singer, J. David. *Deterrence, Arms Control, and Disarmament.* Ohio State University Press, Columbus, 1962.

Singer, J. David, Stuart Bremer, and John Stuckey. "Capability Distribution, Uncertainty, and Major Power War, 1820– 1965." In *Peace, War, and Numbers,* edited by Bruce M. Russett. Sage Publications, Beverly Hills, 1972.

Singer, J. David, and Melvin Small. "Formal Alliances, 1815– 1939: A Quantitative Description." *Journal of Peace Research,* 1 (1966), 257– 282.

Singer, J. David, and Melvin Small. "National Alliance Commitments and War Involvement, 1815– 1945." *Peace Research Society (International) Papers,* 5 (1966), 109– 140.

Singer, J. David, and Melvin Small. "Alliance Aggregation and the Onset of War, 1815– 1945." In *Quantitative International Politics,* edited by J. David Singer. Free Press, New York, 1968.

Singer, J. David, and Melvin Small. *The Wages of War, 1816 – 1965: A Statistical Handbook.* Wiley, New York, 1972.

Singer, Marshall R. "The Foreign Policies of Small Developing States." In *World Politics,* edited by James N. Rosenau, Kenneth W. Thompson, and Gavin Boyd. Free Press, New York, 1976.

Sivard, Ruth. *World Military and Social Expenditures 1976.* WMSE Publications, 1976.

Small, Melvin, and J. David Singer. "Formal Alliances, 1816– 1965: An Extension of the Basic Data." *Journal of Peace Research,* 1 (1966), 1– 32.

Solberg, Carl. *Oil Power.* New American Library, New York, 1976.

Spanier, John. *World Politics in an Age of Revolution.* Praeger, New York, 1967.

Spanier, John. *Games Nations Play,* 2d ed., Praeger, New York, 1975.

Spero, Joan Edelman. *The Politics of International Economic Relations.* St. Martin's Press, New York, 1977.

Staar, Richard F. "The Warsaw Treaty Organization." In *Alliances,* edited by Francis A. Beer. Holt, Rinehart, and Winston, New York, 1970.

Stephenson, Hugh. *The Coming Clash.* Saturday Review Press, New York, 1972.

Stern, Geoffrey. "Soviet Foreign Policy in Theory and Practice." In *The Foreign Policies of the Powers,* edited by F. S. Northedge. Free Press, New York, 1974.

Stoessinger, John G. *Why Nations Go to War.* St. Martin's Press, New York, 1974.

Stone, I. F. *The Hidden History of the Korean War.* Monthly Review Press, New York, 1952.

Sullivan, Michael. *International Relations: Theories and Evidence.* Prentice-Hall, Englewood Cliffs, N.J., 1976.

Surrey, A. J., and A. J. Bromley, "Energy Resources." In *Models of Doom,* edited by H. S. D. Cole, Christopher Freeman, Marie Jahoda, and K. L. R. Pavitt. Universe Books, New York, 1973.

Sweetser, Arthur. *The League of Nations at Work.* Macmillan, New York, 1920.

Szulc, Tad. "Fractious Common Market." *The New Republic,* November 20, 1976.

Tanter, Raymond. "Dimensions of Conflict Behavior Within and Between Nations, 1958– 1960." *Journal of Conflict Resolution,* 10 (March 1966), 41– 64.

Tatu, Michael. "The Great Power Triangle: Washington-Moscow-Peking." In *International Politics,* edited by Robert J. Art and Robert Jervis. Little, Brown, Boston, 1973.

Truman, David. *The Governmental Process.* Knopf, New York, 1951.

Tuchman, Barbara. *The Guns of August.* Macmillan, New York, 1962.

Tucker, Robert. *The Radical Left and American Foreign Policy.* Johns Hopkins Press, Baltimore, 1971.

Ulam, Adam B. *Expansion and Coexistence,* 2d ed. Praeger, New York, 1974.

United Nations Department of Economic and Social Affairs. *Statistical Yearbook of 1969,* United Nations, New York, 1970.

United Nations Population Division. "World Population Prospects, 1970– 2000, as Assessed in 1973." ESA/P/WP. 53, March 1975.

United States Bureau of Mines. *Minerals Yearbook.* Government Printing Office, Washington, D.C., 1967.

United States Bureau of Mines. *Commodity Data Summary*. Government Printing Office, Washington, D.C., 1971.

Uri, Pierre. *Development Without Dependence*. Praeger, New York, 1976,

Vallier, Ivan. "The Roman Catholic Church: A Transnational Actor." *International Organization*, 25 (Summer 1971), 479–502.

Verba, Sidney, and Richard A. Brody. "Participation, Policy Preferences, and the War in Vietnam." *Public Opinion Quarterly*, 34, No. 3 (1970), 325–332.

Vernon, Raymond. Foreword. In *International Labor and the Multinational Enterprise,* edited by Duane Kujawa. Praeger, New York, 1975.

Vernon, Raymond. *Sovereignty at Bay*. Basic Books, New York, 1971.

Waltz, Kenneth. *Man, the State, and War*. Columbia University Press, New York, 1954.

Waltz, Kenneth. "The Stability of a Bipolar World." *Daedalus*, 93 (Summer 1964), 881–909.

Waltz, Kenneth. "International Structure, National Force, and the Balance of World Power." In *International Politics and Foreign Policy,* 2d ed., edited by James N. Rosenau. Free Press, New York, 1969.

Warth, Robert P. *Soviet Russia in World Politics*. Twayne Publishers, New York, 1963.

Weinberg, Nat. "The Multinational Corporation and Labor." In *The New Sovereigns: Multinational Corporations as World Powers,* edited by Abdul Said and Luiz R. Simmons. Prentice-Hall, Englewood Cliffs, N.J., 1974.

Whiting, Allen S. *China Crosses the Yalu*. Macmillan, New York, 1960.

Wilkenfeld, Jonathan. "Models for the Analysis of Foreign Conflict Behavior of States." In *Peace, War, and Numbers,* edited by Bruce M. Russett. Sage Publications, Beverly Hills, 1972.

Wilkinson, David. "World Order Models Project: First Fruits." *Political Science Quarterly*, 91 (Summer 1976), 329–336.

Willrich, Mason, and Theodore B. Taylor. *Nuclear Theft: Risks and Safeguards*. Ballinger Publishing, Cambridge, Mass., 1974.

Wolfers, Arnold. "The Pole of Power and the Pole of Indifference." In *International Politics and Foreign Policy,* edited by James N. Rosenau, Free Press, New York, 1961.

Wolfers, Arnold. "Alliances." In *International Encyclopedia of the Social Sciences,* edited by David Sills. Macmillan and Free Press, New York, 1968.

Wolpin, Miles D. *Cuban Foreign Policy and Chilean Politics*. Heath, Lexington, Mass., 1972.

Worldmark Press. *The United Nations*. Wiley, New York, 1977.

Yalem, Ronald J. "The Level of Analysis Problem Reconsidered." *The Yearbook of World Affairs*, 31 (1977), 306–326.

Yearbook of International Organizations, 15th ed. Union of International Associations, Brussels, Belgium, 1974.

Yeselson, Abraham, and Anthony Gaglione. "The Use of the United Nations in World Politics." In *At Issue: Politics in the World Arena,* edited by Steven L. Spiegel. St. Martin's Press, New York, 1977.

Zinnes, Dina. "Coalition Theories and the Balance of Power." In *The Study of Coalition Behavior,* edited by Sven Groennings, E. W. Kelley, and Michael Leiserson. Holt, Rinehart, and Winston, 1970.

Zinnes, Dina, and Jonathan Wilkenfeld. "An Analysis of Foreign Conflict Behavior of Nations." *Comparative Foreign Policy: Theoretical Essays,* edited by Wolfram F. Hanreider. McKay, New York, 1971.

Author Index

AUTHOR INDEX

Spanier, John, 96, 119, 297
Spero, Joan Edelman, 191, 310
Staar, Richard F., 181
Stephenson, Hugh, 226, 229, 244
Stern, Geoffrey, 120
Stoessinger, John G., 30, 70, 175
Stokes, Donald E., 50
Stone, I. F., 28
Stuckey, John, 105, 273, 315
Sullivan, Michael, 160
Surrey, A. J., 336
Szulc, Tad, 193

Tanter, Raymond, 162
Targ, Harry R., 358

Tatu, Michael, 40
Taylor, A. J. P., 374
Taylor, Theodore, 218
Truman, David, 53, 54
Tuchman, Barbara, 69, 71
Tucker, Robert, 312

Ulam, Adam B., 115, 117, 118
Uri, Pierre, 367
Usher, Abbot P., 14

Vallier, Ivan, 256
Verba, Sidney, 47, 48, 51

Subject Index

Bourbon dynasty, in France and
  Spain, 93
Boxer Rebellion (1900), 122
Brazil, 79–80, 153, 302
Brest-Litovsk, Treaty of, 113
Brezhnev, Leonid, Soviet president,
  121
  and Brezhnev Doctrine, 121
Brief History of Modern China, A, 120
British Empire, *see* Great Britain
Brown, George, Chairman of the Joint
  Chiefs of Staff, 63
Buddhism, 257
Bulgaria, 3, 112
bureaucratic politics
  and Alliance for Progress, 78–83
  and Cuban Missile Crisis, 72–75
  and foreign policy, 66–84
  military technology, 3–5
  origins of First World War, 69–71
  policymaking, 76–78
  Vietnam War, 75–76
Burma, independence, 24

Calvinism, 91
Cambodia, U.S. invasion of, 37
Canada, 64, 146, 305
capitalism
  as a cause of First World War, 5
  and imperialism, 306–315
Carter, Jimmy, U.S. president, 42, 291,
  305, 326, 368
Castro, Fidel, Cuban premier, 78, 82,
  239–240
Central American Common Market
  (CACM), 202–204
Central Intelligence Agency (CIA), 34,
  53, 309
  in Chile, 42, 238–239
  and U-2 flights, 78
Central Treaty Organization
  (CENTO), 174, 177
Ceylon, independence, 24
Chaco War, 204
Chad, 65
Chamberlain, Joseph, 312
Chamberlain, Neville, British prime
  minister, 19, 148
Chiang Kai-shek, Chinese Nationalist
  president, 27, 123–124
Chicago, 351–353
Chile, 80–82, 238–239
  and CIA, 42, 111, 238
  as a threshhold nuclear power, 302
China, 15, 16, 30, 39, 98, 100, 105,
  174, 342–343

aftermath of Second World War, 281
civil war, 26–27
collectivization, 127
Five-Year Plan, 127
and Indian sub-continent, 129,
  174–175
and Japan, 16
in Korean War, 28–29, 98
as a nuclear power, 289, 301·
rapprochement with the
  United States, 38–39
rise of, 112, 122–131
and Second World War, 23
Sino-Japanese War, 306
and Soviet Union, 36, 39–40, 118,
  119–120, 124–126, 130–131
and Tibet, 314
and Vietnam, 30, 130
Chou En-lai, Chinese Communist
  premier, 127, 128, 131
Christianity, 255–257
Chrysler Corporation, 245
Churchill, Winston, British prime
  minister, 182
  at Yalta, 25
civil wars, in Pakistan, Nigeria, and
  Yemen, 204
Clemenceau, Georges, French premier,
  and "collective security," 9
Club of Rome, 264–265, 330–357
  passim
coalitions, 280
Cold War, 24, 26, 31, 33, 167
collective security, 10, 16, 209,
  211–212
Commerce Department, U.S., 82
  and Alliance for Progress, 78–79
Common Market, *see* European
  Community
Communist Information Bureau
  (Cominform), 118
Communist International (Comintern),
  see Third International
Concert of Europe, 205
Confederation of French Industry, 340
Confucianism, 257
Congress, U.S., and the Alliance for
  Progress, 79
conservation, 333–334, 355–357
containment, 118
Continental Can Company, 245
cost over-runs, in military contracts, 57
Council of Europe, 182
Croats, in Yugoslavia, 64
Croix de Feu, 137
Cuba, 77
  Bay of Pigs, 34–35

and Castro, 239–241
  Cuban Missile Crisis, 35
  and the United States, 109
Cuban Missile Crisis, 35–36, 58,
    72–75, 77–78, 120
customs union, 187
Cyprus, 64
Czechoslovakia, 19, 182, 195, 376
  Communist coup d'etat in, 98
  and Soviet Union, 121, 143, 314
  Sudeten crisis (1938), 18

Dalai Lama, 129
"Declaration on Liberated Europe," 25
Deere (John) & Company, 81–82
Defense Department, 78
  and the U.S. Senate, 59–60
defense spending, 57
De Gaulle, Charles, French president,
    139, 141–143, 150
  and Fouchet plan, 189
democracy, 6
  and economic growth, 362–363
Denmark, 94
  in Second World War, 21
dependency theory, 44–45, 237–238,
    240–241, 366–369
depression, see Great Depression
de-Stalinization, 118–119
detente, 37–40
deterrence, 285–292
development,
  and foreign aid, 363–364
Dickens, Charles, British author, 350
Diem, Ngo Dinh, see Ngo Dinh Diem
Dien Bien Phu, battle of, 142
diplomatic corps, cosmopolitanism in
    the 18th century, 94
disarmament, 18, 300
Dominican Republic, 38
  and the United States, 110, 111, 181
Dreyfus Affair, 131–132
Dubcek, Alexander, Czechoslovakian
    Communist leader, 121
Dulles, John Foster, U.S. secretary
    of state
  and Hungarian revolution (1956), 32
  and "massive retaliation," 34

Eastern Europe, and the Soviet Union,
    24, 26, 32–33, 117–118,
    314–315
economic development, 359
  and international trade, 364–365
  and NIEO, 366–371

economic growth, 348–355
  and democracy, 362–363
  and foreign investment, 366
economic union, 188
Egypt, 279
  and the Soviet Union, 121
Eisenhower, Dwight D.,
    U.S. president, 29, 36, 129
  and Arbenz regime in Guatemala,
    111
  Hungarian revolution, 32–33, 38
  and Korean War, 38
  and Lebanon, 111
  and "massive retaliation," 34
electoral college, 63
Emergency Quota Act (1921), 15
Ethiopia, 65
  Italy in, 16–17
ethnic groups, subnational, 61–66
Eurocommunism, 195
Europe, 47, 110
European Coal and Steel Community,
    141, 149, 184
European Community, 141–143,
    150–151, 184–197
European Court of Justice, 184–185
European Defense Community,
    140, 183
Export-Import Bank, 79
export platforms, 228

Facts on File, 161
Fascism, 17
Federal Water Quality Act (1972), 350
"Finlandization," 196
First Indochina War, 141–142
First World War, 18, 19, 31, 51, 57, 83,
    105, 138, 160, 174, 286, 306,
    309, 312, 314, 316
  American entry, 110
  Battle of the Marne, 134
  bipolarity versus multipolarity, 280–
    281
  British role, 145–146
  and bureaucratic response to crisis,
    69–71
  Hitler in, 86–87
  Italy at beginning of, 133
  overview of origins and effects, 2–8
  post-war alliances, 166–167, 176,
    180, 375
  power benefit to U.S., 108
  reaction of scholars, 40
Food and Agricultural Organization,
    323
Food and Drug Administration, U.S., 353

and United States, 149
in Vietnam, 30
Great Depression, 13–14, 17, 19, 115, 136, 147
Great Leap Forward, 128–129, 130
great-man theory of history, 84–89
Great Proletarian Cultural Revolution, 129–130
Greece, 24, 31, 112, 149
Green Berets, 34
Grotius, 91
Groups of 77, 366–371
group theory, 53–54
Guarantee, Treaty of, 135
Guatemala, CIA and, 111, 309
Guevara, Che, Latin American revolutionary, 256
Guyana, 64

Haiti, 110
Hapsburg dynasty, 93
Hawley-Smoot Act, 13
Heath, Edward, British prime minister, 150
Helsinki Declaration, 121
Hindenburg, Paul von, German field marshal and president, 11
Hindus, and Hinduism, 31, 257
Hitler, Adolf, German dictator, 14, 86–88, 138, 170, 176, 376
  becomes chancellor, 13–14
  and Czechoslovakia, 18–19, 148
  and the "final solution," 62
  and Mussolini, 17
  pact with Stalin, 20–21, 116–117
  rise of, 7, 10, 14, 115
  and Second World War, 21–22
Ho Chi Minh, 31, 376
Hohenzollern dynasty, 10
Holland, see Netherlands
Holy Roman Empire, 91, 92
Hong Kong, 122
Hoover, Herbert, U.S. president, 13
Hua Kuo-feng, Chinese Communist leader, 131
human rights, and Jimmy Carter, 42
Hundred Flowers Campaign, 128
Hungary, USSR and, 32–33, 38, 119, 314

idealist-realist debate, 8
Imperial Defense Committee, 133
imperialism, 5, 305–315
India, 29, 80, 128, 153, 174–175, 324, 325, 363, 372

British in, 31
China conflict, 129
independence, 24, 31, 148
nuclear power, 301–302, 305
Pakistan conflict, 31, 301
individuals, and world politics, 84–89, 320–321
Indonesia, 23
inflation, post-First World War, 12, 14, 17
Inter-American Commission on Human Rights (OAS), 260
interest groups, ethnic, 61–66
International Atomic Energy Agency, 305
International Bank for Reconstruction and Development, see World Bank
International Confederation of Free Trade Unions, 246
International Federation of Airline Pilots Association, 218, 245
International Federation of Chemical and General Workers Unions, 245, 247
International Harvester, 82
international labor organizations, 244–253
International Metal Workers Federation, 245, 246
International Monetary Fund, 367–368
International Political Science Association, 263
International Seabed Resources Agency, 370
international system, 45, 267–271
International Telecommunications Organization, 205
International Telephone and Telegraph (ITT), 238
international trade and economic development, 364–365
International Trade Secretariats, 246–247
investments, "multiplier effect," 233
Iran, 111
  CIA in, 309
  Soviet troops in, 26
  as a threshhold nuclear power, 303
Iraq, 64, 180–181
Ireland, Northern, 64, 151
Islam, 31, 257
Israel, 104, 204, 279
  creation, 32, 62
  nuclear weapons, 303
  and the Soviet Union, 63–64
  and United States, 62–63, 311

Italy, 16–17, 18, 88, 94, 105, 176, 204, 272, 375, 376
  alliance with France, 133
  in First World War, 3
  Great Depression, 19
  and Locarno Treaty, 12
  in Second World War, 23

Jainism, 257
Japan, 3, 15–16, 18, 19, 47, 88, 102, 105, 122–124, 148, 153, 275, 305, 375
  annexation of Korea, 27
  "Asia for Asians," 23
  and Britain, 144
  and China, 16, 27, 306
  Nazi-Soviet Pact, 21
  Russo-Japanese War (1904–5), 112
  Second World War, 22–23, 111
  and the United States, 44
  in Vietnam, 29–30
Jews and Judaism, 257
  Balfour Declaration, 7
  as ethnic interest group, 62–64
  in Palestine, 31
  in USSR, 63–64
Johnson, Lyndon B., U.S. president, 38, 81, 190–191
  in Dominican Republic, 111
  in Viet Nam, 37
Joint Chiefs of Staff, and Cuban Missile Crisis, 73

Katyn Forest massacre, 25
Keesing's Contemporary Archives, 161
Kellogg-Briand Treaty, 40, 136
Kennedy, John F., U.S. president, 34–37 *passim,* 191
  Alliance for Progress, 78
  Bay of Pigs, 111
  Cuban Missile Crisis, 73–74
  missile gap, 33
Kenya, 199–200
Kerensky, Alexander, Russian revolutionary, 113
Keynes, John M., British economist, 19
Khrushchev, Nikita, Soviet Communist leader, 118–120, 128–129
  Cuban Missile Crisis, 35
  de-Stalinization, 32
  and Sputnik, 33
Kim Il-Sung, North Korean dictator, 28
Kissinger, Henry, U.S. secretary of state, 38–39, 111–112

Korea, 40
  North, 27–29, 376
  South, 27–29, 302
Korean War, 27–29, 98, 111, 126, 183, 321, 376
Krupp family, German industrialists, 57
Kulaks, 115
Kuomintang, 27, 123–124
Kuwait, Palestinians in, 64

labor unions, transnational, 244–253
Labour Party, in Britain, 147, 150–151
Laos, invasion (1970), 37
Latin America, 60, 84, 176, 181, 201–204, 342
  and Alliance for Progress, 78
  and CIA, 111
  Monroe Doctrine, 110
Latin American Free Trade Association (LAFTA), 201
Law of the Seas Conferences, U.N., 370
law of uneven development, 315
League of Nations, 8–9, 15–18, 40, 110, 116, 134, 167, 206–208
Lebanon, 64
Lenin, Vladimir Ilyich, Russian revolutionary, 5, 27, 113–114, 313
  defense of Leninism, 311–312
  on imperialism, 306–311
  and Sun Yat-sen, 123
  Treaty of Brest-Litovsk, 20
Libya, 65, 303
Limits to Growth (Meadows et al.), 330–357
Locarno pact, 13, 136, 147
Lodge, Henry Cabot, 109
London Naval Treaty (1930), 298
Louis XIV, king of France, 94
Luftwaffe, German air force, 138
Lutheranism, 92

MacArthur, Douglas, U.S. general, 29, 30, 321
McCarthyism, 38
McNamara, Robert, U.S. secretary of defense, 34
Maginot Line, 138, 375
Malaysia, 64
Malthus, Thomas, British economist, 337
Manchester Examiner, 285
Manchu dynasty in China, 122
Manchuria, 15–16, 127, 376

Venezuela, 302
Versailles, Treaty of, 10, 18, 19, 147, 376
  Article 231, 11
Vienna, Congress of, 95, 166, 205
Vietnam, and the Vietnam War, 29–31, 36–37, 44, 51–52, 56, 58, 75–76, 80, 81, 83, 97–98, 103, 111, 130, 143, 190–192, 204, 309, 313

Wales, 152
Wallace, George, American politician, 268–269
war, and human nature, 315–320
war debts, after First World War, 13
Warsaw Pact Organization, 177, 181
Washington, George, U.S. president, 110
Washington Naval Treaty (1922), 298
Watergate scandal, 121
Waterloo, battle of, 95
West Berlin, 33, 35, 47
Westphalia, Peace of, 91–92, 93
Wilhelm II, German kaiser, 3–4, 69
Wilson, Harold, British prime minister, 150

Wilson, Woodrow, U.S. president, 8–10, 15, 51
World Bank, 342, 367
World Confederation of Labor, 246
World Conference on Religion and Peace, 257
World Council of Churches, 256
World Events Interaction Survey (WEIS), 158, 159
World Federation of Trade Unions (WFTU), 246
world government, 40
World Order Models Project, 263, 357–361, 372
world politics, and individuals, 320–321

Yalta, 25
Yemen, 204
Yuan Shik-k'ai, 122
Yugoslavia, 64

Zanzibar, 199
zero sum game, 171
Zoroastrianism, 257